Lecture Notes in Computer Science 3047

Commenced Publication in 1973
Founding and Former Series Editors:
Gerhard Goos, Juris Hartmanis, and Jan van Leeuwen

Springer
Berlin
Heidelberg
New York
Hong Kong
London
Milan
Paris
Tokyo

Flavio Oquendo   Brian Warboys
Ron Morrison (Eds.)

Software Architecture

First European Workshop, EWSA 2004
St Andrews, UK, May 21-22, 2004
Proceedings

Springer

Volume Editors

Flavio Oquendo
Université de Savoie
Ecole Supérieure d'Ingénieurs d'Annecy - LISTIC
B.P. 806, 74016 Annecy Cedex, France
E-mail: Flavio.Oquendo@univ-savoie.fr

Brian Warboys
University of Manchester, Department of Computer Science
Manchester M13 9PL, UK
E-mail: bwarboys@cs.man.ac.uk

Ron Morrison
University of St Andrews, School of Computer Science
St Andrews, Fife KY16 9SS, UK
E-mail: ron@dcs.st-andrews.ac.uk

Library of Congress Control Number: 2004105864

CR Subject Classification (1998): D.2

ISSN 0302-9743
ISBN 3-540-22000-3 Springer-Verlag Berlin Heidelberg New York

Springer-Verlag is a part of Springer Science+Business Media

springeronline.com

© Springer-Verlag Berlin Heidelberg 2004
Printed in Germany

Typesetting: Camera-ready by author, data conversion by Olgun Computergrafik
Printed on acid-free paper   SPIN: 11007821   06/3142   5 4 3 2 1 0

Preface

The last decade has been one of great progress in the field of software architecture research and practice. Software architecture has emerged as an important subdiscipline of software engineering. A key aspect of the design of any software system is its architecture, i.e. the fundamental organization of a system embodied in its components, their relationships to each other, and to the environment, and the principles guiding its design and evolution (as defined in the Recommended Practice for Architectural Description of Software-Intensive Systems – IEEE Std 1471-2000).

The First European Workshop on Software Architecture (EWSA 2004) provided an international forum for researchers and practitioners from academia and industry to discuss a wide range of topics in the area of software architecture, and to jointly formulate an agenda for future research in this field.

EWSA 2004 distinguished among three types of papers: research papers (which describe authors' novel research work), experience papers (which describe real-world experiences related to software architectures), and position papers (which present concise arguments about a topic of software architecture research or practice).

The Program Committee selected 19 papers (9 research papers, 4 experience papers, and 6 position papers) out of 48 submissions from 16 countries (Australia, Brazil, Canada, Chile, Finland, France, Germany, Italy, Japan, Korea, The Netherlands, Spain, Switzerland, Turkey, UK, USA). All submissions were reviewed by three members of the Program Committee. Papers were selected based on originality, quality, soundness and relevance to the workshop. In addition, the workshop included five invited papers presenting European Union projects related to software architecture: ARCHWARE, CONIPF, FABRIC, MODA-TEL, and OMEGA. Credit for the quality of the proceedings goes to all authors of papers.

We would like to thank the members of the Program Committee (Ilham Alloui, Dharini Balasubramaniam, Jan Bosch, Harald Gall, David Garlan, Mark Greenwood, Valérie Issarny, Volker Gruhn, Philippe Kruchten, Nicole Levy, Radu Mateescu, Carlo Montangero, and Dewayne Perry) for providing timely and significant reviews, and for their substantial effort in making EWSA 2004 a successful workshop.

The EWSA 2004 submission and review process was extensively supported by the Paperdyne Conference Management System. We are indebted to Volker Gruhn and his team, in particular Dirk Peters and Clemens Schäfer, for their excellent support.

The workshop was held in conjunction with the 26th International Conference on Software Engineering (ICSE 2004). We would like to acknowledge Michael Goedicke and the other members of the ICSE Organizing Committee for their assistance, during the organization of EWSA 2004, in creating this co-located event.

We would also like to acknowledge the prompt and professional support from Springer-Verlag, who published these proceedings in printed and electronic form as part of the Lecture Notes in Computer Science series.

May 2004

Flavio Oquendo
Brian Warboys
Ron Morrison

Program Committee

Program Chairs

- Flavio Oquendo
  University of Savoie – LISTIC, Annecy, France
  flavio.oquendo@univ-savoie.fr
- Brian Warboys
  University of Manchester, UK
  bwarboys@cs.man.ac.uk

Committee Members

- Ilham Alloui
  University of Savoie – LISTIC, Annecy, France
  ilham.alloui@univ-savoie.fr
- Dharini Balasubramaniam
  University of St Andrews, UK
  dharini@dcs.st-and.ac.uk
- Jan Bosch
  University of Groningen, The Netherlands
  jan.bosch@cs.rug.nl
- Harald Gall
  Technical University of Vienna, Austria
  gall@infosys.tuwien.ac.at
- David Garlan
  Carnegie Mellon University, USA
  garlan@cs.cmu.edu
- Mark Greenwood
  University of Manchester, UK
  markg@cs.man.ac.uk
- Valérie Issarny
  INRIA Rocquencourt, France
  valerie.issarny@inria.fr
- Volker Gruhn
  University of Leipzig, Germany
  volker.gruhn@informatik.uni-leipzig.de
- Philippe Kruchten
  University of British Columbia, Vancouver, Canada
  kruchten@ieee.org
- Nicole Levy
  University of Versailles – PRiSM, France
  nicole.levy@prism.uvsq.fr
- Radu Mateescu
  INRIA Rhône-Alpes, Grenoble, France
  radu.mateescu@inria.fr

- Carlo Montangero
  University of Pisa, Italy
  carlo.montangero@di.unipi.it
- Dewayne Perry
  University of Texas at Austin, USA
  perry@ece.utexas.edu

Organizing Committee

- Ron Morrison (Chair)
  University of St Andrews, UK
  ron@dcs.st-andrews.ac.uk
- Ferdinando Gallo
  Consorzio Pisa Ricerche, Italy
  n.gallo@cpr.it
- Hilary Hanahoe
  Consorzio Pisa Ricerche, Italy
  h.hanahoe@trust-itservices.com

Sponsorship

EWSA 2004 was sponsored by the ArchWare European R&D Project: Architecting Evolvable Software – *www.arch-ware.org*. ArchWare is partially funded by the Commission of the European Union under contract No. IST-2001-32360 in the IST-V Framework Program.

Table of Contents

Research Papers

Experience Papers

Position Papers

Invited Papers:
European Projects in Software Architecture

Sotograph - A Pragmatic Approach to Source Code Architecture Conformance Checking

Walter Bischofberger, Jan Kühl, and Silvio Löffler

Software-Tomography GmbH
{wb,jk,sl}@software-tomography.com
www.software-tomography.com

Abstract. In our experience the implementation of software systems frequently does not conform very closely to the planned architecture. For this reason we decided to implement source code architecture conformance checking support for Sotograph, our software analysis environment. Besides providing a conformance check for a single version of a system, Sotograph supports also trend analysis. I.e., the investigation of the evolution of a software system and the changes in architecture violations between a number of versions.

Sotograph

Sotograph extracts information about a number of versions of a software system from source and byte code and manages this information in a relational database. The data model represents the information that can be extracted from C++ and Java. The information in a database can be analyzed and visualized with a closely integrated set of tools supporting source code architecture conformance checking, cycle analysis, metric based analysis, cross referencing between artifacts on different abstraction levels. Custom metrics and custom analyses can be implemented in an SQL extension.

Supported Architecture Model

From our point of view software architectures describe how the architecture-level artifacts of a software system are intended to cooperate and between which artifacts relationships are forbidden.

The artifacts that are explicitly defined in source code such as classes, packages and name spaces are too fine-grained to serve as architecture-level artifacts. For this reason we aggregate fine-grained artifacts to architecture-level artifacts which we call subsystems. In software systems implemented in Java, subsystems consist typically of a number of packages. In software systems implemented in C subsystems are usually aggregations of the artifacts defined in the source code located in a number of directories. C++ subsystems consist either of aggregations of directories or name spaces.

In defining subsystems it makes sense not just to define the artifacts they consist of, but also the artifacts that form their export interfaces. This permits for a first level of architecture conformance checking.

F. Oquendo et al. (Eds.): EWSA 2004, LNCS 3047, pp. 1–9, 2004.

Architectures can either be described as graphs or as layered architectures. In a graph the arcs define for artifact pairs which references between them are allowed or forbidden. In a layered architecture the layering implicitly forbids upward references and in some cases multi-layer downward references.

We decided to use layered architectures because

- the layers provide a further abstraction level which makes a layered architecture much easier to understand than an arbitrary graph,
- layered architectures are simple to define because the restrictions they impose are inherently given by the layering,
- architects frequently define their top-level architectures as layered systems.

The disadvantage of layered architectures compared to arbitrary graphs is that they are less expressive. This means that sometimes several layered architecture models are needed to describe all relevant architectural restrictions.

Basic Idea of Architecture Conformance Checking

Figure 1 depicts an example of a subsystem based layered architecture and the kind of illegal relationships a source code architecture conformance checker can automatically detect.

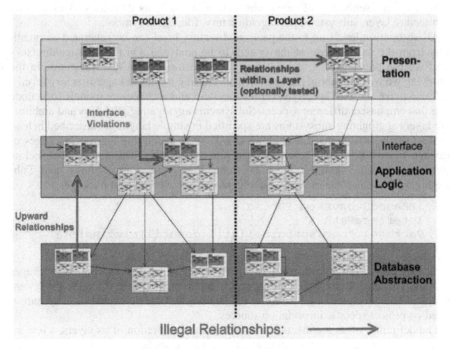

Fig. 1. Sample layered architecture.

Illegal Upward Relationships. It is inherent to layered architectures that references from lower to upper layers are not allowed.

Interface Violations. Usage of non interface artifacts of subsystems by other subsystems is not allowed.

Several Layer Downward Relationships. Depending on the kind of modeled architecture this may be legal or illegal. In our example it is illegal that the presentation layer uses the database abstraction layer directly.

Illegal Relationships within a Layer. These can be illegal for several reasons. A typical example is a line of products where products are flexibly configured based on a set of services and tools. In such an architecture groups of services and tools implementing independent functionality should not know each other.

Architecture Conformance Checking

Architecture conformance checking consists of specifying an architecture which is to be checked, and in checking whether the source code adheres to this architecture.

Specifying an Architecture

Sotograph represents the following abstraction levels in its databases: Architecture, architecture layer, subsystem, package/directory, file, class, symbol.

All abstraction levels up to the package/directory level can be generated automatically from the source code of the system to be analyzed. On the package/directory level we use packages for java systems and directories for C/C++ systems. In the following we will talk about packages when referring to the package/directory level.

It can make sense to specify several subsystem and architecture models for a code base that emphasize different aspects. Subsystems aggregating packages and architecture layers aggregating subsystems are specified in simple languages described below.

Most often subsystems can be defined with rules specifying the root packages of package trees that should be aggregated into subsystems. The source code below shows an example defining the subsystems Public.util, Public.guiutil, and Public.plugins. The interface of these subsystems consists of their root packages.

```
RuleBasedSubsystem Public {
   InterfacePath "";
   Packages "com.sotogra.'(util|guiutil|plugins)'";
}
```

Typically, only a few exceptions have to be specified by enumerating the packages belonging to subsystems. Enumerating specification makes sense when the subsystem model can be generated, e.g., based on the jar files that are generated for a system or based on project specific information sources.

The definition of an architecture consists of an enumeration of its layers, a few attributes, and the packages they contain. The source code below shows an excerpt of Sotograph's overview architecture model.

```
ArchitectureModel Overview {
   Uses Default; // underlying subsystem model
   ArchitectureLayer Manager {
      // this layer is allowed to use all lower layers
      InterLayerUsage = True;
      // the subsystems pertaining to this layer may us
      // each other
      IntraLayerUsage = True;
      // the list of subsystems pertaining to the layer
      Subsystem Tools.manager;
      Subsystem Access;
   }
   ArchitectureLayer ToolsAndServices {
      InterLayerUsage = True;
      // the subsystems pertaining to this layer
      // may not us each other
      IntraLayerUsage = False;
      // the subsystems pertaining to the layer selected
      // with a regular expression
      Subsystems "Tools.([^m]|met).*";
   }
   ArchitectureLayer ToolInfrastructure {
      InterLayerUsage = True;
      IntraLayerUsage = True;
      Subsystem Base.annotation;
      Subsystem Base.dbupdate;
      Subsystem Base.migration;
   }
```

Investigating the Correspondence between Architecture and Source Base

Sotograph can detect the references in a source base that do not correspond to an architecture model and the corresponding subsystem model. Figure 2 shows the number of illegal references on subsystem level for the code bases of Sotograph version 0.95 and 0.96. The rows are sorted according to the difference between the two versions (the last column). This view shows at a glance between which subsystems which kinds of illegal references were added and removed.

This information can then, for example, be visualized to get an overview of how many of the subsystems are illegally used. Figure 3 shows the subsystem inheritance graph with the illegally referenced subsystems marked.

Finally it is possible to zoom in by double clicking the rows of the table displayed in Figure 2. Zooming in means to first investigate the illegal references aggregated on package-level and then on the level of basic references. Figure 4 shows a basic reference-level view, which enumerates the new and existing illegal references between package *architecture* and package *jflex*. The next double click displays the source code defining the illegal reference in the IDE of choice.

Exceptions of Trend Architecture Model Sotograph for v1 = 0.95 and v2 = 0.96

sub...	subRefing	su...	subRefed	errorKind	v1	v2	diff
65965	Default.Db	65962	Default.Base.table	UPWARD	829	788	-41
65965	Default.Db	65959	Default.Base.guiutil	UPWARD	364	359	-5
65966	Default.Tools.architecture	65976	Default.Tools.subsystem	INTERFACE	30	28	-2
65958	Default.Base.annotation	65959	Default.Base.guiutil	INTERFACE	39	39	0
65959	Default.Base.guiutil	65972	Default.Tools.manager	UPWARD	11	11	0
65961	Default.Base.projecttree	65969	Default.Tools.dbview	UPWARD	1	1	0
65962	Default.Base.table	65959	Default.Base.guiutil	INTERFACE	8	8	0
65963	Default.Base.tool	65969	Default.Tools.dbview	UPWARD	2	2	0
65963	Default.Base.tool	65971	Default.Tools.graph	UPWARD	15	15	0
65963	Default.Base.tool	65975	Default.Tools.result	UPWARD	8	8	0
65963	Default.Base.tool	65976	Default.Tools.subsystem	INTERFACE	2	2	0
65964	Default.Base.util	65959	Default.Base.guiutil	UPWARD	19	19	0
65965	Default.Db	65958	Default.Base.annotation	UPWARD	123	123	0
65965	Default.Db	65964	Default.Base.util	INTERFACE	7	7	0
65965	Default.Db	65972	Default.Tools.manager	UPWARD	26	26	0
65965	Default.Db	65976	Default.Tools.subsystem	INTERFACE	6	6	0
65965	Default.Db	65977	Default.Tools.trend	UPWARD	28	28	0
65973	Default.Tools.metric	65977	Default.Tools.trend	INTRA	139	139	0
65975	Default.Tools.result	65972	Default.Tools.manager	UPWARD	3	3	0
65976	Default.Tools.subsystem	65964	Default.Base.util	INTERFACE	42	42	0
65964	Default.Base.util	65963	Default.Base.tool	UPWARD	0	2	2
65974	Default.Tools.query	65964	Default.Base.util	INTERFACE	94	96	2
65964	Default.Base.util	65972	Default.Tools.manager	UPWARD	56	60	4
65966	Default.Tools.architecture	65964	Default.Base.util	INTERFACE	38	42	4
65963	Default.Base.tool	65959	Default.Base.guiutil	INTERFACE	31	36	5
65966	Default.Tools.architecture	65977	Default.Tools.trend	INTRA	74	80	6
65965	Default.Db	65963	Default.Base.tool	UPWARD	738	802	64

Fig. 2. Architecture violations table.

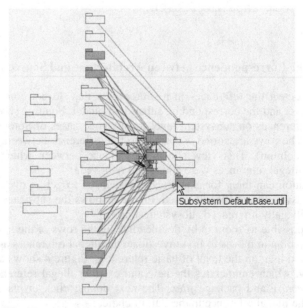

Subsystem Default.Base.util

Fig. 3. Illegally referenced subsystems marked in subsystem inheritance graph.

refi...	refingSymbol	refe...	refedSymbol	referenceType	loc...	changes
189...	me_parseArchitectureModel()	189...	cl_SyntaxErrorException	TYPEACCESS	LO...	NEW
189...	me_parseArchitectureModel()	189...	cl_SyntaxErrorException	TYPEACCESS	LO...	NEW
189...	me_parseArchitectureModel()	189...	me_getLine()	CALL	LO...	NEW
189...	me_parseArchitectureModel()	189...	me_getColumn()	CALL	LO...	NEW
189...	me_parseArchitectureModel()	189...	cl_SyntaxErrorException	TYPEACCESS	LO...	SAME
189...	me_parseArchitectureModel()	189...	cl_SyntaxErrorException	TYPEACCESS	LO...	SAME
189...	me_parseArchitectureModel()	189...	cl_SyntaxErrorException	TYPEACCESS	LO...	SAME
189...	me_parseArchitectureModel()	189...	cl_SyntaxErrorException	TYPEACCESS	LO...	SAME
189...	me_parseArchitectureModel()	189...	cl_SyntaxErrorException	TYPEACCESS	LO...	SAME
189...	me_parseArchitectureModel()	189...	cl_SyntaxErrorException	TYPEACCESS	LO	SAME
189...	me_parseArchitectureModel()	189...	cl_SyntaxErrorException	TYPEACCESS	LO...	SAME
189...	me_parseArchitectureModel()	189...	cl_SyntaxErrorException	TYPEACCESS	LO...	SAME
189...	me_parseArchitectureModel()	189...	cl_SyntaxErrorException	CATCH	LO...	SAME
189...	me_parseArchitectureModel()	189...	me_getLine()	CALL	LO...	SAME
189...	me_parseArchitectureModel()	189...	me_getLine()	CALL	LO...	SAME
189...	me_parseArchitectureModel()	189...	me_getColumn()	CALL	LO...	SAME
189...	me_parseArchitectureModel()	189...	me_getColumn()	CALL	LO...	SAME
189...	me_parseArchitectureModel()	189...	me_getColumn()	CALL	LO...	SAME

Fig. 4. Detailed information about architecture violations.

Checking Other Architectural Aspects

Besides checking that a source base corresponds to an architecture it makes also sense to check for other potential architectural problems in a source base. Sotograph provides cycle analysis and metrics based analysis for this purpose.

Cycle Analysis

Cyclical relationships between architecture level components are very common in mid-sized to large software systems. They make it more difficult to build, test, and understand software systems. For this reason it is important to recognize such cycles just after they were introduced, while it is still easy to eliminate them.

With Sotograph cyclical relationships between artifacts can be found on class, file, package and subsystem level. During continuous analysis we usually only look for artifacts that are coupled with an increasing number of other artifacts.

On analyzing a system the first time we usually look for large numbers of cyclically coupled artifacts. Figure 5 shows as example the graph of all relationships between packages that are cyclically coupled with Sotograph's tool framework package.

Metrics Based Analysis

Metrics can help to identify further potential architectural problems such as
- unused artifacts,
- deep, complex inheritance structures
- very large and very small artifacts
- bottlenecks (artifacts that are used by many artifacts and use many artifacts)

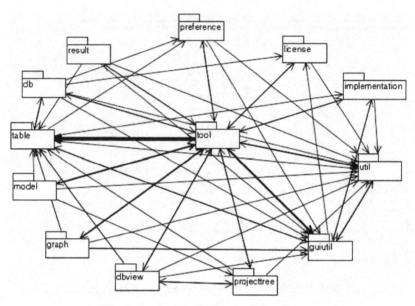

Fig. 5. Graph of cyclically coupled packages.

Related Work

There are a number of published approaches to tool based source code architecture conformance checking. They mainly differ in two respects.

Systems [1] and [2] parse the source code and store the information about artifacts and relations between them into files. Systems [3] and [4] extract information about file inclusion for C/C++ and store the information in files.

Systems [1] and [2] can be used to check the conformance of the source code to arbitrary graphs defining the allowed relations between artifacts. Systems [3] and [4] use layered architectures to specify restrictions.

A major advantage of Sotograph compared to these four systems is the storage of the extracted information in a relational database. This gives the experienced user the possibility to implement custom analyses and metrics in a short time. Furthermore a Sotograph database can contain information about a set of databases allowing for trend analysis.

All systems described in [1] to [4] provide mechanisms to aggregate artifacts in subsystems. None of them provides mechanisms to define the interface through which a subsystem should be used.

All the papers describing these four systems present reengineering scenarios as examples of the application of their tools. The systems are not suited for continuous architecture checking because they do not provide trend support. Furthermore it seems that the setting up and carrying out of an analysis requires considerably more time and experience than a similar analysis carried out with Sotograph.

Experience

As of today, we have checked the architecture conformance of about 50 commercial software systems implemented in Java, C++ or C, in sizes from 100'000 to 4'000'000 lines of code. A basic architecture check, including the filling of the repository, takes usually between one and three hours depending on the size of the investigated software system. For the definition of the subsystem and top-level architecture models, we need the support of a developer understanding the planned overall architecture. This process takes between 15 and 30 minutes.

We found large numbers of architecture violations and cycles in all but a handful of the systems we analyzed. The few exceptions were mostly applications that consisted of a number of weakly coupled modules implementing independent functionality.

Based on this experience we conclude that it is very difficult to implement medium sized to large software systems without considerably breaking the planned architecture. We believe that there are three major factors causing these problems:

The larger a team and a software system the more difficult it is to clearly communicate the architecture to be implemented.

During implementation and code reading developers have a focus on solving a specific problem and frequently forget about the impact on the overall architecture.

The cleaning up of prototypes and quick and dirty solutions that were written under time pressure is frequently forgotten. This happens because nothing reminds architects and technical project leaders about architectural problems as long as the solution works.

Our chief architect is using Sotograph weekly to analyze the modifications and extensions of the last week. This makes it possible to recognize architectural problems in an early stage where it is still cheap to fix them. A weekly analysis that includes the gaining of an overview of new and modified artifacts, layered architecture analysis, cycle based architecture analyses, metric based analysis, and rule checking takes between 15 and 30 minutes. This time does not include the filling of the repository database because the repository is generated weekly by an automated batch job. Filling a database for Sotograph's source code base and calculating information about the differences between the last two versions and calculating, architecture violations, cyclic references, and metric values takes about 15 minutes for the 250'000 LOCs.

Setting up architecture checking for customers and coaching them to carry out the weekly analysis themselves takes about two days. This does not depend on the size of the code base.

References

1. G. C. Murphy, D. Notkin and K. J. Sullivan. Software Reflection Models: Bridging the Gap between Design and Implementation. In IEEE Transactions on Software Engineering, vol. 27, no. 4, pp. 364-380, April 2001
2. R. T. Tvedt, P. Costa and M. Lindvall. Does the Code Match the Design? A Process for Architecture Evaluation. Proceedings of the International Conference on Software Maintenance (ICSM 2002) , IEEE Computer Society, 2002

3. L. Feijs, R. Krikhaar and R. van Ommering. A Relational Approach to Support Software Architecture Analysis. In Software - Practice and Experience, vol. 28(4), pp. 371-400, 10. April 1998
4. B. Laguë, C. Ledue, A. Le Bon, E. Merlo and M. Dagenais. An Analysis Framework for Understanding Layered Software Architectures. In Proceedings of the 6th IEEE International Workshop on Program Comprehension (IWPC 1998), IEEE Computer Society, 1998

Formal Analysis of Architectural Patterns

Mauro Caporuscio, Paola Inverardi, and Patrizio Pelliccione

Dipartimento di Informatica
Università dell'Aquila
I-67010 L'Aquila, Italy
{caporusc,inverard,pellicci}@di.univaq.it

Abstract. Architectural patterns characterize and specify structural
and behavioral properties of (sub)systems, thus allowing the provision of
solutions for classes of problems.

In this paper we show the use of architectural patterns as an abstraction
to carry on, and reuse, formal reasoning on systems whose configuration
can dynamically change.

This kind of systems is hard to model and to reason about due to the
fact that we cannot simply build a model with fixed topology (i.e. fixed
number of components and connectors) and validate properties of interest
on it.

The work presented in this paper proposes an approach that given an
architectural pattern which expresses a class of systems configurations
and a set of properties of interest (i) selects, if any, a *minimal* configuration for which the specified properties make sense, (ii) an abstraction
of the chosen architectural model erformed, in order to reduce the complexity of the verification phase. In this stage, abstractions are driven
by the properties of interest. The output of this abstraction step can be
model-checked, tested and analyzed by using a standard model-checking
framework. (iii) The verification results obtained in the previous step are
lifted to generic configurations by performing *manual* reasoning driven
by the constraints posed by the architectural pattern.

The approach will be applied by using an event-based architectural pattern to a publish/subscribe system, the SIENA middleware, in order to
validate its features and its mobility extension.

1   Introduction

Architectural styles [12] provide solutions for classes of problems, by supporting
reuse of underlying implementations. They can be divided into two subsets: *patterns* and *reference models*. While *patterns* describe global organizational structures, such as layered systems, client-server organizations, event-based systems,
reference models include system organizations defined by specific and parameterized configurations of components and connectors for specific application areas
(i.e. a compiler is composed of lexer, parser, typer, optimizer, code generator).

In this paper we show the use of architectural patterns as an abstraction
to carry on, and reuse, formal reasoning on systems whose configuration can

F. Oquendo et al. (Eds.): EWSA 2004, LNCS 3047, pp. 10–24, 2004.
© Springer-Verlag Berlin Heidelberg 2004

dynamically change. That is systems evolving at run-time either by instantiating or removing components. This kind of systems is hard to model and verify do to the fact that they may have infinite different configurations. Checking properties over these systems would require the ability to build suitable systems models which can take into account the architectural variability in terms of number of components instances and connectors. This would lead to complex specifications and to models which might require, when possible, infinite-based checking techniques.

Then the key idea is to consider only a specific instance of the system and validate the properties of interest on it. This instance has a fixed number of components and connectors and must be carefully selected. In this context, since architectural patterns generically describe a system in terms of structure and semantic, they can be exploited to identify the suitable abstraction of the real system. Of course, proving that a certain property is true for a given instance is not enough in general to assure the correctness of the system.

In this work we propose an approach that derives, from the system specification and the properties to be verified, an architectural abstraction on which a standard verification approach can be carried on. This process gives us an instance of a closed system that can then be verified, with the standard approach, with respect to the properties that drive the choice of the model.

In order to reduce the system complexity, we can perform a further step: we use the properties to slice the architectural model in order to isolate and model only those parts of the system that affect (or are affected-by) the properties we are interested in. Usual techniques to do this kind of analysis (called dependence analysis) are *Chaining* [22,23] and *Architectural Slicing* [24]. The aim of this step is to obtain a system model abstract enough to prove the validity of the properties on interest. The output of this abstraction step can then be model-checked, tested and analyzed.

While other works on model checking event-based architectures [4,13] focus on the analysis of the applications built on top of the event notification system, in this work we focus on the study of the behavior of the event-based architecture itself. To illustrate the approach, we analyze the SIENA middleware and its proposed extension for mobility. SIENA is an event-based system and can be analyzed by resorting to a hierarchical event-based architectural pattern. This allows us to establish a set of characterizing properties of the architectural pattern that will be then (re-)used to prove that the proposed mobility extensions behaves as expected.

The model checking framework we use is CHARMY(*CH*ecking *AR*chitectural *M*odel consistenc*Y*). In CHARMY [16,17,15], we assume to start from a system specification described by means of state machines and scenarios [18] for the behavioral aspects. CHARMY, built on top of the SPIN [14] model checker engine, is used to check the consistency between the software architecture and the functional requirements expressed by means of a Promela specification and Büchi Automata [1] respectively, which are both derived from the source notations.

Section 2 introduces our methodology for modelling and verifying Architectural Styles. Section 3 provides a background on the CHARMY environment. The approach is detailed in Section 4 by applying it to the SIENA case study. Finally in Section 5 we draw some conclusions summarizing our experience and discussing future developments.

2   The Verification Approach

By referring to architectural elements components and connectors, we will make use of the following definitions:

Weakly-Closed System: A *Weakly-Closed System* is a system with a fixed number of components.

Closed System: A *Closed System* is a system with fixed number of component instances and fixed connectors.

Weakly-Open System: A *Weakly-Open System* is a system with variable number of component instances and with fixed connectors.

Open System: An *Open System* is a system with variable connectors and number of component instances.

Our approach for verifying architectural patterns is based on the standard verification methodology summarized in Figure 1.a used for closed system. Figure 1.b shows how this approach is extended in order to achieve validation and verification of architectural patterns.

The key idea relies on (i) choosing a suitable architecture instance (that is a closed system), (ii) applying the standard verification methodology and finally (iii) *manual* reasoning on the obtained verification results in order to scale them to the generic case.

The approach we follow does not rely on a completely automatic analysis. From the system specification and a set of elicited properties, it is identified an architectural reduction on which the standard verification approach can be carried on.

The challenge is to select a configuration which to some extent is minimal with respect to all the possible system configurations for which the specified properties make sense. This process gives us an instance of a closed system that can then be verified, with the standard approach, with respect to the properties that drive the choice of the model. The model configuration must be selected by exploiting both the structural and semantics rules implied by the architectural pattern that characterize the system.

At this point we can slice the system architectural model in order to reduce the complexity of the verification step. By using dependence analysis techniques [22,23,24] and by making suitable abstractions [9] we can reduce the complete model to the part which is needed to verify the properties of interest. These techniques are used to cut off those parts of the system, if any, that are not relevant to verify the properties of interest.

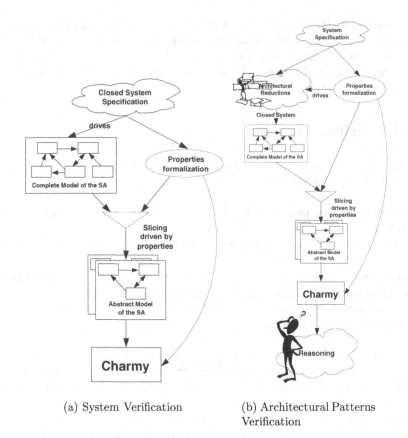

(a) System Verification   (b) Architectural Patterns
                                     Verification

Fig. 1. The Verification Approach.

Proving that there is something wrong in this model should easily allow to assess that it will be wrong also in any *larger* model. Of course, for assessing validity, things are slightly more complex. In fact, the validity of a property on a generic system configuration cannot simply rely on structural arguments. Therefore analysis is carried on in two steps. First the automatic analysis is carried out on the simplest model, then formal reasoning is used in order to scale the analysis results to generic model configurations.

Obviously the possibility to carry on this kind of formal reasoning depends on the considered system and on the properties of interest. There is no automatic way to instantiate the methodology since it depends on the system characteristics (e.g. topology, interactions, communications,...) and properties. This also implies that there can be unscalable systems or unscalable properties such that this methodology cannot be applied on.

In the follow, we will detail this approach by formally analyzing the SIENA middleware and its extension for mobility. To this extent we first characterize and validate the properties of SIENA and then we carry on the analysis of the set of functionalities that are introduced in order to support mobility.

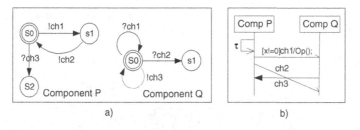

Fig. 2. State Diagram and Sequence formalism.

3   CHARMY: A Framework for Model Based Validation and Verification

This section presents a brief overview of the CHARMY framework.

CHARMY is a framework that, since from the earlier stage of the software development process, aims at assisting the software architect in designing software architecture and in validating them against functional requirements. State machines and scenarios are the source notation for specifying software architectures and their behavioral properties. Model checking techniques and in particular the chosen model checker *SPIN* [14] are used to check the consistency between the software architecture and the functional requirements by using a Promela specification and Büchi Automata [1] which are both derived from the source notations. The former is the *SPIN* modeling language, while the latter is the automata representation for Linear-time Temporal Logic (LTL) formulae [19] that expresses behavioral properties.

CHARMY currently offers a graphical user interface which aids the software architecture design and automates the machinery of the approach.

Technical details on CHARMY may be found in [15,16], while an approach to integrate CHARMY into a real software development life-cycle can be found in [15,16,10].

4   Event-Based Architectural Patterns: SIENA

In this Section we formally analyze SIENA [6,7], a publish/subscribe event notification service developed at the University of Colorado. Following the methodology described in Section 2, we identify the architectural pattern that underlines SIENA. That is, the Event-Based Architectural Pattern [5,21] where components communicate exchanging one or more events rather than invoking directly a procedure or sending a message to a component. The communication between components is assured by an Event Service that reacts to a publish request by forwarding the corresponding event notification to all components subscribed for it.

SIENA specializes this general Event-Based architectural pattern by implementing the Event Service as a network of servers connected in a hierarchical topology[1].

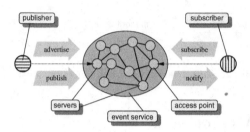

Fig. 3. A Common Publish/Subscribe Architecture.

Figure 3 represents the SIENA software architecture where two entities may be distinguished: *clients* and an *event-service*. The *event-service* is composed by a number of servers which provide clients with *access points* by offering an extended publish/subscribe interface. The *clients* are both *publishers* and *subscribers*. *Publishers* are the generators of events (notification) and use the access points to *publish* the notifications. *Subscribers* are the consumers of notifications and use the access points to *subscribe* for events of interest. Subscribers express their interest in such kind of events by supplying a *filter*. A *filter* is applied to the content [8] of notifications and it allows the *event-service* to deliver events to the subscribers that are interested in them.

Since event-based systems allow loose-coupling components, they seem to be well suited to support systems in which computational components may change location, in a voluntary or involuntary manner, and move across a space that may be defined to be either *logical* or *physical* [20,11]. Then a *mobility extension*, called CoMETA (Component Mobility using an Event noTification Architecture) has been designed and implemented within the SIENA publish/subscribe system [2]. This extension allows applications to receive notifications that are published while they are traveling to a new destination (i.e. access point). The flow of notifications and their subscriptions is restored when they reconnect to the SIENA network at their new destination.

CoMETA provides the above solution by means of *Events-Download* service. It simply consists of allowing the client to download stored events and to modify routing information, after it has reached a new location.

Events-Download: Referring to Figure 4.a, the new access point (called T) downloads the stored events from the old access point (called H) and, then send them to the client (called C).

---

[1] Actually the SIENA specification also defines other types of topologies (acyclic and generic peer-to-peer, hybrid). However the actual Java implementation allows only the hierarchical one [http://www.cs.colorado.edu/serl/siena].

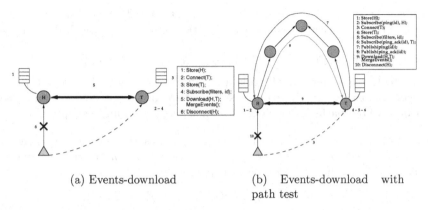

(a) Events-download   (b)   Events-download   with
                                          path test

Fig. 4. Events Download Service.

We start from the SIENA and CoMETA specifications (both behavioral and
structural), given as state machines and scenarios. In order to fully characterize
the correct behavior of the system we identify the following four properties.
Properties from 1 to 3 characterize SIENA, while the fourth property defines a
desired Behavior of CoMETA:

Property 1 asserts that if a client C_1 publishes an event for which client C_0 has
    already expressed interest, then client C_0 must receive the event notification.
Property 2 asserts that a server must process a sequence of events according
    to the reception order.
Property 3 expresses that the events received by a client C_0 and generated by
    the same source maintain the publication order.
Property 4 asserts that when a client reaches its destination and reconnects
    to the SIENA event service than it receives all events published while it was
    disconnected.

4.1   Properties Formalization

In this Section we formalize the above properties. In order to simplify the writing
of LTL formulas we assume the existence of a predefined atomic predicate $Prec$
that checks if a sequence of actions is ordered with respect to the time in which
each action occurs[2]. In our implementation this predicate is provided by the
framework and it is defined as follows:

Definition 1. *Let $\preceq$ be an ordering relation. $Prec(e_1, e_2, e_3 \cdots, e_n)$ is a predicate that returns* **true** *if and only if $e_1 \preceq e_2 \preceq e_3 \ldots e_{n-1} \preceq e_n$.*

---

[2] Note that in the following we use LTL and the predicate in Definition 1 because of its
more intuitive and compact representation. In practice we use the Büchi automata
formalism because CHARMY automatically generates Büchi automata starting from
graphical representations of temporal properties [16].

Property 1: When C_0 subscribes a filter $(SUBC_0)$ and C_1 publishes an event $(PUBC_1)$ then C_0 receives an event notification identified by the $NOTC_0$ message.

$$\Box(Prec(SUBC_0, PUBC_1) \Rightarrow \Diamond(\neg UNSC_0 \wedge NOTC_0))$$

Due to the way our model works (i.e. after an $UNSC_0$ the client C_0 disconnects and, then shuts down), it is sufficient to add the $\neg UNSC_0$ in order to select only whose paths in which C_0 does not perform an unsubscription.

Property 2: Let $m_0, m_1, \ldots, m_n$ be a sequence of messages received by a generic server S. If S receives m_0 at time t_0, m_1 at time t_1, ..., m_n at time t_n, where $t_0 < t_1 < \cdots < t_n$, then S will process m_0 before $m_1 \ldots$ before m_n.

$$\Box(Prec(MSG_s(m_0), MSG_s(m_1), \ldots, MSG_s(m_n))$$
$$\Rightarrow \Diamond Prec(\tau_s(m_0), \tau_s(m_1), \ldots, \tau_s(m_n)))$$

where $\tau_s(m_i)$ represents the internal operations performed by S in processing m_i and, $MSG_s(m_i)$ represents a generic message received by S.

Property 3: The events received by a client C_0 and generated by the same source maintain the publication order.

$$\Box(Prec(SUBC_0, SUBS_0MASTER, PUBC_1(e_1), PUBC_1(e_2))$$
$$\Rightarrow \Diamond Prec(NOTC_0(e_1), NOTC_0(e_2), UNSC_0))$$

where $PUBC_1(e_i)$ means that C_1 published e_i and, analogously $NOTC_0(e_i)$ indicates that C_0 receives the event e_i. $SUBS_0MASTER$ means that S_0 forwards to S_1 the subscription received from C_0

Property 4: Let C_0 be a client subscribed for a given filter f. Let C_0 move after it has received the event e_i. When C_0 will connect to the server S_2 (refer to Figure 6.a), it will receive all events $e_{i+1}, e_{i+2}, \ldots, e_n$ published during its disconnection period.

$$\Box(Prec(SUBC_0, \tau_{moveC_0}, PUBC_1(e_{i+1}), \cdots, PUBC_1(e_n), MVIC_0))$$
$$\Rightarrow (\neg UNSC_0 \wedge Prec(NOTC_0(e_{i+1}), \cdots, NOTC_0(e_n)))$$

where τ_{moveC_0} indicates that C_0 is moving and, $MVIC_0$ indicates that C_0 is connecting to a new access-point.

4.2   Abstract Model of SIENA

Architectural Reduction: The goal is to build a system that is as smallest as possible, but meaningful for the analysis of the properties. We have considered the configuration obtained by putting together 3 servers and 2 clients (as showed in Figure 5.a) in a tree-like topology. This model respects the hierarchical architecture defined by the SIENA specification (where C_0 and C_1 represent clients) and it is meaningful for proving *Properties 1-3*. In fact only considering at least three servers it is possible to fully model all the intra-server communication semantics.

Architectural Slicing: Although a SIENA client is able to both publish and subscribe events, in order to verify *Properties 1-3* it is sufficient to consider one publisher C_1 and one subscriber C_0. This means that in our abstract model, every event will be generated by C_1 and delivered to C_0 through the path $< S_2, S_1, S_0 >$. In other words C_0 is able to submit subscriptions and unsubscriptions, to receive notifications, but it cannot publish any event. Analogously C_1 is able to publish events but it does not submit subscriptions and, therefore it is not able to receive notifications. This allows us to build servers which have only the needed features. For example S_2 is not able to accept subscribe-requests, S_0 cannot receive publish-messages (Figure 5.b) and, S_1 is simply able to route messages from S_2 to S_0 (Figure 5.c). This allows the reduction of the number of parallel processes and of the exchanged messages in the system model.

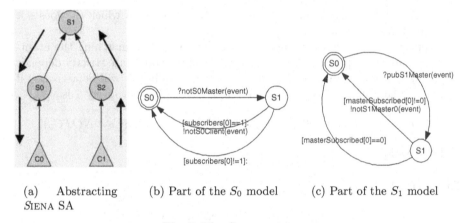

(a)   Abstracting   (b) Part of the S_0 model   (c) Part of the S_1 model
SIENA SA

Fig. 5. The SIENA system.

Moreover the events set has been simplified by defining one event type only. That is, the client can subscribe and publish only events of *integer* type. Therefore our system model does not distinguish between different kinds of events or filters.

Properties Verification and Reasoning: In this section we show the results of the analysis for *Properties* 1-3.

Property 1:

$$\Box(Prec(SUBC_0, PUBC_1) \Rightarrow \Diamond(\neg UNSC_0 \wedge NOTC_0))$$

This property is not valid on the SIENA model. The MSC in Figure 7.a shows the counter-example: (i) Client$_0$ and Client$_1$ connect to Server$_0$ and Server$_2$ respectively, (ii) Client$_0$ subscribes a filter to Server$_0$ and Client$_1$ publishes an event to Server$_2$ which is then forwarded to Server$_1$. (iii) At this point the subscription request is forwarded to Server$_1$. The published event is therefore lost.

The invalidation of this property means that in the Event-Based distributed Architectural Patterns it is important to focus on the filters *activation* rather than on the filters *subscription*. Then, given a predicate *Active* defined as in Definition 2, Property 1 must be rewritten:

Definition 2. *Let Active(f) be a predicate that returns* **true** *if and only if the filter f has been activated into the event-service.*

Property 1.b: When a filter f, subscribed by C_0, has been activated and C_1 publishes an event ($PUBC_1$) matching such a filter then C_0 receives an event notification identified by the $NOTC_0$ message.

$$\Box((Active(f) \land PUBC_1) \Rightarrow \Diamond(\neg UNSC_0 \land NOTC_0))$$

$\neg UNSC_0$ is introduced in order to select only the paths in which C_0 does not perform an unsubscription.

Property 1.b describes the behavior that every system matching the event-based architectural pattern should satisfy. The *Active* predicate strictly depends on the system under analysis. In our SIENA model, a filter f will be activated if and only if the variable $masterSubscribed[0] == 1$. Then Property 1 is

$$\Box(((masterSubscribed[0] == 1) \land PUBC_1) \Rightarrow \Diamond(\neg UNSC_0 \land NOTC_0))$$

and it is valid.

Property 2:

$$\Box(Prec(MSG_s(m_0), MSG_s(m_1), \ldots, MSG_s(m_n))$$
$$\Rightarrow \Diamond Prec(\tau_s(m_0), \tau_s(m_1), \ldots, \tau_s(m_n)))$$

This schema formula can be instantiated with actual messages. For example we checked the following instance referring to S_0:

$$\Box(Prec(SUBC_0(f_0), SUBC_0(f_1))$$
$$\Rightarrow \Diamond Prec(SUBS_0 MASTER(f_0), SUBS_0 MASTER(f_1)))$$

with a valid result that implies that the SIENA model maintains the subscription order. Since in SIENA servers are independent from each other and from the topology of the event-service, this formula is also valid in more general instances of the event-service model.

Property 3:

$$\Box(Prec(SUBC_0, SUBS_0 MASTER, PUBC_1(e_1), PUBC_1(e_2))$$
$$\Rightarrow \Diamond Prec(NOTC_0(e_1), NOTC_0(e_2), UNSC_0))$$

This formula is another instance of the schema formula in property 2 referring to the messages sequence $SUBC_0$, $SUBS_0MASTER$, $PUBC_1(e)$, $PUBS_2MASTER(e)$, $NOTS_0MASTER(e)$, $NOTC_0(e)$.

Note that a $SUBS_0MASTER$ message has been added in order to force the filters activation.

The check reports a valid result. Since the SIENA event-service is built in a hierarchical topology, two consecutive messages, emitted by a given source and addressed to the same destination, will follow the same path and will touch the same nodes. Thus, since this is true for every instance of the event-service and, since property 2 is valid for every node in the event-service, then this property is also true for any general model.

4.3   Abstract Model of CoMETA

Architectural Reduction: In extending the architectural model presented in Figure 5.a for integrating the CoMETA features, we maintained C_1 as publisher and C_0 as subscriber. As showed in Figure 6.a C_1 is connected to S_1 and C_0 is able to move from S_0 to S_2. This model represents a weakly-closed system.

Architectural Slicing: In this case S_1 must be modified in order to route messages to both S_0 and S_2 and to manage publications submitted by C_1 (Figure 6.c). S_2 must be modified in order to receive notifications and to deliver them to C_0 and, in S_0 the notification persistence must be added (Figure 6.b). Thus, before C_0 moves, the events published by C_1 will be delivered to C_0 through S_0 and, after C_0 has moved, they will be routed to S_2.

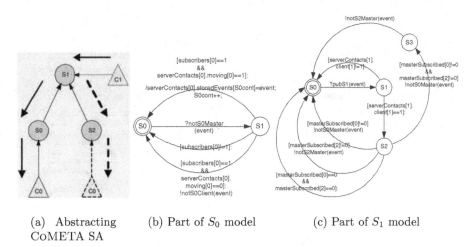

(a) Abstracting
CoMETA SA

(b) Part of S_0 model

(c) Part of S_1 model

Fig. 6. The CoMETA System.

Properties Verification and Reasoning: Property 4 is not valid in our model. This means that our solution does not avoid loss of events and thus it violates the expected behavior.

Studying the trace obtained as result of Property 4 violation from CHARMY (showed in Figure 7.b), we can note that the loss of events is due to delays that may occur during the messages propagation through the servers. In fact, since the SIENA event-service is built as a distributed-system, propagation delay may occur in forwarding routing information through the SIENA servers. Thus, when the client requests to download stored events from the old server (and then to shutdown the event-persistency active on such server), routing information may be not yet changed through the event-service. Therefore, new events continue to be delivered to the old location but, since in that place nobody is waiting for them, they will be lost.

Since Property 4 is not valid in a minimal model, then it is also not valid in more general instances of the event-service. In fact, the event-service is built as a tree-like topology and then, since our model represents the minimum possible tree (excluding trees composed by one or two nodes), any general model will contain this minimal architecture. That is, our model represents a minimal complete sub-tree of any given event-service architecture. Thus, lost events may occur, each time the event-download involves two servers located in two different branches of the same root.

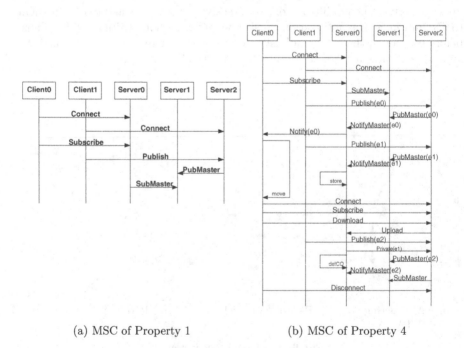

(a) MSC of Property 1   (b) MSC of Property 4

Fig. 7. MSC of the Properties.

In order to solve the above described problem, a synchronization between the two master servers involved in the events-download procedure (let H be the old server and T the destination one) is required. Moreover, before requesting the download, the client should test if routing information spread in the event-service are active (as shown in Figure 4.b). This guarantees that new events will be delivered to the right location and, that the client will be able to receive them.

Since routing information are set up by subscribing filters (for more information refer to [6]) the idea is to test if submitted filters are active and then perform the event-download procedure. Since SIENA does not provide any native method to know if and when a certain filter is active through the event-service, we can think of subscribing a filter for a special event right after all the others and then publish an event that matches it. Validity of Property 2 in SIENA (refer to Section 4.1) guarantees that this special filter will be processed only after the others. Therefore, if it results active, the other (subscribed before it) will be active too.

This solution is based on the filters activation process thus it implicitly refers to the validity of Property 1.b. Therefore, it is possible to apply this solution to those systems that implement a hierarchical event-based architectural pattern, by properly defining the notion of filters activation. An example of applying the "event-download with path test" solution to others event-based systems can be found in [3].

5   Conclusions

In this paper we have proposed an approach for verifying systems based on architectural patterns. Starting from system specification, the approach derives an architectural abstraction on which a standard analysis can be carried on. Once the architectural pattern, matching to the system under analysis, has been recognized and, a set of properties of interest has been defined, the approach defines the following steps: (i) to find out, if there exists, a *minimal* configuration for which the specified properties make sense, (ii) to abstract the chosen architectural model in order to reduce the complexity of the verification phase. In this stage, abstractions are driven by the properties of interest. The output of this abstraction step can be model-checked, tested and analyzed by using a standard model-checking framework. (iii) The verification results obtained in the previous step are lifted to generic configurations by performing *manual* reasoning driven by the constraints posed by the architectural pattern.

In the case of a property of interest characterizing a desired behavior common to all systems that match the selected pattern, then the property can be lifted to the architectural pattern level (i.e. Property 1). Furthermore this property can be embedded into the semantic specification of the pattern itself and then it should be satisfied by all those systems that implement such a pattern.

In order to validate the approach, it has been applied to the SIENA middleware by using an event-based architectural pattern. Moreover, it has been shown how to reuse architectural pattern properties in order to validate possible extensions of the pattern itself (the mobility extension of SIENA).

In this direction on going works concern different aspects. First, more investigation is due to understanding unscalable systems and properties, then, the automation of both the architectural slicing driven by the properties of interest and, the scaling process.

Acknowledgments

The authors would like to thank Antonio Carzaniga and Alexander L. Wolf for their contributions to the work about CoMETA.

The authors would also like to acknowledge the Italian national project C.N.R. SP4 that partly supported this work.

References

1. R. Buchi, J. On a decision method in restricted second order arithmetic. In *Proc. of the International Congress of Logic, Methodology and Philosophy of Science*, pages pp 1–11. Standford University Press, 1960.
2. M. Caporuscio. CoMETA - Mobility support in the SIENA publish/subscribe middleware. Master's thesis, Università degli Studi dell'Aquila - Dipartimento di Informatica, L'Aquila - Italy, March 2002.
3. M. Caporuscio, A. Carzaniga, and A. L. Wolf. Design and evaluation of a support service for mobile, wireless publish/subscribe applications. *IEEE Transactions on Software Engineering*, 29(12):1059–1071, Dec. 2003.
4. M. Caporuscio, P. Inverardi, and P. Pelliccione. Compositional verification of middleware-based software architecture descriptions. In *Proceedings of the International Conference on Software Engineering (ICSE 2004)*, Edimburgh, 2004. To appear.
5. A. Carzaniga, E. Di Nitto, D. S. Rosenblum, and A. L. Wolf. Issues in supporting event-based architectural styles. In *3rd International Software Architecture Workshop*, Orlando, Florida, Nov. 1998.
6. A. Carzaniga, D. S. Rosenblum, and A. L. Wolf. Achieving Scalability and Expressiveness in an Internet-Scale Event Notification Service. In *Proceedings of the Nineteenth Annual ACM Symposium on Principles of Distributed Computing*, pages 219–227, Portland, OR, July 2000.
7. A. Carzaniga, D. S. Rosenblum, and A. L. Wolf. Design and Evaluation of a Wide-Area Event Notification Service. *ACM Transactions on Computer Systems*, 19(3):332–383, Aug. 2001.
8. A. Carzaniga and A. L. Wolf. Content-based networking: A new communication infrastructure. In *NSF Workshop on an Infrastructure for Mobile and Wireless Systems*, number 2538 in Lecture Notes in Computer Science, pages 59–68, Scottsdale, Arizona, Oct. 2001. Springer-Verlag.
9. E. M. Clarke, O. Grumberg, and D. A. Peled. *Model Checking*. The MIT Press, Massachusetts Institute of Technology, 2001.
10. D. Compare, P. Inverardi, P. Pelliccione, and A. Sebastiani. Integrating model-checking architectural analysis and validation in a real software life-cycle. In *the 12th International Formal Methods Europe Symposium (FME 2003)*, number 2805 in LNCS, pages 114–132, Pisa, 2003.

11. A. Fugetta, G. Picco, and G. Vigna. Understanding Code Mobility. *IEEE Transaction on Software Engineering*, 24(5), 1998.
12. D. Garlan, R. Allen, and J. Ockerbloom. Exploiting style in architectural design environments. In *Proceedings of SIGSOFT'94: The Second ACM SIGSOFT Symposium on the Foundations of Software Engineering*. ACM Press, December 1994.
13. D. Garlan, S. Khersonsky, and J. S. Kim. Model Checking Publish-Subscribe Systems. In *Proceedings of The 10th International SPIN Workshop on Model Checking of Software (SPIN 03)*, Portland Oregon, May 2003.
14. G. J. Holzmann. *The SPIN Model Checker: Primer and Reference Manual*. Addison-Wesley, September 2003.
15. P. Inverardi, H. Muccini, and P. Pelliccione. Automated Check of Architectural Models Consistency using SPIN. In *the Automated Software Engineering Conference Proceedings (ASE 2001)*. San Diego, California, Nov 2001.
16. P. Inverardi, H. Muccini, and P. Pelliccione. Charmy: A framework for model based consistency checking. Technical report, Department of Computer Science, University of L'Aquila, January 2003.
17. P. Inverardi, H. Muccini, and P. Pelliccione. Checking Consistency Between Architectural Models Using SPIN. In *Proc. the First Int. Workshop From Software Requirements to Architectures (STRAW'01)*, year 2001.
18. Object Management Group (OMG). Unified Modeling Language (UML) Version 1.5. http://www.omg.org/uml/, March 2003.
19. A. Pnueli. The temporal logic of programs. In *In Proc. 18th IEEE Symposium on Foundation of Computer Science*, pages pp. 46–57, 1977.
20. G.-C. Roman, G. P. Picco, and A. L. Murphy. Software Engineering for Mobility: A Roadmap. In A. Finkelstein, editor, *The Future of Software Engineering*, pages 241–258. ACM Press, 2000. Invited contribution.
21. M. Shaw and P. Clemens. Toward boxology: preliminary classification of architectural styles. In *Proc. on the second International Software Architecture Workshop (ISAW2)*, S. Francisco, CA USA, Oct. 1996.
22. J. A. Stafford, D. J. Richardson, and A. L. Wolf. Chaining: A software architecture dependence analysis technique. Technical Report CU-CS-845-97, Department of Computer Science, University of Colorado, Boulder, Colorado, September 1997.
23. J. A. Stafford and A. L. Wolf. Architecture-level dependence analysis in support of software maintenance. In *Third International Software Architecture Workshop*, pages 129–132, Orlando, Florida, November 1998.
24. J. Zhao. Software Architecture Slicing. In *Proceedings of the 14th Annual Conference of Japan Society for Software Science and Technology*, 1997.

Architectural Modelling in Product Family Context

Rodrigo Cerón[1,*], José L. Arciniegas[1,*], José L. Ruiz[1], Juan C. Dueñas[1],
Jesús Bermejo[2], and Rafael Capilla[3]

[1] Department of Engineering of Telematic Systems,
Universidad Politécnica de Madrid,
ETSI Telecomunicación, Ciudad Universitaria, s/n, E-28040 Madrid, Spain
{ceron,jlarci,jlruiz,jcduenas}@dit.upm.es
http://www.dit.upm.es/
[2] Telvent, Spain
[3] Department of Informatics and Telematics, Universidad Rey Juan Carlos, Madrid, Spain
rcapilla@escet.urjc.es
Tel: +34 91 6647458, Fax: +34 91 6647490

Abstract. The software development community pursues the development of software systems with a higher degree of reuse, reduction of costs, and shorter time to market. One of the successful mechanisms followed to achieve these goals is based on sharing the development efforts, producing sets of similar products. This approach is known as Product Family Engineering (PFE). Architectural modeling (producing architectural models) in product families is a key issue in PFE activities and it will be the main focus of this paper. First, we will propose an architectural UML meta-model for PFE, able to represent the different variations in products. This meta-model will set up the conceptual basis for two valuable sets of activities that reflect industrial best practices: one deals with effectively building and maintaining the product family architecture and the other with the automatic derivation of architectures of specific products. A small example of automatic derivation is included.

1 Introduction

For many years, software industries have been trying to achieve the development of software intensive systems with a higher degree of reuse, cost reduction, and shorten of time to market. Product Family Engineering (PFE) is considered as one of the most successful approaches to do it. It is based on the development of sets of similar products, called product families.

---

* Jose L. Arciniegas and Rodrigo Cerón are visiting professors from Universidad del Cauca, Colombia. Rodrigo Cerón is sponsored by COLCIENCIAS - Colombia. The work performed by José L. Arciniegas has been partially developed in the project TRECOM, granted by Spanish Ministry of Science and Technology under reference TIC2002-04123-C03-01. The work done by Rodrigo Cerón, Jose L. Ruiz, and Juan C. Dueñas has been partially performed in the project FAMILIES (Eureka 2023, ITEA ip02009), partially supported by the Spanish company Telvent and by the Spanish Ministry of Science and Technology, under reference TIC2002-10373-E.

F. Oquendo et al. (Eds.): EWSA 2004, LNCS 3047, pp. 25–42, 2004.

One of the main areas of interest in our research group is conceptual modelling for product families. There are many works in this arena [1–9], in consequence there is a need for common understanding, which can be facilitated with the usage of conceptual models providing a framework to organize and structure the knowledge. The models provide a way of communication and a common vocabulary for the people within the organization [10]. As a result, the assets for a product family include not only the software itself but also its models. The Unified Modelling Language (UML) provides guidelines to modelling in a general sense [10], [11]; it is a broadly adopted standard and it has been the modelling language used in some companies for years. UML is the language that we have chosen for this work; many UML advantages can be mentioned but are outside the scope of the present paper [5], [10], [11].

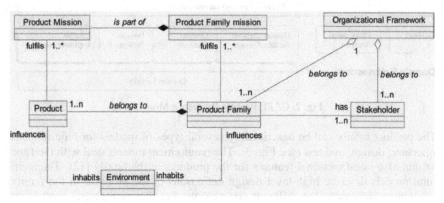

Fig. 1. Product Family Environment.

The first step that has to be done is to understand the Product Family Environment in its context: we have defined a conceptual model (see Fig.1), following and extending the general ideas of the standard IEEE 1471-2000. The product family belongs to an organizational framework and its development is thus justified within this context. The stakeholders also belong to the organizational framework, and they work in the development of the product family as a whole. The product family and each specific product will be developed to fulfil at least one mission, so obviously product missions should be aligned with product family missions. The product family should be understood as a mean to facilitate the product development. The external environment will influence the development of the product family as a whole and it also has to be taken into account.

The basic work behind the results presented here has performed in the CAFÉ project [9]. The CAFÉ reference framework (CRF) gives a guide to classify the activities and models related with PF development. In summary, CRF can be divided in two main parts CAFÉ Process Reference Model (CAFÉ – PRM, shown in **Fig. 2**) and CAFÉ Assets Reference Model (CAFÉ - ARM). The objective of this model is to represent the major activities and methods operating on the core assets, to allow the mapping of the contribution/tools against a common reference. Our research work is aimed to solve problems in the transition from Domain Design to Application Design, although also the transition from the design to implementation is also considered in our research work.

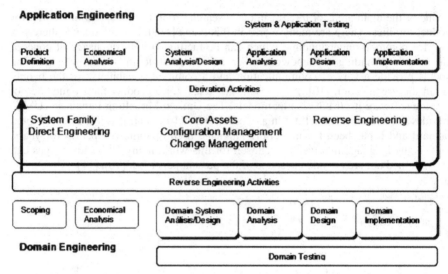

Fig. 2. CAFÉ Process Reference Model.

The product family can be described by several types of models for requirements, architecture, design, and test (see **Fig. 3**). The requirement models deal with the functional but also non-functional features for the products in the family [12]. The architectural models describe high-level design definitions of the products in the family; the design models show the different components that the architectural models describe; and finally, test models contain the tests that the PF must satisfy; they are usually based on the PF requirements.

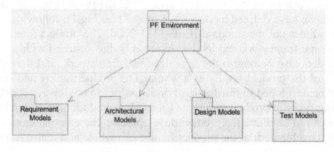

Fig. 3. Product Family and some of its assets.

Our goal in this document is to present our ongoing efforts towards the representation and efficient management of product family architectures, which includes:

- The identification of an architectural process taking into account the specificities in product family engineering.
- The identification of the elements that are required in order to support the modelling of the architectural elements that appear in each of the product family system, as well as those appearing in a subset of the family. The way these elements are related is called "variation point" in the literature, and we link the concept to the actual architectural models in this work.

- The selection of a modelling mechanism to express the decisions that can be taken in order to create product architecture models from the family reference architecture and how the application of these decisions can be partially automated.
- The presentation of an easily usable approach that imposes a low entry barrier to the designers and companies in use of it.

The rest of article is organized as follows: in the next section, we will present a meta-model for the representation of variability in the architecture. In section 3, we describe our processes for building and maintaining the Product Family Architecture (PFA). Section 4 contains the processes for the derivation of single product architectures from the PFA; these are illustrated in section 5 some simple case studies that show how automatic support may help in apply the decisions to the PFA. In section 6, we conclude with some remarks and future research.

2 Architectural Meta-model

In this section we present our architectural meta-model, as a conceptual framework to cope with variability in architecture [13]. **Fig. 4** shows the different relationships among the models in Product Family Environment, including requirements, architectural and test models. Following the conventional forward engineering process, the architectural and test models are obtained from the requirements model. There must be traces among these three models, in order to keep an integrated and updated model repository (the traceability package shows these relations).

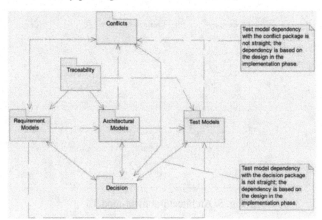

Fig. 4. PF models and relationships.

In order to know how to face variability, first we need to understand it. A definition may help: "Variability is what can be different among members of a collection (of problems, solutions or products)" [14]. Variability aspects can be managed at different stages: requirements description, architectural description, design documentation, source code, compiled code, linked code and running code.

The variation point concept can be used in order to express variability explicitly. A variation point identifies one or more locations at which variability will occur. Each variation point will be related to a decision. Once the decision is made, a set of variant elements will remain and others will be left apart; as a result, the variation point will have changed its state.

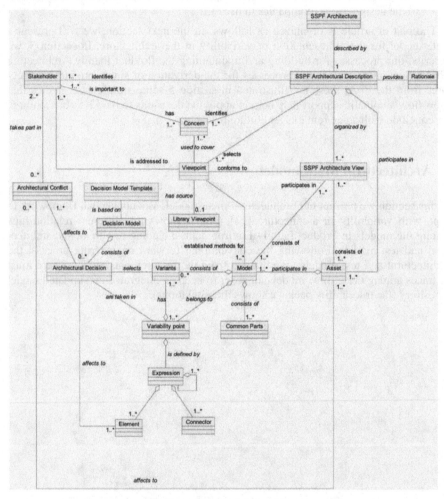

Fig. 5. Architectural meta-model.

Effectively handling variability is the main challenge an organization has to cope with in PFE. It gives us the chance to gain flexibility in the products involved in the PF. As a consequence, variability modelling is an essential concern in order to build flexible PF arquitectures.

Tightly linked to the concept of variability, the decisions are part of the product family; therefore they are related to the models in the PF. In order to obtain specific products, decisions have to be taken to deal with variability: either in the requirement, or architectural or testing phases. The later the variability issues are solved the more flexible the product family is. Conflicts are a consequence of the variability in the product family; they have to be fixed in order to obtain coherent products. Different alternatives may lead to different conflicts, but there should be at least one solution for each conflict.

Our architectural meta-model proposal is shown in the **Fig. 5**. To fully understand the diagram, assume that Element in our meta-model denotes a ModelElement in UML sense. The top of the architectural meta-model is based on the IEEE Std. 1471-2000 [15], where models are organized in views, which makes modelling simpler and easier to understand for different stakeholders. System Software PF (SSPF) provides the rationale for this architecture; it is captured by an architectural description.

Variability is explicitly represented in the architecture through variation points. For us, each variation point is composed of one or more variants and it is formally defined by an algebraic expression. The expression denotes the relationships among elements, using as syntax operators the ones available in Boole Algebra. Expressions are composable, therefore an expression can be created as a combination of others. While the variation point concept appears several times in the literature (see [1], [3], [4], [13], [14]), attaching logical expressions about the composability of the different variants is a novel contribution of ours. Later some examples will be given. Due to its expressivity power, simplicity and independence of the modelling language used, we consider this solution very useful in real, industrial contexts.

The reference architecture obtained for a product family is a series of models in different views; each element in a model is labelled as variable to the set of products in the product family. The architecture for a single product can be obtained by a derivation process from the PFA. Functional issues are captured by means of the algebra expressions mentioned previously. Non functional issues are captured by means of decisions and the decision model used. Object Constrain Language (OCL) can be used to express the decision model; this is one of the features we are currently researching on.

3 Reference Architecture Modelling

In order to automate the production of models, a series of systematic activities have to be provided. In this section, we propose two processed for Reference Architecture Modelling, based on our experience with the best practices identified in several companies in the CAFÉ project. **Fig. 6** shows the first practice. Its basic purpose is to obtain an appropriate architecture for the PF that will only include the common aspects of the PF. This activity is closely related to scoping and requirements elicitation tasks which are already classical activities in product family engineering.

First, based on the domain and product scoping, a product architectural scoping and a product scoping assessment is carried out with different kinds of products, in order to include them or not into the product family. After that, considering the PF requirements, an architectural style for the product family has to be chosen [16], [17], [18]. Before going on, it is necessary to verify that the common requirements are fulfilled by the obtained architecture. If the architectural style is fulfilled, the Core Reference Architecture can be developed, taking into account the architectural style, the PF requirements and the Engineering Assets Repository. Otherwise, the process should return to the product architectural scoping in order to change the members of the family.

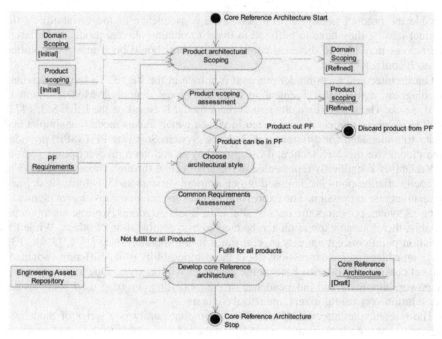

Fig. 6. Development of the core Reference Architecture.

Fig. 7 shows the second practice. Its main goal is to obtain the complete architecture for the PF. The architecture reached by this process will include both common and variable aspects of the PF. As input for this process we will need: the reference architecture (obtained as a result of the previous process), existing assets and specific product requirements.

First, based on the platform repository (descriptions of quality, physical and logical features of the platforms), the Core Reference Architecture will be enhanced. Then a validation will be carried out to check its internal coherence. If this architecture is coherent, variation points have to be provided, by adding all the variants and identifying all the possible relations among them. Otherwise, it would be necessary to go back to the beginning of this process.

The addition of variants must take into account the available assets; this should be made automatically using the Engineering Assets Repository. Functional and non-functional features for each asset should be provided. Once this is finished, the architecture has to be assessed against the Product Specific Requirements of all the products included in it. If it does not fulfil the requirements it will be necessary to come back to the beginning of this process. If fulfilled, in order to obtain the PF reference architecture in its initial state, the last step would be to identify the variation point ranges. The addition of variation points and the relations among them are manual activities. On the contrary, the selection of components from its repository should be automatic.

Dealing with evolution of the architecture is an important issue in this process. As it is now, there are two main limitations to the changes a reference architecture may suffer: first the set of common requirements the product family is meeting should be

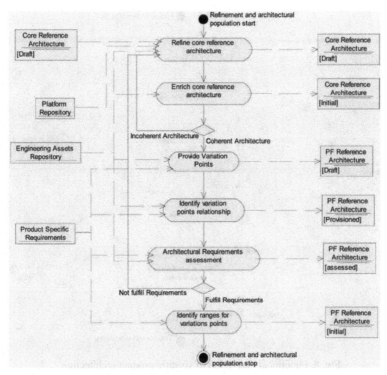

Fig. 7. Refinement and architectural population.

stable, and second, the architectural style should remain stable. The evolution of the product family architecture will mainly focus on adding or removing variation points, and the sets of variants for them. Also interesting is to notice that before a new element is inserted in the reference architecture (a new component, for example) its compatibility to the previous elements must be checked.

4 Derivation from PF Architecture

In this section, we are going to propose two best practices for the derivation of product architectures from the PFA. **Fig. 8** shows the first practice, whose basic purpose is to obtain the functional product architecture. It only considers functional requirements of the product. Inputs needed for this process are: the product requirements, PFA and existing components.

Initially, a functional-based decision has to be taken on the basis of the product specific requirements, the PF Reference Architecture and the Component Repository [19]. Then decisions will have to be taken, and as a result, a set of variants will be selected, according to the three mentioned inputs [20]. After that, these selections have to be matched against components contained into the repository. If there is no adequate match, it will be necessary to return to the selection of variants (and take a decision about using COTS, open source or developing the components). If all match,

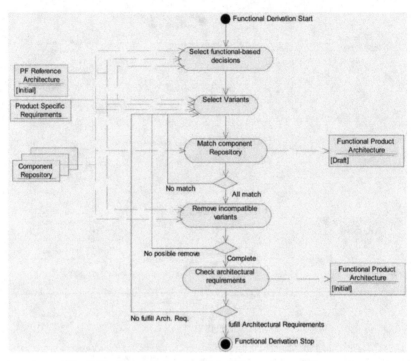

Fig. 8. Functional derivation of specific product architecture.

the process can continue in order to remove all the incompatible variants that could exist. Automatic support is needed in the architectural transformations from an architecture with full variation points to a functional product architecture and to provide help to remove incompatible solutions.

This automatic support is currently given by a prototype tool that takes as inputs: the architectural models described using UML and annotated with the identification of specific elements, the variation points including the logic expressions about the compatibility of their variants (and also compatibility between variants in different variation points), and the decisions the architect may take, expressed by means of the names of the elements to be selected, or to be removed (a decision can be also described by means of a logical expression).

Fig. 9 shows the second practice. Its basic purpose is to obtain the specific product architecture. It takes into account non-functional requirements of the product. This process will need the following inputs: PF functional architecture, product requirements, existing components and quality models.

Initially, non-functional-based decisions have to be taken, using: the product specific requirements, the Functional Product Architecture and the Component Repository [19]. Then, the variants needed have to be chosen, according to the three mentioned inputs. After that, these selections have to be matched against the component repository. If there is no adequate match, it is necessary to return to the selection of variants. If all match, the process can continue in order to check completeness in the model. If the model is complete, or it is incomplete but it is possible to defer this absence, the process can continue. If not, the process must return to select the vari-

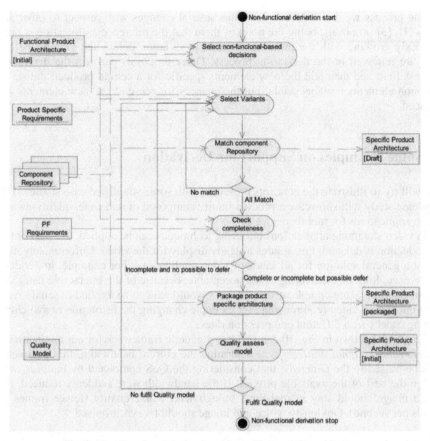

Fig. 9. Non-functional derivation of specific product architecture.

ants. Finished this step, the specific architecture can be packed and assessed against a quality model. If the architecture model does not fulfil the quality model, again the process must return to the selection of variants, otherwise the specific product architecture with functional and non functional requirements is obtained. Automatic support is needed in the architectural transformations from functional product architecture to non-functional product architecture, in order to remove incompatible solutions and to check completeness.

It might be argued that this division between the functional and non-functional derivation activities may not be so useful, because the interrelations between those two kinds of decisions to be made. However, let us remind that a first decision affecting the non-functional requirements is taken right starting the architectural process: the selection of the architectural style of the product family, that imposes a threshold to the overall quality of the specific systems in the family. Another reason to divide the derivation activities into functional and non-functional is that the current practices in industry show that the design of elements in the architecture dealing with the satisfaction of functional requirements is made in different time and by different people than those dealing with non-functional requirements.

The process we are describing contains several changes with respect to other authors [1], [3] proposals, being the main of them that the reference architecture is continuously growing with the introduction of new variation points and variants before they are removed in the derivation process. Other proposals perform the derivation process first, and then add the new elements specific for a certain product; the set of common elements remains stable, but the chances for reuse of the new elements are reduced.

5 Some Examples on Support for Derivation

We will try to illustrate the concepts presented with some simplified case studies. The first case study will showcase a product family composed of real-time, quality-aware, video applications for mobile devices.

In video streaming applications buffering techniques can be applied, the start of the reproduction is delayed; this assures a steady display for the video. Unfortunately, this is not a general solution for all kinds of video applications. For example, in a video-conference, long time buffering is not acceptable, because of the interactive nature of a conversation. More complicated techniques would have to be applied to satisfy real-time interactive video requirements, for example changing the resolution or switching among codecs with different compression rates.

The model shown in Fig. 10 can serve as a generic framework for our applications. The *Feedback signal analyzer* will determine the current bandwidth, this parameter will be passed to the *Gateway*, that considering the QoS contracted by the user, will assign the best of the available proxies. If the bandwidth were suddenly reduced, the video image should stay in real-time, though with worse quality (fewer frames or pixels per second). Obviously, voice and image should be synchronised.

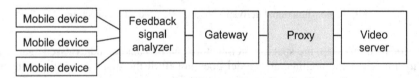

Fig. 10. Real time video for mobile systems.

The key aspect in what concerns to QoS is the proxy, which will determine the quality and, as a result, the codec chosen. The architecture of the proxy is described in the **Fig. 11**, where several variants can be identified (being tagged with {variant} in the UML class diagram): MPEG-4 or H.263 for video coding, GSM or AMR for audio, JPEG for still image coding and MPEG-4 file format for media storage. The proxy can be used for encoding still images in JPEG format, decoding JPEG images to raw RGB pictures and for recording, storing and playing video from a file.

The variability points in this particular case can be identified with interfaces in **Fig. 11**, and will determine which codec type should be used to process video or audio with a specific quality. For each variation point, the architect has to provide an algebraic expression (in terms of Boole Algebra):

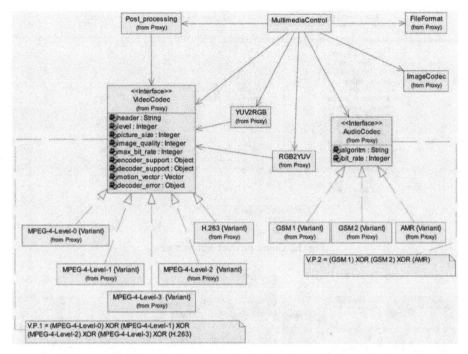

Fig. 11. Logic view of the the codecs product family.

- **Variation Point 1:** related to the interface VideoCodec. Depending on the encoding level: picture size, image quality, bit rate and so on, a specific video codec will be chosen. In this case the algebraic expression is:
  VP1 = (MPEG-4-Level-0) XOR (MPEG-4-Level-1) XOR (MPEG-4-Level-2) XOR (MPEG-4-Level-3) XOR (H.263).
- **Variation Point 2:** related to the interface AudioCodec, similar in functionality to the VideoCodec. Depending on the coding algorithm or bit rate used, the audio codec will be chosen. The algebraic expression for this variation point is:
  VP2 = (GSM 1) XOR (GSM 2) XOR (AMR)

Given these two variation points, 15 different configurations (product architectures) would be available before any decision is taken. Once defined the PF architecture, a variability-aware tool could be used to derive specific product architectures. For example, if the architect had chosen the variants: MPEG-4 and GSM 1, the result shown in **Fig. 12** would have been obtained.

The second case study represents a product family of client-server systems whose essential purpose is to control electronic devices at home. To simplify the exposition we will restrict the example to a bind control product line. The model which is shown here contains: variant and common components related to the client, related to the server and a variant set of classes that can be attached either to the client or to the server, therefore here we have a variant association.

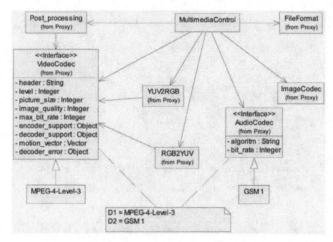

Fig. 12. Codec product architecture.

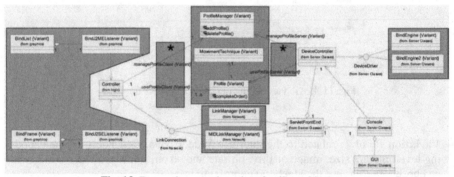

Fig. 13. Domestic control product family architecture.

The diagram (see Fig. 13) tries to illustrate five different variation points in order to show how they would be described by the use of equations:

- **Variation Point 1:** describes the possibility of using J2ME or J2SE graphic classes to construct the GUI of the client. In other words, if the client will run on a computer with full availability of graphical elements, or it will be running on a reduced environment, such as a mobile phone or another embedded system with less resources for human interaction.
  VP1 = (BindList AND BindJ2MEListener) XOR (BindFrame AND BindJ2SEListener)
- **Variation Point 2:** describes the possibility of using J2ME or J2SE network classes to construct the network implementation of the client. In essence, this variation point reflects the availability of network elements, allowing the selection of a different manager that allows itself for variability during execution (selection of different communication protocols during run-time). The MIDLinkManager refers to the piece of software in the J2ME platform for mobile phones that is able to control the communications using the mobile network.
  VP2 = LinkManager XOR MIDLinkManager

- **Variation Point 3:** describes the possibility of controlling different types of electronic binds. As said, the example is a control for a bind in a domestic environment. The different engines can be identified as different "device drivers" for each of these machines.
  VP3 = BindEngine XOR BindEngine2
- **Variation Point 4:** describes an optional functionality, the use of control profiles. The system may store different profiles for the automatic adaptation of the light in the room to the user needs. This functionality is optional: it does not appear in all the products in the family and this fact is reflected by this variation point.
  VP4 = OPT (ProfileManager AND MovementTechnique AND Profile)
- **Variation Point 5:** describes the possibility of associating the optional components inside the VP4 to the server or to the client. If a profile manager is included, it can be allocated to the client or to the server. Thus, a decision about the quality of the system (in terms of maximum number of profiles to be stores, speed to access the profiles, availability of the profiles) must be taken whose results are to put this function in either of those places.
  VP5 = VP4 AND ((manageProfileClient AND useProfileClient) XOR (manageProfileServer AND useProfileServer))

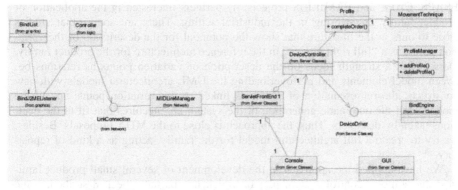

Fig. 14. Domestic control product architecture after decisions.

Given these two variation points, 24 different configurations (product architectures) would be available before any decision is taken. Once defined the PF architecture, a variability-aware tool could be used to derive specific product architectures. The Fig. 14 represents an example of how the process of derivation of a specific product architecture from the reference PFA can be done by a series of decisions that are automated by giving values to the different elements of the variation points. Thus, the decisions taken are:

Decision 1 = BindList, BindJ2MEListener
Decision 2 = MIDLinkManager
Decision 3 = BindEngine
Decision 4 = TRUE
Decision 5 = manageProfileServer, useProfileServer.

This second example is obviously very simple because its main objective is to illustrate the processes explained in previous sections. However, it is large enough to show important issues in variability modeling:

- The variability of functional elements must be represented.
- Unconnected regions of models can be part of the variation point; other approaches link each of the possible variants to a single point in the architecture.
- Different rules for relations are included, not only the selection (xor), but mandatory and optionality.
- Associations between elements in the model can also be affected by the variability points and henceforth they can be affected by the rules and decisions.
- Non-functional issues, such as quality crosscutting or adaptations to different deployment settings, must be dealt with in the variability representation (for example, the allocation to the client or the server of a certain functionality).

6   Conclusions and Further Work

The approach taken is based on the best practices studies and described during the ESAPS, CAFÉ and FAMILIES projects, by partners interested in the application of product family engineering in the industrial setting. There are some other studies close to ours in the literature that show the potential for the description of the variation points as a "full right citizen" in the reference architecture for the product family. Ours makes a strength focus on the description of variation points as relations between model elements and not overloading the UML architectural models with new constructs; the representation of decisions linked to the variation points and to the models; and the automatic generation of the system architectures that fit to the decisions taken by designers. Thus, the approach is close to the MDA proposals. Besides, we try to create a full architectural model for the family, acting as a kind of repository.

We have applied the approach in the development of several small product families: the domotic control system part of which has partially been described, some games to be executed on mobile platforms, a video streaming server, a deployment framework for distributed services, an Internet service control system, a network management service and the kernel of a mixed civil-militar simulator. In all of them we have made from two to five prototypes (not actual commercial products).

Our experience in the application is that it is a medium to long-term effort whose benefits are made clear if variability-in-the-large or variability-in-the-long is involved. The main conclusion of designers applying our approach is that the most important value is the recognition of variation points and the decisions, and the capability of documenting them. Another important contribution is the capability that the approach holds for the evolution of the systems. The results of the evaluation of third-party components can be documented with respect to the full range of products in the family (in the best case), thus giving support to the architectural assessment documentation.

As it has been mentioned in the article, we have tried to provide a method for description of common and variable elements in the reference architecture in a product family context, as a conceptual framework an architectural meta-model has been presented. Best practices for PFA Modelling and for the derivation of specific product architectures from the reference architecture have been described, in terms of how and when to apply the set of decisions that architects take for the creation of a product in the family. For these purposes, we have used part of the standard UML language and its extensibility mechanisms, but we have not changed the meta-model, thus making our approach applicable, regardless the in-house tool support (provided it handles standard UML modelling facilities).

A complete logical language has been defined (including the "not", "or", "xor", "and" operators) and a prototype of tool for execution of the derivation process has been developed. Using this prototype, we have performed several experiments in order to check the usability in a real context. The largest experiment so far is composed by 55 classes, 6 interfaces, 25 inheritance associations, 20 composition associations, 20 implementation associations, 60 attributes and 120 methods, which yields 281,474,976,710,656 possible product architectures. Applying decisions iteratively a satisfactory solution can be found in seconds.

With respect to the activities described in the paper and their application in the development cycle, let us remind that we are focusing on the product family engineering activities described by the CAFÉ reference framework, and very especially in the derivation of product architectures from reference product family architectures. It is important to note that we are not imposing any other requirement to the development process, neither having done domain analysis activities, nor having a domain implementation platform; if these were available, then our approach could be used and its real potential improvements obtained, but in the case of not having them, we are still providing a means for the incremental growing of the family architectural models.

Among the main points that, in our view, need improvement in the approach and should need more work before transferring it to companies, these can be cited:

- Semantic checking between UML models and views when the variants are in place and when the derivation process has been performed. UML has still a lack of consistency among views. The described approach suffers from the same problem, but extended because perhaps variation points could cross among views. Very especially, we still have to provide support for the expression of variability in dynamic models. As some authors suggest, dealing with variability in state-charts or message sequence chart models has special implications.
- New relations, the application of variation points to other elements in models than packages or classes (methods, attributes, constants), and the incorporation of other kinds of rules about other elements not directly present in the models, such as memory occupation. In this case, and using ranges of numbers, we could think about architectural tuning to certain configurations, which in the case of embedded systems has realized to be key for the effective usage in industry.
- Methodological support for the management of decisions, hierarchies of decisions and logical ordering of decisions and restrictions. It is our view that having a flat space of decisions will render useless as the number of these grows (and it is a very likely situation). Even more, not all decisions can be taken by the same set of stakeholders, therefore, some guidelines for the separation and clustering of decisions must be given (activities such as ordering of requirements would be a help for this). Another possible way to solve the scalability problem could come from the logic programming area, or the use of expert systems.

– Support for traceability among common parts in domain analysis, architecture and implementation is still a problem, which is even more acute for the variable elements. Variable attributes in each of these fields should be identified, and links among variants at these three levels would allow for a higher reuse degree in the family. Also, support for reverse engineering activities would be a great improvement that would help many companies with the adoption of product families. Finally, linking the variation points and decisions through the system lifecycle, including the maintenance (and requirements, testing, configuration) may lead to an effective means for the kind of evolution some systems require.

Our future research work will deepen methods and techniques to transcend these identified weaknesses. Special attention will be paid to tool support and automation of the best practices presented in the article and execution of experiments of application to commercial or open source system families. In general, a global view for the PF development is needed in order to define requirements for tool support in PFE.

References

1. Bosch, J.: Design and Use of Software Architectures-Adapting and Evolving a Product Line Approach. ACM Press, Addison-Wesley, Harlow, England (2000)
2. Coplien, J., Hoffman, D., Weiss, D.: Commonality and Variability in Software Engineering. IEEE Software, Vol. 15 No. 6. IEEE Computer Society, Los Alamitos, CA (1998) 37-45
3. El Kaim, W.: Managing Variability in the LCAT SPLIT/Daisy Model. In: Gacek C., Jourdan J., Coriat M. (eds.): Product Line Architecture Workshop, First Software Product Line Conference (2000) 21-31
4. Griss, M.: Implementing Product-Line features by Composing Component Aspects. In: Donohoe P. (ed.): Software Product Lines: Experience and Research Directions: Proceedings of First International Software Product Line Conference. The Kluwer International Series in Engineering And Computer Science, Volume 576. Kluwer Academic Publishers (2000) 271-288
5. Jacobson, I., Griss, M., Jonsson, P.: Software Reuse, Architecture, Process and Organization for Business Success. ACM Press, Addison-Wesley, New York (1997)
6. Keepence, B., Mannion, M.: Using Patterns to Model Variability in Product Families. IEEE Software, Vol. 16 No. 4. IEEE Computer Society, Los Alamitos, CA (1999) 102-108
7. Lane, T.G.: Studying Software Architecture through Design Spaces and Rules. Technical Report, CMU/SEI-90-TR-18, Software Engineering Institute (1990)
8. van der Linden, F. (ed.): Development and Evolution of Software Architectures for Product Families. Proceedings of the Second International ESPRIT ARES workshop, Las Palmas de Gran Canaria. Lecture Notes in Computer Science, 1429. Springer-Verlag, Berlin (1998)
9. van der Linden, F.: Software Product Families in Europe: The Esaps & Café Projects. IEEE Software, Vol. 10 No. 4. IEEE Computer Society, Los Alamitos, CA (2002) 41-49
10. Krutchen, P.: The Rational Development Process, An Introduction. 2nd edn. Prentice Hall, Englewood Cliffs, NJ, (2000)
11. OMG: Unified modeling language specification. Version 1.5. Object Management Group (2003)
12. Kang, K., Cohen, S., Hess, J., Novak, W., Peterson, A.: Feature-Oriented Domain Analysis (FODA) Feasibility Study. Technical Report CMU/SEI-90-TR21, November (1990)

13. Jazayeri, M., Ran, A., van der Linden, F. (eds.): Software architecture for product families. Addison Wesley, Boston (2000)
14. El Kaim, W.: System Family Software Architecture Glossary. ESAPS project, Technical Report WP2-0002-(ESAPS-0015) (2001)
15. IEEE-SA Standards Board: IEEE Recommended Practice for Architectural Description of Software-Intensive Systems. IEEE std 1471, 2000. Institute of Electrical and Electronics Engineers, New York, NY (2000)
16. Gamma, E., Helm, R., Johnson, R., Vlissides, J.: Design patterns, Elements of Reusable Object-Oriented Software. Addison-Wesley, Boston (1995)
17. Bachmann, F., Bass, L.: Managing Variability in Software Architectures. In: Proceedings of the 2001 Symposium on Software Reusability. ACM SIGSOFT (2001) 126-132
18. Buschmann, F., Meunier, R., Rohnert, H., Sommerlad, P., Stal, M.: Pattern – Oriented Software Architecture, A System of Patterns. John Wiley & Sons, New York, NY (1996)
19. Szyperski, C.: Component Software, Beyond Object-Oriented Programming. 2nd edn. ACM Press, Addison-Wesley, New York, NY (1998)
20. Alonso, A., León, G., Dueñas, J.C., de la Puente, J.A.: Framework for Documenting Design Decisions in Product Families Development. In: Proceedings of the Third IEEE International Conference on Engineering of Complex Computer Systems. IEEE Computer Society, Los Alamitos, CA (1997) 206-211.

Reflection-Based, Aspect-Oriented Software Architecture

Carlos E. Cuesta[1], M. Pilar Romay[2],
Pablo de la Fuente[1], and Manuel Barrio-Solórzano[1]

[1] Departamento de Informática (Arq., Cc.Comp., Leng.)
Universidad de Valladolid *
{cecuesta,pfuente,mbarrio}@infor.uva.es
[2] Departamento de Programación e Ingeniería de Software
Universidad Europea de Madrid
pilar.romay@uem.es

Abstract. The Software Architecture discipline is devoted to the study and description of structures, created by the composition of software modules. At the same time, the most important merit of Aspect Orientation is the fact that it introduces a new kind of modularization, deployed in a range of new dimensions, orthogonally to traditional models. These fields are able not only to combine, but also to complement and extend each other. They show also remarkable coincidences in some of their key concepts, such as multiple viewpoints and connectors. This paper explores their relationship, in particular from the point of view of the specification of "aspect-oriented architectures" in terms of existing Architecture Description Languages (ADLs). Specifically, we consider the language $\mathcal{P}i\mathcal{L}ar$: a reflective, process-algebraic ADL conceived for the description of dynamic architectures. It has three conceptual foundations which have also been proposed as a basis for aspect-orientation, namely reflection, superimposition and process algebras. We show how, due to the semantics of its reification relationship, $\mathcal{P}i\mathcal{L}ar$ is capable to directly describe "architectural aspects" with no need for syntactic extensions. At the same time, we suggest that the addition of these extensions could be very useful anyway. The discussion is supported by an example of a coordination aspect in $\mathcal{P}i\mathcal{L}ar$, based on the classical Paxos Consensus algorithm.

1 Introduction

Software Architecture is the branch within Software Engineering which deals with the design, study and description of the structure of software systems. This structure is usually expressed as an *architecture* composed by a set of *components* and their relationships. This refers both to analysis – the way a system can be decomposed – and synthesis – the way its parts can be composed –.

The notion of component in Software Architecture is intended to be general and doesn't depend on any particular conception; but it's also true that their origins are

---

* First author supported by the Spanish Ministry of Science in the Research Project MCYT-TIC2003-07804-C05-01. First, third and fourth authors also supported by the Autonomous Government of Castilla y Leon in the Research Project JCYL-VA117/03.

F. Oquendo et al. (Eds.): EWSA 2004, LNCS 3047, pp. 43–56, 2004.

strongly related to encapsulation and information hiding. For this reason, most usual descriptions are divided in parts, very similar to those of traditional modular schemas. In recent years, Aspect Orientation – a popular name for which is more generically known as *advanced separation of concerns* – has emerged as a reaction to the limitations of those approaches. New kinds of modules, which break internal barriers and affect simultaneously wide areas within the system, are conceived, and thus novel kinds of non-classical decomposition, orthogonal to conventional structures, are proposed.

In this paper we suggest that Software Architecture and Aspect Orientation can be considered as complementary notions, and discuss the way in which both could be combined for their mutual benefit. Thus, aspects provide Architecture with a strategy to modularize the specification of behaviour, and to deal with multiple viewpoints. On the other hand, architectural description endowes Aspect Orientation with the means to make explicit both their global structure – which tends to be underspecified and even scattered – and the relationships between elements placed in distinct dimensions.

The combination of these two fields can be approached in a number of ways and using different abstraction levels. This paper focuses mainly in just *one* of those approaches: the way in which *aspect-oriented software architectures*, that is architectures of systems structured using both components and aspects, can be specified by using an Architecture Description Language (ADL). Our hypothesis is that standard (static) ADLs, which describe rigid modular structures, are unfit for the specification of aspects; on the other hand, probably this could be successfully achieved by using a much more flexible language, like a (dynamic) *reflective* ADL.

In this paper we use the $\mathcal{P}i\mathcal{L}ar$ language [6], an ADL which provides Reflection as a means to specify dinamism, and which seems to be perfectly fit for our purposes. Thus we make a first tentative attempt to solve the problem of the architectural description of aspects, laying the foundations for a more detailed treatment.

2   Architecture and Aspects

The notion of *architectural view* was probably the last one to appear in the field. It springs from a very natural analogy: just like in building architecture we have distinct blueprints describing distinct aspects of the same building – walls and spaces, electric wiring, water conducts –, it sounds reasonable to conceive a software architecture description as the composition of several structural specifications (*views*) reflecting several perspectives (*viewpoints*) of the same software system.

The concept itself has gained immediate acceptance. However, its use has been quite irregular. Now it happens that it is frequently applied in informal approaches to Software Architecture, such as several proposals extending UML to cope with architecture, or even the Unified Process itself. However, at the same time there are hardly any proposals to *formally* introduce the concept of views in an ADL.

The adequate specification of views in an ADL is then one of the open problems in the field or architecture description. Here we suggest that an analogy between views and aspects could be quite natural, and probably useful from our point of view.

2.1 Convergence and Coincidences

Many authors have already noted the coincidences between Software Architecture and Aspect Orientation, coming either from one field [25] or the other [3,12]. The most complete study of this topic comes from the work of KandÚ and Strohmeier [10,11] in the context of UML. Besides, we should also note that Software Architecture itself provides already an implicit *separation of concerns*: by describing the structure, we are also separating computation from *configuration*. However, during the specification of behaviour we could tangle some other abstractions, such as coordination.

Both fields are clearly converging. This is more apparent by examining two basic concepts. As discussed in the previous section, the correspondence between architectural views and aspects is quite straightforward, in particular if the latter are considered from the perpective of *multiple dimensions* [23]. Here Aspect Orientation appears as a possible way to relate the different views in architecture [12]; on the other hand Software Architecture provides the means to describe the way in which aspects are organized to build an structure, something which is becoming ever more critical.

The other concept is that of *connector*. First, there is a certain analogy between some proposals to introduce aspects, such as contracts, roles, interceptors or composition filters, and architectural connectors. Second, aspects can be easily used to implement connectors, being in fact a very good mechanism for this purpose. On the other side, connectors might serve as the support to introduce join points and advices, and in fact they provide the means for intercepting interaction, one common strategy for Aspect Orientation. Finally, a formal translation of both notions in terms of superimposition [13] is indeed very similar, particularly at the higher level. Incidentally, we could extend this reasoning to include any kind of wrappers, adaptors or mediators, including reflective ones: all of them can be seen as instances of the same abstract notion.

3   Considering Foundations

The ultimate purpose of this paper is the description of aspect-oriented architectures in terms of an ADL, then using already existing techniques in the field of Software Architecture. In a sense, what we are trying to do is to "encode" the notions of Aspect Orientation in terms of architecture. Regarding this, it should be quite useful to consider some of the existing proposals for the foundations of aspects.

There are already a number of proposals dealing with the definition of formal foundation for Aspect Orientation. We are able to distinguish at least four groups of proposals. The first one gathers those techniques which describe aspect weaving by using existing compilarion models, such those based on monads, graph rewriting systems or adaptive programming. A second group tries to provide direct semantics for aspectual constructions [24]. It is quite close to the third category, which defines more active models, able even to describe *dynamic weaving*, such as execution monitors [7], interactional aspects in the μ^2 model [20], and the variant of Andrews' proposal with process algebra [1] which we discuss in section 3.2.

The final group gathers the most abstract proposals, and is directly related to the theoretical notion of *superimposition* [2,13], which in a sense is identical to aspects. We devote the next section to deal in great detail with this notion, and the closely related notion of *reflection* [4]. Both of them are also intimately related to Software Architecture, in particular within the frame of the $\mathcal{P}i\mathcal{L}ar$ language: a process-algebraic, reflective ADL which supports superimposition.

3.1 Superimposition and Reflection

The notion of *superimposition* [2,13,14] appeared in the field of concurrency. It describes a kind of composition, in which a (base) process is subsumed by one or more processes executing in parallel, with the objective to ensure that the former complies with some properties. To do so, superimposed processes must have access to internal states in the first one; in the end, actions composing the behaviour of the whole set *interleave*, creating just one process. Currently, this mechanism is used quite often as a method for stepwise refinement for concurrent systems [14,18].

There are several definitions for superimposition. The most complete is due to Shmuel Katz [13]: in it, the superimposed process is defined as a pattern or template with holes (*roletypes*) to accomodate several base processes, and which could be assimilated both to the roles in a connector and to join points in the aspect weaving process. Over time, Katz himself has dealt both with theoretical development of the notion and with its application to Aspect Orientation [12,22]. Indeed, aspects and superimpositions are almost the same idea, as already stated in existing work [14].

The notion of superimposition has been also used in Software Architecture, in both its most theoretical [26,27] and practical [13] forms. Usually the concept has been introduced to assist in the definition of connectors, though it has been also used to define alternative ways to deal with composition.

Reflection [4,19] is the capability of a system to reason and act upon itself. It causes an implicit division of a system in a base level, which carries out normal operation, and one or several meta levels, which observe and alter the first one. This abstraction provides an adequate platform for the specification of aspect-oriented systems. More than that: some of the topics in Aspect Orientation, and in particular dynamic weaving, are nearly always related to the presence of reflective capabilities.

Despite the fact that the tranlation of aspects in terms of reflection is straightforward, it has been suggested that this notion is perhaps too powerful, and thus it may compromise the consistency of the specification, unless we limit the means for composition in the meta-level somehow. We suggest that a reflective ADL provides this sort of limit; however, these won't prevent the architect to describe a conflicting system *when this is actually what he's intending to do*.

The origins of Aspect Orientation are intimately related to Reflection, and not just historically. That said, it's also true that the real essence of the first, *separation of concerns*, is not reflective at all. Indeed, there isn't actually a real dependency between the two concepts. However, both the analysis of targets, which provides the basis for pointcut evaluation, and even the idea of aspect weaving has a clear metaprogramming nature. Then, a reflective foundation for aspects should not pose any kind of conflict; quite the opposite, it is probably the best basis for such a description.

However, we're not saying here that aspectual notions can be simply subsumed into a reflective scheme; but just that this can be an useful starting point. And of course, by means of Reflection we also acquire some other capabilities which *a priori* were unrelated to Aspect Orientation. There's at least an interesting study [15] suggesting that we can identify a distinct interface for every combination, including not only aspectual capabilities in reflection, but also reflective capabilities in "aspects".

The similarity of superimposition and reflection is maybe less clear, though is sometimes implicitly assumed [9]. Actually the two concepts are *not* equivalent: the notion of reflection is more powerful, albeit at the conceptual level. But in a modular and concurrent environment, interposition mechanisms used to implement reflection are just the same ones used to provide interception for superimposed processes. In particular, both of them have the capability to break encapsulation using a privileged interface. We can conclude that, in a context where components can be *superimposed*, we are able to define a *reflective* architecture.

3.2   The Role of Algebra

Algebra has an intrinsic modular nature which makes it particularly useful for the description of composition structures. That's probably the reason why the (process-) algebraic approach is the most popular foundation and representation strategy in the field of Software Architecture. This makes particularly attractive James Andrews' proposal [1] for the semantics of Aspect Orientation conceived in terms of a CSP-like process algebra. This way we share a common vocabulary relating all the involved fields, and thus making their similarities more apparent.

Andrews' formal treatment is perhaps quite technical, but his global idea is simple: any aspect – including the base system – is described as a process definition using algebra. Join points are conceived as *synchronizations* between those processes, and thus are simple designated as common channels. Interactions between aspects are carried out as communications over those same points, using free variables. The body of each aspect is given by non-synchonized sections, and the parallel composition – *conjunction* – of all these processes results in aspect weaving. We should remark that this operation might be non-deterministic.

We should note, however, that Andrews' vision is static. He conceives Aspect Orientation as a program transformation, which is completely carried out during the compilation phase. In fact, aspect weaving is done by means of the systematic elimination of synchronizations between processes, to finally obtain just one process: an "hypermodule" [23]. And all of this is previous to the execution phase.

However, to make a trivial extension of this proposal, such that it is capable of doing *dynamic weaving* [24], is fairly simple. Let's just suppose that all the defined processes are effectively being executed in parallel, and then synchronizations are produced as a part of normal activity. This means that join points are indeed dynamically resolved. In fact, this suffices to make this proposal reminiscent of the way concurrent processes interact inside a superimposition.

4   The PiLar Language

$PiLar$ is an ADL of the process-algebraic kind, which was designed to serve as a general framework for the specification of Dynamic Architectures. For this reason, it was conceived as a reflective ADL [6]: the notions from the field of Reflection are incorporated into the language, and then they are used to provide a description of dynamism. This is possibly the only language in its class.

There isn't enough space here to describe $\mathcal{P}i\mathcal{L}ar$ syntax, albeit briefly. There is however a complete definition available [4], as well as several shorter descriptions [5,6], so we refer the reader to them for further detail. Anyway we summarize some concepts in the following, to ease the discussion.

An architectural description in $\mathcal{P}i\mathcal{L}ar$ is standardly structured as a set of component types (archtypes) and instances, whose definition is similar to that of other ADLs. Behaviour is specified by means of *constraints*, described in a process-algebraic-like syntax, which is inspired in CCS.

There is just one reflective notion in $\mathcal{P}i\mathcal{L}ar$, namely *reification*. Here it is defined as a bidirectional structural relationship, describing a causal connection between the component instances it binds. A reified instance is known as a base-component or *avatar*, while the reifier is named a *meta-component*. The set of all such meta-components sets up the meta-level of the architecture; when considered within it, they behave just like any other instance. But at the same time they have total access to *their* avatars in the lower (base) level, including their internals; this implements a grey-box approach. Meta-components are then capable of doing full introspection and intercession. Besides they can be reified themselves by other components, thus building a meta-meta level. This way the architecture is implicitly statified in *meta-layers* as required; even a dynamic system has usually enough with two or three layers. There is also a notion of *metaspace*: the subset of a meta-layer which gathers all the meta-components (directly or indirectly) related to a particular reification link.

$\mathcal{P}i\mathcal{L}ar$ semantics are specified in terms of a π-calculus dialect, and it's technically quite complex. The concept of reification is no doubt the most complex one, and possibly it's the only one which requires a detailed explanation, as the rest of the language is quite conventional. Obviously, it has a reflective interpretation, but we are also able to describe it here in terms of concurrent processes, for simplicity and convenience.

From this point of view, reification can be compared with a superimposition of processes. From an avatar's point of view, the corresponding meta-component can be perceived as a superimposed process, able to access all its internal elements, and specifically its ports. Control over the behaviour of the avatar is not achieved by active supervision; instead, both components evolve concurrently, and the influence is expressed by means of interactions or synchronizations at the same ports.

$\mathcal{P}i\mathcal{L}ar$ allows the definition of many reifications on one avatar and vice versa. Whenever this happens, meta-components exert their influence in parallel, and optionally synchronizing. Then one of them could possibly leave all the other unaffected; but at the same time they could also compete for the same resources (ports). These conflicts are treated as non-deterministic choices, just like in any process algebra.

4.1   Aspects in PiLar

In the light of $\mathcal{P}i\mathcal{L}ar$ semantics and some of the proposed foundations for Aspect Orientation, a direct translation for aspects within the language becomes apparent. It suffices to assume that the base level in an architecture provides the basic structure to be augmented: each additional aspect is introduced by using the meta-level.

The correspondence between notions is almost perfect. Every *aspect* – here meant in the restricted sense also covered by the term *hyperslice* [23] – is encoded as a meta-component: this means that it maintains a direct reification link with (at least) an avatar. Constraints in meta-components act as *advices*, and their composites define *hypermodules*; so they are always subsets of (or equated to) metaspaces.

Each "aspectual" reification is also referring to a concrete dimension (concern); of course, several reification links may refer to the same dimension. In fact, as a first step we could say that a reification defines a *pointcut*, as it provides access to a (potential) set of *join points*: these are each one of the ports in a reified avatar, as they are the places where synchronizations would take place. Of course, we could also generalize the notion of pointcut, not limiting it to a single reification, but gathering several ones by means of some kind of predicate, or even using explicit labels. In summary, by using just the simple rule "aspects are described as meta-components" we obtain a natural encoding for all the required abstractions.

PiLar's reflective structure makes possible to apply this kind of separation of concerns in any place of an architecture. Aspects can be superimposed over components, but also over *connections*. In short, using the same mechanism we can define adaptors and connectors, aspects and multiparty interactions. Almost every one of these has been proposed as a foundation to implement the other: we can use connectors to introduce aspects via interception, but we can also simulate a connector by superimposing a certain protocol over a connection. In *PiLar*, nonetheless, the idea is that all of them can be conceived as *distinct facets of the same mechanism*.

5   A Case Study: Paxos Consensus Algorithm

In this section we provide an example to show how aspect definition and superimposition could be applied in the context of architecture description in *PiLar*. The example defines a *coordination aspect* in terms of *PiLar* components, and then superimposes it over a conventional, static architecture, thus "augmenting" it[1]. This way we obtain a new system in which both structure and behaviour result from a consistent mixture of these two independent descriptions. This result is also particularly elegant from a purely architectural point of view, as it is implicitly divided in two layers, which respectively provide configuration and coordination. But at the same time this layering is just conceptual: there's no explicit separation between these layers, defining explicit composite components. So this is not an instance of the layered architecture style.

In this example, the base architecture would be irrelevant, as our purpose is just to show how a coordination aspect can be superimposed (weaved) over it. The interesting part is, then, the definition of this aspect. To achieve coordination we have decided to use the *Paxos consensus algorithm*, which is a classic in distributed systems literature.

The main purpose of this example is to show how two independently defined – or oblivious – aspects can be combined so they can work together. Both Paxos consensus

---

[1] The language makes perhaps easier to conceive aspect weaving as the augmentation of a base system, and superimposition semantics provide the same impression. But there's nothing in the syntax or semantics preventing us of doing a true composition of models in the spirit of MDSoC [23], which would be described in a very similar way.

and the base Pipe-Filter architecture (see Fig. 2) are generic notions; and they could be combined in many ways. So we prefer to abstract out irrelevant notions; that's why some parts of the behaviour are defined as internal (**tau**) or even left implicit.

Someone could feel that to use a "coordination aspect" is an easy choice, as Coordination has a close conceptual relationship with Architecture [5]. But it's precisely this relationship which makes more interesting to achieve separation of concerns between them. Indeed, though Software Architecture provides itself a basic conceptual separation between computation and configuration, the subsequent separation between *configuration* and *coordination* has always being a problem, and there are conflicting opinions about how to deal with this subject [21,25].

Succintly, the Paxos algorithm describes a coordination mechanism which can be used to implement a fault-tolerant distributed system. At its heart, it is basically a *consensus* algorithm, which makes possible for an (arbitrarily large) number of processes – components – to reach an agreement about an (arbitrarily complex) common value v they all need to use – let it be a number –. They lack any kind of shared memory, so they must use just asynchronous interaction, *and* in the possible presence of non-Byzantine failure: messages can be lost, but they are never corrupted.

The Paxos consensus algorithm was defined and described by Leslie Lamport [16] and since then it has been applied and adapted to a wide range of distributed systems. It is described using the metaphor of a parliament – in the imaginary ancient Greek island of Paxos, thereby its name – in which senators are not assumed to be present, as they can enter or leave the sessions anytime. Laws must be approved in the Senate, by consensus of a majority; but at the same time senators involved in the discussion might be absent during the voting process, and vice versa; their number may vary unexpectedly. The algorithm provides a safe mechanism to ensure that consensus is reached anyway.

The algorithm depends on the notion of a *majority* of acceptors: the perceived agreement of such a majority defines the desired consensus. Lamport himself refuses to choose a particular definition for this majority [17]. He simply assumes an abstract majority. To maintain this generality, and also to simplify the specification of the algorithm, we use an abstraction too. So the Boolean pseudo-function (process) *MajAcc(n)* gets true if a majority (whichever definition) of acceptors provided an answer to the proposal numbered n, leading into consensus.

We are not going to explain in detail the Paxos algorithm, given that its author has provided a short description himself [17], and it is well-known anyway. We will just outline its behaviour to make the specification in Figure 1 comprehensible, but we won't try to justify the roles, phases and steps of the algorithm.

Figure 1 provides a description of the algorithm, separated in three components which correspond to the three roles in it: proposers, acceptors and learners. The description is conceived here as a *coordination aspect* or hypermodule, composed by three basic components – hyperslices – and an auxiliary component (**Paxos**) providing an implicit and *variable* pattern to compose them.

It has no meaning by itself: it is not describing an architecture nor a style. It just defines some basic vocabulary and composition rules, which only make sense when superimposed over a base architecture. The description does not include any instance, it just defines *types*. Even the composition pattern is given as a set of bindings between

```
\component Proposer (
  \metaface (
    port prepareA | port acceptA )
  \constraint (
    \rep ( \new(hvalue: Int); hvalue!(0);
      /- = Phase One = -/
      tau(propn); prepareA!(prop_n);        /- request to prepare for proposal -/
      /- = Phase Two = -/
      \rep ( prepareA?(recv_n,recv_v);    /- promise message is received -/
        \if ( recv_v = prop_n )
          ( hvalue?(v); \if ( v < recv_v ) ( hvalue!(recv_v) );
            \if ( MajAcc(recv_n) )
              ( hvalue?(v); \if ( v = 0 ) ( tau(v) );
                acceptA!(recv_n, v)        /- request to accept this proposal -/
  ) ) ) ) ) )
```

```
\component Acceptor (
  \metaface (
    port prepareP | port acceptP | port toLearn )
  \constraint (
    \new (hnum, hvalue: Int);
    hnum!(0); hvalue!(0);
    ( \rep (
      /- = Phase One = -/
      loopSet(prepareP); prepareP?(prop_n);   /- request to prepare is received -/
      hnum?(n); \if ( prop_n > n )
        ( hnum!(prop_n); hvalue?(v);
          prepareP!(prop_n, v) ) )              /- promise message is sent -/
    | \rep (
      /- = Phase Two = -/
      loopSet(acceptP); acceptP?(acc_n, acc_v);
      hnum?(n); \if ( acc_n <= n )
        ( hvalue!(acc_v); toLearn!(acc_n, acc_v) )  /- accepted -/
  ) ) ) ) )
```

```
\component Learner (
  \metaface (
    port toAccept )
  \constraint ( \rep ( toAccept?(num,val);
    \if ( MajAcc(num) ) ( tau(val) )  /- CONSENSUS -/
) ) )
```

```
\component Paxos (
  \config ( \bind (
    Proposer.prepareA = Acceptor.prepareP |
    Proposer.acceptA = Acceptor.acceptP |
    Acceptor.toLearn = Learner.toAccept ) ) )
```

Fig. 1. Roles of the Paxos algorithm in a coordination "aspect".

interfaces in the meta-level (*metafaces*). This describes a relationship between archtypes themselves, which would later propagate to their instances, and thus is able to adapt to any particular configuration.

The algorithm was defined to be independent of the underlying communication medium. Lamport simply assumes it; the algorithm itself guarantees safety anyway. So, the way in which the different roles are bound together is actually irrelevant. The mechanism which uses a direct connection between meta-components is probably not the best[2], but it is the simplest one. We have chosen it because it has the lowest impact on the rest of the system, and thus the description of the algorithm is not affected. A practical example could possibly use some other kind of connector.

Agents in the aspect must be capable of coordinate by agreeing on the same value. To do so, they discuss about a number of *proposals*, temporarily accepting or discarding some of them, till a majority of members of the synod agrees in an specific value. Proposals are issued by *proposers*. In the simplest incarnation, a proposal consists of an identifier (an unique number) and a certain value, which at first is still unknown. Proposer must send their proposals to *acceptors*. Acceptors form the fuzzy set of agents who must reach consensus. On principle, they are always willing to accept any proposal they receive, but at the same time they always keep their word, so they can't lie or contradict themselves. Consensus is obtained when a majority of acceptors agree on a proposal. But as they need not to know each other, they don't know when this happens either. Thus the role of *learners*. These are agents who simply listen each time an acceptor accepts a proposal; they count these acceptance messages, and eventually learn that a certain proposal has been accepted by a majority. Then consensus has been reached, and this finishes the algorithm.

The algorithm unfolds in two phases, as indicated by comments in the $\mathcal{P}i\mathcal{L}ar$ description. In the first one, a proposer ellaborates a proposal in an internal action, and send a *prepare* request to acceptors, which consists of a message including the proposal number. Meanwhile, an acceptor waits to receive such a prepare request. Upon reception, it compares the new proposal number with the highest-numbered proposal it has received till now. If the new number is greater, the acceptor sends a *promise* response. By sending the promise, the acceptor compromises itself not to accept any lower-numbered proposal, and also informs the proposer of the value contained in the most recent proposal it has accepted, if any.

Then the algorithm enters phase two. The proposer is waiting for *promise* responses to each one of its proposals. Upon reception, it stores the received value and checks if a majority of the acceptors has promised to consider this proposal. When this is the case, it sends all the acceptors – possibly not exactly the same set as before – an *accept* request indicating both the proposal number and the last value it has stored.

Also in phase two, the acceptor waits for accepting requests. Upon receipt, it checks if during this time it has promised to consider another higher-numbered proposal. If this is not the case, it *accepts* this proposal, and sends a message to all learners telling them so. This message is similar to the accept request: it consists also of the pre-accepted proposal number and value. Finally, a learner is continuously listening about accepted

---

[2] We use the meta-level as a kind of shared space. This could cause unexpected synchronizations: that's why we use the **loopSet** command, which acts basically as a broadcaster.

component Filter ((**port** prev | **port** next))

component Pipe ((**port** left | **port** right))

component PipeLine (
  (**port** input | **port** output)
  config (
    F1, F2, F3: Filter | P1, P2: Pipe |
    bind (
      F1.prev = input | F1.next = P1.left | P1.right = F2.prev |
      F2.next = P2.left | P2.right = F3.prev | F3.next = output))
  reify (F1, F2, F3 : Acceptor)
  reify (F1, P2 : Proposer)
  reify (P1, P2 : Learner))

Fig. 2. Superimposing (weaving) the aspect over a Pipeline.

proposals; each time it checks if some proposal has appealed to a majority of acceptors. When this is the case, consensus has been reached.

The "aspect" is completely self-contained. To work it doesn't need anything else, just to be applied to concrete instances. It does not make use of connections in these instances, as it defines its own connections (in the meta-meta level). Reflected instances just have to provide a name to store the datum obtained by consensus in the aspect. For the sake of simplicity we just introduce it by means of an internal action **tau**. Thus base components, whichever their definition may be, under any configuration or style, get to coordinate in the end anyway.

As we said, the base architecture we are going to *weave* with the Paxos algorithm is irrelevant for the purposes of this case study. Our purpose is to show how a coordination aspect can be superimposed in terms of $\mathcal{PiLar}$; the aspect has been defined independently and should work fine over any configuration. So we have chosen one of the most basic and well-known architectures at hand, to keep the presentation as simple as possible. The base architecture in Figure 2 is obviously an instance of the Pipe-Filter style: it is indeed one of the most static and linear architectural patterns, and it provides a rigid and unsurprising configuration.

The system describes a pipeline of three filters connected by means of two pipes. In $\mathcal{PiLar}$ those pipes would be usually described as connections, not components; but this presentation maintains better the flavour of the original definition. Base behaviour has been left implicit, but it is quite obvious: data flows enter the pipeline and pass the first filter, then throught the first pipe to the second filter, and so on.

Now we superimpose a coordination protocol over this configuration. In this case, the original data flow is left unaffected, and Paxos consensus is achieved in a completely independent process. Of course we could later use the obtained value as desired; for example, the behaviour on filters could be parameterized using this value.

To do the weaving we need just to define the poincuts; that is, the reification links which would map coordination roles to particular instances in the Pipe-Filter configuration. Here we have decided that the three filters are acceptors, the two pipes are learners, and one pipe and one filter are proposers. This has been a completely arbitrary decision: the algorithm doesn't depend on this mapping, and it doesn't even depend on the original nature of the superimposed components. It just requires the presence of at least one proposer, at least one learner, and probably an odd number of acceptors.

Incidently, we should remark that the superimposition of a fault-tolerant coordination layer is not completely pointless, even in the presence of reliable channels. Probably it is of no much interest for a static architecture like the one in Figure 2; but we should have in mind that $\mathcal{P}i\mathcal{L}ar$ was conceived to describe *dynamic* architectures, so the continued existence of connections is not assured: messages can be lost and communication as a whole could be unreliable. On the contrary, the Paxos consensus algorithm was designed to work in a mutable environment, so it would still behave consistently. Then in the end it appears indeed as a good idea to use it to provide coordination in the top of dynamic architectures, the intended design target for $\mathcal{P}i\mathcal{L}ar$.

6   Conclusions and Future Work

The main purpose of this paper was to support the thesis that an ADL with reflective capabilities, like $\mathcal{P}i\mathcal{L}ar$, is expressive enough to describe architectural models while separating concerns. This is not surprising, considering their respective foundations; but anyway some interesting conclusions can be deduced from this experience.

The structure defined by aspects is not self-evident in a pure $\mathcal{P}i\mathcal{L}ar$ description, but the meta-level scheme isn't either. The first case is more complex however, for the same aspect can be simultaneously described by several meta-components; they probably relate with distinct join points in the base architecture, by using potentially independent reification links. But in principle all of them are situated in the same meta-level. On the other hand, we doesn't have the necessary data to decide which meta-components or reifications relate to a particular aspect or dimension.

In summary, in its current version $\mathcal{P}i\mathcal{L}ar$ is capable to describe the separation of concerns by using aspect modules; but it doesn't provide the means for their identification. This is related to another fundamental requirement [8]: the quantification of join points, which we discuss below. However at the same time it does provide the support for their *composition*. On the one hand, it makes possible to describe the relationships between meta-components of the same aspect (hyperslices in the same dimension) once identified, thus effectively outlining the structure for this aspect (the architecture of this view). On the other hand, it even allows the interaction between hyperslices in different dimensions, thus creating the analogous of hypermodules [23].

That said, it still sounds reasonable to suggest some kind of syntactic extension for the language, able to specifically deal with the description of (multiple) aspects. Currently, there are not many ADLs with this capability, except some of the proposals related to UML [11] . Actually, $\mathcal{P}i\mathcal{L}ar$ doesn't strictly require such an extension; the core of the language alone is expressive enough to tackle this sort of description. But that's basically a *semantic* capability: even when aspectual notions can be encoded within the language, this not always results in a natural construction. So it becomes clear that the specification of Aspect Orientation in $\mathcal{P}i\mathcal{L}ar$ would be much easier and clearer with the addition of some syntactic sugar.

Tentatively, we could propose two such extensions. The first one would consist of the addition of an optional *annotation* in reifications, to state if they refer to a particular concern and which one if this is the case. This would make possible to explicitly *identify* the meta-components building a particular aspect. The second one might be the introduction of an *hypermodule* notion or similar. It is not strictly necessary, but probably it would ease the comprehension of the resulting model. This concept should be provided anyway, at least as a semantic construction.

That's just syntactic sugar: it doesn't alter the semantics of the language at all. All the required notions can be defined in terms of already existing ones. We should also consider a more complex extension, which could affect the semantics: the addition of an explicit syntax for complex pointcuts. At present, we have related pointcuts to reification links, but probably we should add the option to consider *sets* of reifications, identified either by another annotation or by some sort of predicate.

In summary, there are many relationships and analogies between Software Architecture and Aspect Orientation, and so there's a huge potential in their combination. In this paper we have just outlined some of the consequences of this combination, studying one of them in greater detail. But of course work in this context is still recent, as are the involved fields themselves, and must be further developed. In this regard, it is probably one of the most fruitful research directions in the near future.

References

1. James H. Andrews. Process-Algebraic Foundations of Aspect-Oriented Programming. In *Reflection 2001: Third International Conference on Metalevel Architectures and Separation of Crosscutting Concerns*, Lecture Notes in Computer Science, 2001.
2. Jan Bosch. Superimposition: A Component Adaptation Technique. *Information and Software Technology*, 41(5):257–273, March 1999.
3. Constantinos A. Constantinides and Tzilla Elrad. On the Requirements for Concurrent Software Architectures to Support Advanced Separation of Concerns. In *OOPSLA'2000 Advanced Separation of Concerns*, October 2000.
4. Carlos E. Cuesta. *Reflection-based Dynamic Software Architecture*. ProQuest Information & Learning, May 2003.
5. Carlos E. Cuesta, Pablo de la Fuente, Manuel Barrio-Solórzano, and Encarnación Beato. Coordination in a Reflective Architecture Description Language. In Farhad Arbab and Carolyn Talcott, editors, *Coordination Models and Languages*, volume 2315 of *Lecture Notes in Computer Science*, pages 141–148, York, UK, April 2002. Springer Verlag.
6. Carlos E. Cuesta, Pablo de la Fuente, Manuel Barrio Solórzano, and M. Encarnación Beato. Introducing Reflection in Architecture Description Languages. In Jan Bosch, Morven Gentleman, Christine Hofmeister, and Juha Kuusela, editors, *Software Architecture: System Design, Development and Maintenance*, pages 143–156. Kluwer Academic Publishers, 2002.
7. Rémi Douence, Olivier Motelet, and Mario Südholt. A Formal Definition of Crosscuts. In *Proceedings of Third International Conference on Metalevel Architectures and Separation of Crosscutting Concerns (Reflection 2001)*, volume 2192 of *Lecture Notes in Computer Science*, pages 170–186. Springer Verlag, September 2001.
8. Robert E. Filman and Daniel P. Friedman. Aspect-Oriented Programming is Quantification and Obliviousness. In *OOPSLA 2000 Advanced Separation of Concerns*, October 2000.

9. Ira R. Forman. Superimposition: A Form of Separation of Concerns for Distributed Systems. In *Proceedings of First OOPSLA'2000 Workshop on Advanced Separation of Concerns (ASoC1)*, October 2000.

10. Mohamed Mancona Kandé. *A Concern-Oriented Approach to Software Architecture*. PhD thesis, École Polytechnique Fédérale de Lausanne, 2003.

11. Mohamed Mancona Kandé and Alfred Strohmeier. On The Role of Multi-Dimensional Separation of Concerns in Software Architecture. In *OOPSLA'2000 Workshop on Advanced Separation of Concerns in Object-Oriented Systems (ASoC)*, October 2000.

12. Mika Katara and Shmuel Katz. Architectural Views of Aspects. In *Proceedings of the Second International Conference on Aspect-Oriented Software Development (AOSD'03)*, pages 1–10. ACM Press, March 2003.

13. Shmuel Katz. A Superimposition Control Construct for Distributed Systems. *ACM Transactions on Programming Languages and Systems*, 15(2):337–356, April 1993.

14. Pertti Kellomäki. A Formal Basis for Aspect-Oriented Specification with Superposition. In Gary T. Leavens and Ron Cytron, editors, *FOAL 2002 Proceedings: Foundations of Aspect-Oriented Languages*, pages 27–32, April 2002.

15. Sergei Kojarski, Karl Lieberherr, David H. Lorenz, and Robert Hirschfeld. Aspectual Reflection. In *Sofware engineering Properties of Languages for Aspect Technologies (SPLAT'03)*, March 2003.

16. Leslie Lamport. The Part-Time Parliament. *ACM Transactions on Computer Systems*, 16(2):133–169, May 1998.

17. Leslie Lamport. Paxos Made Simple. *ACM SIGACT News*, 32(4):18–25, December 2001.

18. Antónia Lopes and José Luiz Fiadeiro. Superposition: Composition vs. Refinement of Non-deterministic, Action-Based Systems. *ENTCS*, 70(3), 2002.

19. Pattie Maes. Concepts and Experiments in Computational Reflection. *ACM SIGPLAN Notices*, 22(12):147–155, December 1987. OOPSLA'87 Conference Proceedings.

20. Renaud Pawlak. *La Programmation par Aspects Interactionnelle pour la Construction d'applications Ó Préoccupations Multiples* PhD thesis, CNAM, Paris, 2002.

21. Matthias Radestock and Susan Eisenbach. Coordination in Evolving Systems. In O. Spaniol, C. Linnhoff-Popien, and B. Meyer, editors, *Trends in Distributed Systems - CORBA and Beyond*, volume 1161 of *Lecture Notes in Computer Science*, pages 162–176, 1996.

22. Marcelo Sihman and Shmuel Katz. A Calculus of Superimpositions for Distributed Systems. In *Proceedings of the First International Conference on Aspect-Oriented Software Development (AOSD'02)*, pages 28–40. ACM Press, April 2002.

23. Peri Tarr, Harold Ossher, William Harrison, and Stanley Sutton, Jr. N-Degrees of Separation: Multi-Dimensional Separation of Concerns. In *Proceedings of the 21st International Conference on Software Engineering (ICSE'99)*, May 1999.

24. Mitchell Wand, Gregor Kiczales, and Chris Dutchyn. A Semantics for Advice and Dynamic Join Points in Aspect-Oriented Programming. In Gary T. Leavens and Ron Cytron, editors, *FOAL 2002: Foundations of Aspect-Oriented Languages*, pages 1–8, April 2002.

25. Michel Wermelinger, José L. Fiadeiro, Luis F. Andrade, Georgios Koutsoukos, and Joao Gouveia. Separation of Core Concerns: Computation, Coordination and Configuration. In *OOPSLA'2001 Advanced Separation of Concerns*, October 2001.

26. Michel Wermelinger and José Luiz Fiadeiro Fiadeiro. Algebraic Software Architecture Reconfiguration. In *Software Engineering – Proceedings of ESEC/FSE'99*, volume 1687 of *Lecture Notes in Computer Science*, pages 393–409. Springer Verlag, 1999.

27. Michel Wermelinger, Antónia Lopes, and José Luiz Fiadeiro. Superposing Connectors. In *Proceedings of 10th International Workshop on Software Specification and Design*, pages 87–94. IEEE Computer Society Press, 2000.

Software Architecture Evolution through Dynamic AOP

Paolo Falcarin[1] and Gustavo Alonso[2]

[1] Dipartimento di Automatica e Informatica, Politecnico di Torino,
I-10129 Torino, Italy
Paolo.Falcarin@polito.it
[2] Department of Computer Science, Swiss Federal Institute of Technology (ETHZ)
CH-8092 Zurich, Switzerland
Alonso@inf.ethz.ch

Abstract. Modern computing and network environments demand a high degree of adaptability from applications. At run time, an application may have to face many changes: in configuration, in protocols used, in terms of the available resources, etc. Many such changes can only be adequately addressed through dynamic evolution of the software architecture of the application. In this paper, we propose a novel approach to dynamically evolve a software architecture based on run-time aspect oriented programming. In our framework, a system designer/administrator can control the architecture of an application by dynamically inserting and removing code extensions. It is even possible to replace a significant part of the underlying middleware infrastructure without stopping the application. The novelty of this work is that it allows for a much more flexible development strategy as it delegates issues like middleware choice and adherence to an architectural specification to a framework enhanced by dynamic code extensions.

1 Introduction

Software architectures for distributed systems are a challenge in terms of software development and evolution. Design choices like, e.g., the kind of architecture, and the underlying middleware among the components are often made in an early design phase, and are therefore difficult and expensive to alter or rollback. To minimize the impact and cost of such design changes, the notion of software variability has been introduced [1]. Software variability implies a series of locations in the software where behavior and structure can be configured as well as the ability to change, customize or configure different aspects of the system. Moreover, to keep the evolution under control, variability requires a model-driven and architecture-centric approach that constraints changes and avoids undesired divergences as the specification evolves. In this paper we explore the issue of variability in the area of distributed systems. In particular, we are interested in the interplay between middleware platforms and component models, and how this aspect can be treated as a configurable option, preferably at run time. Our

F. Oquendo et al. (Eds.): EWSA 2004, LNCS 3047, pp. 57–73, 2004.
© Springer-Verlag Berlin Heidelberg 2004

goal is to address some of the challenges encountered when using some of the predominant component platforms [2]: CORBA/CCM [3], J2EE/EJB [4], or Web Services [5]. For instance, in the context of these platforms, it has been argued in favor of agile development processes [6].

Agile methods suggest a continuous process whereby working software is constantly being produced as the development progresses toward the final objectives. Yet, in many applications, particularly in the area of distributed systems, having a working prototype already implies that several crucial design decisions have been made: for example, the component model to use and, by association, the underlying middleware infrastructure. Such early design decisions limit the scope of agility because they may become too costly to revisit or readjust at a later point in time. To address these issues, we propose a mechanism to implement and specify variability at both development and run time. At development time, the idea is to support delaying architectural decisions, such as the type of middleware platform to be used, with minimal impact on reconfiguration and modifications. At run time, the former idea is extended to insert/withdraw connectors and components in the deployed architecture, without interrupting the application.

The framework we propose combines ideas from dynamic Aspect-Oriented Programming (AOP) [7] and dynamic software architectures [8]. Its contribution is to provide a mechanism whereby middleware infrastructure, components, and overall system architecture are treated as software variants that can be easily changed during prototyping or even at run time. Thus, the framework provides the necessary flexibility to adapt to continuous changes either for rapid prototyping purposes or as a result of changes in the computing or network environment. The paper is organized as follows: first of all we introduce the motivation of our work, then we describe our framework in detail, and finally we show a case study and discuss related work.

2   Motivation and Requirements

In this section we discuss the motivation behind the proposed framework and previous work the framework builds upon.

2.1   Middleware and Flexible Development

The early life cycle stages of specification and design are of crucial importance in a distributed system. Typically, it is at these stages that the middleware platform is chosen. Because the middleware platform tends to have such a profound effect on the architecture and properties of the resulting system, decisions related to the underlying middleware are particularly significant. For example, if language independence (or heterogeneity) is a requirement, then CORBA is a natural choice for middleware. However, once CORBA is selected, then the interfaces between components must be specified through the CORBA IDL, middleware services are component managed, and access to middleware services is through a particular programming model whereby the services used are determined at compile time. In contrast, a Java-based system may choose to use Enterprise Java Beans. In this case the middleware services are (by default) container-managed, and access to the services is by a different programming model. The decisions about which services are used and how they are used are made not at compile time but at deployment time. These differences are significant enough to constraint the degree of freedom in the overall design and, in most realistic applications, are very costly to change once development has started. Ideally, services and even the middleware platform itself should be parameters of the system that can be changed, as need dictates. The objective would be to use a declarative specification of all design decisions that are to become variants (to simplify development and separate concerns) but making these decisions explicit by formalizing them in an architectural specification file, and by building a framework that implements it in the current architecture of the system.

2.2 Software Architecture Evolution

Software connectors provide a uniform interface abstraction of communication to other connectors and components of the architecture: thus, designers need not to be concerned with the properties of different middleware technologies, if the technology can be encapsulated within a software connector. Moreover, the advantages of combining multiple middleware technologies, to be used in different parts of a distributed architecture, are even more evident with separation of connector code from component code.

This separation, beyond leading to an easier development, is then a necessary condition to support dynamic evolution of software architectures, i.e. runtime reconfiguration and/or replacement of components and connectors in a running system. We need a specification language that allows to easily define and modify architectural elements, and to be executed by a framework supporting dynamic evolution.

At the implementation level, to support dynamic evolution, the programming style changes: the programmer writes application code that must be independent from middleware-specific mechanisms and thus treating each remote method call as a normal local call; moreover design decisions about technologies used by an architecture are automatically reflected in the running system by means of a framework and must not worry anymore application developer. Following these ideas, our framework will rely on an architectural specification defined with xADL (XML-based Architecture Description Language) [9]; there are several ADLs focused on dynamic software architectures, but we have chosen xADL because: it is designed to be a standard way to express architectural specification; it is extensible and adaptable allowing architects to define new XML-Schemas for extensions that can be referenced in a xADL file; moreover, it is based on XML and it is easier to be automatically parsed than other ADLs. The latter feature is a key point to enable a real mapping between code and its architectural specification, even if they both evolve in time.

2.3   Dynamic Adaptation

Once certain design decisions can be postponed and have been made explicit through a document that the system uses to configure the application, it is possible to take the idea one step further. Rather than making architectural decisions at development or deployment time, they can be made also at run time. For example, it should be possible to dynamically change the middleware platform used at run-time with a new version of the same platform or an even different platform altogether. We will later demonstrate how this can be done by using the proposed framework to change a distributed application running on CORBA to a Web Service based implementation. The change can take place without stopping any system component, and they are done under the control of a specification decided by the system architect and propagated through a centralized configuration application. This is a key issue if components are deployed on remote terminals, where manual reconfiguration is not feasible, and it is very important to maintain application integrity and coherence with the evolving specification. The use of a specification and basing all changes on the specification document allows for all necessary checks to be performed at run-time. Such checks are part of the functionality of our framework, which attaches an instance of the framework to each component to make sure the checks are performed. In addition, our framework can be coupled with a dynamic Aspect-Oriented Programming platform (the PROSE system, discussed later on in the paper) for added flexibility. Using dynamic AOP gives us the possibility to remotely insert middleware code and model-checking features of the framework in advice code. This advice code is then directly tied to the component rather than executed separately, thereby allowing us to dynamically insert and withdraw these aspects at run-time as the specification changes. Thanks to PROSE the dynamic adaptation can be efficient and do not halt normal operations, and changes can be propagated to all distributed components in a reliable and transactional manner.

3   JADDA Framework

In this section we discuss the implementation of our framework: JADDA, Java Adaptive component for Dynamic Distributed Architectures. JADDA has two parts: a Java library used to check architectural specification and to handle middleware concerns, and a System Administrator Console (SAC) used to propagate the xADL architectural specification to all the distributed components using JADDA. SAC is an independent application that is used to send xADL specification files to all involved remote servers of distributed systems, while the JADDA library has to be included in all components of the distributed architecture.

In the following subsections we describe different features of JADDA implementation. First of all we describe its inner architecture and API, then we detail xADL standard extensions created to configure middleware (like CORBA and SOAP); moreover we describe extensions mechanism based on a dynamic AOP platform, and JADDA behavior during run-time reconfiguration due to evolution of architectural specification.

3.1   JADDA Architecture

JADDA library that must be included in each component of the distributed architecture has an inner structure depicted with the UML class diagram of Figure 1.

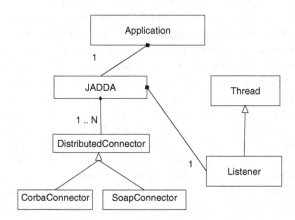

Fig. 1. JADDA UML class diagram.

Each application must include an instance of JADDA class; during its construction and initialization, a Listener instance is created in a separate thread. The Listener has the complex task to listen on the network for incoming xADL specification file and to handle dynamic reconfiguration. Moreover JADDA may include different instances of DistributedConnector abstract class: this defines a common API for middleware: in fact different reifications of this class (like CorbaConnector and SoapConnector) can be added to implement behavior of different middleware standards. During initialization the JADDA instance, running in each component, registers itself in the JADDA System Administrator Console in order to receive the current xADL architectural specification file; then all the needed remote interface references are taken by the CORBA Name server or by the UDDI [10] registry depending on the information contained in the xADL file. Application independence from the middleware used is due to the fact that JADDA wraps on different middleware protocols for remote method invocation, offering to application a simple API, whose typical usage is depicted in Figure 2.

The method "call" is overloaded in order to offer different versions able to call methods with different numbers of parameters; in the different 'call' method signatures, after the first three strings identifying the requested method, the remaining parameters are all Java 'Object' types: they all refer to the main 'call' method implementation with a third parameter made by an array of Object classes. We introduce the Service class to represent a generic remote reference to a service; looking at the previous code the creation of a Service object with the

```
Jadda jadda = new Jadda();

Service s =newService("Server","ChatManager");

String methodName="accessRoom";

String parameter = "Joe";

jadda.call(s, methodName, parameter);
```

Fig. 2. Remote invocation with JADDA API.

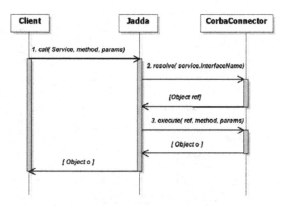

Fig. 3. Sequence diagram of method 'call'.

depicted parameters, creates a generic reference to the interface "ChatManager" of the component "Server". These values have to be present in the specification file, because the method 'call' searches in the current xADL file all the information about the middleware needed to communicate with the requested interface method and it uses Java reflection to execute the remote method invocation, as depicted in figure 2, supposing the case of a CORBA call.

The method "resolve" on the underlying connector implementation is invoked to resolve and cache the remote reference for subsequent calls. The method "execute" realizes the real remote invocation using Java reflection to use middleware-related classes, depending on the used DistributedConnector's subclass (in this case CorbaConnector) and on related data defined in the xADL file. This approach gives a unique and abstract view of different middleware standards. This implementation strategy reduces significant problems in the development and maintenance of software systems and connector code is no more mixed with component code; thus service code is more portable and independent by middleware chosen in the beginning of design and service code can be easily reused or upgraded in future versions.

3.2   xADL Extensions for Distributed Systems

JADDA provides a uniform interface on different software connectors: in this way system designers need not to be concerned with properties of different middleware technologies. The basic schema of xADL is reused to define the architecture's topology but new XML-schemas have been created to specify information related with distributed systems.

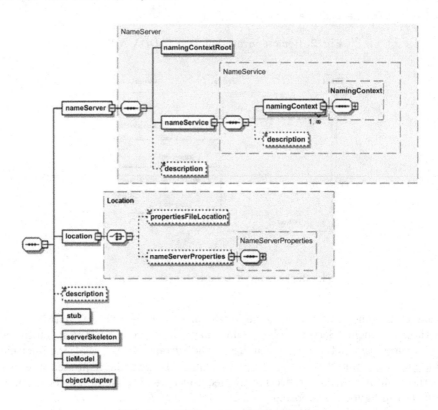

Fig. 4. CorbaConnector XML schema.

For example the communication type defined in a xADL's Connector schema has been extended with a new schema called Distributed-Connector. This is only a basic schema that is specialized by other XML-schemas related to middleware protocol standards, like CorbaConnector for CORBA-IIOP, and SoapConnector for SOAP. A standard protocol like CORBA-IIOP can be implemented by different middleware platforms, offering slightly different APIs to applications. Therefore, including in the same architecture different kinds of CORBA implementations, means having different instances of CORBA-connectors in a xADL file: each CORBA connector instance will define values of tags, defined in the CORBA-connector schema, to qualify its own specializations, as sketched in figure 4.

For example, the CORBA schema defines tags like: "NameServer" that includes all the needed information for binding and retrieving CORBA object references published on a CORBA Naming Service; the tag "Location" gives the runtime information to connect to Naming Service (e.g. hostname and port). The kind of middleware used by a component's interface is defined in the extended-Interface XML-schema: this one extends the xADL's Interface schema and it contains the reference to the connector instance used by a component's interface; other XML-schemas like DistributedLink, and SoapConnector are not detailed for brevity.

3.3 JADDA Reconfiguration

Once described JADDA behavior while the system is running, in this subsection we describe how architecture reconfiguration works. First of all the Listener thread included in JADDA registers its presence to the SAC, sending the IP address and port where it is waiting for a new specification file. Then SAC sends this file to all components of the distributed architecture, i.e. to all their registered JADDA instances. When the file is received the Listener thread has to follow a particular behavior, as depicted in state-chart of figure 5, passing from INIT state to REQUEST state. This Listener's state means that a new specification file has been received and that is waiting the right moment to reconfigure JADDA. In this case it checks if the main application thread containing JADDA instance is IDLE (i.e. no calls are currently in execution) or FREEZE (i.e. JADDA has terminated a remote call and it has found that Listener's state is REQUEST): if the previous conditions hold then Listener can update internal tables of JADDA in a synchronized manner, passing to the state UPDATING. Once finished it comes back to IDLE state, waiting for a new specification file from the network.

To understand the whole behavior we also have to describe the JADDA state-chart, depicted in figure 6. In the beginning and the end of each remote call, JADDA checks Listener's state. If Listener is IDLE then JADDA can execute different remote calls, passing to CALLING state and using the variable 'apps' to count the number of parallel invocations currently in execution: this is due to the fact that the main application can be multi-threaded and different parallel invocations to JADDA are possible. If Listener is in REQUEST state, JADDA has to complete all the current remote calls (eventually suspending new incoming ones): when apps counter reaches zero then JADDA can move to FREEZE state, leaving the full control of its data to the Listener thread, that can start the reconfiguration of JADDA's internal data. The IDLE state can always be reached because of timeouts support of middleware implementations: when a remote call is blocked the timeout triggers an exception that is caught by JADDA, which forces the IDLE state.

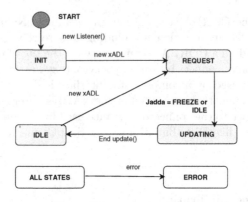

Fig. 5. Listener state-chart.

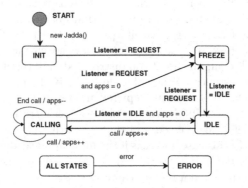

Fig. 6. JADDA state-chart.

3.4   JADDA Extension for Dynamic AOP

Dynamic AOP is used to extend the features of an application at run time. Dynamic creation of aspects by the system designer can lead to unexpected software evolution: in our case, the scope of extensions is constrained to middleware code, i.e., future modifications of the connector implementation and configuration that were not considered in the early phases of the design. The aspects remote transmission in a transactional way allows all the components of the architecture to dynamically upload new classes. The necessary condition to obtain these results is running JADDA enabled with dynamic AOP features; moreover, when dynamic AOP is set, application developer can further run JADDA in two distinct AOP-modes: in the first one, developers can handle each remote method invocation in the code, writing local methods having the same signature as the needed methods on remote interfaces. These local methods, initially with an empty body, will be completed by the JADDA architectural framework, using the code of aspects and classes inserted at run-time by the dynamic aspect-oriented platform PROSE [11], which wraps on a standard JVM, enhancing it with dynamic AOP features.

In the second AOP-mode, developer can use JADDA as usual with its API that wraps on different connectors, but the implementation of available connectors can be updated using dynamic AOP features. PROSE is a dynamic AOP platform to be able to insert and withdraw aspects at runtime, and in our case it is used to totally decouple the application code from middleware and architectural concerns. Using this tool, the adaptability of JADDA is improved allowing the dynamic downloading of new connectors and related middleware components (and related classes, like interface stubs), when a new version or a different vendor's implementation is available for a particular middleware protocol.

In both JADDA AOP-modes aspect code is transmitted by the System Administrator Console (SAC), relying on an application of PROSE that allows remote transmission of aspects bytecode in a transactional way. In the first JADDA AOP-mode, the aspect code is built by SAC using a temporary Java file, called Aspect Template (see figure 7): it contains generic and incomplete Java code of an aspect for the PROSE platform. Depending on the values of the xADL specification file, then the SAC completes the aspect template in order to obtain different Java files, one per each interfaces' method of the whole architecture. In In figure strings here depicted in bold font, like "AspectTemplate", "CLASSNAME", and "METHODNAME" are special keywords that will be replaced by SAC with the string values defined in the current xADL specification file.

```
public class AspectTemplate extends DefaultAspect {
Jadda jadda=Jadda.instance;
public MethodCut crosscut = new MethodCut() {
public void METHOD_ARGS(CLASSNAME c,Service s,REST p){
    try {
        jadda.checkParameters(s, p);
        jadda.call(s, "METHODNAME", p);
    } catch (JaddaException ex) {
    jadda.prose.exception=true;
  }
} protected PointCutter pointCutter() {
    return (Executions.before()).
            AND (Within.type("CLASSNAME")).
            AND (Within.method("METHODNAME"));
} };
```

Fig. 7. Aspect Template source code.

Using the example of figure 2, "CLASSNAME" will be replaced by the Chat client class name and method with the string "accessRoom". The composition logic defined in the "pointcutter" method, is interpreted by the PROSE platform that will call the "METHOD_ARGS" method (i.e. the "advice", in AOP terminology) before each execution of method "METHODNAME" of the class "CLASSNAME". The Aspect name is created by SAC composing the name of the current xADL file, the class name and the method name: a new unique identifier is needed because JVM does not allow namespace conflicts, even if they are due to unloaded classes.

These Java files are aspects code for the dynamic AOP platform and they are compiled to bytecode. Finally, among the different compiled classes, SAC deduces, from the xADL specification, which are the methods invoked by each component of the distributed architecture and it sends, after the new xADL file, the new aspects to each JADDA instance. As an aspect class can refer to new classes (e.g. middleware-related interface stubs), these are also sent to the JADDA instance, through the remote transfer mechanisms offered by the dynamic AOP platform. In the second AOP-mode, SAC sends new connector implementations, depending on the current xADL specification. On the other side, when the Listener thread in the JADDA instance received a new file, it withdraws the current aspects and inserts the new ones, when they are all arrived. Then the previous state-charts are still valid in order to maintain consistency during reconfiguration, even with aspect code insertions/withdrawals.

4   Case Study

We have applied JADDA to a basic example of chat system whose architecture is sketched in figure 8. A chat server publishes its own interfaces ChatManager and ChatRoom on a CORBA Naming Service; the System Administrator Console (SAC) is running and listening for requests on a specified port. Two chat clients using JADDA independently bootstrap and their own JADDA instance register their presences to the SAC and send data (e.g., the port where they are listening for xADL file transmission). The second step is represented by the transmission of the common xADL file, containing the current architectural specification, to all the involved components, i.e. the chat clients. After that, the third step is composed by the creation of aspects code in the SAC and then the consequent transmission to the clients using the remote aspect transmission feature of PROSE. Moreover, not only aspects can be added to a running application but also other additional classes, like middleware stubs, needed to activate the distributed connector used by the clients (e.g. using a CORBA connector like in figure 8).

Once the aspects are all arrived to a chat client, its own JADDA instance activates them and the application code starts its normal execution, resolving remote object references on the CORBA name server whom location is specified in the xADL file, and starting to call remote methods on the CORBA chat server. Let's now suppose that system architect wants to evolve the system in order to use a new middleware like SOAP and the deployed components (the chat clients) would be notified that there is a new instance of the chat server exposing WSDL interfaces on another location. System architect just needs to prepare the new xADL file with the needed information and build all the related aspects and stub classes. Once finished we can upload the new specification and the new aspects to each component currently connected using the remote aspect transmission feature of PROSE, as depicted in the first two steps of figure 9.

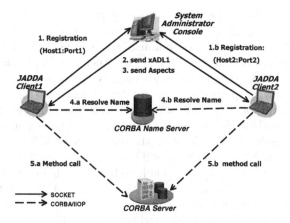

Fig. 8. Set-up scenario.

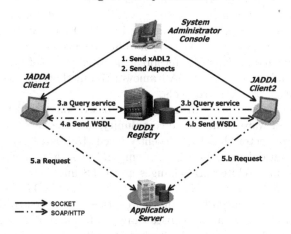

Fig. 9. Switch scenario.

After all the aspects have been inserted in a chat client, it will restart a normal execution resolving remote service address through a query to the UDDI registry (step 3) and then when a WSDL interface will be sent back (step 4) a normal method call will be executed to the new deployed Chat Server. The important result is the portability of the chat application that has neither to be rewritten nor restarted while middleware is changed and components are swapped.

5   Related Work

The discussion on related work touches different fields: dynamic software architectures, middleware, and separation of concerns. Architecture description languages (ADLs) and tools provide a formal basis for describing software architectures by specifying the syntax and semantics for modeling components, connectors, and configurations. Since a majority of existing ADLs, have focused on design issues, their uses have been limited to static analysis and simulate system execution at the architectural level. The other possibility, also used in our approach, is reflecting architecture modifications in an executing system. Arch-Java [12] follows this approach extending Java language with new constructs and providing a compiler to build an application that adheres to its architectural specification. Different kinds of connectors are implemented, usable with an API that has some similarities with the one of JADDA, but there is no support for dynamic architectural changes. These issues are considered by tools like Regis [13], and ArchStudio [8], both made to handle architecture-based runtime software evolution. ArchStudio, like JADDA, relies on xADL architectural specification, and the run-time structure of the application is altered, generating a different arrangement of components and connectors. These must be developed using Java-C2 class framework [14], limiting developer's freedom. While Arch-Studio checks architectural properties on xADL specification, in our approach model checking is implemented at runtime in JADDA instances of each component. Neither ArchJava nor ArchStudio offer connectors relying on off-the-shelf (OTS) implementations of widespread middleware protocols (like SUN's CORBA-IIOP and SOAP in JADDA framework), but they offer its own connector implementation of other protocols.

The key role of connectors in architecture-based software development has been stated by software architecture community, and the issue of reusing OTS middleware in connectors has been recently faced [15], but, in general, existing ADLs support static description of a system, and provide no facilities for specifying both runtime architectural changes and OTS middleware encapsulation. Although a few ADLs, such as Darwin [16], C2 [14], Rapide [17], Wright [18] can express runtime modification to architectures, these are specified during design and included in the application, constraining evolution among a set of predefined alternatives. JADDA follows another approach, based on unconstrained dynamism, i.e. insertion of unexpected modifications of an architecture and incorporation of behavior not anticipated by the original developers: in this case validity of changes must be ensured both before insertion, acting on architectural model, and at runtime, preserving consistency [19]; in fact, some aspects of software architecture evolution are the same of configuration management [20], and therefore dynamic architectural changes can be seen a more generic approach to dynamically reconfigure a software system at run time. Another approach of dynamic reconfiguration is adding configuration elements to components. For instance, Polylith [21] is a specification language for configuration, used to explicitly specify component bindings: in this case reconfiguration sequence consists of two steps: waiting to reach a reconfiguration point; and blocking communication channels (managing messages in transit) during reconfiguration. A third way is delegating reconfiguration to containers [22]. JADDA dynamic reconfiguration tries to take features of the first two approaches, adding a JADDA instance to each component and governing the change with an architecture-centric approach.

Regarding middleware reconfiguration and adaptation, different approaches have been proposed for mobile applications [23] and for context-aware applications [24]. Among these ones, the architecture-centric approach was used to adapt reflective middleware to new requirements [25], using the Aster framework in supporting dynamic adaptation in the context of the Open-ORB middleware platform to accommodate re-configurations due to changing non-functional parameters and environmental conditions. This work is more focused on defining extensions of software architecture techniques to accommodate dynamic change, in order to make the automatic synthesis of component-based configurations, and their subsequent monitoring and adaptation, based entirely on architectural descriptions. It is not clear how much the architectural model is bound to the implementation as in our approach, that is also focused on the implementation of a framework able to substitute at run-time an OTS middleware implementation (not constrained to a particular standard like CORBA) with a different one.

Moreover, several research has been done in quality-aware middleware systems [26] and middleware adaptation to non-functional features. For instance, P. Devanbu [27] proposed a methodology to enhance CORBA components with non-functional features (e.g. security), and the tool Lasagne [28] gives explicit support for CORBA clients runtime-adaptation to fulfill non-functional requirements.

This tool relies on Aspect Components [29], a dynamic aspect-oriented platform for distributed programming. It provides components that integrate system-wide properties (crosscutting concerns) such as distribution and authentication within a core application.

Separation of concerns is an emerging methodology to better modularize non-functional features, decoupled from application code. State-of-the-art separation of concerns techniques such as Aspect-oriented Programming [30], Hyperspaces [31], Mixin Layers [32], and Adaptive Plug and Play Components [33] allow extension of a core application with a new aspect/subject/layer/collaboration, by simultaneously refining state and behavior at multiple points in the application in a non-invasive manner. Therefore we think that JADDA and dynamic AOP are better suited for client-specific integration of extensions, while the above techniques are better suited for providing separation of concerns at the component implementation level. In composition filters approach [34], filters intercept messages sent and received by components. Since they are defined in extensions combined with a superimposition mechanism, they can be dynamically attached to components, but the integration of an extension is scattered across multiple object interactions, thus difficult to update consistently in one atomic action.

In JADDA, the composition logic is completely encapsulated within the composition rules contained in the aspect code (pointcuts) and the components' methods involved are taken by the specification. By doing this, developers do not need worry about architectural issues since these are automatically handled by the framework. Moreover our work extends dynamic reconfiguration to different middleware protocols and it adds basic runtime model-checking features.

6   Conclusions and Future Work

This paper describes the architectural framework JADDA, a component used to reach three main goals. The first one is easing timeline variability (changes that can be applied at either development time or run time) of different middleware implementations used.

The second goal is updating the connectors of a system by acting on its xADL architectural specification. This is edited and propagated by the SAC. In this way, re-configuration can be decided at a higher level than source code and all the needed information are stored in the xADL file.

Finally, dynamic reconfiguration is also handled using dynamic Aspect-Oriented Programming platform to allow additional classes transport in a reliable and transactional manner. As these features could lead to a stronger modification of application and to an unexpected software evolution, the verification of correctness of a new architecture is currently implemented in JADDA to verify specified links. While at boot-time JADDA allows realization of whichever xADL architectural model in the implementation, at run-time the current JADDA implementation is tailored for simple client-server architecture, where a client application (using JADDA) interacts with only one server. For example multiple chat client applications running on mobile terminals could use JADDA to dynamically migrate their connections to a new server implementation. Current work focuses on handling more complex architectures with related consistency issues, and extending JADDA for different middleware standards. Checking xADL correctness before instantiation in the running system, and realization of different interaction styles (e.g. event-based communications) will be part of future work.

Acknowledgements

The authors want to thank Andrei Popovici (ETH Zurich), and Patricia Lago (Politecnico di Torino) for the precious advices given during the realization of this work.

References

1. van Gurp, J., Bosch, J., Svahnberg, M.: The notion of variability in software product lines. Proceedings 2nd Working IEEE / IFIP Conference on Software Architecture (WICSA) (2001)
2. Szyperski, C.: Component software: Beyond object-oriented programming. (1998)
3. OMG: CORBA (common object request broker architecture) specification. (http://www.corba.org/)
4. EJB: Enterprise javabeans specification. (http://java.sun.com/products/ejb/docs.html)
5. Gudgin, M., et al.: http://www.w3.org/TR/soap12-part2/. W3C Recommendation (2003)
6. Newkirk, J.: Introduction to agile processes and extreme programming. Proc. of ICSE 2002 (2002)

7. Popovici, A., Alonso, G., Gross, T.: Just in time aspects: Efficient dynamic weaving for java. Proc. of the 2nd International Conference on Aspect-Oriented Software Development (2003)

8. Oreizy, P., Medvidovic, N., Taylor, R.N.: Architecture-based runtime software evolution. Proc. of International Conference of Software Engineering (ICSE98) (1998) 177–186

9. Dashofy, E.M., van der Hoek, A., Taylor, R.N.: A highly-extensible, xml-based architecture description language. Proc. of Working IEEE/IFIP Conference on Software Architecture (WICSA 01) (2001) 103–112

10. UDDI: Universal discovery and description and integration. (http://www.uddi.org/)

11. PROSE: Programmable service extensions. (http://prose.ethz.ch/)

12. Aldrich, J., Chambers, C., Notkin, D.: ArchJava: Connecting software architecture to implementation. Proc. of International Conference of Software Engineering (ICSE 2002) (2002)

13. Magee, J., Dulay, N., Kramer, J.: Regis: a constructive development environment for distributed programs. Distributed Systems Engineering Journal (1994) 304–312 Special Issue on Configurable Distributed Systems.

14. Medvidovic, N., Oreizy, P., Robbins, J.E., Taylor, R.N.: Using object-oriented typing to support architectural design in the c2 style. Proceedings of the ACM SIGSOFT '96 Fourth Symposium on the Foundations of Software Engineering (1996) 24–32

15. Dashofy, E.M., Medvidovic, N., Taylor, R.N.: Using off-the-shelf middleware to implement connectors in distributed software architectures. Proc. of International Conference of Software Engineering (ICSE 99) (1999) 3–12

16. Magee, J., Kramer, J.: Dynamic structure in software architectures. Fourth SIGSOFT Symposium on the Foundations of Software Engineering (1996)

17. Luckham, D.C., Vera, J.: An event-based architecture definition language. IEEE Transactions on Software Engineering (1995)

18. Allen, R., Garlan, D.: A formal basis for architectural connection. ACM Transactions on Software Engineering (1997)

19. Feiler, P.H., Li, J.: Consistency in dynamic reconfiguration. Proc. 4th International Conference on Configurable Distributed Systems (ICCDS 98) (1998)

20. van der Hoek, A., Mikic-Rakic, M., Roshandel, R., Medvidovic, N.: Taming architectural evolution. Proc. of the Ninth ACM SIGSOFT Symposium on the Foundations of Software Engineering (FSE-9) (2001)

21. Portilo, J.M.: The Polylith software bus. ACM Transactions on Programming Languages and Systems (TOPLAS) (1994)

22. Rutherford, M.J., Anderson, K., Carzaniga, A., Heimbigner, D., Wolf, A.L.: Reconfiguration in the Enterprise JavaBean component model. Component Deployment: IFIP/ACM Working Conference Proceedings (2002) 67–81

23. Inverardi, P., Marinelli, G., Mancinelli, F.: Adaptive applications for mobile heterogenous devices. Proc. of 22nd Intl. Conf. on Distributed Computing Systems Workshops (2002) 410–413

24. Griswold, W.G., Boyer, R., Brown, S.W., Truong, T.M.: A component architecture for an extensible, highly integrated context-aware computing infrastructure. Proc. of International Conference on Software Engineering (ICSE 2003) (2003)

25. Blair, G., Blair, L., Issarny, V., Tuma, P., Zarras, A.: The role of software architecture in constraining adaptation in component-based middleware platforms. Proc. of Middleware 2000 – IFIP/ACM International Conference on Distributed Systems Platforms and Open Distributed Processing (2000)

26. Bergmans, L., van Halteren, A., Ferreira Pires, L., van Sinderen, M., Aksit, M.: A QoS-control architecture for object middleware. Proc. of IDMS 2000 conference (2000)

27. Wohlstadter, E., Jackson, S., Devanbu, P.: DADO: enhancing middleware to support crosscutting features in distributed, heterogeneous systems. Proc. of International Conference on Software Engineering (ICSE 2003) (2003) 174 –186

28. Truyen, E., Vanhaute, B., Joosen, W., Verbaeten, P., Jorgensen, B.N.: Dynamic and selective combination of extensions in component-based applications. Proc. of the 23rd International Conference on Software Engineering (ICSE 2001) (2001) 233–242

29. Pawlak, R., Duchien, L., Florin, G., Martelli, L., Seinturier, L.: Distributed separation of concerns with aspect components. Proc. of TOOLS Europe 2000 (2000)

30. Kiczales, G., Lamping, J., Mendhekar, A., Maeda, C., Lopes, C.V., Loingtier, J., Irwan, J.: Aspect-oriented programming. Proc. of ECOOP97 (1997)

31. Tarr, P., Ossher, H., Harrison, W., Sutton Jr, S.: N-degrees of separation: Multidimensional separation of concerns. Proc. of ICSE 99 (1999)

32. Smaragdakis, Y., Batory, D.: Implementing layered designs with mixin layers. Proc. of ECOOP 98 (1998)

33. Mezini, M., Lieberherr, K.: Adaptive plug and play components for evolutionary software development. Proc. of OOPSLA'98 (1998)

34. Aksit, M., Wakita, K., Bosch, J., Bergmans, L., Yonezawa, A.: Abstracting object-interactions using composition-filters. Object-Oriented Distributed Processing (1993) 152–184

On the Role of Architectural Style
in Model Driven Development

Tommi Mikkonen, Risto Pitkänen, and Mika Pussinen

Institute of Software Systems
Tampere University of Technology
P.O.BOX 553, FIN-33101 Tampere, Finland
{tjm,rike,mtp}@tut.fi

Abstract. Object Management Group's Model-Driven Architecture (MDA) can
be considered as one of the achievements resulting from ever-increasing importance of software architecture. However, based on case studies on using the ideas
of MDA both with UML and in a formal setting, some notions that have been
conventionally associated with architecture-oriented development have no clear
role in the model. In particular, we are referring to architectural styles, which can
be seen as recurring architectures of various systems, especially when designing
product families. In this paper, we analyze architectural styles in the context of
MDA, propose a modification to the model that would allow encapsulation of architectural properties in it, and demonstrate the usage of the approach with two
examples, where interaction and distribution are the essential characteristics of
the used architecture.

1 Introduction

Software architecture has quickly emerged as one of the main artifacts of software development. Following the seminal contribution of e.g. Shaw and Garlan [1], Buschmann
et al. [2], and Bass *et al.* [3], the use of architecture as a first-class design element has become the de-facto design approach in software development. As a result, we can observe
the rise of software platforms and software product lines, which enable reuse of associated architectures and related qualities within different product families. Moreover,
architectural styles, such as *message-passing architecture*, *blackboard architecture*, or
pipes-and-filters architecture, have emerged, which can be used as the philosophy guiding the design, use, and evolution of software architectures as well as systems built on
top of them.

Model-Driven Architecture (MDA) by Object Management Group (OMG) is one
of the later architecture-oriented discoveries, which deals with architectures at meta-
level. In MDA, the distinction between computation independent, platform independent
and platform specific models is explicitly present by allowing each model to include a
structure of their own. Ideally, a mapping is provided for moving between the different
models, allowing a smooth transition between the designs. The transitions then ease
traceability and technology upgrades when new platforms become available.

What becomes problematic with this approach is how to include the notion of architectural styles in the model. The problem is that a system-level architectural style has

F. Oquendo et al. (Eds.): EWSA 2004, LNCS 3047, pp. 74–87, 2004.

been conventionally considered such a pervasive property of the system that it is difficult to see any competing architectural principles at any level of abstraction, because software architecture forms a concept of its own [4].

In order to highlight the role of architectural styles as first-class elements in the design and modeling even when following the MDA conventions, we propose a new layer, called Architecture Specific Model (ASM), that focuses solely on architectural issues. Our argumentation is organized as follows. Section 2 discusses architecture centric software development as well as architectural styles and MDA in more detail. The section also provides a more detailed discussion on the rationale of ASM. Sections 3 and 4 provide justification for the claim of this paper by introducing two cases aiming at following the MDA approach, and the role of Architecture Specific Model in them. The presented examples have been selected so that they represent domains where the use of architecture has long tradition and domain-specific architectural styles have emerged, thus contributing to the importance of being able to obey the architecture. Finally, Section 5 gives a concluding discussion that summarizes our experiences.

2 Architecture-Centric Software Development

Architectures have emerged as an important technical artifact of software systems. The importance of architectures results from their ability to define many system-level properties, like scalability and modifiability. For the purposes of this paper, we will be studying in more detail two topics related to architectures, namely architectural styles and the Model-Driven Architecture initiative (MDA) by Object Management Group (OMG).

2.1 Architectural Styles

The use of patterns and styles of design is pervasive in many engineering disciplines, including software in particular. When regarding an architecture, one can associate phrases such as *client-server system*, *pipe-and-filter design*, or *layered architecture* with it. Moreover, design and implementation techniques add more flavor to the terms, such as e.g. *object-oriented* or *data flow* organizations, as indicated in [1].

In many cases, architectural styles and patterns are associated with a certain family of systems. For instance, a compiler has a relatively well-established structure and model of decomposition, consisting of lexical, syntactic, and semantic analyse and code generation. Similarly, interactive systems including a graphical user interface commonly rely on *Model-View-Controller* architecture, where concerns related to user interface and internal logic are separated. This has been included in e.g. the Symbian application architecture [5]. Another example is the multi-tier style for distributed enterprise systems that divides the application to multiple tiers of functionality, each encapsulating a particular logical slice on the path from a client to a data storage. This model has been included in e.g. J2EE [6].

The way an architect chooses to configure components and connectors of a system is what makes the difference between different architectural styles. In order to keep the selected configuration a valid abstraction of the system, the associated architectural style(s) and related patterns must be followed. This obedience then results in valid applications that enable reuse of architecture-related concepts.

2.2   Model-Driven Architecture

Model-Driven Architecture initiative by Object Management Group is a model for the design of software systems. In order to ease focusing on important issues during design, MDA separates three different levels of abstraction in them [7]. These levels are listed in the following.

- *Computation Independent Model* (CIM) is the most abstract model of the system. It can be considered as a model representing the domain of the system, where the implemented system is modeled together with its environment.
- *Platform Independent Model* (PIM) is a model of the system given at a level that includes no platform specific issues. PIM is obtained by refining the associated CIM. Usually, this refinement is manual, although methodological guidelines may support this task.
- *Platform Specific Model* (PSM) is the most concrete model, which takes also platform specific issues into account. PSM is obtained by refining the corresponding PIM by introducing platform information. This is often advocated as an automated task, but in cases where a complex mapping is required, manual design decisions are often needed.

In this paper, we will be focusing on the relation between PIM and PSM, as the selected architecture should be fit to implement PIM and allow its realization in PSM.

When architectures of PIM and PSM are identical, the situation is trivial. However, with the introduction of platforms that require obedience to platform-dependent practices, architectural differences between platform independent and platform specific models are becoming more and more common. For instance, many of the architecturally significant items of an EJB application arise from the implementation domain rather than the problem domain. An example of such issue is the treatment of e.g. *home interface*, which requires certain measures in modeling but actually originates from the selected implementation technique.

Such subtle details imply that PIM should be more general than any particular implementation, and PSM should include all the implementation details. This raises a question: which of the models should introduce the selected architectural style of an application? On the one hand, this is a decision that is not connected to any platform dependent issue, indicating that PIM should include it. On the other hand, platform specific details often imply a certain style for applications by requiring that a certain framework is followed even if this is not included in higher-level designs. Thus, PSM would seem to be the natural place for the implementation architecture.

The description given in [8] does not resolve this conflict. It simply states that PIM may be architecture style specific, but it may also allow several possible styles, implying that architecture can be overlooked for platform independence. In contrast, at PSM level, the platform must provide the implementation primitives that the selected style requires. As many platforms assume a certain prescribed architecture, they may be restricted to implement some of the available architectural styles only.

2.3   Architecture Specific Model

Based on the above, the selected architectural style can reside in PIM, PSM, or be distributed between them. PIM includes the elements of the style that the designer wants

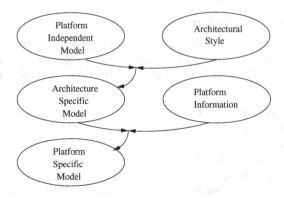

Fig. 1. Introducing Architecture Specific Model.

to highlight at that level of abstraction. However, this may be a partial view only, potentially lacking some architecturally significant aspects, because there is no direct requirement to complete architecting to some predefined level. In contrast, PSM includes all the implementation level details that potentially blur the architecture. As there is no unique place for architecturally significant design decisions, following a prescribed architectural style is hardened.

As a solution, we propose to add one more layer to the model. This layer, called *Architecture Specific Model* (ASM), is dedicated to describing architecture (Figure 1). The purpose of the layer is to make architectural styles, design patterns, and other important design decisions explicit in the model. Centralizing this decision into one layer then results in improved clarity regarding architectural properties, because the decisions cannot be made in isolation from one another.

For practical purposes, ASM alleviates transformation from PIM to PSM by introducing in the model architectural concepts that have platform specific counterparts in some set of platforms with similar facilities. This is often necessary as a mapping from an arbitrary PIM to PSM is likely to either be too generic to result in an effective and useful implementation or require extensive model marking [8]. The latter alternative would in fact leave platform independent architectural issues outside the scope of the actual model.

In the following, we will introduce two approaches to MDA based development, that demonstrate the role of ASM. The work has been inspired by tool-development projects, where different levels of abstractions in modeling have been focused at. The first case uses UML for modeling and patterns for PIM-ASM-PSM transformation. The second case uses a formal approach, where different formalisms constitute the levels.

3   UML-Based Approach

In this case study we have decided to capture architecture and platform specific knowledge into patterns. Patterns are stored in pattern specifications containing knowledge and documentation about the destination architecture and the destination platform. The

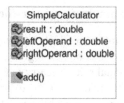

Fig. 2. PIM for simple calculator.

tool that has been used both to build and deploy pattern specifications has been introduced in [9].

In this case, we use Model-View-Controller (MVC) architectural style and Symbian OS as architecture and implementation platforms.

3.1   Using Patterns in Transformation Process

MDA Guide [8] presents the use of platform specific patterns as an alternative for describing transformation between PIM and PSM. In that proposal PIM is marked with pattern and role names. Transformation to PSM will happen based on the marked PIM as patterns are applied to marked elements based on name matching (Figure 3-5 in [8]). In our approach a developer binds the classes of a PIM to roles of patterns i.e. does the marking and name matching phases. By establishing bindings the developer assigns certain architectural responsibilities to the bound elements. The pattern engine of the tool uses the information stored into pattern specifications and creates task lists that guide the semi-automatic transformation process from PIM to ASM, and further from ASM to PSM. In addition to just binding existing elements to roles, patterns can be used to generate new architectural or platform specific elements. The binding and transformation processes are not totally separate ones; instead, they are interleaving. Establishing a binding produces a set of tasks and each performed task produces a transformation step. The order of doing steps needed during a transformation process is partly defined in a pattern specification and partly decided by the developer. When all roles of patterns have been bound to target elements and all mandatory tasks have been performed, the transformation process is complete.

Bindings are stored into pattern instances that are the images of original pattern specifications in which role names have been replaced with names of concrete design elements. We have decided to favor user-driven semi-automatic process showing to the developer a little bit of what is happening under the hood in order to offer better understanding on the target architecture. In principle the method itself does not prevent full automation after patterns have been bound to the elements they should be applied to.

As patterns are explicitly bound to concrete design elements, binding information is preserved both in the ASM and PSM level. There is a route from patterns representing architectural entities to design elements implementing those. It is possible to select a role from a pattern instance and query for the concrete element that is bound to the role. This enables later tracking of architectural entities also from the final PSM via pattern roles bound at the architectural level.

3.2 MVC Architectural Style and Platform Specific Issues

The MVC architectural style is not so much about what each individual role must do, but more about what they have to accomplish together. ASM must provide necessary infrastructure that enables individual roles to carry out their responsibilities regardless of destination platform. This information is used to extend PIM with necessary glue interfaces and classes enabling those reponsibilities. The ASM used in the case study is based on the following slightly simplified responsibilities between the roles forming MVC style.

Model is responsible for storing the state of the application and the logic that implements state changes. Model has to have means to inform Views about changes in its internal state without actually knowing the concrete views.

View is responsible for giving to the user of the application a presentation of the current state and necessary widgets to initiate changes that may alter the internal state of the application. View is responsible to provide a mapping from the changed widget to the corresponding state variable stored into the model.

Controller is responsible for mapping user interface events to calls that invoke operations on the model, which may change its internal state.

When using MVC style most of the responsibilities of View and Controller are platform specific issues. In Symbian OS the platform specific application architecture offers placeholder classes for each of the main roles, but does not define how communication between the roles should happen [5]. As this communication is in fact a more abstract issue, we use ASM to ensure that communication structure between different roles and interfaces separating application logic from presentation and user interaction is established. Applications developed on top of this platform must conform to a platform specific version of the MVC architecture.

3.3 An Example Transformation Using Patterns

Figure 2 depicts a very simple calculator class that offers only a service to add two operands belonging to the class into a third attribute storing the result of the addition. The model should evolve into an application with a proper user interface offering the same functionality in the destination platform, which in our case is Symbian OS.

Figure 3 represents the pattern defining and guiding the transformation process from PIM to ASM. The pattern used in the case study is not dependent on any particular platform but uses C++ in accompanied code templates thus making it language dependent.

By binding an attribute to *ObservedStateVariable* role, tasks asking to create corresponding methods for getting and setting the value of the state variable are created. The pattern introduces Observer [10] between View and Model taking care that changes in Model are propagated properly to View. As value of the observed attribute is set by the operation representing *setStateVariable* role, the attached code template takes care that observers are notified after the state change. ASM also introduces an interface class between Controller and Model. The decision of having this separate interface class is not mandatory in MVC but it can make Controller independent of the name given to the actual Model class. This is essential for our example destination platform because in it Model is implemented as a separate DLL. Still, the decision does not prevent using other platforms.

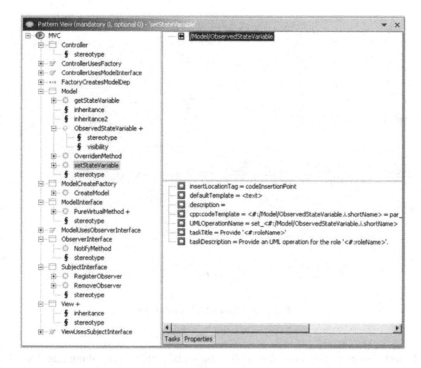

Fig. 3. Pattern for MVC ASM.

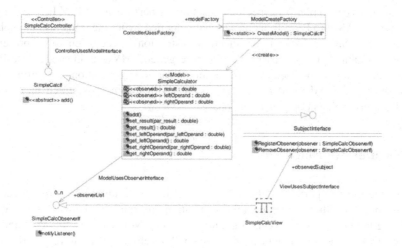

Fig. 4. ASM for simple calculator.

Figure 4 depicts the UML model after the pattern describing the transformation from PIM to ASM has been applied.

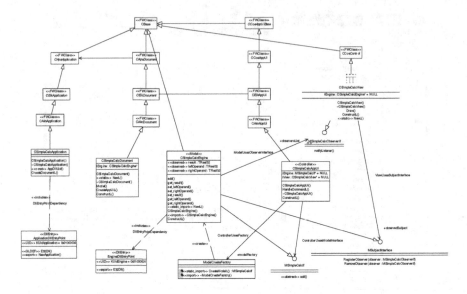

Fig. 5. PSM for simple calculator.

Figure 5 depicts the UML model after the set of patterns describing transformation from ASM to PSM have been applied. Transformation itself is similar to the previously described pattern-guided process. Only difference is that mapping from platform independent datatypes to platform specific ones must be performed on PIM before the patterns guiding ASM to PSM transformation are applied. After the transformation phase the resulting PSM conforms to architectural restrictions and conventions represented by the destination platform as well as to more general MVC architecture. The PSM is detailed enough to be used as a source model for code generation. The information expressed in the UML model is complemented with information stored into pattern specifications during code generation phase.

4   Formal Approach

One of the most important goals of MDA is to achieve a higher level of abstraction than is possible with conventional third generation programming languages, i.e. to use modeling languages as programming languages [11]. Motivated by this goal and endeavor towards precise semantics for incremental development, we have experimented with using the DisCo [12, 13] specification method as the backbone of a model-driven approach (see [14] for a preliminary report of the full results). The approach is summarized in Fig. 6, its main components being languages for platform independent and architecture specific modeling, a model execution tool, and an experimental code generator. In the following, we discuss how our findings relate to the role of architecture in model driven development.

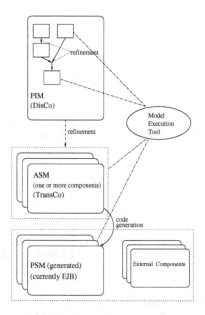

Fig. 6. Formal Model Driven Approach.

4.1   Platform Independent Modeling in DisCo

DisCo is based on the joint action paradigm [15, 16] and Temporal Logic of Actions [17]. Models are written in an incremental, refinement-based manner using a variant of *superposition* which preserves safety properties. The basic building blocks of a specification are *layers*, which are units of superposition. *Classes*, *actions*, *relations* and *assertions* along with some other constructs may be introduced and refined inside layers.

As an example, let us investigate a fragment taken from a model of a library:

```
dynamic class Title is
    isbn, author, title: String;
end;

action add_title(t: new Title; isbn, author, ti: String) is
when not (∃ t2: Title :: t2.isbn = isbn) do
    t.isbn := isbn || t.author := author || t.title := ti;
end;

action remove_title(t: Title) is
when not (∃ c : Copy :: c.of_which = t) do
    delete t;
end;
```

The level of abstraction is higher than in conventional object-oriented modeling languages, as communication is modeled in terms of multi-object actions instead of messages or methods. Although an action has a list of parameters, it is never explicitly called, and there is no notion of explicit control flow. Instead, actions are scheduled in a nondeterministic manner based on the values of their guard expressions in the current system state. For example, action remove_title may be picked for execution whenever

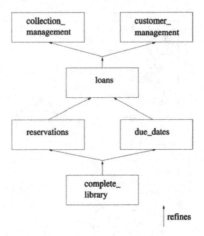

Fig. 7. Possible layer structure for library model.

no copies of the title to be removed exist in the collection[1]. If several actions (or several combinations of parameters for the same action) are enabled at the same time, the choice between them is nondeterministic. While this is appropriate for specification, using such a nondeterministic execution model in an implementation would be both inefficient and inappropriate due to not having control over which actions the system should perform in which order.

Specifications are organized in an aspect-oriented fashion, each layer describing concepts relating to a particular concern. Figure 7 depicts a possible layer structure for a library specification. While refinements can be written manually, also the application of pre-verified archived superposition steps has been studied [18]. Using archived steps is interestingly similar to pattern application as discussed in [8] and Sect. 3 of this paper.

Models written in DisCo can be animated in a graphical tool. As depicted in Fig. 6, the model execution tool will in the future be integrated with other stages of the approach as well, enabling model-implementation interaction as well as model-based testing and other advanced features.

4.2   Introducing an Architecture

A model written in DisCo is usually both platform and architecture independent. Multi-object actions abstract away from details of communication, enabling implementation using various paradigms and styles. Automatic code generation directly from a DisCo model is not feasible in the general case, because there are design decisions to be made before an implementation can be obtained. First, DisCo models are closed, i.e. they include both the system and its environment, and subsystem borders and interfaces are not explicitly indicated. Second, actions describe nondeterministically scheduled interactions between objects, without specifying who calls them, or which of the parameters

---

[1] Class **Copy** is defined in the model, but it is not shown here to save space.

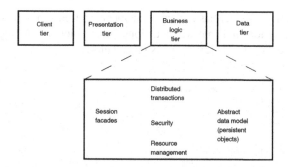

Fig. 8. Multi-tier architectural style.

are required inputs. A parameter list must include all objects and values the action refers to or modifies, some of which might be inputs, the rest being outputs or just auxiliary values. In fact, an action might be implemented using asynchronous messaging as well as synchronous method calls.

Model transformation is thus required in order to obtain a model adequate as a basis for code generation, and input from a designer is needed in this transformation. At this experimental stage we have decided to use an extended version of DisCo language called TransCo to manually specify a refinement which produces an ASM. This method also allows further refinement of the model, enabling the developer to add e.g. new classes and functionality specific to the platform independent architecture. In the future, tool support could be added to assist in this transformation.

Architectural style, which is a required input to the PIM–ASM mapping in our generic modeling architecture (Fig. 1), is embedded in TransCo itself, as it is a language specifically designed for modeling of business logic of multi-tier systems (Fig. 8). Enterprise computing platforms such as J2EE are based on an architectural style which divides the system into client, presentation, business logic and data tiers (in some cases there may be more or fewer tiers). In this architectural style, business logic contains the core functionality of the system, which has been separated from both its presentation to the client (such as dynamic web pages) and the concrete data storage model (such as relational database). Business logic platforms, for example Enterprise JavaBeans, offer various automatic and explicitly callable services to business logic components, including resource management, threading, distributed transactions, persistence and security.

TransCo can be compared to certain architecture description languages that have a specific architectural style embedded in them, such as C2SADEL based on the C2 style [19]. The main difference is that in TransCo an explicit link to an architecture-independent model exists.

For further details on TransCo the reader is referred to [14].

4.3   Architecture Specific Modeling in TransCo

The first class constructs of TransCo include for example *components, persistent classes* and *transactions*, all of which are core concepts of many multi-tier business logic platforms. A TransCo model has a clear refinement relationship with a DisCo model: for example transactions indicate which actions they implement. A fragment from the TransCo refinement of the library model is given below:

```
class implementation Title is
  attribute isbn : String (primary key);
  attribute author : String;
  attribute title : String;
  unique key (author, title);
end;

transaction add_title(isbn: String; author: String;
                      title: String)
  t: new Title;
of complete_library.add_title(t, isbn, author, title)
is
  when Title._find(isbn) = null;
  t.isbn := isbn;
  t.author := author;
  t.title := title;
end;
```

As seen in the fragment, syntax resembles that of DisCo. A class implementation implements a DisCo class in a persistent manner. Variables are implemented as attributes, which may form keys. The primary key of a class implementation defines a class method _find(), which returns an object with the corresponding key. Additional keys may be either unique (the corresponding finder method returns an object) or non-unique (the corresponding finder method returns a set of objects). Finders are usually used for implementing parameter bindings and quantifications. An example of the latter is the guard statement of the transaction add_title above: Title._find(isbn) = null implies the original action guard not ($\exists$ t2: Title :: t2.isbn = isbn).

4.4   Producing a PSM

Producing a PSM or generating code from a TransCo model is relatively straight-forward as discussed in [14], provided that the target platform has support for the key constructs. Such platforms include e.g. Enterprise JavaBeans and CORBA. What makes the difference between straightforward and impossible transformation is the architectural style embedded in the TransCo language. In our approach, the architecture-independent DisCo model is transformed into an architecture-dependent model expressed in TransCo. The language itself forces us to refine the model in such a way that it becomes implementable using the chosen architectural style, supported by the target platforms.

In our approach, targeting DisCo models towards other architectural styles besides multi-tier means that different architecture-specific languages need to be defined. This is some kind of a trade-off between genericity and simple, architecture-specific expressiveness. Previous experiences with using DisCo for modeling application-specific hardware [20] and implementing models using VHDL suggest that quite different domains and architectural styles can be supported as well.

5 Discussion

We conclude that architectural styles can be embedded in the Model-Driven Architecture framework, but unfortunately this embedding may be difficult to represent explicitly. The reason for this is that in many cases the representative of the architectural style implicitly resides somewhere between Platform Independent and Platform Specific Models.

In order to lift architecture as a first-class model element, one more level is needed in MDA, called Architecture Specific Model (ASM), which introduces the required architectural style. While this element is not always explicitly needed because it can also be considered as a some kind of a design convention to obey when refining a PIM into a PSM, a documented architectural connection eases the transition from PIM to PSM in many practical cases.

Our first experiences suggest that a transition from PIM to ASM cannot be a fully automated one. Instead, a lot of engineering is required, because the definition of architecture is an important design decision. In contrast, transition from ASM to PSM can be computer-aided, assuming that a mapping from ASM to PSM is predefined. Obviously, in order to create the mapping, PSM must include primitives that are suited for implementing ASM, which further emphasizes the importance of architecture.

The unclear role of CIM and vagueness of the mapping between CIM and PIM give possibilities for other interpretations as well, assuming that the contents of different modeling levels of models can be interpreted freely. Then, one could interpret CIM as an architecture independent model, PIM as an architecture specific model as sometimes suggested but not required in [8], and PSM as a platform specific model. This interpretation has been already used in [14]. Then, CIM becomes an important technical artefact of the development, instead of being a simple environment description that can be overlooked, as many authors have done.

Acknowledgements

This research has been supported by the Academy of Finland (project Abesis 5100005) and National Technology Agency of Finland (project Archimedes 40183/03).

References

1. Shaw, M., Garlan, D.: Software Architecture: Perspectives on an Emerging Discipline. Prentice-Hall (1996)
2. Buschmann, F., Meunier, R., Rohnert, H., Sommerland, P., Stal, M.: Pattern-Oriented Software Architecture: A System of Patterns. Wiley (1996)
3. Bass, L., Clements, P., Kazman, R.: Software Architecture in Practice. Addison-Wesley (1997)
4. Laine, P.: The role of software architectures in solving fundamental problems in object-oriented development of large embedded sw systems. In: Proc. the Working IEEE/IFIP Conference on Software Architecture, Amsterdam, IEEE Computer Society (2001) 14–23
5. Tasker, M., Allin, J., Dixon, J., Shackman, M., Richardson, T., Forrest, J.: Professional Symbian Programming: Mobile Solutions on the EPOC Platform. Wrox Press Inc (2000)

6. Sun Microsystems: (J2EE WWW site) At http://java.sun.com/j2ee/.
7. OMG: (Model-Driven Architecture WWW Site. At URL http://www.omg.org/mda/)
8. OMG: (MDA guide version 1.0.1. OMG Document Number omg/2003-06-01, June 2003. At URL http://www.omg.org/mda/specs.htm)
9. Hammouda, I., Pussinen, M., Katara, M., Mikkonen, T.: UML-based approach for documenting and specializing frameworks using patterns and concern architectures. The 4th AOSD Modeling With UML Workshop in conjunction with UML 2003, San Francisco, CA (2003)
10. Gamma, E., Helm, R., Johnson, R., Vlissides, J.: Design Patterns: Elements of Reusable Object-Oriented Software. Addison-Wesley (1994)
11. Selic, B.: The pragmatics of model-driven development. IEEE Software **20** (2003) 19–25
12. Järvinen, H.M., Kurki-Suonio, R.: DisCo specification language: marriage of actions and objects. In: Proceedings of the 11th International Conference on Distributed Computing Systems, IEEE Computer Society Press (1991) 142–151
13. DisCo WWW site: (http://disco.cs.tut.fi)
14. Pitkänen, R.: Formal model driven development of enterprise systems. Technical report, Institute of Software Systems, Tampere University of Technology (2004) http://disco.cs.tut.fi/reports/formalmdd.pdf.
15. Back, R.J.R., Kurki-Suonio, R.: Distributed cooperation with action systems. ACM Transactions on Programming Languages and Systems **10** (1988) 513–554
16. Kurki-Suonio, R.: Action systems in incremental and aspect-oriented modeling. Distributed Computing **16** (2003) 201–217
17. Lamport, L.: The temporal logic of actions. ACM Transactions on Programming Languages and Systems **16** (1994) 872–923
18. Kellomäki, P., Mikkonen, T.: Design templates for collective behavior. In Bertino, E., ed.: Proceedings of ECOOP 2000, 14th European Conference on Object-Oriented Programming. Number 1850 in Lecture Notes in Computer Science. Springer–Verlag (2000) 277–295
19. Medvidovic, N., Rosenblum, D., Taylor, R.: A language and environment for architecture-based software development and evolution. In: Proceedings of the 21st International Conference on Software Engineering (ICSE'99), Los Angeles, CA, IEEE Computer Society (1999) 44–53
20. Pitkänen, R., Klapuri, H.: Incremental cospecification using objects and joint actions. In Arabnia, H.R., ed.: Proceedings of the International Conference on Parallel and Distributed Processing Techniques and Applications (PDPTA'99). Volume VI., CSREA Press (1999) 2961–2967

UML 1.4 versus UML 2.0
as Languages to Describe Software Architectures

Jorge Enrique Pérez-Martínez[1] and Almudena Sierra-Alonso[2]

[1] Universidad Politécnica de Madrid, Departamento de Informática Aplicada
Campus Sur de la U.P.M., 28031 Madrid, Spain
jeperez@eui.upm.es
[2] Universidad Autónoma de Madrid, Escuela Politécnica Superior
Ctra. de Colmenar, km. 15, 28049 Madrid, Spain
Almudena.sierra@ii.uam.es

Abstract. UML 1.4 is widely accepted as the standard for representing the various software artifacts generated by a development process. For this reason, there have been attempts to use this language to represent the software architecture of systems as well. Unfortunately, these attempts have ended in representations (boxes and lines) already criticized by the software architecture community. Recently, OMG has published a draft that will constitute the future UML 2.0 specification. In this paper we compare the capacities of UML 1.4 and UML 2.0 to describe software architectures. In particular, we study extensions of both UML versions to describe the static view of the C3 architectural style (a simplification of the C2 style). One of the results of this study is the difficulties found when using the UML 2.0 metamodel to describe the concept of connector in a software architecture.

1 Introduction

UML 1.4 [18] has become the standard for representing the software products obtained in the various activities (like requirement acquisition, requirement analysis, system design, or system deployment) of a software development process. For this reason, it is not surprising that there have been attempts to use UML 1.4 to represent the software architecture of an application. However, the language is not designed to syntactically and semantically represent the elements of software architectures, neither using its constructors as they are defined nor adding stereotypes to them. Some works analyzing this problem are [1][5][7–10][12][14][16][22–25][29]. Consequently, the only solution is to make a heavyweight extension to the UML 1.4 metamodel. However, this type of extension requires the modification of the language, which in turn implies that the tools processing it would need to be changed, deviating from the standard. The appearance of UML 2.0 [19][20] in the near future could solve (or at least ease) this problem. As indicated in [3], UML 2.0 promises a significant improvement in the way systems are architected.

F. Oquendo et al. (Eds.): EWSA 2004, LNCS 3047, pp. 88–102, 2004.
© Springer-Verlag Berlin Heidelberg 2004

In this work we present a set of extensions to the UML 1.4 metamodel and to the UML 2.0 metamodel to describe the static view of the C3 architectural style. This style is a variation of the C2 style [15]. UML 1.4 has been selected versus UML 1.5 because UML 1.4 is more popular and it is more extended than UML 1.5.

The rest of the paper is organized as follows. In Section 2 we describe basic concepts related to software architecture, trying to establish a conceptual reference framework. In Section 3 we describe how we change the C2 architectural style to obtain the C3 style. In Section 4 we present the extension to the UML 1.4 metamodel to represent the static view of the C3 style. In Section 5 we approach this problem using UML 2.0. Section 6 presents a comparison between the results of the two previous sections. Finally, Section 7 presents conclusions and future lines of research.

2 Software Architecture

Due to the recent appearance of the software architecture discipline, there are still several definitions of this concept. For example, in [2] we find: "The software architecture of a program or computing system is the structure or structures of the system, which comprise software components, the externally visible properties of those components, and the relationships among them." In [28] we can read: "Abstractly, software architecture involves the description of elements from which systems are built, interactions among those elements, patterns that guide their composition, and constraints on these patterns." IEEE Standard 1471 [11] defines architecture as: "the fundamental organization of a system embodied in its components, their relationships to each other, and to the environment, and the principles guiding its design and evolution." Our work assumes the definition of software architecture given by [11] since it is the most complete of those referenced.

On the other hand, this work takes the definition of architectural style provided by [4]: "an architectural style is a specialization of a viewtype's elements and relationships, together with a set of constraints on how they can be used. A style defines a family of architectures that satisfy the constraints."

3 The C3 Architectural Style

C3 is an architectural style derived from the C2 style [15]. We briefly describe now the C2 architectural style. "The C2 architectural style can be informally summarized as a network of concurrent components hooked together by message routing devices" [15]. Every component has its own control flow and no assumptions are made about the existence of a shared addressing space. The key elements of the C2 architecture are components and connectors.

Components communicate through asynchronous message passing. There are two types of messages: notifications and requests. Notifications are announcements of changes in the state of the internal object of a component. Requests sent by a component indicate service requests to components on top of it. A notification is always sent downward through a C2 architecture while a request is always sent up.

Both components and connectors must have top and bottom domains. The top domain of a component can only be connected to the bottom domain of a connector and its bottom domain can only be connected to the top domain of a connector.

A connector can be connected to any number of components and/or connectors. Components can only communicate through connectors since direct communication between components is forbidden. Two connectors can only be connected from the bottom of one to the top of the other. Connectors are responsible for routing and, potentially, multicasting messages. A secondary responsibility of connectors is message filtering. Connectors can provide the following policies for filtering and delivery of messages: no filtering, notification filtering, message filtering, prioritized, and message sink

The modifications introduced in the C2 style to obtain C3 are the following:

- There is no predetermined type of inheritance between components.
- Interface operations only allow input arguments.
- The type of component and its internal structure are not predetermined.
- Connectors only support the policies of message filtering and message sink.
- Operations in the interface can define preconditions and postconditions.

4   A Proposal of Heavyweight Extension to UML 1.4 Metamodel to Describe the Static View of the C3 Architectural Style

This section presents our proposal to extend the UML 1.4 metamodel to describe the static view of the C3 style. This proposal has been previously presented in [21]. To extend the metamodel we have followed two rules:

- We do not remove existing metaclasses nor modify their syntax or semantics.
- The new metaclasses must have as few relations as possible with the metaclasses already defined, i.e., they must be self-contained (as much as possible).

The objective behind these rules is to simplify the implementation of this extension in tools that already support the current UML 1.4 metamodel.

We will introduce the new metaclasses to the UML 1.4 metamodel to represent the structural aspects of the C3 architectural style in a new package which we call *C3Description*, located in the package *Foundation*. The abstract syntax for the package *Foundation::C3Description* is shown in Figure 1. In this Figure, the new metaclasses added to the UML 1.4 metamodel appear shading.

Although not shown in that figure, the new constructors (except for *Role* and *Port*) are added to the UML 1.4 metamodel as subclasses of *ModelElement*, which defines the metaattribute *name*. *ModelElement* is a subclass of *Element*, the root metaclass. Constructors *Role* and *Port* will be subclasses of *Element* since they do not need to have a name. As shown in Figure 1, we use the constructors *Attribute*, *Constraint* and *Parameter* defined in package *Core*, and types *Boolean* and *ProcedureExpression* defined in package *Data Types*. A detailed description of the *Foundation::C3De-scription* package can be found in [21]. To summary we can say:

- The metaclasses *Component, Connector* and *Architecture* represent the concepts of component, connector and configuration of the C3 style. The association *con-tains* between *Component/Connector* and *Architecture* indicates that a component and a connector can be composite elements.
- The metaclasses *Port* and *Role* represent the interaction points of a component and a connector, respectively. The cardinality (2) between *Component* and *Port* indicates that a component has two domains: top and bottom. The cardinality (1..*) between *Connector* and *Role* indicates that a connector has several interac-tion points. The association between *Port* and *Role* models the connection be-tween a component (at one domain) and a connector. The association *conTocon* between *Role* and *Role* models the connection between two different connectors.
- The metaclass *InterfaceElement* models the interface of a C3 component in both domains. An interface element has a name (inherited of *ModelElement*), a direc-tion that indicates whether the component provides this operation to the environ-ment (prov) or whether the component requires that operation from environment (req), a parameters set and, probably, a precondition and a postcondition.
- The state variables of a component are modeled with the metaclass *Attribute* and the invariant of the component with the metaclass *Constraint*.
- Lastly, the metaclass *Filter* models the filter mechanisms supported by C3.

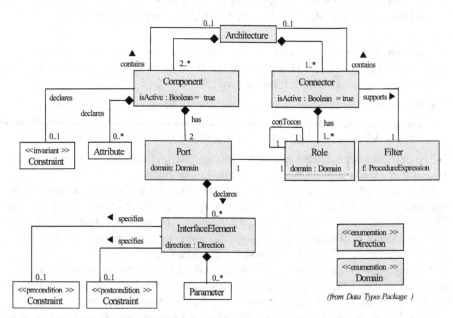

Fig. 1. Abstract syntax of the package Foundation::C3Description in UML 1.4 to describe the static view of the C3 architectural style (from ACM/SIGSOFT 28(3)).

5   Description of the Static View of the C3 Architectural Style with UML 2.0

To investigate how to use UML 2.0 to describe the static view of the C3 architectural style we can follow this strategy:

1. Use the elements of UML 2.0, as they are defined by the language.
2. If the previous option is unable to represent the C3 style, the only possibility is extending UML 2.0. We can extend UML 2.0 in two ways:

   - We can define a new dialect of UML 2.0 by using Profiles to customize the language for particular platforms and domains. This implies making use of the package *InfrastrutureLibrary::Profiles*.
   - We can specify a new language related to UML 2.0 by reusing part of the *InfrastructureLibrary::Core* package and augmenting it with appropriate metaclasses and metarelationships. With this approximation we define a new member of the UML 2.0 family of languages.

In the following, we study each of these approximations to evaluate the capabilities of UML 2.0 to describe the static view of the C3 architectural style.

5.1   Using UML 2.0 "as Is"

In this case we try to use the constructors defined by the package *UML* to represent the architectural elements of the C3 style. Unfortunately, the constructors defined in UML 2.0 do not allow specifying many of the architectural aspects of the C3 style. Some sample problems are:

1. The semantics of a connector is different in UML 2.0 and in C3. For example, UML 2.0 [20] defines an assembly connector as follows: "is a connector between two components that defines that one component provides the services that another component requires." In C3, a connector can be connected to any number of connectors and not only to components.
2. A component in UML 2.0 (metaclass *Components::Component*) can have any number of associated ports. In C3, each of the two component domains could be modeled by a port, so that a component would only have two associated ports.
3. In C3 an operation in the specification of an interface does not return any result, while the same concept of operation in UML 2.0 (metaclass *Classes::Kernel::Operation*) allows a result to be returned.
4. In UML 2.0 the declaration of an interface (metaclass *Classes::Interfaces::Interface*) can have some attributes (*properties*) associated while interfaces in C3 only allow to declare operations.

We could point out more problems of UML 2.0 to describe the architectural style C3, but one is enough to require a different strategy. In the next section we describe an approximation to describe the static view of the C3 architectural style by defining a new dialect of UML 2.0.

5.2   Defining a Dialect of UML 2.0

With this approximation, the package *InfrastructureLibrary::Profiles* is used to characterize elements of the package *UML* so that they can be used to describe elements of the architectural style C3. Every package referenced in this section is supposed to be contained in the package *UML* except when its name starts with *InfrastructureLibrary*. For every element of style C3, we will describe which element of UML 2.0 looks more appropriate to represent it and the constraints on such element. Those constraints are written in Object Constraint Language, OCL [18].

5.2.1   Component

To characterize a component of C3 we will use the metaclass *Component* of the package *Components* as the base class. The resulting stereotype will be named *C3Component* (see Figure 2).

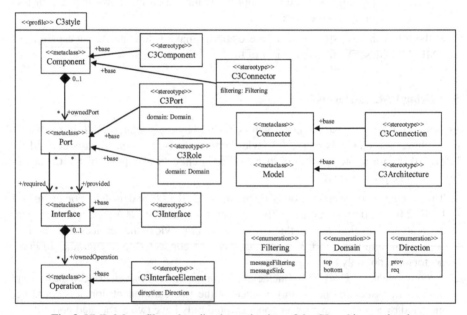

Fig. 2. UML 2.0 profile to describe the static view of the C3 architectural style.

We define the following constraints in the context of this stereotype:

1. A *Component* in UML 2.0 is a subclass of *Class* so that it can define attributes and operations. In C3, these features are private of the component.

   > self.base.ownedAttribute-> forAll (at| at.visibility = VisibilityKind::private) **and**
   > self.base.ownedOperation-> forAll (op| op.visibility = VisibilityKind::private)

2. A C3 component has two ports representing its top and bottom domains. Metaclass *Component* inherits from *Class* and this one inherits from *EncapsuledClassifier*, which declares the association +*ownedPort* (with respect to *Port*).

   > self.base.ownedPort -> size() = 2

3. A C3 component can be a simple element or a composite element. This means that it can contain other components and connectors. Metaclass *Component* specifies the relation *+ownedMember,* which extends the concept of basic component to formalize it as a "building block" with a set of modelling elements. The relation *ownedMember* is defined between metaclasses *Component* and *PackageableElement.* This implies that both component and connector must be *PackageableElement.* In the case of *C3Component* there is no problem since it is a stereotype of *Component* and inherits (indirectly) from *PackageableElement.* However, the case of connector is very different. If we define *C3Connector* as a stereotype of *Connector* (see Section 5.2.5), the inheritance chain of the latter does not go across *PackageableElement.* In fact, *Connector* inherits from *Feature* and this one from *NamedElement* (which inherits from the root metaclass *Element*).

4. In UML 2.0 component interfaces are supported by the component itself (or one of the classifiers implementing it) or are the type of one of its ports. Here we decided to support component interfaces in C3 by the ports of the component.

> self.base.provided -> size() = 0 **and** self.base.required -> size() = 0

5. A component in C3 is an active element. *Component* inherits the attribute *isActive* from *Class* (defined in *CommonBehaviors::Communications*).

5.2.2 InterfaceElement

This constructor represents an operation involved in the interaction of a component with its environment. To characterize an interface element in C3 we take as base class the metaclass *Operation* from the package *Classes::Kernel.* The resulting stereotype will be named *C3InterfaceElement* (see Figure 2). An interface element in C3 defines a direction that indicates if the element represents an operation provided to the environment (*prov*) or an operation required from the environment (*req*). In the context of this stereotype we define the following constraints:

1. An operation declared in the interface does not return any results.

> self.base.returnResult -> size() = 0

2. The parameters from an interface operation of a C3 component can only have *in* direction.

> self.base.parameter -> forAll (p| p.direction = ParameterDirectionKind::in)

3. Only interface operations with direction *prov* can have preconditions and/or postconditions.

> self.direction = Direction::req **implies**
> > self.base.precondition -> empty() **and** self.base.postcondition -> emtpy()

5.2.3 Interface

An interface in C3 is a set of public operations assigned to a component port. To characterize a C3 interface we take as the base class the metaclass *Interface* from the package *Classes::Interfaces.* The resulting stereotype will be named *C3Interface* (see Figure 2). In the context of this stereotype we define the following constraints:

1. A C3 interface does not declare attributes.

> self.base.ownedAttribute -> size() = 0

2. All the operations described in an interface must be of type *C3InterfaceElement*.

> self.base.ownedOperation -> forAll (op|
>> stereotype (op).name = 'C3InterfaceElement')
> where: stereotype (c: Class): Stereotype; stereotype = c.extension.ownedEnd.type

3. All the operations defined in the same interface have the same direction

5.2.4 Port

To characterize a port in C3 we will take the metaclass *Port* of the package *CompositeStructures::Ports* as the base class. The resulting stereotype will be called *C3Port* (see Figure 2). A C3 port defines a *domain* corresponding to that of the component it belongs to. In the context of this stereotype, we define the following constraints:

1. The attributes in the metaclass *Port* are constrained by the stereotype as follows. The attribute *isService* is constrained to a value *true* since ports in C3 are external to the component. The attribute *isBehavior* is constrained to have the value *false* since the object or objects inside the component (not the component itself) support this behavior.

2. The interface provided of a port contains only operations with *prov* direction.

> self.base.provided.ownedOperation -> forAll (op|
>> stereotype(op).direction = Direction::prov)

3. The interface required of a port contains only operations with *req* direction.

> self.base.required.ownedOperation -> forAll (op|
>> stereotype(op).direction = Direction::req)

5.2.5 Connector

The description of a C3 connector in UML 2.0 is not as immediate as for the preceding C3 elements. As we pointed out in Section 5.1 the semantics of connectors in UML 2.0 (metaclass *Connector*) does not correspond to the semantics of the same concept in C3. In the following, we describe how some semantic differences between the two constructors can be overcome through the use of constraints. To characterize a C3 connector we will take the metaclass *Connector* from the package *CompositeStructures::InternalStructures* as the base class. The resulting stereotype will be called *C3Connector*. We have to consider the following problems:

1. UML 2.0 [20] defines an assembly connector as follows: "is a connector between two components that defines that one component provides the services that another component requires." In C3, a connector can be connected to any number of connectors, and not only components. In UML 2.0 the end points of a connector must be constructors of the type *ConnectableElement*. UML 2.0 only defines the following metaclasses of this type: *Property, Variable, Port,* and *Parameter*. Since in UML 2.0 the metaclass *Connector* is not of type *ConnectableElement*, a connector cannot be connected to other connectors. This makes it impossible for *Connector* or any of its stereotypes to represent a C3 connector. The core problem is that the

metaclass *Connector* is not a type of *Classifier* as *Component* is. So, connectors in UML 2.0 do not appear to be first class entities.

2. In C3, a connector, like a component, can be formed by components and connectors. However, the metaclass *Connector* is not a *PackageableElement* and consequently it cannot be contained in any component (see Section 5.2.1) nor it can contain other connectors.

3. In C3 a connector has one or more points of interaction with its environment. Each of these points is a role. In UML 2.0, a connector only has two end points, while in C3 a connector can have more than two roles.

Considering the problems we have pointed out, we conclude that the metaclass *Connector* is not valid as the base class for a stereotype representing a connector in C3. The next obvious option is using the metaclass *Component* as the base class. On the other hand, C3 connectors have a filtering policy associated. So, we add the attribute *filtering* to specify this policy. The resulting stereotype will be named *C3Connector* (see figure 2). In the context of this stereotype we define the following constraints:

1. A C3 connector does not define attributes or operations.
   > self.base.ownedAttribute -> size() = 0 **and** self.base.ownedOperation -> size() = 0

2. A C3 connector may have several roles in each domain. If we represent each role with a stereotype of *Port* (see next section), we can describe this constraint as follows:
   > self.base.ownedPort -> size() >= 1 **and**
   > self.base.ownedPort -> forAll (p| stereotype(p).name = 'C3Role')

3. A C3 connector can be a simple element or a composite element. Specifically, a connector can contain other components or connectors. Observe that by stereotyping the metaclass *Component* to represent a connector we solve the problem pointed out in constraint [3] of section 5.2.1.

4. A C3 connector does not support any interfaces.
   > self.base.provided -> size() = 0 **and** self.base.required -> size() = 0

5. A C3 connector defines a filtering policy.
   > self.filtering = Filtering::messageFiltering **xor**
   > self.filtering = Filtering::messageSink

5.2.6 Role

As we saw in the previous section, we call role to each point of interaction of a connector with its environment. To describe a C3 role in UML 2.0 we find similar problems to those faced to describe a connector. A C3 role represents a point of interaction of a connector with a component (through its port) or with another connector (through its own role). On the contrary, the concept of role in UML 2.0 is defined in the context of a collaboration [20]: "Thus, a collaboration specifies what properties instances must have to be able to participate in the collaboration: A role specifies (through its type) the required set of features a participating instance must have." We can model a role as a stereotype of the metaclass *Port*. The resulting stereotype is named *C3Role* (see Figure 2). In the context of this stereotype we define the following restrictions:

1. A role in C3 does not support any interface.
2. A role associated to a connector in C3 does not support any behavior.

> self.base.isService -> size() = 0 **and** self.base.isBehavior -> size() = 0

5.2.7 Connection Component-Connector and Connector-Connector

In C3, the component port may be linked to the role of a connector. On the other hand, the role of a connector can be linked to the role of another connector or to the port of a component. We have to remember that both *C3Port* and *C3Role* are stereotypes of *Port*. So, how could we state this relationship? It is necessary to define an association between *C3Port* and *C3Role*. However, an association between stereotypes is only possible if it is a subset of the existing associations in the reference metamodel between the base classes of those stereotypes. This means that there must be an association between *Port* and *Port*. Here comes into play the metaclass *Connector*, establishing a link between two instances of type *ConnectableElement* (like instances of *Port* are). Then, to characterize the connection in C3 between a component port and the role of a connector, or between two roles of two different connectors, we will define a stereotype of the metaclass *Connector* called *C3Connection* (see Figure 2). In the context of this stereotype we define the following constraints:

1. A connection in C3 links two elements.

> self.base.end -> size() = 2

2. A connection in C3 links a component port with a connector role or two roles of two different connectors.

> **let** ports: Set = self.base.end.role -> select (el| stereotype(el).name = 'C3Port')
> **let** roles: Set = self base.end.role -> select (el| stereotype(el).name = 'C3Role') **in**
>   ports -> size() = 1 **implies** roles -> size() = 1 **and**
>   roles -> size() = 2 **implies** roles -> forAll (r1 r2|
>   r1.end.connector <> r2.end.connector)

3. A connection in C3 cannot link two ports.

> **let** ports: Set = self.base.end.role -> select (el| stereotype(el).name = 'C3Port') **in**
>   **not** ports -> size() = 2

5.2.8 Composite Components and Connectors

A C3 architecture is a set of components and connectors whose connectivity respects a set of topological constraints. In Sections 5.2.1 and 5.2.5 we indicated that both a component and a connector may be formed by components and connectors. This means that both a component and a connector may contain an architecture. To characterize a architecture with C3 style we will define a stereotype of *Model* (which is a subclass of *Package*) named *C3Architecture* (see Figure 2). In the context of this stereotype we define the following constraints:

1. A C3 architecture is a composition of components and connectors.
2. A C3 architecture is formed by two or more components and one or more connectors.

5.2.9 An UML 2.0 Profile to Describe the Static View
of the C3 Architectural Style

Figure 2 describes the set of stereotypes defined thus far, which have been grouped under the profile *C3style*.

Since style C3 imposes certain topological constraints in relation with the connectivity between components and connectors, it is interesting to show the relationships among the different stereotypes defined. Figure 3 shows those relationships.

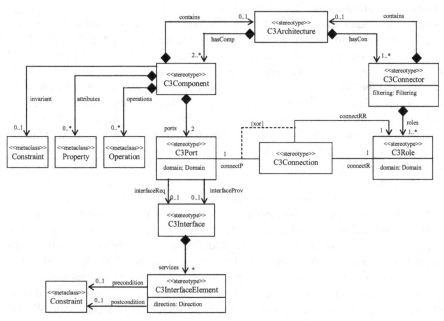

Fig. 3. Abstract syntax of a dialect of UML 2.0 to describe the static view of the C3 architectural style.

5.3 Defining a New Member of the UML 2.0 Language Family

As indicated in the previous section, a connector (represented by the metaclass *Connector*) in UML 2.0 does not appear to be a first class entity. This observation seems to go against the general opinion in the software architecture community, which considers that connectors and components deserve a similar treatment [6][17][26][27]. Moreover, from the document defining the superstructure [20], it seems that a connector in UML 2.0 is limited to connect ports (*ConnectableElement*). The software architecture community assigns more complex semantics to the concept of connector than that represented by the metaclass *Connector*. In this direction, Garlan and Kompanec [7] indicate that: "From a run-time perspective, connectors mediate the communication and coordination activities among components. Examples include simple forms of interaction, such as pipes, procedure calls, and event broadcast. Connectors may also represent complex interactions, such as a client-server protocol or a SQL link between a database and an application. Connectors have interfaces that define the roles played by the participants in the interaction." In [17], Mehta, Medvidovic and Phadke indicate that: "Connectors can also provide services, such as persistence, invocation, messaging, and transactions, that are largely independent of the interacting components' functionality." The same authors [17] say: "Connectors can also have an internal architecture that includes computation and information storage. For example, a load balancing connector would execute an algorithm for switching incoming traffic among a set of components based on knowledge about the current and past load state of components."

On the other hand, the concept of connector found in some architectural styles also assigns to it more complex semantics than the one represented by the metaclass *Connector*. For example, in style C3, we have already seen that a connector is responsible for routing messages and implementing the filtering policy defined for it. In the architectural style pipe&filter a connector is responsible for transmitting information from the output of a filter to the input of another one. In this case, the connector does not route messages but transports information flows. Besides, specializations of this style characterize and restrict attributes of the connector like its storage capacity (bounded pipes) or the type of information transported by the connector (typed pipes). In a layered architectural style, connectors are defined by the protocols determining how layers interact.

In short, the metaclass *Connector* as defined in UML 2.0 does not seem to represent the concept of connector assumed by the software architecture community. As we say in section 5.2.5, the metaclass *Connector* can not represent a C3 connector. From our point of view, it would be necessary to define a new metaclass in UML 2.0 to characterize an architectural connector. This new metaclass should be added to the package *InfrastructureLibrary::Core*. Of course, extending the infrastructure will imply extending also the superstructure with the purpose of defining user level constructors. The same would apply to the concept of role linked to a connector. We are studying the correct way to do these extensions.

6   UML 1.4 vs. UML 2.0 to Describe the Static View of the C3 Architectural Style

In this section we are not going to do a comparison between UML 1.4 and UML 2.0 since other works already treat this problem [13]. The content of this section is limited to present the differences between the results obtained when UML 1.4 is used to describe the static view of the C3 architectural style (Section 4) and the results obtained when UML 2.0 is used to the same goal (Section 5).

The most important difference between the two approaches is that to use UML 1.4 it was necessary to realise a heavyweight extension to the metamodel. The reasons are that there were not constructors which could represent the semantics of the architectural elements of C3 and that we have dismissed the stereotyping mechanism because this mechanism is not able to characterise correctly those architectural elements. Thus we added to the metamodel the following metaclasses: *Architecture, Component,*

Connector, Filter, Port, Role and *InterfaceElement,* and the new enumerated types *Direction* and *Domain.* On the contrary some metaclasses, like *Constraint, Parameter* and *Attribute,* and the predefined types *Boolean* and *ProcedureExpresion,* were reused. Nevertheless, a heavyweight extension to the metamodel implies that the tools processing UML 1.4 are not able to process this new extension.

With UML 2.0 the problem is easier to solve because UML 2.0 has incorporated metaclasses to represent architectural elements. The static view of the C3 architectural style has been able to be represented completely using the existing metaclasses and stereotypes over those metaclasses. As we mentioned in section 5.2.5, the only dark point is the treatment of connectors. Bellow we indicate some differences between the two approaches:

- With UML 2.0 the metaclass *Model* has been stereotyped to represent a C3 architecture. With UML 1.4, that concept was represented by adding the metaclass *Architecture* to the metamodel.
- With UML 2.0 the metaclass *Component* has been stereotyped to represent a component. With UML 1.4, that concept was represented by adding to the metamodel the metaclass *Component* that declared the attribute *isActive.* In UML 2.0, the metaclass *Component* inherits this attribute from the metaclass *Class.*
- With UML 2.0 the metaclass *Component* has been stereotyped to represent a C3 connector. We saw that this is not the best solution. However, it is better than to add two new metaclasses to the metamodel (*Connector* and *Filter*) as we did with UML 1.4.
- With UML 2.0 the metaclass *Port* has been stereotyped to represent the concepts of port and role of C3. With UML 1.4 we had to add the metaclasses *Port* and *Role* to the metamodel.
- With UML 2.0, to represent the interfaces of a component in C3, the metaclasses *Operation* and *Interface* have been stereotyped. With UML 1.4 we added the metaclass *InterfaceElement* to the metamodel. Furthermore, with UML 2.0 it is easier to distinguish the interfaces provided by a component from the interfaces required by that component because in the metamodel the relationships provided and required are already defined between the metaclasses *Component* and *Interface.*

As a conclusion, UML 2.0 provides more features than UML 1.4 to model aspects of a software architecture; mainly the aspects related to the concepts of component, port and interface. Nevertheless, we think that UML 2.0 has not introduced enough semantic power to model the concept of connector as defined by the software architecture community.

7 Conclusions and Future Work

In this work we have proposed an extension to the metamodels of UML 1.4 and UML 2.0 to describe the static view of the C3 architectural style. As we said in Section 4, it was necessary to add new metaclasses to the UML 1.4 metamodel to represent most of the C3 architectural concepts. On the contrary, with UML 2.0 it has been enough to define stereotypes of metaclasses already defined in its metamodel to realise the same function. This shows that the new constructors of UML 2.0, like *Connector* and *Port*, and the new semantics of the metaclass *Component*, allow to describe architectural aspects contrary to happens with UML 1.4. Nevertheless, we found several problems when trying to define the constructor connector in C3 since the metaclass *Connector* of UML 2.0 has different semantics. In fact, in Section 5.2.5 we illustrated some important differences between both concepts that made it impossible for that metaclass to be used as the base class for stereotype *C3Connector*. The core problem is that the metaclass *Connector* defined in UML 2.0 is not a type of *Classifier*, while *Component* is. In UML 2.0 connectors do not appear to be first class entities. From our point of view a revision of UML 2.0 is necessary in order to support the software connector.

In the short term, we plan to do an analysis of the capabilities of UML 2.0 to represent a dynamic (behavioral) view of architectural style C3. Then, our research will focus on the different architectural styles defined nowadays with the purpose of capturing their similarities and establish a set of metaclasses needed to add in UML 2.0 to be able to represent them. The proposed extensions, derived from that study, will define a new member in the UML family of languages. This set of extensions could be sent to the RTF (Revision Task Force) corresponding to OMG so that they could be considered in the next language review.

References

1. Abi-Antoun, M. and Medvidovic, N. (1999). Enabling the refinement of a software architecture into a design. In Proc. of The Second International Conference on The Unified Modeling Language. CO, USA: Springer-Verlag.
2. Bass, L., Clements, P. and Kazman, R. (1998). Software architecture in practice. Reading, Massachusetts: Addison-Wesley
3. Björkander, M. and Kobryn, C. (2003). Architecting systems with UML 2.0. IEEE Software, 20, 4, 57-61.
4. Clements, P., Bachmann, F., Bass, L., Garlan, D., Ivers, J., Little, R., Nord, R. and Stafford, J. (2003). Documenting software architectures, views and beyond. Boston, Massachusetts: Addison-Wesley.
5. Egyed, A. and Medvidovic, N. (2001). Consistent architectural refinement and evolution using the Unified Modeling Language. In Proc. of the 1st Workshop on Describing Software Architecture with UML. Toronto, Canada, 83-87.
6. Garlan, D., Allen, R. and Ockerbloom, J. (1994). Exploiting style in architectural design environments. In Proc. of SIGSOFT'94: The Second ACM SIGSOFT Symposium on the Foundations of Software Engineering, 175-188.
7. Garlan, D. and Kompanek, A.J. (2000). Reconciling the needs of architectural description with object-modeling notation. UML 2000 – The Unified Modeling Language: Advancing the Standard. Third International Conference. York, UK: Springer-Verlag.
8. Gomaa, H. and Wijesekera (2001). The role of UML, OCL and ADLs in software architecture. In Proc. of the Workshop on Describing Software Architecture with UML, ICSE'01. Toronto, Canada.
9. Hilliar, R. (1999). Building blocks for extensibility in the UML. Response to UML 2.0 Request For Information". Available from OMG as ad/99-12-12.

10. Hofmeister, C., Nord, R.L. and Soni, D. (1999). Describing software architecture with UML. In Proc. of the First Working IFIP Conf. on Software Architecture. San Antonio, TX: IEEE.

11. IEEE (2000). IEEE Recommended practice for architectural description of software-intensive systems.

12. Kandé, M. M. and Strohmeier, A. (2000). Towards a UML profile for software architecture descriptions. UML 2000 – The Unified Modeling Language: Advancing the Standard. York, UK: Springer-Verlag.

13. Kramler, G. (2003). Overview of UML 2.0 abstract syntax. Available from http://www.big.tuwien.ac.at/staff/kramler/uml/uml2-superstructure-overview.html.

14. Lüer, C. and Rosenblum, D.S. (2001). UML component diagrams and software architecture- experiences from the WREN project. In Proc. of the Workshop on Describing Software Architecture with UML, ICSE'01. Toronto, Canada.

15. Medvidovic, N. (1999). Architecture-based specification-time software evolution. (Doctoral Dissertation, University of California, Irvine, 1999).

16. Medvidovic, N., Rosenblum, D.S., Redmiles, D.F. and Robbins, J.E. (2002). Modeling software architectures in the unified modeling language. ACM Transactions on Software Engineering and Methodology, 11 (1), 2-57.

17. Mehta, N.R., Medvidovic, N. and Phadke, S. (2000). Towards a taxonomy of software connectors. In Proc. of ICSE'00, ACM. Limerick, Ireland, 178-187.

18. OMG (2001). Unified Modeling Language specification (version 1.4).

19. OMG (2003a). Unified Modeling Language (UML) Specification: Infrastructure, version 2.0 (ptc/03-09-15). http://www.omg.org/uml.

20. OMG (2003b). Unified Modeling Language: Superstructure, version 2.0 (ptc/03-08-02). http://www.omg.org/uml.

21. Pérez-Martínez, J.E. (2003). Heavyweight extensions to the UML metamodel to describe the C3 architectural style. ACM SIGSOFT Software Engineering Notes, Vol. 28 (3).

22. Rausch, A. (2001). Towards a software architecture specification language based on UML and OCL. In Proc. of the Workshop on Describing Software Architecture with UML, ICSE'01, Toronto, Canada.

23. Riva, C., Xu, J. and Maccari, A. (2001). Architecting and reverse architecting in UML. In Proc. of the Workshop on Describing Software Architecture with UML, ICSE'01, Toronto, Canada.

24. Rumpe, B., Schoenmakers, M., Radermacher, A. and Schürr, A. (1999). UML + ROOM as a standard ADL? In Proc. of Fifth International Conference on Engineering of Complex Computer System, Las Vegas, Nevada.

25. Selic, B. (2001). On modeling architectural structures with UML. In Proc. of the Workshop on Describing Software Architecture with UML, ICSE'01. Toronto, Canada.

26. Shaw, M. (1994). Procedure calls are the assembly language of software interconnection: Connectors deserve first-class status. Tech. Rep. CMU-CS-94-107, Pittsburgh, PA: Carnegie Mellon University, School of Computer Science and Software Engineering Institute.

27. Shaw, M., DeLine, R. and Zelesnik, G. (1996). Abstractions and implementations for architectural connections. In Proc. of 3rd International Conference on Configurable Distributed Systems, Annapolis, Maryland.

28. Shaw, M. and Garlan, D. (1996). Software architecture. Perspectives on an emerging discipline. N.J., USA: Prentice-Hall.

29. Störrle, H. (2001). Turning UML-subsystems into architectural units. In Proc. of the Workshop on Describing Software Architecture with UML, ICSE'01, Toronto, Canada.

From Acme to CORBA: Bridging the Gap

Márcia J.N. Rodrigues[1], Leonardo Lucena[2], and Thaís Batista[1]

[1] Informatics and Applied Mathematics Departament,
Federal University of Rio Grande do Norte, Brazil
`marciaj@dimap.ufrn.br, thais@ufrnet.br`
[2] Federal Center of Technological Education of Rio Grande do Norte, Brazil
`leonardo@cefet-rn.br`

Abstract. Software architecture and middleware platforms are different abstraction levels of component-based development that have been evolved separately. In order to address the gap between these two areas, in this paper we discuss the integration of a generic and extensible architecture description language, Acme, with a standard middleware platform - CORBA. We propose mapping rules to transform an ACME description into a CORBA IDL specification. To make it possible, we define some extensions to Acme to include some features according to the CORBA IDL specification. These extensions explore the facilities provided by Acme for expressing additional information. We use a case study to illustrate the mapping proposed.

1 Introduction

Software architecture [1] is an important field of software development that focus on the early design phase of component-based development. It concerns the design and specification of the high-level structure of an application. This is especially important to solve design problems in the initial stages of development. Architectural description languages (ADLs) are used to describe software architectures in terms of components and the relationship among them.

Although various architectural languages are available at the moment [2], each of them has its own particular notation and some are designed for specific application domains. This makes them inappropriate for expressing a broad range of architectural design and also for sharing and reusing architectural descriptions. In order to address this problem, the Acme Architecture Description Language [3] provides a common language for the support of the interchange of architectural descriptions. It provides a generic and extensible infrastructure for describing software architectures.

At the implementation level of component-based development, middleware platforms are playing an important role as an underlying infrastructure that offers transparent communication between distributed and heterogeneous components. In this context, CORBA has been successful because it is a language and platform independent model.

F. Oquendo et al. (Eds.): EWSA 2004, LNCS 3047, pp. 103–114, 2004.

Software architecture and middleware platforms deal with different levels of abstraction of component-based development and share some common characteristics. Both offer support for the management of large, complex and distributed applications as well as to reduce the costs of applications development by promoting components reuse. Besides, both focus on composing systems by assembling components. They are complementary approaches to a component-based development. However, there are few interactions between the two research areas. In [4] is showed that it is necessary to integrate such areas in order to use existing component middleware technologies to implement systems modeled with architectural languages.

An important challenge for software developers today is the ability to translate a software architecture description into a corresponding description for a target implementation platform. They have to know details about the two models in order to identify the mapping between the concepts. In general, this task is done in an ad-hoc way because there is a lack of reference models and tools to identify and relate the concepts of the two research areas. Thus, the mapping is an error-prone task that can lead to inconsistencies between the architectural description and the corresponding description in the target implementation platform.

In this paper we address the integration between this two research areas, discussing how the concepts of the Acme architecture description language can be translated into corresponding concepts of CORBA IDL. Our goal is to provide mapping rules in order to reduce the gap between the Acme architecture description and the CORBA IDL specification. Besides, the rules can be used in the development of automatic transformation tools.

In order to evaluate our proposal we present a case study of a distributed application: a multiagents system for buying and selling goods [5,6].

This paper is structured as follows. Section 2 presents the background of this work: Acme and CORBA. Section 3 discusses the mapping from Acme to CORBA. Section 4 presents the case study that illustrates the application of the mapping. Section 5 regards about the related works. Finally, Section 6 contains the final remarks.

2   Background

2.1   Acme

Acme [3,7] is a software architectural description language whose main goal is being an interchange language among different ADLs. Acme was projected to consider the essential elements of the different ADLs and to allow extensions to describe the most complex aspects of others ADLs.

An Acme architecture is structured by using the following aspects: structure, properties, constraints, types and styles [7]. In this section we will present each aspect and then we will illustrate their use with an example.

Structure. Acme has seven entity types to architectural representation: components, connectors, systems, ports, roles, representations, and rep-maps.

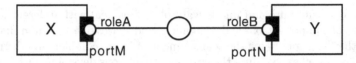

Fig. 1. Example of an architectural description in Acme

The **components** are the basic elements of an Acme description. They represent primary elements of a system. The Acme component can model hardware and software elements or both. The Acme component has interfaces, named **ports**, that represent interaction points with the computational environment. Each port represents an interface that is offered or required by the component. However, the ports do not distinguish between neither what is offered nor what is required by a component.

The Acme **connectors** represent interactions among components. A typical connector may define a communication synchronization model, a communication protocol or features of a communication canal.

Acme provides a way to explicitly document the system communication, thus, it is necessary to provide the concept of connector. This is an important feature of the architectural modeling: the interactions are considered first class concepts. In contrast, in object-oriented project approaches, the interactions are implicit within diagrams that describe classes and objects. The connectors have a set of interfaces represented by **roles**. Each role defines a participant in the interaction defined by a connector. A role is seen as an interface, in a communication canal, defining an interface to the connector just as a port provides an interface to a component.

Acme **systems** are defined as graphs in which nodes represent components and edges represent connectors. Therefore, a graph of a computational system is defined by a set of attachments. Each attachment represents an interaction between a port and a role.

The Acme language uses **representations** that allows the components and connectors to encapsulate subsystems. Each subsystem may be seen as the most concrete description of the element that it represents. This allows the analysis of the system in various abstraction levels.

When a component or connector has an architectural representation, it should have a way of showing correspondence between internal system representation and external interfaces of components or connectors that are being represented. The **rep-maps** define this correspondence. They associate internal ports/roles to external ports/roles.

Figure 1 shows an example of an architectural description in Acme. The System has two components, X and Y, joined by a connector. The connector has its `roleA` attached to `portM` of component X while `roleB` is attached to `portN` of component Y. The textual description is shown in Figure 2.

Properties. The components, as well as other Acme elements, have **properties** that are used to describe their structural and functional aspects. Each property

```
System System1 {
  Component X{
    Ports {portM;}
  };
  Component Y{
    Ports {portN;}
  };
  Connector C{
    Roles {roleA; roleB;}
  };
  Attachment X.portM to C.roleA;
  Attachment Y.portN to C.roleB;
};
```

Fig. 2. Textual description of the architectural description of Figure 1

has a name, an optional type and a value. The properties do not define semantics in Acme, but their values have meaning in tools that analyze, translate, show or manipulate Acme descriptions.

Constraints. Acme may define the constraints that should be used by the computational system. These constraints are a special type of properties that are associated with any Acme description element. This association determines the scope of the constraint. This means that if one constraint is associated to a system, then every element comprised within the element also is associated to this constraint.

The constraints may be associated to design elements in two ways: using invariants or heuristics. The violation of invariants makes the system invalid, while the violation of heuristics is treated as a warning.

Types and Styles. The ability to define system styles (families) is an important feature for an architecture description. **Styles** allow the definition of a domain-specific or application-specific design vocabulary.

The basic block for defining styles in Acme is a **type** system that is used to encapsulate recurring structures and relationships. In Acme there are three ways to define these structures: property types, structural types, and styles. Property types have been previously showed.

Structural types enable the definition of types of components, connectors, ports, and roles. Each type provides a type name and a list of necessary substructure, properties and constraints.

The other existent type in Acme is style, also named family. Just as structural types represent sets of structural elements, a family represent a set of systems.

2.2   CORBA

CORBA (Common Object Request Broker Architecture) is a standard proposed by OMG that allows interoperability between applications in heterogeneous and

```
module People{
    interface Student{

    //Attributes
        attribute string name;
        attribute string phone;
        readonly attribute long identification;

    //Operations
        void RegistrationInDisc(in long ident);
    };
```

Fig. 3. IDL Description

distributed environment. CORBA determines the separation between object interface and object implementation. An object interface is described using the *Interface Definition Language (IDL)*. Object implementation can be done using a programming language with a binding to CORBA.

A CORBA architecture is composed by a set of functional blocks that use the communication support of ORB (Object Request Broker) - the element that coordinates the interaction between objects intercepting the client invocations and directing them to the appropriate server.

The entities that compose the syntax of IDL are: modules, interfaces, operations, attributes and exceptions.

Module is the element that groups other elements. An interface defines a set of operations provided by an object and its attributes. The declaration of attributes initiates with the keyword **attribute**. Attributes types can be: basic, built, templates or interfaces.

Figure 3 shows a simple IDL interface definition with attributes and operations.

3   Mapping Acme to CORBA

This section shows our proposed mapping strategy of Acme architecture descriptions to IDL specifications.

Acme is a generic language for architectural description and, thus, it has a small number of elements. Therefore, architectural descriptions using only Acme's basic elements are, semantically, very poor. For this reason, some extensions are proposed in this paper in order to make architectural descriptions more meaningful for transformation into IDL specifications. In this way, in addition to the mapping, we show the structures that must be part of the Acme descriptions to make them suitable for mapping to IDL.

3.1 Systems

Both Acme and IDL contain structures that aggregate other elements. Acme uses Systems and Families (Styles), while IDL uses Modules. The mapping preserves this grouping by transforming systems and families in IDL modules.

3.2 Components

Components are the main elements of an architectural description. They are mapped directly to IDL interfaces by a one-to-one relationship. The structural types that define components are also mapped into interfaces. The internal details of the interfaces are obtained through ports and connectors.

3.3 Ports

Ports define the points of interaction of each component with the environment. The details of the interaction are described through the properties of the ports. These properties do not have semantics in Acme but they are interpreted at the moment of the transformation in IDL specifications.

In the mapping strategy used in this article, the ports that compose each component are combined to comprise a single IDL interface. Figure 4 shows a specification in Acme that corresponds to the IDL specification of Figure 3.

```
System People {
  Component Student{
    Port personal : InputPort = {
      Properties {
        // Attributes
        name : idl_attribute = "attribute string name";
        phone: idl_attribute = "attribute string phone";
        // Operation
        registration: idl_operation =
                      "void RegistrationInDisc(in long ident)";
      };
    };
    Port school : InputPort = {
      Properties {
        // Attribute
        id : idl_attribute = "readonly attribute long identification";
      };
    };
  };
};
```

Fig. 4. Acme Specification

```
interface X{
    //require
    attribute Y roleB;
    ...
};
```

Fig. 5. Mapping Output Ports

The types `idl_attribute` and `idl_operation` indicate that the properties of these types have significance in IDL. The properties `name`, `phone` and `id` represent attributes, while `registration` represents an operation.

Another aspect that must be considered is that ports can offer and request services. This leads to the classification of the ports as input ports (offers services), output ports (requires services), and input and output ports (offers and requires services)[1]. The example of Figure 4 shows input ports (`InputPort`). The other options are `OutputPort` and `InputOutputPort`.

The output ports are represented in IDL through attributes. Each output port (or input and output port) is mapped into an attribute. The name and the type of the attribute depend on the connector that is attached to the port. For the example in Figure 1, if `portM` is an output port then the corresponding IDL interface of component `X` will have an attribute called `roleB` of type `Y`. Figure 5 shows the result of this transformation.

The use of constraints allows better specification of the interface required by Output ports. Invariants can specify which roles can be attached to a port. In the example of Figure 1, constraints can be used to state that `portM` can only be attached to `roleA`.

3.4   Connectors and Roles

The connectors specify how components are combined into a system. They do not have a corresponding representation in IDL. Instead, the connectors are used to determine the type of interface that output ports require, as seen in Section 3.3. In the same way, the roles contribute to determine the names of the attributes that are related to output ports.

3.5   Representations

Representations enable the existence of architecture descriptions with different levels of abstraction. Representations allow elements to enclose internal subsystems. However, IDL descriptions cannot be encapsulated. Only the most concrete (internal) elements are mapped to IDL. The mapping process creates an

---

[1] The original semantics of Acme does not make distinction among these types of ports.

Table 1. Summary of the Mapping Rules of Acme to IDL

Element	Acme	IDL

System	**System** {
	 ...
	 }
		module {
		 ...
		 }

Component	**Component** X = {
	 ...
	 }
		interface X {
		 ...
		 }

Component Type	**Component Type** X = {
	 ...
	 }
		interface X {
		 ...
		 }

Input Port	**Component** X = {
	 ...
	 Port p : InputPort =
	 new InputPort **extended with** {
	 Properties {
	 attr : idl_attribute = "[idl attribute]";
	 oper : idl_operation = "[idl operation]";
	 }
	 }
	 ...
	 }
		interface X {
		 ...
		 // *Port p*
		 [idl attribute]
		 [idl operation]
		 ...
		 }

Output Port	**Component** X = {
	 ...
	 Port px : OutputPort =
	 new OutputPort **extended with** {
	 ...
	 }
	 ...
	 }
	 Component Y = {**ports** {pY;}}
	 Connector C = {**roles** {roleA;roleB;}}
	 Attachment X.px to C.roleA;
	 Attachment Y.pY to C.roleB;
		interface X {
		 ...
		 // *Require (output port)*
		 attribute Y roleB
		 ...
		 }
		 ...
		 interface Y {
		 ...
		 }
		 ...

auxiliary version of the system with only one level of abstraction. The complex elements are *blown up* displaying their internal representations[2].

The mapping rules of Acme to IDL are summarized in the Table 1. The style `IDLFamily` (Figure 6) aggregates the extensions that makes Acme descriptions suitable for mapping to IDL. The family also has some constraints, not shown here, that checks if the descriptions are valid.

4   Case Study

To illustrate the mapping from Acme to IDL CORBA we use an e-commerce multi-agents system [6].

A Multi-agents system is a society of agents that cooperates with each other to solve a specific problem. Thus, a problem is divided in more specific problems that are attributed to agents, according to their individual capability.

---

[2] When there are two or more representations for the same element, one of them must be chosen to be mapped.

```
Family IDLFamily = {
  Port Type InputPort = {}
  Port Type OutputPort = {}
  Port Type InputOutputPort = {}
  Property Type idl_attribute = String;
  Property Type idl_operation = String;
}
```

Fig. 6. Style IDLFamily

In the case study the agents are distributed through a net and need to interact with each other to negotiate goods. The system has three types of agents. The buying and selling agents are negotiating agents that buy or sell goods.

The market agent plays as a facilitator that presents an agent to other negotiators.

These agents are modeled by software components. The features that agents needed such as autonomy and communication are founded in the components.

The distribution of the components must allow communication among components implemented in different platforms without worrying about the communication details.

Figure 7 shows how a fragment of the Acme architectural description is mapped into IDL. The `Buyer` component are transformed into `Buyer` interface. The two ports of the component are combined and their `idl_operation` properties are transported to the component interface. The ports are output ports therefore produce `seller` and `market` attributes. The other components are mapped in the same way.

5   Related Works

The integration of ADLs and middleware platforms is a current trend in component-based development. Following this trend, OMG has published a specification of a standard to support all the systems lifecycles: MDA [8]. MDA is a vendor and middleware independent approach language that uses UML to build system models [9]. MDA does not specify mapping models between UML and platform-specific models. Some works [10] are addressing this issue by defining mapping rules to transform UML descriptions into CORBA IDL specifications.

The ABC environment [11] does a gradual mapping from an ADL to a middleware platform. It offers an ADL, named JBCDL, whose descriptions are mapped to an OO design model described in UML and then mapping rules are applied to convert the OO model to a CORBA IDL description. The authors mention that an OO model adds more flesh to perceive components and connectors specified in the architecture description. We argue that using a generic ADL, such as Acme, that is flexible and provides annotation facilities, it is not necessary to have an intermediate model to enhance the expressiveness of the architecture description.

112   Márcia J.N. Rodrigues, Leonardo Lucena, and Thaís Batista

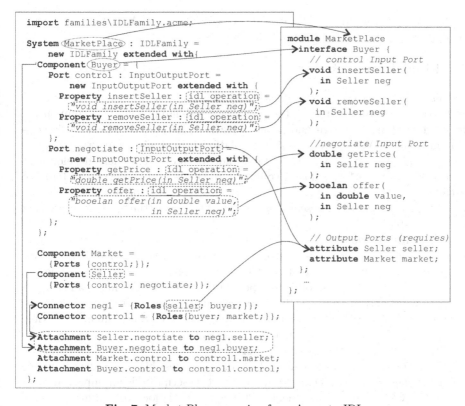

Fig. 7. Market Place mapping from Acme to IDL

Darwin [12] is an ADL that has been a pioneer in the integration of an ADL with CORBA. In the mapping from Darwin to CORBA, the Darwin compiler translates a Darwin component to the IDL interface. Each provision in the Darwin specification is translated into a read only attribute of the object reference type. Each requirement is similarly mapped into an attribute which is not read only because it is set externally to reflect the binding of the component instance. While this work uses a particular ADL, we choose to use a generic ADL in order to allow the integration between other ADLs and CORBA via Acme. Since Acme provides a means to integrate the features of existing ADLs and to share architectural descriptions between these ADLs, it is possible to transform specifications of other ADLs into Acme and then into CORBA.

A mapping from an ADL, named ZCL, to a component-based environment that uses CORBA components is proposed in [13]. This work defines structural mapping from the ADL to the environment. However, this mapping does not only address the CORBA description but also the features of the scripting language used in the environment. Although this work aims to shorten the gap between design and implementation, they rely on the same problem of many works: to use a particular ADL. Besides, the mapping is restrictive to the specific environment. In contrast, in our work we join an ADL that allows interoperability of ADLs with a standard middleware platform. We consider that this combination will be appropriate for different classes of applications.

6   Final Remarks

In this paper we investigated the feasibility of combining the use of two different technologies in order to reduce the gap between different phases of component-based development: design and implementation. Software architecture description languages (ADLs) and middleware platforms deal with composing systems from compiled parts. However, ADLs do not focus on component development and middleware platforms do not cope with the high-level model of a system. An architecture description should be implemented in a specific development platform, thus bringing these research areas together is essential to the composition of large systems.

We identified the common features of a generic architecture description language - Acme - and a component-based development platform - CORBA. We proposed a mapping from Acme to CORBA. In order to make it possible, we improve the expressiveness of Acme specifying the concept of input and output ports and properties that will be transformed into attributes and operations. This extension clarifies the mapping to CORBA IDL. Since Acme is flexible and provides facilities for additional ADL-specific information, we explore these facilities to specialize the concept of ports.

Using the mapping proposed in this work, it is possible to generate interface definitions described in CORBA IDL. The IDL description is an important part of the CORBA-based development and it is the basis for programmers to produce the implementation code. Thus, once the interface has been defined, the programmer will be able to reuse existing components or coding components according to the architectural description. Besides, IDL description can be automatically mapped into client and server languages by using an IDL compiler.

A tool, named ACMID, that performs an automatic transformation from Acme to CORBA IDL using the mapping proposed by this work is under development. ACMID implements a conversion algorithm that does such transformation. The transformation is based on XML (eXtensible Markup Language) [14]. ACMID receives as input an XMI (XML Metadata Interchange Format) [15] file that contains the meta-model description of the Acme architecture model. A modified version of Acme Studio [16] is used to produce the Acme model. The conversion rules are described in XSLT (eXtensible StyleSheet Language Transformations) [17] and they produce a specific model to the CORBA platform represented in IDL (Interface Definition Language).

As a future work we intend to observe the enhancement provided by the ACMID in the development of a number of practical cases of component-based development.

Acknowledgments. We thank CNPq (Brazilian Council for Development of Science and Technology) - process 552007/2002-1 - and PRH-22-ANP/MCT for their finantial support.

References

1. Shaw, M., Garlan, D.: Software Architecture: Perspectives on an Emerging Discipline. Prentice-Hall (1996)
2. Medvidovic, N.: A classification and comparison framework for software architecture description languages. Technical Report UCI-ICS-97-02, Department of Information and Computer Science, University of California, Irvine (1997)
3. Garlan, D., Monroe, R., Wile, D.: ACME: An architecture description interchange language. In: Proceedings of CASCON'97, Toronto, Ontario (1997) 169–183
4. Oreizy, P., Medvidovic, N., Taylor, R., Rosenblum, D.: Software architecture and component technologies: Bridging the gap. In: Digest of the OMG-DARPA-MCC Workshop on Compositional Software Architectures, Monterey, CA (1998)
5. Chavez, A., Maes, P.: Kasbah: An agent marketplace for buying and selling goods. In: First International Conference on the Practical Application of Intelligent Agents and Multi-Agent Technology (PAAM'96), London, UK, Practical Application Company (1996) 75–90
6. Maes, P., Guttman, R., Moukas, A.: Agents that buy and sell: Transforming commerce as we know it. Communications of the ACM **42** (1999)
7. Garlan, D., Monroe, R.T., Wile, D.: Acme: Architectural description of component-based systems. In Leavens, G.T., Sitaraman, M., eds.: Foundations of Component-Based Systems. Cambridge University Press (2000) 47–68
8. Miller, J., Mukerji, J.: Model-driven architecture - mda. Technical report, OMG (2001) ormsc/2001-07-01. www.omg.org/mda.
9. Booch, G., Rumbaugh, J., Jacobson, I.: The Unified Modeling Language User Guide. Addison-Wesley (1999)
10. Nascimento, T., Batista, T.: Tupi - transformation from pim to idl. In: Proceedings of the International Symposium on Distributed Objects and Applications - DOA2003, Catania, Sicily, Italy (2003)
11. Mei, H., Chen, F., Wang, Q., Feng, Y.: Abc/adl: An adl supporting component composition. In George, C., Miao, H., eds.: Proceedings of the 4th International Conference on Formal Engineering Methods, ICFEM2002, LNCS 2495. (2002) 38–47
12. Magee, J., Tseng, A., Kramer, J.: Composing distributed objects in CORBA. In: Proceedings of the Third International Symposium on Autonomous Decentralized Systems, Berlin, Germany, IEEE (1997) 257–63
13. de Paula, V., Batista, T.: Mapping an adl to a component-based application development environment. In: Proceedings of FASE2002 - Lecture Notes in Theorical Computer Science (LNCS) - 2306. (2002) 128–142
14. Birbek, M.: Professional XML. Wrox Press Inc. (2001)
15. OMG: Xml model interchange (xmi). Technical report, OMG (1998) OMG Document ad/98-10-05.
16. AcmeStudio: (AcmeStudio: Supporting architectural design, analysis and interchange) available at http://www-2.cs.cmu.edu/~acme/acme_documentation.html.
17. W3C: Xsl transformations specification. Technical report, W3C (1999) www.w3.org/TR/xslt.
18. Garlan, D., Cheng, S.W., Kompanek, A.J.: Reconciling the needs of architectural description with object-modeling notations. Science of Computer Programming **44** (2002) 23–49

Constraints of Behavioural Inheritance

Ella E. Roubtsova and Serguei A. Roubtsov*

Technical University Eindhoven, Den Dolech 2, P.O. Box 513,
5600MB Eindhoven, The Netherlands
E.Roubtsova@tue.nl, S.Roubtsov@tue.nl

Abstract. We present an approach to component inheritance and reuse
which closes the gap between architectural design and process-oriented
approaches. To apply inheritance checks in design and verification of
a system, one should consider an inheritance relation as a *property* of
the system and specify it as an inheritance constraint. To specify the
inheritance constraints we offer a logic of behavioural inheritance. In a
UML profile with the process tree semantics we show how to use this logic
for architectural design and for verification with respect to the specified
inheritance constraint.

Keywords: Constraint of behavioural inheritance, logic of behavioural
inheritance, process tree semantics, UML profile, behaviour specification
reuse.

1 Introduction

Inheritance of components is one of the accepted instruments for reuse of components in architectural design [1, 2]. However, in architectural approaches, like
CATALYSIS [2] or ISpec [3]), and in Architecture Description Languages
(ADLs), like Rapide, C2 [1] or Koala [4], the notion of component inheritance is
a predefined part of the underlying metamodel. The support of the system evolution in those approaches is restricted by structural subtyping [1] of components.
However, the structural subtyping relation allows defining an infinite set of behaviour inheritance relations on parent and child components. The behaviour of
a parent can be repeated in a child before or after some new behaviour fragments,
it can be repeated for a specific part of the child behaviour or it can be divided
into parts by some new behaviour fragments. Thus, a component-inheritor specification can satisfy one of the behavioural inheritance relations and not satisfy
another. In practice, this usually becomes clear only after producing and testing
the behaviour specification of a component-inheritor, because the current approaches to architectural design do not direct and help designers to think about
the necessary behavioural inheritance relation in advance. Consequently, this
causes semantic mistakes in architectural design.

---

* The research of S.A. Roubtsov was partly supported by PROGRESS (*STW
EES5141*) and EMPRESS (*ITEA 01003*) projects.

F. Oquendo et al. (Eds.): EWSA 2004, LNCS 3047, pp. 115–134, 2004.

There are process-oriented architectural approaches, like SADL [1], which represent ordering constraints among sub-processes of a process. Those approaches come closer to the problem of component behavioural inheritance. But the component behavioural inheritance [5] is defined for the process approaches as a finite set of potential inheritance relations on processes representing components. The relations are classified on the basis of the back transformation of a component-inheritor specification to a component-parent specification. So, if it is possible to transform a component-inheritor specification to a component-parent specification, then a designer can prove that the inheritance of some type is correct. However, the process-oriented approaches do not give us any clue of where to use one or another type of behavioural inheritance relations and how to specify such relations, i.e. the notion of behavioural inheritance given in the process theory [5] has little connection with the tasks of architectural design.

In this paper we present an approach to component inheritance and reuse which closes the gap between architectural design and process-oriented approaches. We suggest that, to apply inheritance checks in design and verification of a system, one should consider an inheritance relation as a *property* of the system. Moreover, we define such a property in terms of architectural design. Any particular type of behavioural inheritance cannot be correct or incorrect in itself. It is for a designer to decide which type of possible behavioural inheritance relations fits the case in question and, then, to prove that such a type holds in the design specification.

In verification methods, specification of properties is always based on an abstraction chosen for the system specification [6, 7]. Our system is a component exchanging messages with the environment and other components. We consider a *behavioural pattern* containing sequences, alternatives and cycles of such messages (e.g., operation calls and returns) as a unit of system specification.

When a new component inherits a parent component, we should give a specification of how exactly the parent's behavioural pattern should be reused. Designers may have different ideas on how to reuse a particular behavioural pattern. One case demands establishing some conditions on reuse of the pattern, another case - fulfilling the pattern for all alternatives. So, there is no sole behavioural inheritance specification, but an infinite set of them. The chosen inheritance specification should become a property of the inheritor's design specification and this property must be kept.

Consequently, we consider behaviour inheritance relations as *constraints*. The standard constraint language OCL [8] is not suitable for the specification of behavioural inheritance relations because it does not manipulate processes as abstract elements. Because of that we offer a *logic of behavioural inheritance* to define inheritance constraints. Constraint languages can be extended on the basis of this logic.

An inheritance constraint describes how the process of a component-parent can appear in the process of a component-child. We consider the component-child to be a correct inheritor of the component-parent with respect to the specified behavioural inheritance constraint if the inheritance constraint holds for the process of the component-child. A predicate of the logic of behavioural inheritance represents the place of the parents's process tree in the child's process tree. A process tree is an abstract variant of a computation tree. Formulas of our logic describe properties of this computation tree. So, our logic is a computation tree logic with a process interpretation.

The logic of behavioural inheritance allows designers to specify what kind of behavioural inheritance they would like to achieve. Moreover, the logic defines types of constraints as logical units and allows us to put a corresponding technique to each type of constraint to prove that this constraint holds. So, the logic provides methodological support for reuse of component behaviour in architectural design.

The paper is organized as follows. In Section 2 we define a component behavioural pattern as a process and a corresponding process tree. An example of the process tree semantics is given for a component specification profile in the UML. In this profile we also demonstrate specification of components using inheritance. Section 3 describes our logic of behavioural inheritance and explains how to use this logic for architectural design and for proving correctness of component behavioural inheritance. Section 4 concludes the paper.

2   A Behavioural Pattern as a Process Tree

In our approach, a **component specification** is a process p of **type**

$$P = (A, SP, T) \; [5], \; p \in P, \; where$$

- A is a finite set of actions.
- $SP = \{sp, sp_1, sp_2, ..., sp_F\}$ is a finite set of abstract states from the unique initial state sp to the unique final state sp_F.
- T is a set of transitions. Transition $t \in T$ defines a triple (sp', sp'', a), such that state sp'' is reachable from state sp' as a result of action $a \in A$: $sp' \stackrel{a}{\Longrightarrow} sp''$.

We construct a *process tree* for a component behaviour specification.
A **process tree** is a process graph [9] $G_p = (N, E)$ which has a unique path from the node *root* to every other node. Each process tree corresponds to its process p so that:

- Each node $n \in N$ of the process tree corresponds to an abstract state from set SP. The *root* corresponds to the initial state sp.
- Each node, except final nodes, is labelled by the process name which represents the process starting from the state corresponding to this node. Final nodes, labelled by $\sqrt{}$, correspond to the final state sp_F.
- Each edge $e = (n', n'', a) \in E$ of the process tree corresponds to a transition from set T. An edge is labelled by an action $a \in A$. Edges to final nodes carry the termination label $\downarrow$.

Thus, a **path** in a process tree is a sequence of arcs

$$((n_1, n_2, a_1), (n_2, n_3, a_2), ..., (n_{m-1}, \sqrt{}, \downarrow)).$$

There is a unique sequence of actions that corresponds to each path: $a_1, a_2, ..., a_{m-1} \downarrow$. A path which starts from the root is called a *root path*. The node labels, the final nodes labelled by $\sqrt{}$ and the edges labelled by $\downarrow$ can be omitted [9] to simplify process tree graphical representation.

If a component behaviour specification contains cycles, then we represent each cycle by two paths: one path for the cycle's body and the other path for the cycle's exit. Repeated cycle's bodies are replaced by dots: "...".
Computation trees similar to our process tree are widely accepted as internal models for specification languages. Computation tree semantics has been defined for automata specifications [6, 10] and for UML profiles containing statecharts [7]. In the next subsection, we define a process tree semantics for our UML profile for component specification and reuse.

2.1   Process Tree Semantics for Our UML Profile

Our UML profile is one in the family of UML-like languages [11]. We specify a process of a component in a role language. This role language is represented in an identified subset of the UML metamodel [12].

The elements of a process are specified in terms of roles communicating via interfaces. A role is a UML class with stereotype $\ll$ *Role* $\gg$. In general, a role can have several players (instances), but we do not refer to players in this paper. An interface comprises a semantically close group of operations of a role. An interface is always provided by a particular role which implements operations of this interface. The interface can be required by other roles or, maybe, by the role itself. These *provide* and *require* relations specify actions of our process graph. To refer to a particular action we use the conventional "dot"-notation. In this notation an operation call, for example, is denoted as
$role_{requirer}.role_{provider}.interface.operation(parameter : type)$
and its return (callback) as
$role_{requirer}.role_{provider}.interface.operation(parameter : type) : result$.
The notation above provides uniqueness of operation names within the entire component specification. In all examples of this paper each interface has exactly one operation with different results. So, it is possible to use the shortened notation for action names:
$role_{requirer}.role_{provider}.interface(parameter : type)$
$role_{requirer}.role_{provider}.interface(parameter : type) : result$.

The actions and the component behavioural pattern built from such actions are specified by an **interface-role diagram** IR and a **set of sequence diagrams** $S_1...S_k$.

An interface-role diagram (Fig. 1a, 2) is a graph $IR = (R, I, PI, RI, RR)$ with two kinds of nodes and three kinds of relations:

– R is a finite set of roles. Each role $r \in R$ is depicted by a box.

– I is a finite set of interfaces depicted by circles. In this paper, each interface $i \in I$ has one operation identified by the interface name. Each operation has a set of results Res_i.

– $PI \subseteq \{(r, i)|\ r \in R, i \in I\}$ is a *provide relation* on roles and interfaces. Each role provides a finite set of interfaces. An element of the relation is depicted by a solid line between a role and an interface.

– $RI \subseteq \{(r', (r, i))|\ r', r \in R, i \in I, (r, i) \in PI\}$ is a *require relation* on roles and interfaces. Each role requires a finite set of provided interfaces. An element of the relation is drawn by a dash arrow connecting a role and a provided interface. The arrow is directed to the interface.

– $RR \subseteq \{(r, r')|\ r, r' \in R\}$ is a *relation of inheritance* on the set of roles. An element of the relation is shown by a solid line with the triangle end $r' \rhd r$ directed from role-child r' to role-parent r.

A sequence diagram (Fig. 1b) is a UML sequence diagram [8]

$$S = (B, A_s, \aleph \rightarrow A_s),$$

– $B = \{b_i\}$ is a set of boxes with dash lines drawn down from each box and representing the time dimension. In our profile, box $b_i \in B$ represents a player (an instance) of a role from the interface-role diagram. We have assumed that each role has only one player, so a box represents a role.

– A_s, is a set of labelled arcs.

An arc $(b_i, b_j, l) \in A_s$ is depicted as an arrow that connects the dash line running from box b_i to the dash line running from box b_j. An arc has a label l which represents an operation, for example,

$\quad l = interface.operation(parameter)$ for an operation call or

$\quad l = interface.operation(parameter) : result$ for an operation return

$\quad$ (or $l = interface(parameter)$ and

$\quad l = interface(parameter) : result$, if each interface has only one operation.)

– $\aleph \rightarrow A_s$, $\aleph = \{1, 2, 3...\}$ is a function defined on a subset of natural numbers that orders arcs.

Process tree. From each specification in the described above profile we construct a process tree.

S-tree. A sequence diagram corresponds to a process tree $G = (N, E)$ which contains one path. We name such a tree *s-tree*: $e_1, ..., e_k = (n_1, n_2, a_1), ..., (n_k, n_{k+1}, a_k)$, where $e_x = (n_x, n_{x+1}, a_x)$, $x = 1, ..., k$, $a_x = x \rightarrow (b_i, b_j, l)$, $(b_i, b_j, l) \in A_s$.

Operation Fusion: Let a *process tree* and an *s-tree* be given.

– If a root path of the *process tree* and a root subsequence of the *s-tree* have the same sequence of labels of arcs, then this path and this subsequence are fused, i.e. joined in one path.

– The first arc of the *s-tree*, the label of which differs from the label of the current arc in the root path of the *process tree*, starts a new branch from the last fused node of the *process tree*.

Process tree construction.
1. *S-tree constructed from a sequence diagram is a process tree.*
2. *The result of the fusion of a process tree with an s-tree is a process tree.*
3. *There are no other process trees.*

The detailed description of the algorithms can be found in [13].

For a component specification in our profile, the set E of arcs of the process tree $G_p = (N, E)$ is exactly defined from the set of arcs of all the sequence diagrams: $E = A_{s_1} \cup \cdots \cup A_{s_k}$. In turn, the set of arcs of all the sequence diagrams $A_{s_1} \cup \cdots \cup A_{s_k}$ is a multiset on the require relation set RI from the interface-role diagram of this component (some operations can be called several times). The process tree of a component can be easily transformed back to its sequence diagrams: each root path of the process tree is mapped onto an s-tree corresponding to a sequence diagram. In the next subsection, we give an example of a component specification in our profile.

2.2 Specification of Component *Web Service* in Our UML Profile

Let us consider an abstract component *Web Service*. Like most services on the Web, this service sends back some data in response to a user's request. (Even if you buy something, Internet itself never sends you goods, it only promises you to send goods later.) The component provides an opportunity to choose one of Web services from a list. Usually, before responding, the server asks the client for some additional information. For example, to get access to search engines the client should identify a kind of information to be retrieved; to buy things in an e-shop the customer should choose them and provide data that guarantees the purchase, and so on. In all cases the process is essentially the same; the differences (what kind of response is required, what additional information is needed and how to ask it) can be hidden in the server's software. This allows us to consider such an adjustable service as a reusable component in the Web service interaction model. Fig. 1 shows the specification of component *Web Service*, which we intend to reuse.

The interface-role diagram of component *Web Service* is shown in Fig. 1a. Role *Web Server* provides two interfaces: *IServiceList* : $\{ID : integer\}$, which returns identifier ID of a chosen service and *IService(ID:integer)* : $\{true, false\}$, which has two return values: *true* that means the successful result of a service request and *false* that means the unsuccessful result.

Role *Web Client* requires interfaces of *Web Server* and provides interface *IFillForm(Form:structure)* : $\{correct\ structure,\ incorrect\ structure\}$. Two types of the return value indicate two possible results of interaction via this interface: the *correct structure*, if the form is filled in correctly, and the *incorrect structure*, if some fields of the form are filled in incorrectly.

Two sequence diagrams present the behavioural model of component *Web Service* (Fig. 1b). The first sequence diagram models the successful behavioural pattern. *Web Client* chooses the service defined by parameter ID from the list and requests this service. In response *Web Server* sends back the form defined by the parameter *Form* to be filled in. After the correct data structure has been

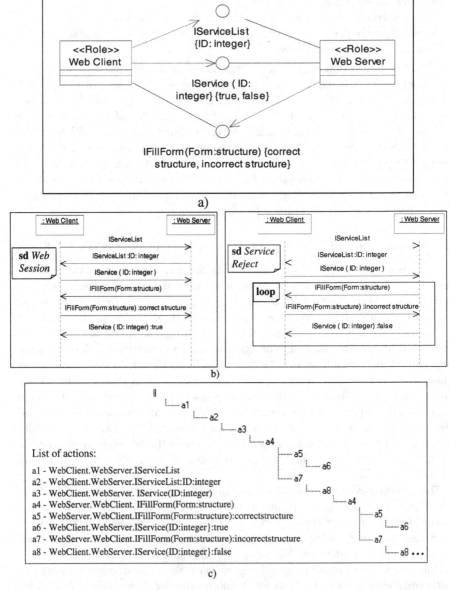

Fig. 1. The specification of component *Web Service*: a) interface-role diagram; b) sequence diagrams; c) process tree

filled in and sent to *Web Server*, it fulfils the service (return value *true*) and the session ends. The second sequence diagram corresponds to the case when the client's data for some reason is inappropriate. In such a case *Web Server* responds by the *false* return value and requests the data again.

This is a usual behavioural pattern for Web services: you can escape repetition of data requests by cancelling the connection or navigating to another Web page. Of course, more robust variants exist, e.g., a client may also be allowed to cancel the session within a requested form, the number of attempts may be restricted, and so on. However, in our component we have decided to rely on the common Web ideology. So, here we have a cycle, which is depicted by operator **loop** from the UML2.0 notation [14] newly adapted by OMG group.

The process tree representing behaviour of component *Web Service* is shown in Fig. 1c. In this figure and later we show action names only; the node labels, the final nodes labelled by $\sqrt{}$ and the edges labelled by $\downarrow$ are omitted to simplify the picture.

From action $a_4 = WebServer.WebClient.IFillForm(Form : structure)$ (the request from *Web Server* to *Web Client* to fill in the *Form*) the process tree branches out: one branch ends after the service has been completed and the other runs a possibly infinite cycle. Let the name of the process of component *Web Service* be $p=$*Web Service*. We shall use this process as a unit of behaviour to inherit from.

2.3   Component Specification by Inheritance

Inheritance of components in interface-role diagrams is specified by the inheritance relation on roles RR.

Definition 1. *Let two interface-role diagrams be given:*

$$IR_p = (R_p, I_p, PI_p, RI_p, RR_p), \quad IR_q = (R_q, I_q, PI_q, RI_q, RR_q).$$

Interface-role diagram IR_q inherits interface-role diagram IR_p, if and only if there is an interface-role diagram $IR_{new} = (R_{new}, I_{new}, PI_{new}, RI_{new}, RR_{new})$, (Fig. 2) such that

1. *$R_q = R_p \cup R_{new}$. Role sets R_p and R_{new} are disjoint, i.e. $R_p \cap R_{new} = \emptyset$.*
2. *$I_q = I_p \cup I_{new}$. Interface sets I_p, I_{new} are disjoint, i.e. $I_p \cap I_{new} = \emptyset$.*
3. *Only new roles can inherit roles of the parent interface-role diagram. Parent roles cannot inherit new roles.*
   $RR_q = RR_p \cup RR_d$, where
   $RR_d = \{(r_p, r_d) \mid r_p \in R_p \wedge r_d \in R_d \wedge R_d \subseteq R_{new}, \wedge r_d -\triangleright r_p\}$, $RR_d \neq \emptyset$.
   So, the relation RR_d defines subset of roles $R_d \subseteq R_{new}$ which have parents in the set R_p.
4. *Elements of the provide relation from roles-parents are duplicated in the interface-role diagram IR_q by roles-inheritors because of the inheritance relation RR_d.*
   $PI_q = PI_p \cup PI_d \cup PI_{new}$,
   $PI_d = \{(r_d, i) \mid r_d \in R_d \wedge i \in I_p \wedge (\exists r \in R_p \mid r_d -\triangleright r \wedge (r, i) \in PI_p))\}$.
   Sets PI_p and $(PI_d \cup PI_{new})$ are disjoint, i.e. $PI_p \cap (PI_d \cup PI_{new}) = \emptyset$.
5. *Elements $(x, (r, i))$ of the require relation RI_p are duplicated in the interface-role diagram IR_q if both role r that provides interface i and role x that requires interface i are inherited.*
   $RI_q = RI_p \cup RI_{new} \cup RI_d$, where
   $RI_d = \{(x_d, (r_d, i)) \mid r_d, x_d \in R_d \wedge i \in I_p \wedge (\exists r, x \in R_p, \mid (r_d -\triangleright r \wedge x_d -\triangleright x \wedge (r, i) \in PI_p \wedge (x, (r, i)) \in RI_p))\}$.
   Sets RI_p and $(RI_{new} \cup RI_d)$ are disjoint, i.e. $RI_p \cap (RI_{new} \cup RI_d) = \emptyset$.

The inheritance relation RR_d in the interface-role diagram IR_q defines a duplicating function $\rho_{RI_p}^{RI_d}$ which maps the parent require relations onto the subset of the child require relations. Elements of the set RI_d are not depicted in the interface-role diagram IR_{new}, although they are inherited from the parent.

As we have mentioned already, a name of an action in our specification includes names of the role-provider and the role-requirer. If both the $role_{provider}$ and the $role_{requirer}$ of a parent component are inherited by a new $role_{inheritor-of-the-provider}$ and a new $role_{inheritor-of-the-requirer}$ correspondingly, then the actions defined by the role-provider and the role-requirer are inherited by the new component.

The sequence diagrams of the child component are constructed from the actions specified by its interface-role diagram. If the parent process is inherited, then its actions are renamed using the duplicating function $\rho_{RI_p}^{RI_d}$ and the parent process p is transformed to the duplicated process $p' = \rho_{RI_p}^{RI_d}(p)$ which is equivalent to p under duplicating. Here and later we indicate a duplicated process by the prime mark (e.g. p').

2.4   An Example of Component Specification by Inheritance

Let us design component *Corporative Provider* which inherits component *Web Service*. The new component enables all the possibilities of component *Web Service* but "for members only". Membership is supposed to be obtained somewhere outside the Web, using security ID cards, for example. For non-members a corporate server should simply deny access. Of course, the alternative behaviour is quite rudimentary but it could easily be extended by some predefined service, a kind of survey for guests, for example. The behaviour of component *Web Service* should be inherited by the new component just in one case, for a corporate member. Therefore, the predefined process of a membership check must come before the choice of a service.

Fig. 2 shows the interface-role diagram of component *Corporative Provider*. Two new roles *Member* and *Corporative Server* interact via the two new interfaces *IMemberAccess* and *IMemberInfo*: *Member* asks for access and afterward *Corporative Server* requests information via *IMemberInfo*. Depending on the return value of *IMemberInfo* role *Corporative Server* allows or denies access.

Role *Member* inherits role *Web Client*; role *Corporative Server* inherits *Web Server* from component *Web Service*. This means that roles *Member* and *Corporative Server* are able to perform all actions which roles *Web Client* and *Web Server* use in communication. So, the new component *Corporative Provider* is able to utilize the complete parent behaviour of component *Web Service*. This is depicted in sequence diagrams shown in Fig. 3. All three sequence diagrams are started by obligatory process $q = Check\ Membership$. The first two sequence diagrams are started with subprocess $s = CorrectMembership$ after which the inherited process $p' = WebService' = \rho_{RI_p}^{RI_d}(p)$ (which is equivalent to the parent process $p = WebService$ under duplication) fulfils itself. The third sequence

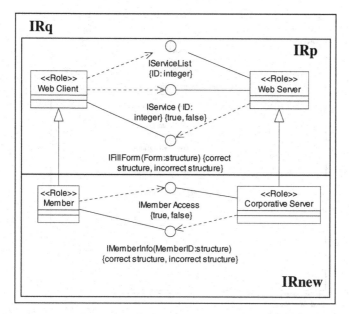

Fig. 2. The interface-role diagram of component *Corporative Provider*

diagram in Fig. 3 shows the alternative process *Incorrect Memberships*, i.e. the membership is not confirmed.

Thus, our UML profile allows a designer to specify the processes that should be inherited. The next section discusses how to help him/her formally specify the goal of inheritance and how to prove that this goal is achieved.

3 A Logic of Behavioural Inheritance

3.1 An Existential Definition of Behavioural Inheritance

Behavioural inheritance has been defined in [5]. Generalizing this definition we have the following:

Process c inherits process p if and only if there exist disjoint sets of actions $H, I \subseteq A_c \backslash A_p$, such that it is possible to derive process p from process c by

- *blocking actions from H in process c using blocking function $\delta_H(c)$;*
  $\delta_H(c) : P \to P$;
  $a \in H \to \delta_H(a) = \delta$; δ *is a blocked action;*
  $a \notin H \to \delta_H(a) = a$;
- *hiding actions from I in process $\delta_H(c)$ using hiding function $\tau_I(\delta_H(c))$;*
  $\tau_I(\delta_H(c)) : P \to P$;
  $a \in I \to \tau_H(a) = \tau$; τ *is a hidden action;*
  $a \notin I \to \tau_I(a) = a$;

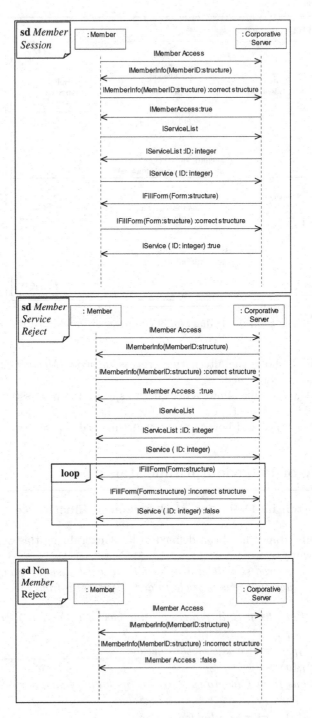

Fig. 3. The sequence diagrams of component *Corporative Provider*

- *and simplifying the resultant process using axioms of ACP (Algebra of Communicating Processes) with replacement of the parallel composition by the left merge) [9] and axioms for hidden and blocked actions [5]:*

$x + \delta = x; \qquad \delta \cdot x = \delta;$

$x \cdot \tau = x; \qquad x \cdot (\tau \cdot (y + z) + y) = x \cdot (y + z);$

where x, y, z are actions; δ is a blocked action; τ is a hidden action.

Intuitively, the blocking of action a means that the process which follows this action will not be considered any more. The hiding of action a makes this action invisible, but the rest of the process which follows this action is taken into consideration.

The above definition is an existential one. The definition leaves unanswered an important practical question: how would we like to inherit the parent process? In other words, the definition given in [5] does not address the tasks of architectural design.

3.2 Behavioural Inheritance from the Designer's Point of View

Studying architectural design in practice [15] we have found that designers think about behavioural inheritance in terms of named processes (e.g. "Check Membership" or "Choose a Service from the List"). Composing such processes on the basis of their intuition, designers sometimes make semantic mistakes. So, designers need methodological support to use inheritance intentionally.

In this paper, we propose composing processes in the process tree model. A behavioural inheritance relation on processes of a component-child and a component-parent has to be specified by a constraint in our logic of behavioural inheritance. This logic has the process tree semantics which we define following the semantic definition given in [16].

Let AP be a set of atomic propositions. An atomic proposition $\phi \in AP$ can be of two types: $\beta_p = $ "*process p begins*"; or $\epsilon_p = $ "*process p ends*". So, each atomic proposition has a parameter (the name of the parent process) represented by its index. Each inheritance constraint ψ can be specified by a formula inductively defined as follows:

$$\psi ::= \phi \mid \neg\psi \mid \psi_1 \wedge \psi_2 \mid \psi_1 \vee \psi_2 \mid \psi_1 AU \psi_2 \mid \psi_1 EU \psi_2;$$

To define the semantics of the logic we construct a Kripke structure [10]: $M = (SP, T, \mu)$, where SP is a finite set of states; T is a binary relation on states which defines the initial state and the possible transitions; $\mu : SP \rightarrow 2^{AP}$ assigns true values of atomic propositions to each state. The satisfaction relation for formulas in states $(M, sp) \models \psi$ is defined inductively:

1. $sp \models \phi$ iff $\phi \in \mu(sp)$.
2. $sp \models \neg\psi$ iff $sp \not\models \psi$.
3. $sp \models \psi_1 \wedge \psi_2$ iff $sp \models \psi_1$ and $sp \models \psi_2$.
4. $sp \models \psi_1 \vee \psi_2$ iff $sp \models \psi_1$ or $sp \models \psi_2$.

5. $sp \models \psi_1 AU \psi_2$ if *for every path* $sp_0, sp_1, \ldots$ with $sp = sp_0$,
for some $i \geq 0$ $sp_i \models \psi_2$ and $sp_j \models \psi_1$ for $0 \leq j < i$.
6. $sp_i \models \psi_1 EU \psi_2$ if *for some path* $sp_0, sp_1, \ldots$ with $sp = sp_0$,
for some $i \geq 0$ $sp_i \models \psi_2$ and $sp_j \models \psi_1$ for $0 \leq j < i$.

Using this logic we now give our own definition of behavioural inheritance: behavioural inheritance from the designer's point of view.

Definition 2. *Process tree c inherits process tree p if the inheritance constraint* ψ_p *specified for c is satisfied in the root of process tree c.*

For example, constraint $\beta_p \ AU \ \epsilon_p$ means that process tree c inherits process tree p if for every path of process tree c starting from the root there is a node where process p begins, i.e. $\beta_p = true$, and then there is a node where process p ends, i.e. $\epsilon_p = true$.

The definition of a process p includes a reachability relation on the process's states $sp, sp_1, \ldots, sp_F$. Let $sp \overset{a_1}{\Longrightarrow} sp_1$ and $sp_1 \overset{a_2}{\Longrightarrow} sp_2$ specify the reachability relation of a process p. This relation is represented by formula $(\beta_{a_1} AU(\epsilon_{a_1} \wedge \beta_{a_2}))AU\epsilon_{a_2}$. Recursively applying the formulas of our logic to each reachability relation, it is easy to derive the logic formula which describes the reachability relation of a given process. That is why we use predicate Φ_p to represent a complete process p which starts in state sp and literally fulfils itself without interruptions till its final state. The satisfaction relation for predicate Φ_p is the following:

$sp \models \Phi_p$ if *for every path* $sp_0, sp_1, \ldots$ with $sp = sp_0$, for some $i \geq 0$ $sp_i \models \epsilon_p$ and for $0 \leq j < i$ $sp_j \models \beta_p$ (i.e. $sp \models \beta_p \ AU \ \epsilon_p$) and every path $sp_0, sp_1, ..sp_i$ with $sp = sp_0$ and $sp_i = sp_F$ is a path of process p.

The logic of behavioural inheritance solves the following problems:
Firstly, this logic allows designers to specify what kind of behavioural inheritance they would like to achieve. Moreover, in the case of composition without modification, the behaviour specified by a constraint can be constructed automatically as a composition of process trees.
Secondly, this logic defines types of constraints (AU or EU) and allows us to set the correspondence between the type of constraints and the proving technique.

For example, to prove constraint $\beta_q \ AU \ (\epsilon_q \wedge \Phi_p)$ (Fig. 4 (1)), we should choose, one after the other, each $s - tree$ from process q and block all other s-trees. In the path with the chosen s-tree we check that process p starts and literally fulfils itself after finishing of the chosen $s - tree$. To prove constraint $\beta_q \ EU \ (\epsilon_q \wedge \Phi_p)$ we should check that process p starts and literally fulfils itself for at least one s-tree from q (Fig. 4 (2)). For the derivable constraints these two basic techniques are combined.

Sometimes designers need to insert new processes into the parent behavioural patterns. Doing this designers usually mean to keep the parent behavioural pattern in form of one or another inheritance constraint. However, they can make mistakes *modifying* the parent process. The correctness check of modification (Fig. 5) begins when a starting node of the parent process tree has been found in the child process tree. From this point the tree transformation rules (Fig. 6),

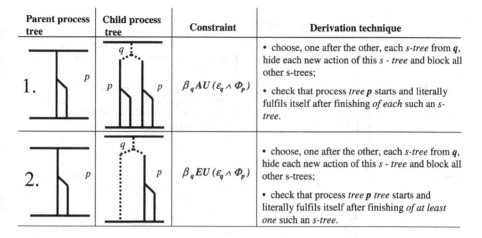

Parent process tree	Child process tree	Constraint	Derivation technique
1.		$\beta_q AU(\varepsilon_q \wedge \Phi_p)$	• choose, one after the other, each *s-tree* from *q*, hide each new action of this *s - tree* and block all other s-trees; • check that process *tree p* starts and literally fulfils itself after finishing *of each* such an *s-tree*.
2.		$\beta_q EU(\varepsilon_q \wedge \Phi_p)$	• choose, one after the other, each *s-tree* from *q*, hide each new action of this *s - tree* and block all other s-trees; • check that process *tree p* tree starts and literally fulfils itself after finishing *of at least one* such an *s-tree*.

Fig. 4. Examples of Behavioural Inheritance

which we have constructed on the basis of the axioms defined in [5], can be used to check correctness of insertions. Sequential insertions of new actions are hidden (axiom 3). Alternatives started by new actions with the structure corresponding to axiom 4 are transformed according to the transformation rule 4 (Fig. 6). Alternatives of other structures starting by new actions are blocked using axiom 1. Axiom 2 is a restrictive one: a blocked action cannot be eliminated from the sequential branch and, this way, the point of incorrect inheritance can be found.

3.3   An Example of Behavioural Inheritance without Modification of the Parent Process

The informal inheritance constraint for component *Corporative Provider* specified in Fig. 2,3 is the following: *Only in the case of correct membership, process p= Web Service is fulfiled without changes.* The formal variant of this constraint is: $\epsilon_s \, EU \, \Phi_p \wedge \neg(\neg \epsilon_s \, EU \, \Phi_p))$.

Component *Corporative Provider* is a correct inheritor of component *Web Service* if the process tree of *Corporative Provider* has a path starting from the root such that there is a node on this path where process $s=CorrectMembership$ ends and then there is a node on this path where process $p = WebService$ literally fulfils itself. Also the process tree should not contain paths where there is no end of process $s = CorrectMembership$ but process p fulfils itself.

The process tree representing behaviour of component *Corporative Provider* is shown in Fig. 7. Thinking in terms of processes designers can "drag-and-drop" processes manually, like in a Lego-game, pointing out the connections between process trees. In such a way the composing of formal constraints can be done automatically by an appropriate tool.

We have developed a prototype of such a tool (see, [17]), which is included into the Rational Rose design environment as an Add-In. The tool allows visualizing

Parent process tree	Child process tree	Constraint	Derivation technique
1.	q	$\beta_q AU\,(\varepsilon_q \wedge \Phi_p)$	• choose, one after the other, each *s-tree* from q, hide each new action of this *s - tree* and block all other s-trees; • check that process tree p starts and fulfils itself after finishing *of each* such an *s-tree* provided that new actions in p are hidden and/or blocked according to the graph transformation rules (Fig. 6)
2.	q	$\beta_q EU\,(\varepsilon_q \wedge \Phi_p)$	• choose, one after the other, each *s-tree* from q, hide each new action of this *s - tree* and block all other s-trees; • check that process *tree p* starts and fulfils itself after finishing *of at least one* such an *s-tree* provided that new actions in p are hidden and/or blocked according to the graph transformation rules (Fig. 6)

Fig. 5. Examples of Behavioural Inheritance with Modification of a Parent Process

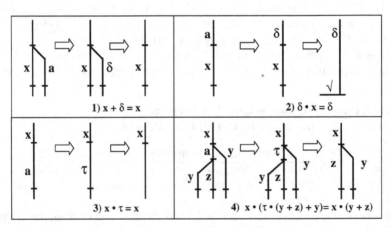

Fig. 6. Graph transformation rules; x, y, z - parent actions; a - new action; δ - blocked action; τ - hidden action

process trees and checking inheritance. The inheritance relation that we have defined on roles in the interface-role diagram (Fig. 2) allows us to duplicate actions of the parent process p. Actions of *Web Service* $a_1 \ldots a_4$ (Fig. 1c) are renamed $b_5 \ldots b_8$ of *Corporative Provider* (Fig. 7); actions a_5, a_6 are renamed b_9, b_{10}; actions a_7, a_8 are renamed b_{11}, b_{12}. Predicate $\epsilon_q = Correct\ Membeship\ ends$ is satisfied after action b_4. This path has all states of process p on it. So, according to the given constraint, component *Corporative Provider* is a correct inheritor of component *Web Service*.

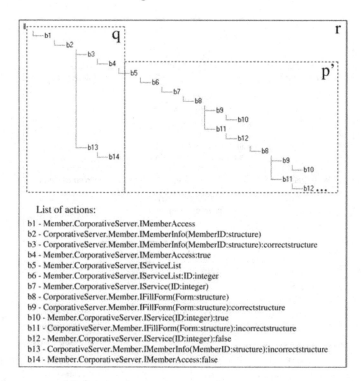

List of actions:

b1 - Member.CorporativeServer.IMemberAccess
b2 - CorporativeServer.Member.IMemberInfo(MemberID:structure)
b3 - CorporativeServer.Member.IMemberInfo(MemberID:structure):correctstructure
b4 - Member.CorporativeServer.IMemberAccess:true
b5 - Member.CorporativeServer.IServiceList
b6 - Member.CorporativeServer.IServiceList:ID:integer
b7 - Member.CorporativeServer.IService(ID:integer)
b8 - CorporativeServer.Member.IFillForm(Form:structure)
b9 - CorporativeServer.Member.IFillForm(Form:structure):correctstructure
b10 - Member.CorporativeServer.IService(ID:integer):true
b11 - CorporativeServer.Member.IFillForm(Form:structure):incorrectstructure
b12 - Member.CorporativeServer.IService(ID:integer):false
b13 - CorporativeServer.Member.IMemberInfo(MemberID:structure):incorrectstructure
b14 - Member.CorporativeServer.IMemberAccess:false

Fig. 7. Process tree of component *Corporative Provider*. Process r comprises processes p' and q

3.4 An Example of Behavioural Inheritance with Modification of the Parent Process

Assume that component *Paid Web Service* is constructed by inheritance from component *Web Service* with some altering: after the choice of service, but before getting one a customer should guarantee his payment sending requested information (e.g. a credit card number) back to component *Paid Web Service*. The new component should be able to utilize process $p=$ *Web Service* of component *Web Service* in the case of confirmed payment represented by some process $cf=Confirmed$ payment. If the payment is not guaranteed, then the session has to be terminated. The informal inheritance constraint may look like this: *Only in the case of confirmed payment, component Paid Web Service fulfils process $p = WebService$.*

The formal variant of the constraint is

$$((\beta_p \ EU \ \Phi_{cf}) \ AU \ \epsilon_p) \ \wedge \ \neg((\beta_p \ EU \ (\neg\Phi_{cf})) \ AU \ \epsilon_p).$$

Component *Paid Web Service* is a correct inheritor of component *Web Service* if the process tree of *Paid Web Service* has a path starting from the root such that there is a node on this path where process p begins, then there is a node on

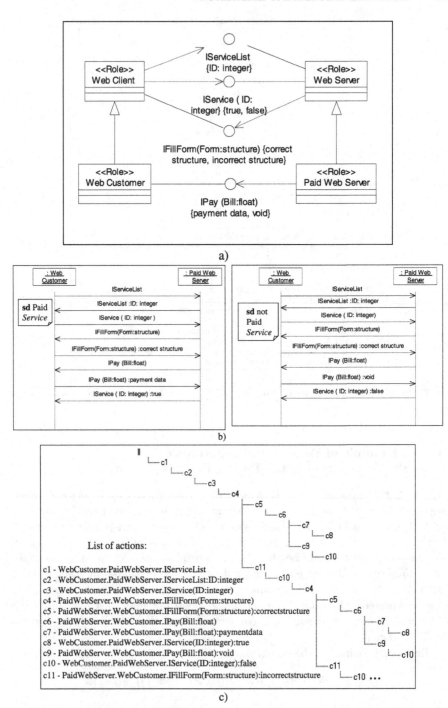

Fig. 8. The specification of component *Paid Web Service*: a) interface-role diagram; b) sequence diagrams; c) process tree

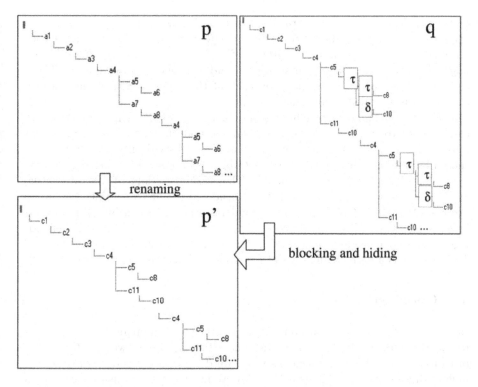

Fig. 9. *Paid Web Service* inherits *Web Service*

this path where process cf begins and literally fulfils itself and then for all paths starting from this node there is a node where process p ends. Also the process tree should not contain paths where process cf is not fulfilled but process p is fulfilled. The specification of component *Paid Web Service* is shown in Fig. 8. The interface-role diagram of component *Paid Web Service* is shown in Fig. 8 a. New roles *Web Customer* and *Paid Web Server* inherit corresponding roles of the component-predecessor. One sequence diagram corresponding to the case when the information required to perform the service is incorrect, is completely the same as for the predecessor (see the second sequence diagram in Fig. 1b.) We do not show this case in Fig. 8b. The new behaviour is provided by new interface *IPay*. Its return value *payment data* is regarded as a confirmed payment and return value *void* corresponds to a not confirmed payment. Two sequence diagrams (Fig. 8b) show that two actions using interface *IPay* are inserted between inherited actions. (Compare these two diagrams and the first diagram in Fig. 8).

Process tree q representing behaviour of component *Paid Web Service* is shown in Fig. 8c. Actions $a_1, ..., a_5, a_6, a_7, a_8$ of component *Web Service* (Fig. 8) are renamed $c_1, ..., c_5, c_8, c_{11}, c_{10}$ (Fig. 9). In the specified process tree of the new component (Fig. 8c) process p starts from the root and we are looking for states where predicates β_{cf} = "Confirmed   Payment begins" and ϵ_{cf} = "Confirmed Payment ends" are satisfied. Process $cf=$ Confirmed Payment is a sequence constructed from actions $c_6 = IPay(bill : float)$ and $c_7 = IPay(bill : float)$: payment data. We choose each such path and continue to investigate it. There exists the final state of process p on each of these paths. So, our inheritance constraint is satisfied. This case is of process modification without composition and the technique with hiding and blocking described in subsection 3.1 can be used to prove the constraint. Our method supports this technique by information to define the actions that should be blocked and the actions that should be hidden. The alternative Not Confirmed Payment is started by action $c_9 = IPay(bill : float) : void$ of new interface $IPay$. Actions of this alternative are blocked because this process is not considered in our constraint. Actions of process $cf=$ Confirmed Payment are hidden because we consider this process in our constraint. This way, process tree $p' = WebService'$ (Fig. 9) is derived. Hence, we may conclude that according to the given constraint component Paid Web Service is a correct inheritor of component Web Service.

4   Conclusion

Inheritance of behaviour is a promising technique for component reuse and architectural design. Involving behavioural inheritance in design, we inevitably give birth to additional inheritance constraints on design results and we have to formulate those constraints. This is the price we have to pay to ensure correctness of reuse in design. In this paper, we have proposed to extend existing architectural approaches by specification of how a child-component inherits behaviour of its parent-component. We have defined a logic to represent these relations as behavioural inheritance constraints. The behavioural inheritance constraints can be constructed and proved with the help of tools. The technique described in this paper has been built into the specification tool [17], which we have developed to investigate correctness of components specified by inheritance.

References

1. Medvidovic N., R.Taylor: A Classification and Comparison Framework for Software Architecture Description Languages. IEEE Transaction on Software Engineering **26** (2000)
2. D'Souza D.F., A.C.Wills: Objects, Components and Frameworks with UML. The CATALYSIS Approach. Addison-Wesley (1999)
3. Jonkers H.B.M: Interface-Centric Architecture Descriptions. In proceedings of WICSA, The Working IEEE/IFIP Conference on Software Architecture (2001) 113–124
4. Ommering R. van, F. van der Linden, J. Kramer, J.Magee: The Koala component model for consumer electronics software. IEEE Computer **11(3)** (2000) 78–85
5. Basten T., W.M.P. van der Aalst: Inheritance of behaviour. The Journal of Logic and Algebraic Programming **46** (2001) 47–145
6. Clarke E.M.,Jr. O. Grumberg, D. A. Peled: Model Checking, Cambridge (1999)

7. Harel D., O. Kupferman: On Object Systems and Behavioural Inheritance. IEEE Transactions On Software Engireering **28** (2002) 889–903

8. OMG: Unified Modeling Language Specification v.1.5, http://www.omg.org/ technology/documents/formal/uml.htm. (2003)

9. Baeten J.C.M.,W.P. Weijland: Process Algebra. Cambridge University Press (1990)

10. Alur R., C.Courcoubetis,D.L.Dill: Model-Checking in Dense Real-Time. Information and Computation **104(1)** (1993) 2–34

11. Clark T., A. Evans, S. Kent, S. Brodsky, S. Cock: A Feasibility Study in Rearchitechtoring UML as a Family of Languages using a Precise OO Meta-Modeling Approach. (2000)

12. OMG: Requirements for UML profiles, OMG document ad99-12-32. (1999)

13. Roubtsova E.E., S.A.Roubtsov: Behavioural Inheritance in the UML to Model Software Product Lines. (Accepted for Elsevier journal "Science of Computer Programming", Editor J. Bosch. (2004))

14. OMG: UML2. http://www.omg.org/uml/. (2003)

15. Roubtsov S.A., E.E. Roubtsova, P. Abrahamsson: Evolutionary product line modelling. In: Proc. International Workshop on Evolution of Large-scale Industrial Software Applications (ELISA), Amsterdam, The Netherlands. (2003) 13–24

16. Manna Z., Pnueli A.: The Temporal Logic of Reactive and Concurrent Systems. V.1. Specification. Springer-Verlag (1992)

17. Roubtsova E.E., S.A.Roubtsov: UML-based Tool for Constructing Component Systems via Component Behaviour Inheritance. ENTCS, Editors T.Erts, W. Fokkink **V.80** (2003)

Software Architectures
for Designing Virtual Reality Applications

Rafael Capilla and Margarita Martínez

Department of Informatics and Telematics,
Universidad Rey Juan Carlos, Madrid, Spain
{rcapilla,mmartinez}@escet.urjc.es

Abstract. Software architectures are particularly useful when designing complex systems. Apart from facilitating the design, development and evolution processes, software architectures help developers who are new in the domain to understand the design issues involved, reducing the learning effort. In this work we present a software architecture for virtual reality systems. This architecture applies patterns common in other interactive systems, such as the Model-View-Controller, and also identifies new patterns proper of the VR domain, such as the scene graph. In addition, in the proposed architecture we have identified the variability points needed for adapting and evolving such VR systems.

1 Introduction

The challenge of a virtual reality system (VR-system) is to simulate the real world in a virtual environment, making it real for the user who is immersed in the system [8]. Among the characteristics of virtual reality systems that make them complex to develop we can cite the following.

- Use of special hardware devices: head-mounted displays, 3D haptics, etc.
- Complexity of user interfaces and multimodal interaction.
- 3D modeling techniques.
- Complex graphic operations, such as object collision and deformation.
- Presence of the user in the virtual scene.
- Real-time requirements.

We believe that all these factors can preclude a quick development of virtual reality software applications. The challenge to facilitate the construction of such systems is the motivation of this paper. Therefore we have tried to provide some guidance for understanding and designing VR systems from a software engineering perspective. Our proposal analyses the use of *software architectures* [2] [4] [21] for building virtual reality applications in order to reduce the effort needed in the development process by making more modular and reusable its most relevant parts. The organization of the paper is as follows. Section 2 presents the related work in this field. Section 3 describes our approach for building software architectures for VR systems. Section 4 evaluates our work through the construction of a VR system and section 5 provides the conclusions obtained.

F. Oquendo et al. (Eds.): EWSA 2004, LNCS 3047, pp. 135–147, 2004.

2 Software Architectures in Virtual Reality Systems

We have found only a few proposals in the literature describing virtual reality systems employing software architectures. Schöntage and Eliëns [18] describe the problems for developing distributed VR systems and they mention four architectural styles for classifying object-oriented software under distributed environments. In [19] the DIVA Distributed Architecture Visualization is presented as an example of the use of architectural patterns [5] to achieve a software architecture [20] for building distributed VR systems. Another example is the Dragon system, which is a real-time battlefield visualization virtual environment [10]. The architecture is shown in figure 1.

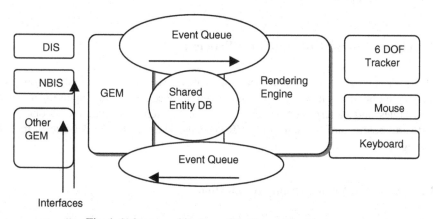

Fig. 1. Software architecture of the Dragon System.

The Dragon system is composed by two major subsystems: the *rendering engine* (RE) and a *generic entity manager* (GEM). RE draws the virtual environment, processes the user input and creates requests and events that are sent to the GEM subsystem. GEM is responsible to collect data from external sources and represent them under a common format. Both subsystems interact through a pair of unidirectional event queues and a shared entity database. DIS (Distributed Interactive Simulation) and NBIS (Joint Maritime Command Interaction) are interfaces of the system. In [3], the authors mention the requirements that software architectures must fulfil for supporting the design of VR systems as well as to perform rapid prototyping. Some of these requirements refer to the modularization and extensibility as a practical point of view in the design process.

In general terms, the lack of flexibility is a common point in many of the VR systems already developed. One of the problems in the development of Large Scale Virtual Environments [14] comes from the use of monolithic architectures, blocking some important aspects such as *maintenance, reusability* and *extensibility* among others. Therefore, a more modular design of VR applications based on good software architectures can improve the development and maintenance of these complex systems.

Other approaches that mention the use of software architectures in the construction of VR systems can be found in [1] [7] [9] but from our point of view, some of the references mentioned only show a global view of the system but not a more detailed one of the modules of the architecture. Moreover, the proposed architectures don't exhibit clearly the variation points needed for supporting the evolution of the systems we want to build. This is a key aspect for evolving the architecture through specific variability mechanisms as a way to avoid monolithic approaches. Finally, none of the proposals mentioned before describe the process by which they have obtained the architecture or which design techniques they have employed. In our opinion this is important if we need to develop other VR systems or evolve the existing ones as new requirements appear.

3   Architectural Construction Process

The process we have followed to obtain the software architecture is first analyzing the domain to obtain a domain model and build a reference architecture applying architectural styles and patterns. Finally we refine the reference architecture to obtain the software architecture for describing VR systems. These steps are detailed in the following sections.

3.1   Analysis of Virtual Reality Applications

A domain analysis process [17] is a key step for understanding the terminology and elements employed in most VR applications. Thus, the output of this process, that is a domain model, is used for representing those elements, characteristics and relationships that can be employed in the construction of the future software architecture. First, a d*omain scoping* process was performed to establish the limits of the domain and try to determine which VR systems will be inside or outside the domain. In this work we have included both immersive and non-immersive systems but we didn't consider distributed VR systems as well as those based on the CAVE (Cave Automatic Virtual Environment is a visualization device in which the images are projected in the floor and walls). The design of distributed VR applications is more complex because there are other factors such as communication cost, distribution of data and functions and coherence, while CAVE systems need a high cost hardware infrastructure not affordable for everybody. Finally, we didn't analyze VR engines because is not the main goal for VR application developers. Instead of this, we have preferred to analyze the most common types of VR applications that don't need stronger requirements. After this, in the *analysis phase* we identified the domain vocabulary extracted from several knowledge sources (e.g.: technical documentation, experts, web pages, technical guides, etc.), providing a classified list of terms. VR applications are implemented in several programming languages, so we had to compare similar concepts in order to classify them properly. Finally, we obtained several relationships between the elements, its properties, actions and VR devices and other relevant parts of a VR application that we used us in the construction of the software architecture.

Before we produce the domain model we did a reverse engineering process from existing VR code in order to obtain additional information that leads us to a more accurate architecture. The code inspected belongs to small VR applications written in different languages: 5 VRML, 3 Java 3D, 4 C code with OpenGL and FreeVR functions and 2 Multigen's Vega examples. The process was done manually due to the diversity of code analyzed. The terminology may vary depending on the programming language used but elements of VR applications share similar concepts. For instance, a VRML [13] node can be associated to a Java 3D object. Some of the elements identified in this step were objects, properties, events, routes and behaviors. The identification of properties associated to the aspect of the object (e.g.: shape, color, texture, or size), served for the identification of the variation points in the architecture. Finally, we identified other relationships that were used to discover the structure of a VR application, such as figure 2 shows.

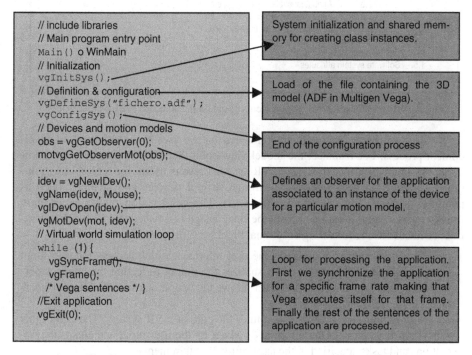

Fig. 2. Structure of a Multigen Vega Virtual Reality application.

3.2 Reference Architecture Development

Once the domain model was finished, we started the construction of the reference architecture. Reference architectures focus on fundamental abstractions for satisfying a set of reference requirements and constitute a previous step before we build the software architecture, because they serve to understand the standard parts of a set of systems. The requirements needed for developing the reference architecture represent those needs that are usually associated to a whole domain for describing the particular characteristics of the problem space. For representing these requirements we used an object-oriented template from the IEEE Std. 830-1998 standard, such as figure 3 shows.

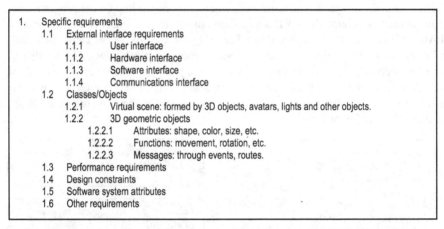

1. Specific requirements
    1.1   External interface requirements
          1.1.1   User interface
          1.1.2   Hardware interface
          1.1.3   Software interface
          1.1.4   Communications interface
    1.2   Classes/Objects
          1.2.1   Virtual scene: formed by 3D objects, avatars, lights and other objects.
          1.2.2   3D geometric objects
                   1.2.2.1   Attributes: shape, color, size, etc.
                   1.2.2.2   Functions: movement, rotation, etc.
                   1.2.2.3   Messages: through events, routes.
    1.3   Performance requirements
    1.4   Design constraints
    1.5   Software system attributes
    1.6   Other requirements

Fig. 3. Partial list of reference requirements based on the standard IEEE Std. 830-1998.

We also evaluated some architectural styles that we used in the architectural development process. For instance, the model-view-controller (MVC) pattern is quite important in interactive systems and in VR systems results useful for representing multimodal interaction (i.e.: interaction through several devices and methods, such as pointing, gestures, force-feedback and more). The construction of the architecture usually takes several iterations before the final design is finished and in our first iteration we identified the following functional blocks.

1. *User interaction layer*: Comprises the user interface, which accepts the user input from several I/O VR devices and visualizes the output reflecting the changes performed in the virtual scene. This layer allows the operations specified in user interface.
2. *Information processing layer*: Constitutes the core of a VR system. The aim of this subsystem is to process the information given by the user input and enacts the operations and tasks specified in the application's requirements.
3. *VR engines layer*: One or more engines realize the operations for re-drawing the objects in the scene. For application developers, VR engines are not very significant because usually they are integrated under the development platform or runtime environment. Therefore we will consider this module as a black box that performs low-level operations for the functions specified in the information processing layer.

We represented the modules described above using a three-layered style [6] because the lower layers or modules provide the functionality needed by the higher ones.

In a second iteration we selected the model-view-controller for representing the higher and middle layers of the architecture because the MVC pattern allows a clear separation between the information being processed (i.e.: the model), the user input coming from different VR devices (i.e.: the controller) and the output (i.e.: the view) shown to the user. The *model* of the MVC style represents the information processing module (i.e.: middle layer of the architecture) whereas the *view* and the *controller* are placed in the higher layer (i.e.: user interaction layer). In some cases the virtual scene is visualized directly, but in other situations we can define several views. Examples of this situation are those VR systems that use the World-in-Miniature (WIM) technique [15] for navigating through the virtual world. A WIM model is a miniature 3D map that permits to the user move across the virtual environment. Finally, in the third iteration we completed the reference architecture specifying the UML classes and packages needed for representing the elements of each layer. For the higher layer we specified the controller and view classes and for the middle layer (i.e.: the model) we included the following ones:

- 3D object package: It represents the scene-graph composed by a hierarchy of 3D objects that form the virtual scene.
- Event package: This package describes the events needed by the objects for communication purposes.
- 3D sound class: Allows sound in the virtual scene.
- Lighting class: Permits the existence of light points in the scene. Several types of lights can be added and customized.
- Other 3D elements (class): To be defined for each particular application.
- Device initialization package: Device initialization can be done in this layer when this task is not supported by the higher level of the architecture.
- Specific packages needed by specific applications (e.g.: other graphic routines).

3.3 Software Architecture for VR Systems

Based on the reference architecture described in the previous section, the development of the software architecture was done by refining the packages and classes of the two higher layers of the design (i.e.: user interaction layer and information processing layer). The refinement process takes the requirements and features of VR applications and defines attributes and methods for each package and class that represents a particular functionality in the system. These attributes and methods are defined taking into account the variability of the future software architecture. For each VR device, software piece or 3D element of a VR application we have defined a set of customizable attributes and methods.

In this work we represent the static view [11] [12] of the system but other ones are possible if needed. In contrast to existing architectures of VR systems that don't provide customization mechanisms, we allow a customization process through specific variation points [4] which are represented by attributes defined in the architecture and customizable parts of the methods. Therefore we can ease the maintenance and evolution against future changes. For instance, in table 1 the *DeviceType* attribute allows several VR devices (e.g.: 3D mouse, tracker, haptic devices or head-mounted displays) for multimodal interaction. This is particularly important in VR systems because one of the methods to achieve realism is providing natural interaction, simulating the ways in which we interact with real objects. Also, the initialization method may depend of the particular VR device employed. Another possibility is the specialization of the controller class by defining subclasses for different devices. On the other hand the *View* class draws and updates the views for a particular observer so we have included it as an attribute inside the view class.

Table 1. Packages, classes and variation points of the User Interaction Layer.

Package	Class	Attributes (Variation Points)	Methods (Customizable parameters)	Description
Subsystem. UI Layer	Controller	DeviceType	Initialization() ProcessEvent()	The controller class accepts the user input from VR hardware devices and processes the events generated by such devices. The controller and view classes are related in the MVC model and we have placed them n the same layer of the architecture. The information from the events processed are passed to the model (i.e.: information processing layer), so the VR application knows what to do when a new event arrives.
Subsystem. UI Layer	View	Observer	DrawView() UpdateView()	The view class draws or updates the views with the data generated by the model. Several views are allowed.

In the information processing layer we have refined the packages and classes already specified in the reference architecture, such as table 2 shows. For instance, we have defined two attributes (i.e.: two variation points) in the lighting class for detailing the type of light source (i.e.: local, infinite, etc.) and the position. Other properties for light sources such as attenuation or color can be also defined and customized afterwards. An interesting point in which there is not much work done from a software architecture point of view is in the definition of the scene-graph (i.e.: a tree representing the object hierarchy) of the virtual model. This is quite important in VR systems because the time needed for loading the virtual model may vary substantially depending on the structure of the object hierarchy (the typical size of a realistic 3D model is measured in Megabytes). The object class shown in table 2 holds properties such as size, color, shape or position, which can be customized.

The packages and classes given in tables 1 and 2 are organized in the software architecture shown in figure 4. As we mentioned in section 2, the existing proposals are usually poorly described and none of them employ UML for modeling the software

Table 2. Packages, classes and variation points of the Information Processing Layer.

Package	Class	Attributes (Variation Points)	Methods (Customizable parameters)	Description
3D objects	Root Group Object Polygons	For the object class(shape, color, texture)		This package contains a hierarchy of objects and elements for processing the 3D model stored in a database (i.e.: the scenegraph).
----	3D Lighting	TypeOfLight Position	Lighting()	One or more light points illuminate the virtual scene or particular objects.
----	3D Sound	TipeOfSound	Activation()	3D sound added to the scene.
----	Other 3D elements	-----	----	E.g.: such as fog or environmental effects.
	Player	MyObserver	MotionModel()	Sometimes we can add a player to an observer which has a specific motion model for animating the objects or avatars in the scene.
Events	Event Sensor	MyEvent MySensor	EventAction() Detection() EventSensor()	Events and information from sensors (e.g.: collision detection or VRML routes) can be manage in the virtual scene.
Specific packages	----	----	----	To be determined. Specific for a particular VR application or family of related systems.

architecture of a virtual reality system. This is important for understanding the key parts of a VR system in order to facilitate the construction of such systems by novice VR developers using standard design methods. From our point of view UML is suitable for representing most of the architectural decisions of VR systems. Other architectural views (i.e.: physical, process view) can be also represented employing other UML diagrams (e.g.: deployment, sequence diagrams, etc.). Perhaps the weakest feature of UML from our point of view is the lack of a way to represent in detail the variation points.

4   Customizing the Software Architecture for a Virtual Church

The evaluation of the architecture of figure 3 was done building a small VR system consisting in the design of a virtual church as well as a virtual tour inside the church. The church is a 12th century Romanesque temple located in a small village in the north of Spain (Cambre's village, http://www.cambre.org) and the shape is similar to old European cathedrals. The application consists in a virtual tour through the church showing its main characteristics and elements with comments that appear in key places. The user interacts with the system through a head mounted display, a tracker and a 3D mouse. For developing the system we used Multigen Paradigm software

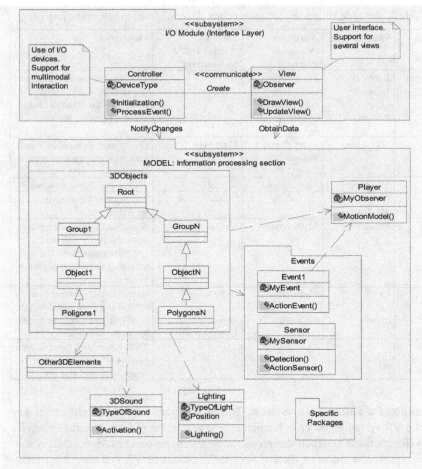

Fig. 4. Software architecture for VR systems.

tools. The application was developed by a novice software engineer not familiarized with the construction of VR systems. In order to facilitate the design of the system, we used the proposed architecture to explain to her the standard parts of the VR system. The customization of the architecture was done through the specific variation points already mentioned by filling the attributes with appropriate values. The requirements for the new application served as a guide for selecting which variation points should be included in the final architecture. Also, we used appropriate values for customizing specific methods that were reused for the final implementation (e.g.: initialization values for different hardware devices) and the final design was quickly obtained such as figure 5 shows.

Once the developer was familiarized with the Multigen Paradigm tools, we took the measures of the church and we started the construction of the 3D virtual model using the Multigen Creator tool. We customized the scene-graph of the 3D model and we decided which elements of the architecture would be used. The Creator database

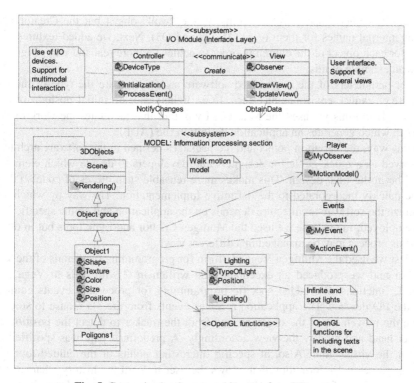

Fig. 5. Customized software architecture for a VR system.

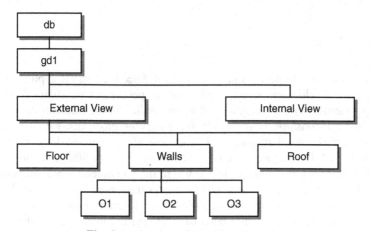

Fig. 6. Partial view of the object hierarchy.

organizes the scene graph starting with a root element called "db" and a generic group "gd1", from which the rest of the objects hang on. We have divided the construction of the church in two main object groups: the external view and the internal one. For instance, the main three elements of the external view are the floor, the walls and the roof. Several objects and polygons compose the "wall" object but the Creator tool assigns internal names for them (e.g.: O1, O2 and O3). Next, we added textures and colors for each object of the church in order to achieve a more realistic view. Figure 6 shows an example of this.

Other parameters of the customized software architecture are the type of motion model (e.g.: walk), environment effects (e.g.: lights) and the initial position of the observer. To do this we used the Multigen Lynx tool that facilitates the work of the designer, which generates an application definition file (ADF).

In this way, the variation points and the packages defined in the software architecture served as a quick guide for designers and developers to decide which elements should be in the final design. This makes more reusable such pieces of code so they can be quickly incorporated to the definitive implementation. The way by which we customize the software architecture depends on the application and on the specific VR tools employed. In our case we used the Multigen Creator and Lynx tools but in other cases this process may be managed in a different way.

At last we used the Multigen Vega platform for programming the details of the virtual tour and we produced an executable file written in C with calls to Vega and OpenGL functions. We added specific programming for processing events coming from the I/O devices. The application receives events from the 3D mouse to stop or initiate the movement of the observer, and from the tracker to detect the position of the user head and modify the view accordingly. A predefined path was specified to perform the virtual tour. Also, at specific interesting points of the guided tour we added some textual information that allows the user to learn the history, characteristics and elements of the church. This feature was performed through OpenGL functions, also reflected in the architecture as a specific or a domain package.

5 Conclusions

In this work we have proposed a new software architecture for VR applications that can reduce the development effort, particularly to people not familiarized with this kind of applications, by providing a good understanding of the elements of a VR system and their relationships. Compared to other existing proposals, we have outlined more accurately the standard parts and functional blocks and we have represented them using the UML notation. Moreover, the definition of specific variation points in the architecture helps designers to decide where the software architecture should be customized for a specific application and facilitates the maintenance and evolution of VR applications over time. The construction of a VR application can be performed more quickly because the standard parts of a VR system have been designed more reusable compared to existing proposals.

Related to this, the modification of the variation points has an immediate effect in the architecture that can be evaluated both at the design of the 3D model as well as viewing what the user sees or feels when interacts with the VR application through specific VR devices. The simulation of the design with a real implementation is the best way to test the proposed architecture.

Another result we obtained refers to the multimodal interaction of VR systems and the use of several hardware devices. This topic has been gathered by the architecture with the controller and view classes of the MVC pattern. The customization of the controller class allows the use of different devices used by modern VR systems and implements different hardware initialization processes if needed. Also, the architecture can support several views if complex graphical user interfaces are needed. For instance, an application could use one view for representing the general layout of a historical place and a detailed view for each for the most interesting parts of the virtual model selected by the user.

Other interesting aspect is that the architecture explicitly represents the scene-graph of the 3D model. This is an important issue in the design and execution of VR systems because many times the performance of the system depends on the organization of the objects in the scene-graph. For the future, we will like to extend our architecture to include other VR applications (e.g.: distributed ones or CAVE-based systems) and test the suitability of our architecture for supporting the evolution against future changes. In addition to this, exploring other scene-graph architectures based on software patterns is an interesting direction for research in VR systems. Finally, quality attributes such as performance, usability and presence are important to be explored for validating non-functional properties in the proposed architecture. Measuring the values obtained through the execution of the system is a way to provide results when defining such quality attributes.

References

1. Alexandre, R.J. F. and Medioni G. G. A Modular Software Architecture for Real-Time Video Processing, Proceedings of the 2nd International Wokshop on Computer Vision Systems, 35-49 (2001).
2. Bass, L., Clements, P., Kazman. Software Architecture in Practice, Addison-Wesley, 2nd Edition (2003).
3. Blach, R., Landauer, J., Rösch A. and Simon, A. A Highly Flexible Virtual Reality System. Future Generation Computer Systems Special Issue on Virtual Environments, Elsevier, Amsterdam (1998).
4. Bosch, J., Design & Use of Software Architectures, Addison -Wesley (2000).
5. Buschmann, F., Meunier, R., Rohnert, H., Sommerland, P., Stal, M. Pattern-Oriented Software Architecture. A System of Patterns. John Wiley & Sons, New York (1996).
6. Clements, P., Bachman, F., Bass, L., Garlan, D., Ivers, J., Little, R., Nord, R. and Stafford, J. Documenting Software Architectures, Addison-Wesley (2003).
7. Fernando, T., Murray, N., Tan K. and Wimalaratne, P. Software Architecture for Constraint-based Virtual Environment, ACM International Symposium on Virtual Reality Software and Technology (VRST'99), London, UK (1999).
8. Gobbetti, E. and Scaneti, R. Virtual Reality, Past Present and Future, Online at: http://www.csr4.it/vvr/bib/papers/vr-report98.pdf
9. Hua, H., Brown, L. D., Gao C. and Ahuja, N. A New Collaborative Infrastructure: SCAPE. IEEE Virtual Reality (VR'03), (2003).

10. Julier, S., King, R., Colbert, B., Durbin J. and Rosenblum, L. The Software Architecture of a Real-Time Battlefield Visualization Virtual Environment, IEEE Virtual reality, Houston, Texas, USA, (1999).

11. Kobryn, C. Applied Software Architecture, Addison-Wesley (2000).

12. Kruchten, P. Architectural Blueprints. The 4+1View Model of Software architecture, IEEE Software, 42-50, (1995).

13. Nadeau, D. R. Building Virtual Worlds with VRML, IEEE Computer Graphics and Applications, 18-29, IEEE Computer Society, (1999).

14. Oliveira, M., Crowcroft, J., Slater M. and Brutzman, D. Components for Distributed Virtual Environments (VRST'99), 176-177, London, IK, (1999).

15. Pausch, R. and Burnette, T. Navigation and Locomotion in Virtual Worlds via Flight into Hand-Held Miniatures, SIGGRAPH'95, ACM, 399-400, (1995).

16. Poupyrev, I. and Ichikawa, T. Manipulating Objects in Virtual Worlds: Categorization and Empirical Evaluation of Interaction Techniques, Journal of Visual Languages and Computing, vol 10, 1, 19-35, (1999).

17. Schäfer, W., Prieto-Díaz R. and Matsumoto, M. Software Reusability, Ellis Horwood, (1994).

18. Schönhage B. and Eliëns, A. From Distributed Object Features to Architectural Styles, Workshop on Engineering Distributed Objects (EDO'99), International Conference on Software Engineering (ICSE), Los Angeles (USA), (1999).

19. Schönhage, B., van Ballegooij, A. and Eliëns, A. 3D Gadgets for Business Process Visualization, International Conference on the Virtual reality Modeling Language and Web 3D Technologies, Monterrey, California, USA, (2000).

20. Schönhage, B. and Eliëns, A. Information Exchange in a Distributed Visualization Architecture: the Shared Concept Space Proceedings of Distributed Objects Applications (DOA'00), Antwerp Belgium, (2000).

21. Shaw, M. and Garlan, D. Software Architecture. Prentice Hall (1996).

Generation and Enactment of Controllers for Business Architectures Using MDA

Günter Graw[1] and Peter Herrmann[2]

[1] ARGE IS KV
graw@iskv.de
[2] University of Dortmund
Peter.Herrmann@udo.edu

Abstract. Model Driven Architecture (MDA) is an initiative of the OMG in which the software development process is driven by various software-related models describing the software to be generated. Moreover, the new upcoming UML 2.0 standard promises to support the execution of models based on several types of actions as well as the inheritance of statecharts. We adapt this new technology in order to generate business controllers. By application of the popular Model View Controller (MVC) architecture, these controllers separate core business model functionality like database management from the presentation and control logic that uses this functionality (i.e., interactive user access). In particular, a controller translates user interactions realized by means of an interactive view into actions on the core business model.

This paper deals with the generation of business controllers applying MDA and UML 2.0 concepts and presents experiences gained in the background of a bigger industrial project. The focus is on statecharts and actions used for the specification and execution of controllers. In particular, in order to deal with the inheritance of statechart diagrams specified for business controllers, we define a couple of transformation rules. These rules support the transformation of abstract PIM statecharts modelling the functionality of business controllers to a flat PSM statechart describing a business controller in a more implementation-like fashion. We outline the application of the transformation rules by means of a business controller example application.

1 Introduction

The Model Driven Architecture (MDA) [5,12] is the most recent initiative of the Object Management Group (OMG) to facilitate the creation of object-oriented software. This approach has the goal to specify software for different independent domains using abstract high level models. These high level models are specified by means of the UML (Unified Modeling Language, cf. [3]) as specification language, which is another standard adopted by the OMG. The UML models are used as input for the generation of code. MDA distinguishes two different kinds of models: platform independent models (PIM) and platform specific models

F. Oquendo et al. (Eds.): EWSA 2004, LNCS 3047, pp. 148–166, 2004.

(PSM). Unfortunately, a drawback of traditional UML was the absence of a sufficiently powerful semantics to specify dynamic behavior, in particular actions. This disadvantage, however, was overcome in 2001 when the UML 1.4 [15] semantics was extended by an action specification language (ASL) [11], which has the aim to enrich the action semantics of the UML.

As if this breath-taking progress is not enough, the new UML major release for UML 2.0 is currently under standardization. Moreover, there exists a proposal for the UML superstructure [14] describing in particular the dynamic aspects of UML models. This draft contains a rich actions semantics refining the results of [11]. Moreover, the syntax and semantics of interaction diagrams were improved based on experiences of the Message Sequence Chart (MSC) community (cf. [10]).

Since actions of the ASL language are declarative by nature, due to the innovations of UML 1.4 and UML 2.0 the generation of executable models based on UML specifications is possible now. This ability is utilized by the xUML (executable UML) profile [13] which enables the execution of UML models. Meanwhile several companies created tools (e.g., bridgepoint, iCCG) which support the execution of xUML models.

Like us, Agrawal et al. [1] concentrate on generative programming of source code based on MDA. In contrast to us, however, they do not focus on behavioral aspects but on the software process of PIM to PSM transformation which is mainly performed by applying graph grammars on UML class diagrams.

This paper concentrates on the application of MDA and UML 1.4 to UML 2.0 concepts for the synthesis of controllers in business software reflecting our experiences in a bigger project of German health care insurances. A controller is used to influence the interaction of views-based graphical user interfaces (GUI) according to business rules and style guides. In particular, it is responsible for the interchange of data between a view defining a user interface and a model describing the business model. Thus, a controller is a main component of the architecture. It is possible to compose controllers of sub-controllers. The architecture of our business system is based on the well-known Model View Controller (MVC, cf. [4]) pattern which is an important architectural pattern for the fulfillment of business system requirements. In a three tier architecture typical for business applications, controllers responsible for database and workflow access are located in the middle tier which is also called application layer. The interaction between the views, which are residing in the presentation layer (i.e., the upper tier), and the controllers are realized by commands from the views to the controllers (i.e., they follow the so-called command concept).

The controller behavior is specified in a platform-independent fashion by means of UML statechart models. Statechart inheritance is used to refine the models facilitating their reuse. Moreover, we use PIM to PSM transformations of UML models to get platform-specific controller models. These PIM to PSM transformations are carried out by means of graph transformation systems (cf. [2]). Finally, the PSM models are used as input for a code generator creating executable Java code. The generated code realizes the complete state machine of

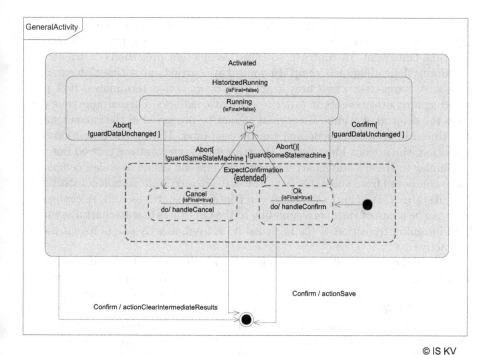

© IS KV

Fig. 1. State chart of the General Activity Controller

the controller and most of the actions specified in the original UML state chart models. For actions which cannot be generated automatically, code fragments are created which, in principle, have to be filled by manually programmed code. Since the tasks realized by this code, however, are often similar, we can avoid additional programming efforts by applying reusable code libraries.

2   State Charts in UML

States can be used in the UML to define the attributes of an object and its behavior in a rather fine-grained way. Here, we apply them in a more abstract fashion in order to model the current situation of an object and its reaction on incoming events. As depicted in Fig. 1, a state description in UML (e.g., *Cancel* or *Ok*) contains an unambiguous name. Moreover, one can add action identifiers which are accompanied by the keywords *entry*, *exit*, or *do*. Based on these keywords the actions are carried out during entering, leaving, resp. remaining in the current state.

In UML, transitions between states can be provided with a statement containing an event name, a guard condition, and action identifiers. A transition is executed if the event specified, in the event name, occurs and the guard condition specified in the statement holds as well. Here, a *call* resp. *send* event is triggered if a call or send action is fired (cf. Sec. 3). In contrast, a change of an object attribute leads to a *change* event whereas a *timed event* refers to a certain real time constraint. In contrast, so-called *completion transitions* or *triggerless transitions* depending on a *completion event* are carried out without an external trigger. A *completion event* fires if an *entry* or *do* action terminates. It is preferred against other events in order to prevent deadlocks. Furthermore, one can allow the deferral of events. If an event cannot be processed in the current state, it is stored in an event queue and can be used later. During the execution of a transition, the actions identified in the transition statement are carried out.

Similar to Harel's statechart diagrams [8], one can define so-called *composite states* composed from substates (e.g., the state *ExpectConfirmation* consisting of the substates *Cancel* and *Ok*) which can contain substates as well. A *composite state* can be a *nested state* corresponding to the OR-states in statechart diagrams. If an incoming transition of the nested state is fired, exactly one of its substates gets active.

A special class of states are pseudostates which have to be left immediately after being reached. Therefore, pseudostates must not contain *do* actions which are only executed if the state remains active for a while. Well-known pseudo nodes are *initial states*. In contrast, *termination states* are not pseudostates since an object remains in this state after reaching it. In nested states, *history states* (e.g., the state H^* in state *HistorizedRunning*) can be applied to store the lastly visited substate of a nested state. By executing an incoming transition of a *history state* the substate stored by it is reached.

To model the processing of events and, correspondingly, the selection of transitions, UML [14] defines a special state machine which is based on the run-to-completion semantics. According to this semantics, only one event may be processed at a point in time and the processing cannot be interrupted by other events. By special state configuration information the state machine describes which state resp. substates are currently active.

Statecharts in UML 2.0 can be inherited. This is reflected in the statechart diagrams by marking the states which are subject to effects of inheritance by dashed lines.

3   Actions in UML 2.0

A major improvement of UML 2.0 is the new Action Semantics defining a metamodel (cf. [14]) for action-based description languages. In contrast to traditional OCL, it facilitates the description of dynamic behavior enabling the generation of implementation code from UML models (cf. [5]). The Action Semantics does not define a particular syntax for action statements but more abstract action class definitions which can be realized by applying various different syntaxes. The standard distinguishes concrete actions from abstract metamodel action class definitions which refer to sets of similar but different action definitions. In concrete syntaxes only concrete actions may be used. Altogether, three main action classes are defined:

- Invocation-oriented actions refer to the object operation calls.
- Read- and write-oriented actions are devoted to the management of object attributes and links.
- Computation-oriented actions are used to compute output values from a set of input arguments.

The invocation-oriented actions are described by an abstract metamodel action class *InvocationAction*. Another, more specialized abstract action class is *CallAction* which is inherited from *InvocationAction*. *CallAction* describes object operations with call parameters and return values. *CallOperationAction* is a relevant concrete action inherited from *CallAction* which realizes operation calls at other objects by triggering the behavioral steps (e.g., a transition of the state machine introduced in Sec. 2) related to the operation in the called object.

Read- and write-oriented actions are distinguished in actions to maintain object attributes and in actions managing object references.

Computation-oriented actions map input arguments directly to output values. An important computation-oriented action is *ApplyFunctionAction* which encapsulates a primitive function. The action arguments are mapped to function arguments and the function result is made available at the output pins (i.e., parameters) of the action. During the computation of the primitive function the executing object is blocked and cannot interact with its environment.

4   Transformation and Generation in MDA

In the Model Driven Architecture (MDA) [12], a PIM (Platform Independent Model) is a model based specification of the structure and functionality on an abstract level neglecting technical details. In our project the PIM, which stems from the domain of health care insurance, can be used for implementations on the platforms of different insurance companies. Moreover, the validation of model correctness is supported, since a PIM supports the technology independent specification of the system. In contrast to this, the PSM (Platform Specific Model) is technology dependent with respect to a certain operating system, programming language, middleware, or application server. Source code of a particular application is generated based on the technology-depending data contained in a PSM.

Transformations are important in MDA. A transformation consists of a set of techniques and rules which are used for the modification of a model m_1 in order to obtain a model m_2. We distinguish three kinds of transformations:

- PIM to PIM transformations are used to get different representations of the same PIM.
- PIM to PSM transformations are applied to obtain the PSM representing a refinement of a specific PIM. This kind of transformation is sometimes called mapping.
- PSM to PSM transformations represent a means to get a different representation of a PSM.

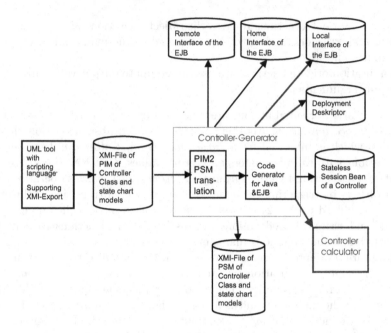

Fig. 2. Integration of Transformation and Generation Tools

Transformations may either be performed manually in iterative elaborations or be automated by means of transformation tools. Often, the automatic transformation of models is performed on the base of templates.

In our approach, we apply a set of tools as depicted in Fig. 2 which are tightly integrated. The integration of a UML modelling tool and the controller generator is performed by means of the XML Metadata Interface (XMI). XMI is a standardized format to represent UML models (cf. [16]). We use a standard UML tool for the export of class and statechart diagrams representing the PIMs of business controllers in the XMI format. In particular, by means of UML class diagrams we define inheritance trees of business controller classes each describing a business controller with a specific functionality defined by the user requirements. Moreover, for each controller class we design a statechart diagram modelling the behavior (cf. Sec. 7).

The second tool is the controller generator consisting of several transformation and generation tools developed within the project. One of these transformation tools is used to perform PIM to PSM transformations by the application of graph rewriting rules. Since it exports the resulting PSM models as XMI files, these can be displayed by an appropriate modelling tool.

Finally, the code generator is used to generate executable Java code from the PSM. It is able to generate distributed applications based on Enterprise Java Bean (EJB) 2.0 technology (cf. [17,18]) and creates the artifacts like interface and descriptor files. The transformation tool is tightly coupled with the Java Code generator.

Moreover, we are experimenting with tools supporting a developer in getting special views of the code generated from the PIM of a business controller. E.g., a small viewer, the so-called controller calculator is able to show all transitions on a given state of a statechart and helps to clarify the execution order of transitions and identifies potential conflicts. This supports the traceability from generated code back to the PIM which is very important for model driven development [19]. Furthermore, it gives some support in estimating the effect of a statechart change before a new XMI export and generator run is started.

5   PIM to PSM Transformation of Business Controller Statecharts

In the following, the PIM to PSM transformation based on graph rewrite rules is explained. Graph rewrite systems (cf. [2]) consist of a set of graph rewrite rules. Each rewrite rule is a tuple of two graph patterns which are called pre-pattern and post-pattern. In our approach, these rules are applied to UML state chart diagrams. A rule may be fired if a state chart diagram contains a subgraph which is an instance of the rule's pre-pattern. This subgraph is replaced by the corresponding instance of the post-pattern (i.e., instances of nodes and vertices carrying identical identifiers in the pre- and post-patterns are retained in the graph transformation). In the Figs. 3 to 7 we quote a number of graph rewrite rules. Here, the pre-patterns are listed on the left side and the post-patterns on the right.

The transformation of PIMs to PSMs is modelled by inheriting the statecharts specifying the behavior of the PIMs and PSMs. Unfortunately, before the submission of the UML 2.0 superstructure document [14] only limited information about the state chart inheritance semantics was available. For instance, the UML 1.4 specification proposed only three different policies dealing with the inheritance issue of state charts. These policies refer to subtyping, implementation inheritance, and general refinement. A more valuable source for insights with respect to statechart inheritance is proposed by Harel and Kupferman [9]. In contrast to UML 1.4, the UML 2.0 superstructure specification [14] contains clear recommendations how to deal with state chart inheritance:

> "A state machine is generalizable. A specialized state machine is an extension of the general state machine, in that regions, vertices and transitions may be added, regions and states may be redefined (extended: simple states to composite states and composite states by adding states and transitions), and transitions can be redefined."

These effects of statechart inheritance may be directly applied to PIM to PSM transformations. In particular, we distinguish the addition of new states to statecharts, the refinement of existing states, the overwriting of existing states, the addition of new transitions, and the redefinition of transitions as classes of transformation steps. For each class we defined a set of graph rewrite rules some of which are introduced below. A statechart may be extended by adding a new

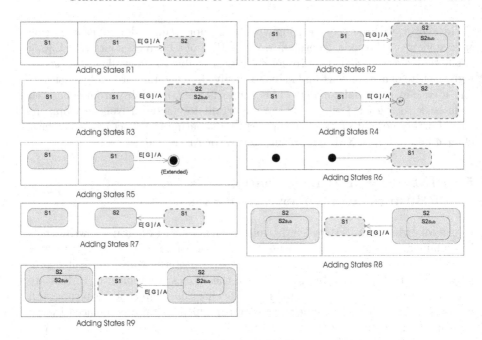

Fig. 3. Adding State Rules

state which is shown by the graph rewriting rules Adding State Rules (ASR) 1-9 depicted in Fig. 3. In order to avoid the addition of isolated states, which could never be reached in the execution, we assume that newly added states have at least one incoming or outgoing transition which is also added by executing a rule. While this restriction is not fundamental, it prevents the introduction of useless model elements which is of particular importance in complex industrial projects. The graph rewrite rule ASR1 handles the extension of a state chart adding a new simple state. ASR2 and ASR3 deal with the addition of a newly introduced nested state where the incoming transition is either connected to the nested state or to a substate of the nested state. ASR4 realizes the addition of a nested state containing a history state. By ASR5 a new final state is added whereas ASR6 handles the addition of an initial state. Due to the UML semantics, however, it is not permitted to add more than one additional initial state. The rewriting rules ASR7 to ASR9 are symmetric with respect to the rules ASR1 to ASR3 but introduce transitions using the new states as source states.

Simple states may be refined to nested states by adding new substates which is performed by the Refining State rules (RSR) 1-3 depicted in Fig. 4. The rules reflect that in PSMs the use of nested states makes only sense if they contain at least two substates. RSR1 handles the transformation of a simple state into a nesting state which contains an initial state and another connected state as substates. The rule RSR2 deals with the introduction of a nested state containing two new substates. Finally, RSR3 handles the addition of a final state

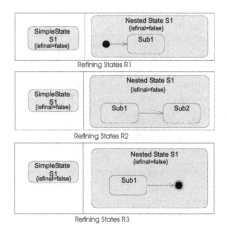

Fig. 4. Refining State Rules

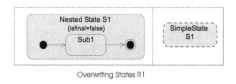

Fig. 5. Overwriting State Rule

into a nested state. Moreover, one can collapse an already existing nesting state consisting of only one substate together with the linked initial and final states to a simple state. This procedure is called overwriting and can be performed by application of the Overwriting State Rule 1 which is listed in Fig. 5.

Moreover, new transitions between existing states might be inserted which is realized by Adding Transition Rules (ATR) like the ATRs 1-5 of Fig. 6. The source and target states of an added transition can be of any type of states supported by our approach. If between the source and target state, however, already an existing transition exists which is fired by the same event as the new transition, the addition may only be done if the existing transition cannot be redefined. This is expressed by the tagged value *isFinal* of the existing transition which has to carry the value *true*. The rules listed in Fig. 6 describe this special case. The rule ATR1 handles the addition of a new transition between two simple states whereas ATR2 and ATR3 describe the addition of a transition in the context of nested states. In particular, ATR2 deals with the introduction of a transition on the nested state while ATR3 handles the addition of a transition on a substate. ATR4 realizes the addition of a transition to a history state of a nested state and ATR5 performs the addition of a transition to a final state. The rules listed in Fig. 6 describe the special case that a non-redefinable transition between the source and target states with an identical event already exists. Similar rules for unconnected source and target states and for existing

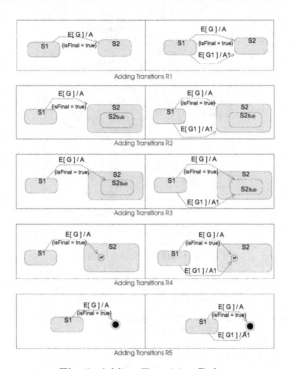

Fig. 6. Adding Transition Rules

Fig. 7. Redefining Transition Rule

transition with different events are also available. If a source and a target node are linked by a redefinable transition, one can apply the Redefining Transition Rule (RTR) 1 which is depicted in Fig. 7. The rule may be only executed if the tagged value *isFinal* is set to *false*. By its application the guard and the action of the transition are altered.

Our tool applies the rules in the following order: At first, RSRs are executed followed by OSRs. Thereafter, the ASRs and ATRs are fired. The graph rewrite rules-based transformation terminates with the application of RTRs. In order to transform a controller PIM to the corresponding PSM, at first the PSMs of its superclasses have to be created by rule applications. Based on these transformation results the tool transforms the state chart of the controller class. The rules are programmed in Java implementing an algorithm visiting the nodes and transitions of a design model parsed from the XMI representation while performing the PIM to PSM transformation.

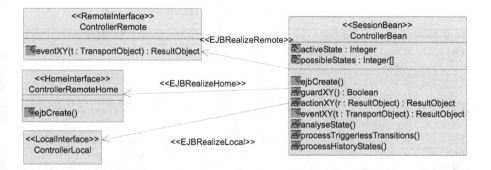

Fig. 8. Structure of a Controller Bean and the Interfaces

If a large number of new transitions is added by the controller model transformations, nondeterminism of the transitions in the resulting model may increase. To support the code generator in resolving this nondeterminism, every transition is supplied by a weight factor indicating the depth of the controller class containing the transition in the class inheritance hierarchy. The weight is a natural number, which is as higher as deeper the controller of the statechart is positioned in the inheritance hierarchy. The weight is made persistent in a tagged value *weight* of the according transition. This value will be used by the code generator to create a useful transition order in the generated stateful session bean realizing the controller. Here, transitions with a higher weight will be prioritized. Moreover, the code generator prefers transitions with guards to transitions without guards. Triggerless transitions without guards have the lowest priority.

6   PIM to PSM Transformation
of Business Controller Classes

In the following, we focus on the structural aspects of the PIM to PSM transformation of a business controller. A business controller is realized by a stateful session bean. Session beans are EJB components providing client access to a business system. In stateful session beans, moreover, the current state of a conversation is maintained whereas stateless session beans have no capability to persist states. A stateful session bean, representing the controller of a PSM, includes the code of a state machine interpreting the statechart of the according PSM Class. The class diagram depicted in figure 8 shows the structure of the PSM of a controller. In table 1 the rules for the creation of a controller PSM are presented which we will explain in the following. Firstly, attributes of a PIM Controller class become member variables of the Controller PSM. Here, we use an algorithm to create the flat representation of all states of all controller states as enumeration type. Moreover, an attribute is introduced to the controller PSM keeping the active state of the statechart which is an element of the enumeration type (Rule *PSM_R1*).

Table 1. Controller PIM To PSM Transformation Rules

Rule Nr.	Rule description	Target
PSM_R1	Creation of enumeration type for states of a controller bean	Controller PSM
PSM_R2	Creation of operations for events of the according state machine of a controller bean	Controller PSM
PSM_R3$_i$	Set of rules for the creation of transport objects transmitted by an event	Controller PSM
PSM_R4	Creation of operations for actions of a controller bean	Controller PSM
PSM_R5	Creation of operations for guards of a controller bean	Controller PSM
PSM_R6$_i$	Set of rules for the creation and of the *analyseState* operation of a state machine	Controller PSM
PSM_R7$_i$	Set of rules for the creation of the *processTrigger-lessTransitions* operation of a state machine	Controller PSM
PSM_R8$_i$	Set of rules for the creation of the *processHistoryStates* operation of a state machine	Controller PSM
PSM_R9	Creation of a remote interface of a controller session bean	Controller PSM
PSM_R10	Creation of a local interface of a controller session bean	Controller PSM
PSM_R11	Creation of the home interface of a controller session bean	Controller PSM
PSM_R12	Creation of an event operation in the remote interface	Controller PSM
PSM_R13	Creation of an operation *ejbCreate* in the home interface	Controller PSM
PSM_R14	Creation of an operation to start the execution of a sub-controller in the local interface	Controller PSM

In our architecure, UML models of Java GUI widgets are used to specify the mapping of selected Java Swing events to logical events of the controller statechart. This mapping is specified by tagged values. Event operations which are called from the views of the GUI of a controller are used to transport values in so called transport objects to the state machine. Vice versa, new data values are sent back to the views as well as result objects containing error states and new values in order to refresh of GUI information. According event operations are introduced to the PSM (Rule *PSM_R2*). The PSMs for transport objects are created by a different generator which is not subject to this paper (Rule *PSM_R3$_i$*).

Each action of the controller's statechart is transformed into an operation with an argument and return type which are both of type ResultObject (Rule *PSM_R4*). A ResultObject is used to retransmit resulting object values to a View of the GUI. For the guards of the statechart parameterless operations with return type boolean are generated (Rule *PSM_R5*). In the project we have the convention that operations for guards and actions are already modelled in the class of a controller PIM. Although this is not necessary, it helps to keep track of what is going on.

Moreover, some operations to realize the correct behavior of controller state machines are required. The method *analyseState* is used to enact entry and exit actions as well as to start doActivities of a state (Rule PSM_R6_i). Furthermore, this operation calls the operation *handleTriggerlessTransition* which is responsible to select triggerless transitions. This selection is based on the result of guard evaluation of the transitions enabled in the active state of the controller state machine as well as the order defined for conflicting transitions (Rule PSM_R7_i). The operation *processHistoryStates* which is also called the method *analyseState* which is responsible for the handling of history states (Rule PSM_R8_i).

The PIM to PSM transformation creates also the home, remote, and local interfaces for the session bean of a controller as shown in figure 8 (Rules *PSM_R9*, *PSM_R10*, and *PSM_R11*). Every event operation is added to the remote interface (Rule *PSM_R12*). An *ejbCreate* operation is added to the home interface (Rule *PSM_R13*). Operations dealing with the enaction of sub-controllers, which are modelled as operations of a controller class are added to the local Interface (Rule *PSM_R14*). Moreover, a doActivity is modelled in a state of the statechart of a controller PIM to compose a controller and a sub-controller. Since a controller requires information about sub-controller termination each sub-controller provides termination information to its controller. To handle different cases of sub-controller termination special transitions are added to the PIM of a controller.

The java code generator generates method frames or complete methods for each operation of the PIM. While, generally, a frame has to be filled by manually created programming code, we can often take reusable code which is inherited from the superclasses of the controller hierarchy applying the inheritance properties of session beans. For read- and write-oriented actions (cf. Sec. 3), the Java method is completely generated whereas for computation-oriented actions only a method frame is created. The PSM operations of guards cause the generation of an according method frame. In contrast to this, the methods for event operations are completely generated since the PIM to PSM transformation of a controller statechart provides all of the required information. This is also applicable to the methods for the operations *analyseState*, *processTriggerless* and *processHistoryStates* of a controller PSM which are completely generated.

A part of the code generator, the so-called *interface generator*, generates the home, local, and remote interfaces which provide the local and remote access to methods of the stateful session bean realizing a controller. Finally, the *descriptor generator* is used to generate the deployment descriptor of a controller bean describing the interfaces of the bean and their behavior. In particular, the deployment descriptor contains the bean's name and type, the names of the home, remote and local interfaces. Moreover, the transaction type of the bean and the transaction attribute of the methods of an interface are declared. A transaction attribute is generated as *required* by default.

7   Business Controller Example

In this section examples of business controller syntheses used in an enterprise application are presented. Fig. 9 depicts the class diagram showing the inheri-

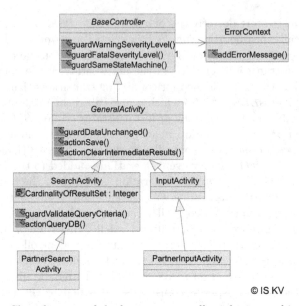

Fig. 9. Class diagram of the business controller inheritance hierarchy

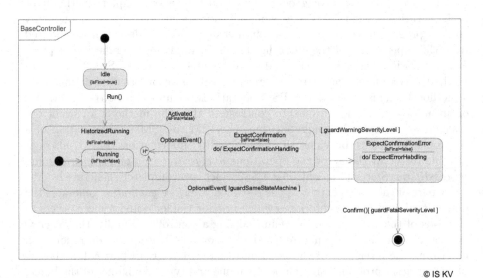

Fig. 10. Statechart of the *Base Controller*

tance hierarchy of business controllers. The abstract class *BaseController* is the root of the class diagram. It is responsible for the error and exception handling as well as for the management of dialogue confirmations. The statechart diagram of *BaseController* outlined in Fig. 10 contains elementary states which are provided for derived business controllers. The controller which is initially in the state *idle* is activated by the event *Run()* and proceeds to the state *Activated*. In particular, the substate *HistorizedRunning* is reached. In a later statechart inheritance, *HistorizedRunning* is refined by the introduction of additional substates in order to store the history of the controller behavior. This is reflected by the history state in *HistorizedRunning*. Moreover, *HistorizedRunning* contains the substate *Running* which is a place holder for later refinements describing the system functionality. Another substate of *Activated* is the state *ExpectConfirmation* which will carry confirmations of dialogue events in refined states. Finally, the statechart diagram contains the state *ExpectConfirmationError* modelling error handling. It is reached by a transition accompanied by the guard *guard-WarningSeverityLevel*. Thus, the transition fires only if the error exception is at least of the severity level *Warning*. According to the severity level the controller may either return to the last active state of historized running or abort due to a fatal error. This is expressed by the transition guards *guardSameStateMachine* resp. *GuardFatalSeverityLevel*. The guards are implemented by the three boolean operations which in the class diagram are contained in the operation compartment of class *BaseController*. This class is associated with the class *ErrorContext* receiving all error messages which result from actions triggered by the business controller.

An inheritance of *BaseController* is the abstract controller class *GeneralActivity* which is mainly responsible for the handling of confirmations initiated by a user in a session. The associated statechart diagram of this controller class was already presented in Figure 1. With respect to *BaseController* the substate *ExpectConfirmation* was refined by adding the two substates *Cancel* and *Ok*. These substates contain do-actions *handleCancel* resp. *handleConfirm* each starting a sub-controller which deals with cancellation or confirmation performed by the user. Moreover, four transitions were added in order to handle logical abort and confirm events of a dialogue. The transitions from the state *Running* to the added states which rely on an *Abort* resp. *Confirm* event refer to the guard *guardDataUnchanged* checking if business data changed since carrying out the last transition. Two other transitions connecting the new states to *Running* are carried out after receiving an *Abort* event if the guard *guardSameStateMachine* holds.

The concrete class *SearchActivity* models a controller which is able to perform a search in a database. The class has an attribute *CardinalityOfResultSet* of type integer holding the number of result entries of a database query. The operation *guardValidateQueryCriteria* is required to check if a query on a database uses the required criteria of the query correctly. Moreover, there is an operation *actionQueryDB* which is an *ApplyFunctionAction* (cf. Sec. 3) performing a query on a database. In the corresponding statechart of *SearchActivity* the state *ValidateSearchResult* and transitions handling the query in a database are added.

In a further refinement of *SearchController* (e.g., the class *PartnerSearchActivity*), controllers with respect to specific business requirements are modelled. Here, the operation *guardValidateQueryCriteria* is overwritten by an operation

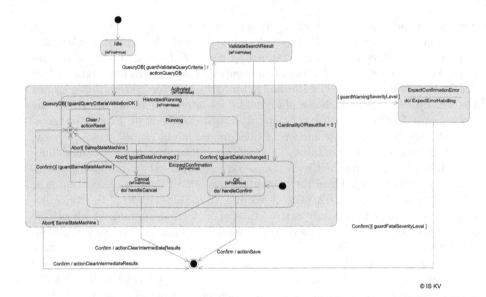

Fig. 11. State chart of the Search Activity PSM

referring to a concrete database application while *actionQueryDB* is refined by an operation containing a concrete database query.

Below, we sketch the PIM to PSM transformation of the statechart of the controller class *SearchActivity*. The resulting PSM of *SearchActivity* is shown in Fig. 11. Moreover, the depicted statechart models the states and transitions of the PIM. We present the states and transitions added to the statechart of the *GeneralActivity* class (cf. Fig. 1) by thick lines. For transformating the PIM to the PSM of *SearchActivity*, we had first to transform the PIM of the superclasses. While for the class *BaseController* no transformations had to be performed, we applied the listed rules to the statechart of the superclass *GeneralActivity* in the following order:

1. Refine nested state *expectConfirmation* by adding the substate *Cancel* which has the action *handleCancel* and the transition from *Running* to *Cancel* (RSR2).
2. Add the substate *Ok* to the nested state *expectConfirmation* which has the action *handleConfimation* and a transition from *Running* to *Ok* (ASR1).
3. Add the initial substate to the nested state *expectConfirmation* with a transition to *Ok* (ASR6).
4. Add a transition from state *Cancel* to the final state (ATR5 variant).
5. Add a transition from state *Ok* to the history state H^* (ATR4 variant).
6. Add a transition from the nested state *Activated* to the final state with the event *Confirm* and the action *actionClearIntermediateResults* (ATR5 variant).

In a second step, we transformed the statechart specifying the *SearchActivity* PIM by application of the following rules:

1. Add state *ValidateSearchResult* with a transition from state *HistorizedRunning* (ASR1).
2. Add a transition from state *Running* to the history state H^* with the event *Clear* and the association action *actionClear* (ATR 4 variant).
3. Add a transition from state *Running* to the history state H^* with the event *QueryDB* and the guard *guardQueryCriteriaValidationOK* (ATR 4 variant).
4. Add a transition from state *ExpectConfirmation* to the history state H^* with the event *QueryDB* and the guard *guardQueryCriteriaValidationOK* (ATR 4 variant).
5. Add a triggerless transition from *ValidateSearchResult* to state *HistorizedRunning* (ATR3 variant).
6. Add a triggerless transition from *ValidateSearchResult* to state *ExpectConfirmation* (ATR3 variant).

All in all, the transformation tool performed the rule application automatically and needed about 125 ms.

8   Concluding Remarks

In this paper we pointed out that new features of UML 2.0 like statechart inheritance and the action semantics extensions are useful means to model business controllers. Moreover, we focussed on MDA-based generation of business controller code. In particular, we use graph rewrite rules for PIM to PSM transformation. The effort to create the transformation tool and the code generator for controllers was about 2 man years and the amount to build the framework of business controllers and the PIM to PSM transformation was about 3 man months. The result is a fast and useful system which reduces the efforts of business controller design drastically. We applied our approach in a first industrial project for health care insurances. Our generated metrics showed that 90 % of the necessary application code could be generated by the application of transformation and generation tools. Moreover, about 60 % of the framework code for the controllers were automatically generated. Performance measurements show that generated controller code is performant. The maintenance of the code is comparatively easy since a lot of information is available in models which makes its complexity more manageable. In spite of the generally exponential complexity of graph isomorphisms, the PIM to PSM transformations of the project could be performed within 400 ms for a standard sized controller due to hard coding of the transformation rules.

In the future, we have to increase the flexibility of rule adoptions which are of interest not only for business controllers. In particular, tools and languages for a suitable generation and application of the transformation rules are of interest in agile software development processes. In complete, we plan to spend several man years of application development using the framework and the transformation tools. Moreover, since the bidirectional traceability from models to code is very fundamental for model driven development appropriate tools are required. We will provide special tools to prepare information concerning traceability in special views, which allow a quick access to the necessary information without using a debugger for Java sources. At third, we will explore the possibility to use the model-based approach for formal-based software development (cf. [6,7]).

References

1. A. Agrawal, T. Levendovszky, J. Sprinkle, F. Shi, and G. Karsai. Generative Programming via Graph Transformations in the Model-Driven Architecture. In *OOPSLA Workshop on Generative Techniques in the Context of Model Driven Architecture*, Seattle, Nov. 2002.
   Available via WWW: www.softmetaware.com/oopsla2002/mda-workshop.html.
2. R. Bardohl, G. Taentzer, M. Minas, and A. Schürr. Application of graph transformation to visual languages. In *Handbook on Graph Grammars and Computing by Graph Transformation, Volume 2*. World Scientific, 1999.
3. G. Booch, J. Rumbaugh, and I. Jacobson. *The Unified Modeling Language User Guide*. Addison-Wesley Longman, 1999.
4. F. Buschmann, R. Meunier, H. Rohnert, P. Sommerlad, and M. Stal. *Pattern-Oriented Software Architecture — A System of Patterns*. John Wiley & Sons, Chichester, 1996.
5. D. S. Frankel. *Model Driven Architecture : Applying MDA to Enterprise Computing*. Wiley Europe, Jan. 2003.
6. G. Graw and P. Herrmann. Verification of xUML Specifications in the Context of MDA. In J. Bezivin and R. France, editors, *Workshop in Software Model Engineering (WISMEUML'2002)*, Dresden, 2002.
7. G. Graw, P. Herrmann, and H. Krumm. Verification of UML-Based Real-Time System Designs by Means of cTLA. In *Proc. 3rd IEEE International Symposium on Object-oriented Real-time distributed Computing (ISORC2K)*, pages 86–95, Newport Beach, 2000. IEEE Computer Society Press.
8. D. Harel. Statecharts: A Visual Formalism for Complex Systems. *Science of Computer Programming*, 8(3):231–274, June 1987.
9. D. Harel and O. Kupferman. On the Behavioral Inheritance of State-Based Objects. In *Proc. Technology of Object-Oriented Languages and Systems (TOOLS 34'00)*, pages 83–94, Santa Barbara, 2000. IEEE Computer Society Press.
10. Ø. Haugen. MSC-2000 Interaction Diagrams for the New Millennium. *Computer Networks*, 35(6):721–732, 2001.
11. Kennedy Carter. *Action Semantics for the UML*. Available via WWW: www.kc.com/as_site/home.html.
12. A. Kleppe, W. Bast, and J. Warmer. *MDA Explained: The Model Driven Architecture: Practice and Promise*. Addison Wesley, 2003.
13. S. J. Mellor and M. J. Balcer. *Executable UML: A Foundation for Model Driven Architecture*. Addison-Wesley, 2002.
14. OMG. *UML: Superstructure v. 2.0 – Third revised UML 2.0 Superstructure Proposal*, OMG Doc# ad/03-04-01 edition, 2003. Available via WWW: www.u2-partners.org/uml2-proposals.htm.
15. Open Management Group. *UML Metamodel 1.4*.
    Available via WWW: www.omg.org/uml.

16. P. Stevens. Small-Scale XMI Programming: A Revolution in UML Tool Use? *Journal of Automated Software Engineering*, 10(1):7–21, Jan. 2003.
17. Sun Microsystems. *Enterprise Java Beans Technology — Server Component Model for the Java Platform (White Paper)*, 1998. java.sun.com/products/ejb/white_paper.html.
18. Ed Roman. *Mastering EJB*, 2002. Available via WWW: www.theserverside.com.
19. Krzysztof Czarnecki, Simon Helsen *Classification of Model Transformation Approaches*, 2003. *Proceedings of the OOPSLA 03 MDA Workshop*. Available via WWW: http://www.softmetaware.com/oopsla2003/czarnecki.pdf.

Formalization of an HCI Style
for Accelerator Restart Monitoring

Olivier Ratcliffe[1], Sorana Cîmpan[2], Flavio Oquendo[2], and Luigi Scibile[1]

[1] CERN, European Organization For Nuclear Research
CH-1211, Geneva 23, Switzerland
{Olivier.Ratcliffe,Luigi.Scibile}@cern.ch
[2] University of Savoie – LISTIC
BP 806, 74016 Annecy Cedex, France
{Sorana.Cimpan,Flavio.Oquendo}@univ-savoie.fr

Abstract. In this paper we present a solution to design and implement a set of high-level standardized Human Computer Interfaces (HCI) for the monitoring of particle accelerators restart. We are developing a software tool, which will generate these HCIs from a predefined model. The architecture-oriented solution presented in the paper can be useful for the design of HCIs for the monitoring of any industrial process, indeed, the requirements are often very similar to those defined in our context. We expose how the architectural development techniques are used to specify and produce a family of process monitoring HCIs. Specifically, we have used an Architectural Description Language (ADL) to formalize an architectural style, which describes the common properties that the HCIs should satisfy in our specific activity domain. This paper presents the different steps of our architectural design process and the integration of the formalized style in a development environment.

1 Introduction

One of the main objectives in the industrial production domain is the optimization of the processes working time. Indeed, the downtime of a production process has a very high cost. An efficient monitoring of the process constitutes a part of the solution to reduce this downtime. If the monitoring system allows the control room operators to determine accurately the cause of a process failure, they are able to solve the problem quickly, the restart time is then reduced, and the process working time is optimized. However, the monitoring of complex processes implies the acquisition, the management and the visualization of a large quantity of information coming from numerous heterogeneous systems. The development of efficient Human Computer Interfaces (HCI) to monitor such a process is then a critical issue. In the specific case of particle accelerators, the system's complexity is very high. Monitoring data are acquired and managed by a lot of different systems, and exploited by operators from several control rooms, having complementary roles, and being geographically separated. It is necessary to provide a unified high level HCI for the monitoring of the entire accelerator operation process. This HCI, and its associated documentation, have to constitute a support to efficiently coordinate the operator's work and skills, and then optimize the operating time of the accelerator.

F. Oquendo et al. (Eds.): EWSA 2004, LNCS 3047, pp. 167–181, 2004.

In this context, CERN's Technical Control Room has implemented a method used to define the monitoring information that is necessary to efficiently restart an accelerator after a major breakdown [1]. This method is the basis for the development of a set of HCIs, which must follow accurate rules in order to be easily understood and efficiently used by the control room operators. Initially, programmers have implemented prototypes of these HCIs taking a specific particle accelerator as example. The work was repetitive, and led to numerous errors on the graphics standardization and data processing levels. Many development iterations have been necessary to obtain satisfying results.

Taking these considerations into account, it has appeared necessary to automate the development process. As significant work was done during the first implementation (especially in data collecting, display standardization and development procedure fields), we want to reuse the design and the acquired experience for the future development of the complete family of applications, which will be used to monitor the restart of all the CERN particle accelerators. In this context, the purpose of SEAM (Software for the Engineering of Accelerator Monitoring) [2] is to automatically generate the monitoring HCIs from predefined properties and rules and from its user interface inputs (cf. figure 1).

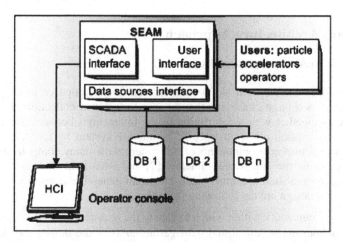

Fig. 1. The SEAM environment is composed by several data sources providing the information concerning the monitored equipments, and by the Supervisory Control And Data Acquisition software (SCADA), which displays the generated HCIs on the operator consoles.

To summarize, the main requirements for this tool are the following:

- reuse the design of the HCI prototypes;
- facilitate the HCI implementation: the operators have to be able to implement the HCI without the help of programmers;
- generate standardized HCIs: these have to follow common graphical, structural and behavioral properties;
- specify and check the properties of the systems represented by the HCIs, like for example, those concerning the equipments data acquisition;
- manage the evolution of the HCI's model according to the evolution of the accelerator restart process.

Most of the current commercial HCIs development tools have functionalities for the creation of domain-specific HCIs, like templates or customizable development environment. These tools are able to help the user to create easily HCIs partially graphically standardized, but none of them can guarantee the conformity with predefined complex properties. Consequently, we think that a tool like SEAM could be very helpful, not only for the accelerator monitoring specific domain, but also for any monitoring process HCIs design.

The requirements listed above, especially the need to have a formal development guide and a framework to reuse the design experience, have led to consider an architecture-oriented solution. Indeed, software architecture's description formalisms provide means to describe the functional, structural, and behavioral properties that the application (set of HCIs in our case) has to comply with.

In this paper, we examine the benefits derived from the use of architectural concepts, languages, and tools to design and implement a set of monitoring applications. Then we present more precisely the Architecture Description Language (ADL) chosen in this context. We expose the formalization of a domain-specific architectural style, and finally, the integration and the exploitation of the style in the SEAM software environment.

2 Software Architecture Approach

2.1 Software Architectures Benefits

Several definitions for the term 'software architecture' are proposed in the literature [3–6], but there is a large consensus that an architecture is a collection of computational elements together with a description of the interactions between them. Formal architectural description allows to specify a software system by formally defining: what types of modules are components of the system; how many components of each type there are; how the components interact [7] and what structural and behavioral properties the system should comply with. The main general reasons to use an architectural-oriented design are the following [8]:

- it provides a framework within which to satisfy the requirements;
- it provides both the technical and managerial basis for the design and the implementation of the system;
- it supports the analysis of the consistency of the design with the architecture;
- it permits architectural design reuse.

Moreover, the use of an architecture-oriented design has advantages for all the persons involved in a software project life cycle, from architects to users, as well as for developers and maintainers.

An architectural style characterizes a family of systems that are related by shared structural and semantics properties [9]. A style is less constraining and less complete than a specific architecture. Styles provide a vocabulary of design elements, which often could be classified as component and connector types such as pipes, filters, clients, servers, databases, etc [10]. They define a set of configuration rules, or topological constraints, which determines the permitted compositions of those elements, and gives a semantic interpretation of these compositions. The styles also define the analyses that can be performed on systems built in that style [11].

The formalized design approach has a lot of advantages compared with informal methods, e.g. the precision, the ability to prove properties and the possibility of structure analysis [12]. The software architecture techniques provide the formal framework that we need to formalize the monitoring HCI's structure, its components, and the communication with the monitored equipment. They simplify the process of building a system, reduce the cost of implementation through reusable infrastructure, and above all improve system integrity through style-specific analysis and tools [13]. The architectural development allows reusing a design already validated, like the one that we have done, and ensures that future applications will respect the previously validated properties [14]. Moreover, the use of an architectural style guides the development of a family of software systems, or monitoring HCIs in our specific case, by providing a common architectural vocabulary that is used to describe the structures of systems and constraining the use of that vocabulary [15]. So the adoption of an architecture-oriented development process provides solutions for at least four of the main requirements listed in the introduction:

- it allows the reuse of the design of the HCI prototypes;
- it should then facilitate the HCI implementation;
- it allows the generation of standardized HCIs that follow common graphical, structural and behavioral properties;
- it allows the specification and the checking of the properties of the systems represented by the HCIs.

2.2 ArchWare ADL

Several architectural description languages and their accompanying toolsets have been proposed to support architecture-based development [16]. They provide formal modeling notations and analyses and development tools that operate on architectural specifications. Any ADL supports at least one style, which can be generic, or in contrary, domain-specific. Some ADLs allow to formalize user specific styles. The ADLs are usually combined with tools dedicated to the exploitation of the formalized architectures and styles [17]. The $\sigma\pi$-ADL [18][19], designed within the ArchWare project (Architecting Evolvable Software), satisfies our needs for several reasons. It is a general-purpose style based-ADL, which supports the expression of architecture structure. The language is a generic ADL, providing a foundation style (component-connector style) [20]. The style mechanism allows the definition of domain specific extensions of the core language, where the domain properties can be explicitly defined and preserved. The later makes the language interesting for the description of our applications, via the definition of a description language specific for our domain. The ADL foundation style has been defined using this mechanism in order to provide a generic language more easily exploitable to define domain-specific styles and architectures. The component-connector style has been chosen to be the foundation style because most of the current software architectures follow this model. The domain-specific languages, like our accelerator restart HCI style described in 3.2, are built on the top of this foundation style. The terms of the new language will be the ones of the chosen domain. Another example of such a construction is presented in [21].

The considered ADL is a formal strongly typed language which is executable, highly customizable, and which enables analysis, refinement, evolution of dynamic architectures, and verification of conformance of architectures against defined style [22]. The $\sigma\pi$-ADL is based on the concept of formal components composition and with a set of operations for manipulating these components – a component algebra. To model component algebra, the ADL supports the concepts of *behaviors, abstractions* of behaviors and *connections* between behaviors. The language also supports all the basic π-calculus [23] operations as well as composition and decomposition.

In the style layer domain properties are expressed using the Architecture Analysis Language (AAL) [24], a sub-language of ArchWare ADL dedicated to property specification. This language has as formal foundation the modal μ-calculus, a calculus for expressing properties of labeled transition systems. The formalism uses both the predicate calculus and the modal μ-calculus in order to represent both structural and behavioral properties. The language provides support for automated verification of property satisfaction by theorem proving and model checking.

3   The Specific Architectural Style of Accelerator Restart Monitoring HCIs

In order to create and use a domain-specific architectural style we have organized our work in four steps (cf. figure 2):

1. analysis of the development of the first HCI's set in order to reuse the acquired experience, deduction of the properties and the constraints to be specified by the style;
2. formalization of the style;
3. instantiation of the HCI architectures from the style;
4. generation of the HCI code from their architectures.

3.1   Analysis of HCI Prototypes

The analysis step is dedicated to the reuse of the HCI prototypes design experience. The analysis of the prototypes permitted to informally specify a model, or style, of HCI, by producing a list of used rules, data constraints, properties, etc. Figure 3 presents the main constituent elements for an HCI.

– **status bloc:** contains the basic elements used for the representation of all systems;
– **system status:** is associated to equipments related to a specific system (like electricity, vacuum,...). A bloc contains the logic used to display the status of any system of the type for which it was created. These blocs compose the individual HCIs described below;
– **individual HCIs:** they are the restart HCIs of the accelerator, for each of its operation modes and geographic areas. An individual HCI displays the status of the systems required to make available a specific part and/or a specific acceleration phase of the accelerator. For example, an individual HCI allows to determine if "the particle beam is accelerated and ready to use on the target";

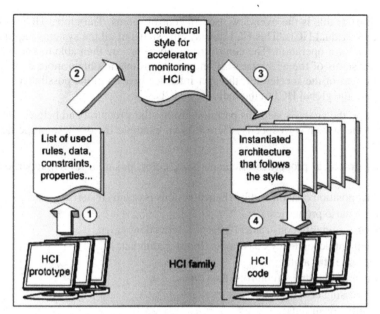

Fig. 2. Our architectural design process: (1) analysis of the HCI prototypes, (2) formalization by using σπ-ADL, (3) definition of HCI architectures by using a style specific environment (SEAM user and DB interfaces), (4) code generation.

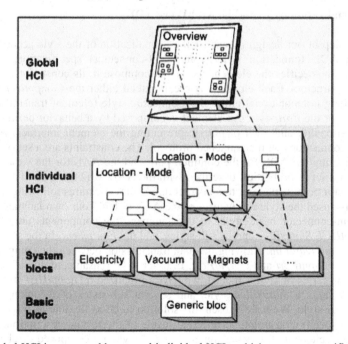

Fig. 3. A global HCI is composed by several individual HCIs, which represent specific parts of the accelerator restart process. These HCIs are composed by "system status" elements giving the state of the equipments essential for the accelerator operation. All these "system status" elements are created from a "status bloc" generic element.

- **global HCI:** this is the overview used in control rooms. The global HCI regroups all the individual HCIs. This HCI displays the status of all the systems required for the accelerator operation. The control room operators are then able to know all the time the status of the accelerator. If an operator wants to obtain more details on a specific part of the accelerator, the user interface gives him the possibility to navigate from the global HCI to the individual HCIs.

Moreover, the analysis step has permitted to list the structural and behavioral properties that the style has to specify. Here it is an example list of these properties and constraints:

- general graphical properties (elements size, color, position, layers, superposition, ...);
- elements position constrained by their functions (systems restart sequence);
- restart scenario properties;
- elements cardinality constraints (presence, redundancy,...);
- inter-element dependency constraints (loops, redundancy, ...);
- allowed states for a bloc;
- bloc inputs and outputs (controls, data types, ...);
- data processing constraints;
- dynamicity constraints;
- ...

3.2 Formalization by Using the ArchWare ADL

The next step of our design process is the formalization of the style according to the Archware-ADL foundation style (component-connector) specifications. The style formalization specifies the element styles that compose it, its constraints, its analysis and its constructors. Each element style can extend either the *Component* style (element making computations) either the *Connector* style (element transmitting an information) or the *Port* style. An element is composed by a behavior defining the element functionality and a set of ports representing the element interface. A port is a group of connections with an attached protocol. The constraints are a set of properties described using the ADL for the common part, and the AAL for the variant part. An analysis is a set of properties, described with the AAL, which is named and reusable. A constructor permits the user to construct quickly architectures following the style.

We have used the style mechanism of the ADL to build our own language from the component-connector basic style. In this language the components are *GlobalHCI*, *IndividualHCI*, *StatusBloc* and its sub-styles, and the *Equipment*. In the same way, the connectors are *DataLink* allowing the data transmission between the components, and the ports are *InputPort* and *OutputPort*. In order to be reusable, all these elements are described in terms of styles. Indeed, we have formalized a *GlobalHCI* style, an *IndividualHCI* style, a *StatusBloc* style, and several sub-styles of it, among them, the *SystemStatus* style. We have chosen this solution to be as flexible as possible, and to be able to specify constraints at different levels of the formal description. Then, the architectural elements following the *GlobalHCI* style are composed of elements following the *IndividualHCI* style. These elements are themselves composed by elements following the sub-styles of the *StatusBloc* style, which permit to display the status of the elements following the *Equipment* style.

We present here only some parts of the styles that we have formalized. They mainly show the way that the various elements of our architectures are organized. The ArchWare ADL and its foundation style make possible to define attributes for each architectural element. Considering the nature of our architectures (graphical applications), these attributes are very numerous, and it was not possible to describe them here. Most of the constraints listed in 3.1 are applied on such attributes, that is why their formalization is not in this paper.

The first extract of formal code concerns the definition of the *GlobalHCI* style (comments are provided after --):

```
GlobalHCI is style extending Component where {
```
-- The *GlobalHCI* style is built from the *Component* style.
```
  styles {
    IndividualHCI is style extending Component where {…}
  }
```
-- The *GlobalHCI* style is composed by elements following the *IndividualHCI*
-- style (described below), which is itself built from the *Component* style.
```
  constraints {
    to components apply {
      forall (c | c in style IndividualHCI)
```
      -- This constraint example specifies that the components used by a
      -- *GlobalHCI* can only be elements following the *IndividualHCI* style.
```
    }
  }
  analysis {…}
}
```

Other constraints are specified in the *GlobalHCI* style. For instance one concerns the graphical relative position of elements following the *IndividualHCI* style on an element following the *GlobalHCI* style.

A part of the *IndividualHCI* style formalization is presented here:

```
IndividualHCI is style extending Component where {
  Styles {                          .
    InputPort is style extending Port where {…}
    OutputPort is style extending Port where {…}
    Equipment is style extending Component where {…}
    StatusBloc is style extending Component where {…}
    MetaStatus is style extending StatusBloc where {…}
    SystemStatus is style extending StatusBloc where {…}
    DataLink is style extending Connector where {…}
  }
```

-- The *IndividualHCI* style is composed by elements following the styles listed
-- here and themselves built from the *Component*, *Connector*, and *Port* styles. Some
-- of these styles are detailed below.

```
constraints {
  to connectors apply {
    forall(c | c in style DataLink),
```
-- The connectors used by an *IndividualHCI* can only be elements following the
-- *DataLink* style.
```
    forall (l1,l2 | l1 in style DataLink and l2 in style
    DataLink implies not attached (l1,l2))
```
-- Two elements following the *DataLink* style cannot be attached together.
```
  }.
  to components apply {
    forall(c | c in style Equipment or c in style Status-
    Bloc or c in style MetaStatus or c in style System-
    Status),
```
-- The components used by an *IndividualHCI* can only be elements following the
-- *StatusBloc*, *MetaStatus*, or *SystemStatus* styles.
```
    forall(c1,c2 | c1 monitored by c2 implies
```
-- "*monitored by*" is an analysis described in the following section of the style
-- definition.
```
    (c1 in style Equipment and c2 in style SystemStatus)
    or
    (c1 in style Equipment and c2 in style StatusBloc)
```
-- This structural constraint example specifies that the components following the
-- *Equipment* style can be monitored only by components following the
-- *SystemStatus* or *StatusBloc* styles.
```
  }
  -- ...
}
analysis {
  monitored is AAL_property {
    parameters {
      bloc1 : AnyElement,
      bloc2 : AnyElement
    }
```
-- This AAL analysis example receives two inputs parameters.
```
    property {
      bloc1 in style Component.
      bloc2 in style Component.
```
-- If these parameters are elements of the *Component* style...

```
to bloc2.ports apply{
  exists(b2ip | b2ip in style InputPort and to con-
  nectors apply {
    exists (dl | to dl.ports apply {
      exists (dlin, dlout | dlin in style InputPort and
      dlout in style OutputPort and to bloc1.ports ap-
      ply {
        exists(blop | blop in style OutputPort and blop
        attached to dlin and dlout attached to b2ip)
      })
    })
  })
}
-- Check if an InputPort of the second element is connected to the OutputPort
-- of the first one via a Connector.
}
} mixfix (bloc1 monitored by bloc2)
-- The analysis is named in order to be easily usable in the constraint definitions as
-- in the previous example.
}
}
```

The next part concerns the *StatusBloc* component formalization. The *SystemStatus* and *MetaStatus* components are not described here, they are sub-styles of the *Status-Bloc* style. The elements following the *SystemStatus* style can only monitor data coming directly from elements following the *Equipment* style. In contrary, the elements following the *MetaStatus* style can monitor data coming from elements following all the other component styles. These constraints have to be specified in the *Individual-HCI* style.

```
StatusBloc is style extending Component where {
  Constraints {
    to ports apply {
      forall (p | p in style OutputPort xor p in style
      InputPort),
      -- This constraint specify that the ports used by a StatusBloc can only be
      -- elements following the OutputPort or InputPort styles.
      exists ([1]p | p in style OutputPort),
      -- This constraint specify that the StatusBloc components have only one
      -- OutputPort.
      exists([1..n]p | p in style InputPort)
      -- This constraint specify that the StatusBloc components have at least one
      -- InputPort.
    }
  }
}
```

In addition of the three constraints formalized here, it is necessary to define the internal computation of the elements following the various components styles.

The formalization of our specific connector style is defined below:

```
DataLink is style extending Connector where (
```
-- The *DataLink* style is built from the *Connector* style.
```
  constraints {
    to ports apply {
      forall (p | p in style OutputPort xor p in style
      InputPort),
```
      -- This constraints specify that the ports used by a *DataLink* can only be
      -- elements following the *OutputPort* or *InputPort* styles.
```
      exists ([1]p | p in style OutputPort),
```
      -- This constraints specify that the *DataLink* connectors have only one
      -- *OutputPort*.
```
      exists([1]p | p in style InputPort)
```
      -- This constraints specify that the *DataLink* connectors have only one
      -- *InputPort*.
```
    }
  }
}
```

Finally, here is the formalization of one of our specific port style, the *InputPort*. The *OutputPort* style is defined in the same way but with a constraint specifying that it cannot receive data.

```
InputPort is style extending Port where {
```
-- The *InputPort* style is built from the *Port* style.
```
  constraints {
    to connections apply {
      forall(c | every sequence{true*.via c send any} leads
      to state{false})
    }
```
      -- This constraint specifies that an *InputPort* has only connections for receiving
      -- data (every sequence including a data sending is impossible).
```
  }
}
```

This formalized style gives the way to produce a family of monitoring HCIs by providing the formal vocabulary to describe their common characteristics, the elements they consist of, the way in which they are arranged, and their behaviors. The exploitation of the style constitutes the steps 3 and 4 of our design process. These steps are achieved by the integration of the style in the software environment, which is the object of the next section.

3.3 Integration in the Software Environment

A first version of SEAM is currently available (cf. Figure 4). Using its graphical user interface, which gives the set of constructing elements, the operators or process specialists are able, without the assistance of programmers, to create monitoring HCIs. Indeed, after the HCIs specification, their XML code is automatically generated from the database. The HCIs are then usable by the SCADA software in control rooms. The HCIs specification and implementation are then easier than during the prototyping phase.

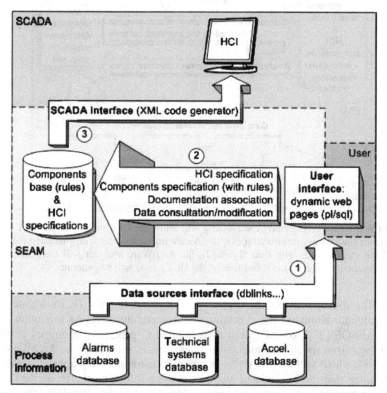

Fig. 4. The SEAM current architecture includes a graphical user interface allowing to browse and to use information coming from the different monitoring and maintenance data sources (1). This user interface is used to specify and store the data and the structural parameters of the monitoring HCIs in the SEAM components database (2). The XML code is then generated from this database (3).

This solution facilitates the design and the implementation of the HCIs, but does not comply with several of the main requirements listed in the introduction. Indeed, the current version of SEAM cannot guarantee the standardization of the generated HCIs, and it does not allow the specification and checking of all the constraints mentioned in 3.1. That is why the objective is now to integrate the formalized style in the SEAM software environment in order to exploit it (cf. Figure 5). In this solution, the user interface will be made of the ArchWare modeler [25] and the ArchWare anima-

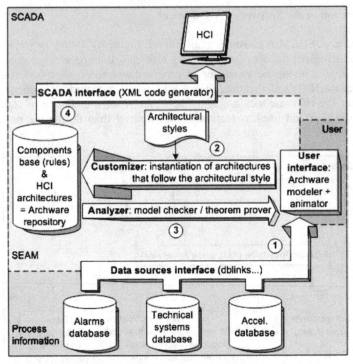

Fig. 5. SEAM future architecture: the modeler will allow the construction of the HCI's architectures from the process information (1); the Archware customizer will guarantee the accordance of the architectures with their styles (2); the ArchWare analyzer will then perform the needed style-specific analyses (3); and finally, the HCI's code will be generated (4).

tor [26]. The modeler allows the user to graphically define the HCI's architectures, and the animator simulates the execution of these architectures. As few other ADLs (such as AESOP [27]), σπ-ADL will soon be able to generate customized graphical environments from specific architectural styles. This is the role of the ArchWare customizer [28], which will use the styles in order to customize the graphical modeler. It will guarantee that the instantiated architectures are following the predefined styles, like those presented in the previous section. This functionality simplifies the specification of valid HCI's architectures. These instantiated architectures will then be stored in the ArchWare components repository. The role of the ArchWare analyzer is to perform style-specific analyses [29][30]. These analyses guarantee coherence, on the one hand, between the monitoring HCIs themselves, and on the other hand, between the HCIs and their reference style. The final step of our design process is the HCIs code generation performed from the validated architectures thus obtained.

4 Conclusions and Future Work

In this paper we have shown how the development of a family of accelerator restart monitoring HCIs can be achieved by the use of software architecture techniques.

Indeed, these techniques, one of which is the use of an architectural style, are particularly efficient to promote design reuse and to assure the satisfaction of user requirements. We have now to upgrade our architectural development environment by adding the ArchWare tools, and to validate the architectural approach including our domain-specific style by producing the monitoring applications for each of the CERN particle accelerators. Thus, the objectives listed in the introduction will be achieved: the design of the prototypes will be reused; the HCIs implementation will be facilitated; the generated HCIs will be standardized and they will verify complex predefined properties. Regarding the management of the evolution of the HCI's model according to the evolution of the accelerator restart process, a first solution is being implemented. This solution is to analyze the process evolution via the monitoring of the changes applied on the related HCI's architectures. The reference style can then be upgraded according to these analyzed evolutions.

This work will validate the architectural-oriented techniques in our specific case, which will be useful for the designers of HCIs for the monitoring of any process, like in industrial production or energy production and distribution domains. Indeed, contrary to SEAM, traditional commercial HCI editors do not provide a style-based development guide allowing the user to implement a set of HCIs following all the needed structural and behavioral properties. Nevertheless, defining and respecting these properties is an essential point to obtain coherent, relevant, and exploitable monitoring information. One of the next objectives is to generalize our architectural style in order to be able to produce the restart monitoring HCIs for any particle accelerator type. This generalized style will then be a basis for the definition of styles for the monitoring   of any process. The overall approach including the definition and the exploitation of an architectural style is not only useful for the development of a set of monitoring HCI, but also for the development of a set of applications in any activity field.

References

1. M. Bätz, An Engineering Method for the Monitoring for Accelerator Equipment and Technical Infrastructure, CERN, 2002.
2. O. Ratcliffe, SEAM User Requirements Document, CERN, 2002.
3. M. Boasson, The Artistry of Software Architecture, Guest editor's introduction, IEEE Software, 1995.
4. L. Bass, P. Clements, and R. Kazman, Software Architecture in Practice, Addison-Wesley, 1997.
5. D. Garlan, M. Shaw, C. Okasaki, C. Scott, and R. Swonger, Experiences with a Course on Architectures for Software Systems, Proceedings of the 6th SEI Conference on Software Engineering Education, 1992.
6. D.E. Perry, and A.L. Wolf, Foundations for the Study of Software Architecture, ACM SIGSOFT Software Engineering Notes, vol. 17, no. 4, 1992.
7. Rapide Design Team, Guide to the Rapide 1.0 Language Reference Manuals, Technical report. Stanforf University, 1997.
8. R. Upchurch, Perspective Foundations: Where does architecture fit in the life-cycle?, 1995.
9. G. Abowd, R. Allen, and D. Garlan, Using style to give meaning to software architectures, Proc SIGSOFT'93: Foundations Eng., ACM, New York, 1993.
10. A. Abd-Allah, Composing Heterogeneous Software Architecture, Doctoral Dissertation, Center for Software Engineering, University of Southern California, 1996.

11. D. Garlan, What is Style, Proceedings of Dagshtul Workshop on Software Architecture, 1995.
12. R. Allen, Formalism and Informalism in Software Architectural Style: a Case Study, Proceedings of the First International Workshop on Architectures for Software Systems, 1995.
13. R.T. Monroe, D. Kompanek, R. Melton, and D. Garlan, Stylized Architecture, Design Patterns, and Objects, 1996.
14. F. Leymonerie, S. Cîmpan, F. Oquendo, Extension d'un langage de description architecturale pour la prise en compte des styles architecturaux : application à J2EE. Proceedings of the 14th International Conference on Software and Systems Engineering and their Applications. Paris, December 2001.
15. R. Allen, HLA: A Standards Effort as Architectural Style, Proceedings of the Second International Software Architecture Workshop (ISAW2), 1996.
16. F. Leymonerie, S. Cîmpan, F. Oquendo, État de l'art sur les styles architecturaux : classification et comparaison des langages de description d'architectures logicielles, Revue Génie Logiciel, No. 62, Septembre 2002.
17. D. Garlan, R. Allen, and J. Ockerbloom, Exploiting Style in Architectural Design Environments, Proceedings of SIGSOFT '94 Symposium on the Foundations of Software Engineering, 1994.
18. F. Oquendo, I. Alloui, S. Cîmpan, H. Verjus, The ArchWare Architecture Description Language: Abstract Syntax and Formal Semantics. Deliverable D1.1b, ArchWare European RTD Project, IST-2001-32360, December 2002.
19. S. Cîmpan, F. Oquendo, D. Balasubramaniam, G. Kirby and R. Morrison, The ArchWare Architecture Description Language: Textual Concrete Syntax. Deliverable D1.2b, ArchWare European RTD Project, IST-2001-32360, December 2002.
20. S. Cîmpan, F. Leymonerie, F. Oquendo, The ArchWare Foundation Styles Library. Report R1.3-1, ArchWare European RTD Project, IST-2001-32360, June 2003.
21. J. Revillard, E. Benoit, S. Cîmpan, F. Oquendo, Software Architecture for Intelligent Instrument Design, Proceedings of the 16th International Conference on Software and Systems Engineering and their Applications (ICSSEA'03), Paris, France, December 2003.
22. F. Oquendo et al., Positioning ArchWare ADL w.r.t. the State of the Art, ArchWare European RTD Project, IST-2001-32360, December 2002.
23. R. Milner, J. Parrow and D. Walker, A Calculus of Mobile Processes, Information and Computation, pp 1-40, 1992.
24. I. Alloui, H. Garavel, R. Mateescu, F. Oquendo, The ArchWare Architecture Analysis Language: Syntax and Semantics. Deliverable D3.1b, ArchWare European RTD Project, IST-2001-32360, January 2003.
25. C. Occhipinti, C. Zavattari, Preliminary ArchWare Architecture Modeller, ArchWare European RTD Project, IST-2001-32360,, Deliverable D2.1a, 2003.
26. H. Verjus, F. Pourraz, S. Azzaiez, Final ArchWare Architecture Animator – Release 1 – Prototype, ArchWare European RTD Project, IST-2001-32360, Deliverable D2.2b, 2003.
27. D. Garlan, A. Kompanek, R. Melton, R. Monroe, Architectural Style: An Object-Oriented Approach (Aesop), Carnegie Mellon University, Pittsburgh, 1996.
28. F. Leymonerie et al., The Style-Based Customizer – Release 1, ArchWare European RTD Project, IST-2001-32360, Deliverable D2.4a, 2003.
29. D. Le Berre et al., Preliminary ArchWare Architecture Analysis Tool by Theorem-Proving – Prototype, ArchWare European RTD Project, IST-2001-32360, Deliverable D3.5a, 2003.
30. F. Leymonerie et al., Preliminary ArchWare Architecture Analysis Tool by Model-Specific Evaluation – Prototype, ArchWare European RTD Project, IST-2001-32360, Deliverable D3.7a, 2003.

Experiences Using Viewpoints
for Information Systems Architecture:
An Industrial Experience Report

Eóin Woods

Artechra Limited
Hamilton House, 6th Floor, 111 Marlowes,
Hemel Hempstead, HP1 3HY, UK
eoin.woods@artechra.com

Abstract. There has recently been an increase in interest, among information systems architecture practitioners, in using viewpoints for architectural definition and description. This has been caused by a number of factors including the publication of IEEE standard 1471 and the increasing adoption of RUP (and its "4+1" viewpoint set). This short experience report outlines the experiences that two software architects have had in evaluating and applying a number of viewpoint sets to information systems development. The strengths and weaknesses found with each viewpoint set are described and some general observations on viewpoint set use and definition are presented.

Introduction and Motivation

As a practicing software architect, I am always interested in techniques that can help to manage the complexity of the architectural design process. Most architects would agree that architecture is a many-faceted discipline and developing a successful software architecture involves considering a lot of different system structures simultaneously. This means that using more than one model to capture your architecture is an intuitively appealing approach and many practicing architects do appear to do this informally. Certainly the software architecture research community appears to have decided that representing architectural designs via a number of related models (or "views") is the only way to do it.

Having said this, if we use a number of models to represent our architectural designs then we need some sort of framework to organize the work and its deliverables, so that the approach doesn't become too unwieldy and disorganized to use.

Some time ago, along with another colleague, I came across IEEE standard 1471 [5] (a standard for architectural description), which was then about to be published. It seemed obvious to us that the view and viewpoint based approach defined in the standard had the potential to help us organize the architectural design efforts of our clients and ourselves. We had also previously come across Phillippe Kruchten's well known "4+1" viewpoint set [7] and we started to further investigate its application to our work.

Researching further, we discovered a number of other viewpoint sets including the Siemens set [4], the RM-ODP set [6] and (much more recently) the Garland and Anthony set [3].

F. Oquendo et al. (Eds.): EWSA 2004, LNCS 3047, pp. 182–193, 2004.
© Springer-Verlag Berlin Heidelberg 2004

We assessed and trialled these viewpoint sets as part of our normal work, considering their application to a number of situations including enterprise and Internet security products, systems integration programmes, and bespoke in-house systems. This process has lead to a number of observations about particular sets of viewpoints and about viewpoint sets in general, and this short paper explains these observations.

The common characteristic across all of our applications of viewpoints is that they are information-oriented systems rather than control systems, and this should be borne in mind when considering our observations.

Our Use of Viewpoints

Views are obviously a useful way of structuring an architectural description (the documentation of the architecture) but in their simplistic form, they are little more than an approach to document organization; ideally an approach based around a set of formal viewpoint definitions should provide us with more than this. In fact, the authors of IEEE 1471 appear to have had more a more ambitious target when they standardized the viewpoint based approach.

From the text of the standard, we find that a viewpoint is a specification of the conventions for constructing and using a view; a viewpoint acts as a pattern or template from which to develop individual views by establishing the purposes and audience for a view and the techniques for its creation and analysis.

Importantly, this definition makes it clear that a viewpoint is not just the name of a section of a document but is a guide for those who which to create views that comply to the viewpoint, explaining how and why the view is to be created.

We feel that a well-defined set of viewpoints has the potential to be applied as:

- A *description* of a particular approach to software architecture.
- A *store* of experience, advice and best practice for a particular aspect of software architecture.
- A *guide* for the novice architect or the architect who is working in an unfamiliar domain (as happens to us all from time to time), who will in all probability be working alone without an expert architect to guide them.
- An *aide-memoir* for the experienced architect, that they can use to avoid overlooking important aspects of the design process, particularly when considering the areas of the architecture that the architect is not an expert in.

We have attempted to consider all of these possible uses of viewpoints as we have applied and assessed them for our work.

Experiences with the Viewpoint Sets

"4+1" Viewpoint Set

When we first starting using architectural views, we started by using the "4+1" set originally defined by Philippe Kruchten and now forming part of the Rational Unified Process [8]. The viewpoints contained in the original set are briefly described in Table 1.

Table 1. 4+1 Viewpoint Catalog.

Viewpoint	Description
Logical	Logical representation of the system's functional structure. Normally presumed to be a class model (in an object-oriented systems development context).
Process	The concurrency and synchronization aspects of the architecture (process and thread model, synchronization approach etc.)
Development	The design time software structure, identifying modules, subsystems and layers and the concerns directly related to software development.
Physical	The identification of the nodes that the system's software will be executed on and the mapping of other architectural elements to these nodes.

We found the strengths of this viewpoint set to be:

- The set is simple, logical and easy to explain. We found that colleagues, clients and stakeholders understood the set with very little explanation.
- The set is quite generic and seems a suitable base to use for describing information system architectures.
- The viewpoint set is really independent of notation, but is normally used in conjunction with UML, which is widely understood and supported.
- The set of viewpoints defined aligns quite well with existing models that architects build and so it is quite an intuitive set to use straight away.
- This appears to be the oldest viewpoint set and is widely known, discussed and supported (partially due to its inclusion in the RUP "architectural profile").

Problems we found when using this viewpoint set were:

- It is difficult to find a good definition of these viewpoints. The original paper only provides outlines of their expected content and we haven't found other fuller definitions in easily accessible sources. This leads to confusion when the viewpoints are applied, with every architect creating different content for each view. The (proprietary) Rational Unified Process product does provide more information on the views but still doesn't define them in a level of detail that we felt that we needed (for example, the Logical View is defined in about 2 pages).
- We found the names of the viewpoints quite problematic:
  - The term "*process*" tended to suggest business process modeling, which caused confusion when people found that the view contains an operating system concurrency model.
  - The terms "*logical*" and "*physical*" aren't terribly descriptive and different people interpret them in different ways.
- The viewpoint set does not explicitly address data or operational concerns. Both of these aspects of a large information system are important enough to warrant their own view (and more importantly guidance relating to these aspects of developing an architecture needs to be captured somewhere).[1]

---

[1] Interestingly Rational appear to, at least partially, agree with us, as they have recently added an optional "Data" viewpoint to the set defined in the Rational Unified Process and renamed "Physical" as "Deployment" (as well as renaming "Development" as "Implementation" which we don't think is as important). Other authors (notably Scott Ambler) have also identified the need for operational considerations to be addressed and have extended RUP to meet these needs [1].

- There is no associated set of cross-viewpoint consistency rules defined for the set (at least we were not able to find such a set).

As a basis for system implementation, architectural descriptions based on this viewpoint set have proved to be quite effective. The views can include most of the information needed to support software development and the Development view can act as an effective bridge between architecture and implementation. The main limitation from the software developer's point of view is the lack of a single place to refer to for an understanding of the system's underlying information structure.

In summary, this viewpoint set appeared to be aimed at the area that we were interested in, although the coverage was not as wide as we would have liked. However we found the lack of readily available, thorough, viewpoint definitions to be an obstacle to initial use of the set by our clients and ourselves. That said, we've had a lot of success applying our interpretations of these viewpoints to our information systems architecture problems.

RM-ODP Viewpoint Set

The Reference Model for Open Distributed Processing (RM-ODP) is an ISO standard framework for describing and discussing distributed systems technology [6]. The framework is defined using a set of five viewpoints, briefly described in Table 2.

Table 2. RM-ODP Viewpoint Catalog.

Viewpoint	Description
Enterprise	Defines the context for the system and allows capture and organization of requirements.
Information	Describes the information required by the system using static, invariant and dynamic schemas.
Computational	Contains an object-oriented model of the functional structure of the system, with a particular focus on interfaces and interactions.
Engineering	Describes the systems infrastructure required to implement the desired distribution of the system's elements. This description is performed using a specific reference model.
Technology	Defines the specific technology that will be used to build the system.

While the RM-ODP approach provides an appealing partitioning of the architectural description, it was actually created to support distributed systems standardization efforts and (as its name suggests) imposes a reference model on the systems being described.

We found the strengths of this viewpoint set to be:

- The structure of the viewpoint set is logical and reasonably easy to explain (although the "Engineering" viewpoint isn't terribly well named).
- The viewpoint set is aimed at distributed information systems.
- The viewpoint set includes an explicit consideration of data architecture via the "Information" viewpoint.

- The viewpoint set is an ISO standard and so is widely accessible and appears to have been widely discussed in the distributed systems research community.

Concerns we had with regards to this viewpoint set were:

- We couldn't find much evidence of this viewpoint set being used by architecture practitioners.
- A particular set of architectural assumptions appears to have been made when defining the viewpoints. In particular, the "Computational" and "Engineering" viewpoints seem to assume that a distributed object system is being created and specify a particular set of primitives that should be used to describe these views.
- A number of the viewpoints appear to assume that RM-ODP's own modeling notations will be used to describe them (which aren't widely understood or supported by tools).
- The viewpoint set doesn't address operational concerns.
- The definition of the viewpoints is quite daunting to approach.
- There doesn't appear to be a set of cross-viewpoint consistency rules available.

We had quite a few concerns as to how effective an RM-ODP based architectural description would be as a basis for implementation. Implementation isn't mentioned much in the RM-ODP literature and even the more tutorial material we found (such as [9]) seemed rather vague on the subject of how the RM-ODP based description would drive the software development process. There is also the problem that many systems aren't created as distributed object systems that would be compliant with the meta-model that appears to be assumed in RM-ODP's Engineering viewpoint. None of this is to say that RM-ODP architectural descriptions couldn't drive software development effectively, but it isn't clear how to do from the material that we could find to refer to. Of course, if a framework that directly implemented RM-ODP's meta-models were available, this could resolve the problem and make RM-ODP a very attractive approach.

Overall, this viewpoint set initially appeared to be very promising, having an intuitive structure and seemingly being aimed at the kind of systems that we are interested in building. However, further investigation suggested that this viewpoint set is quite specialized and perhaps really aimed at supporting standards efforts rather than mainstream information-systems-architecture definition.

Siemens Viewpoint Set

While working at Siemens Research, Christine Hofmeister, Robert Nord and Dilip Soni developed a set of four architectural viewpoints based upon the way that Siemens' software development teams actually operated. The viewpoints in this set are briefly described in Table 3.

We found the strengths of this viewpoint set to be:

- The viewpoints are clearly defined in the very readable primary reference [4].
- Again, this seems to be a logical viewpoint set that can be explained and remembered easily.
- The viewpoints use UML as their modeling notation, which is widely understood and supported.

Table 3. Siemens Viewpoint Catalog.

Viewpoint	Description
Conceptual	The conceptual functional structure of the system.
Module	Defines the subsystems and modules that will be realized in the system, the interfaces exposed by the modules, the inter-module dependencies and any layering constraints in the structure.
Execution	The runtime structure of the system in terms of processes, threads, inter-process communication elements and so on along with a mapping of modules to runtime elements.
Code	The design time layout of the system as source code and the binary elements that are created from it.

- The viewpoints are based directly upon Siemens industrial practice, which gives them some immediate credibility from a practitioner's point of view.
- The viewpoint definitions include tasks required to create them, modeling advice to follow, and common problems ("issues") along with possible solutions to them.

Factors that we found limiting when applying this viewpoint set were:

- The viewpoints are obviously aimed at software engineers working on control systems. The examples and advice in the definitions are control-system rather than information-system centric.
- The deployment, operational and data aspects of the architecture aren't addressed by the viewpoints defined. This makes perfect sense in the control systems environment (as these concerns aren't as relevant or are someone else's problem) but this does limit their application to information systems.
- There is no mention of the applicability of the viewpoints for communication with different stakeholder groups. We suspect that these viewpoints are all aimed at the development team rather than any wider constituency of stakeholders. Again, this may be less of a problem for the architecture of control systems than information systems.
- There is some guidance provided for achieving consistency via traceability rules, but there isn't really a set of clear cross-viewpoint consistency rules.

Architectural descriptions based on this viewpoint set are likely to be a strong basis for system implementation, provided that the system is broadly in the control or real-time systems domain. The Code view forms a good bridge to implementation and all of the aspects of a functionally oriented system, that are important to a developer, can be easily addressed using the other views.

Garland and Anthony Viewpoint Set

Jeff Garland and Richard Anthony are practicing software architects who have recently written a practitioner-oriented guide to software architecture for information systems. In their book they define a viewpoint set aimed at large-scale information systems architecture [3]. Their viewpoints are briefly described in Table 4.

Table 4. Garland and Anthony Viewpoint Catalog.

Viewpoint	Description
Analysis Focused	Illustrates how the elements of the system work together in response to a functional usage scenario.
Analysis Interaction	Interaction diagram used during problem analysis.
Analysis Overall	Consolidation of the contents of all of the Analysis Focused view contents into a single model.
Component	Defines the system's architecturally significant components and their connections.
Component Interaction	Illustrates how the components interact in order to make the system work.
Component State	The state model(s) for a component or set of closely related components.
Context	Defines the context that the system exists within, in terms of external actors and their interactions with the system.
Deployment	Shows how software components are mapped to hardware entities in order to be executed.
Layered Subsystem	Illustrates the subsystems to be implemented and the layers in the software design structure.
Logical Data	Logical view of architecturally significant data structure.
Physical Data	Physical view of architecturally significant data structure.
Process	The runtime concurrency structure (operating system processes that the system's components will be packaged into and IPC mechanisms).
Process State	State transition model for the system's processes.
Subsystem Interface Dependency	The dependencies that exist between subsystems and the interfaces of other subsystems.

This viewpoint set was published fairly recently and so we haven't been able to give them as much consideration as we have given the others over time (and we haven't considered their application to a real system). However, this set looks particularly promising for information systems.

We found the strengths of this viewpoint set to be:

- This set of viewpoints is aimed directly at information systems architects and so tries to address their needs directly.
- The viewpoints are all small and focused, with the content and the use of the viewpoint being immediately apparent.
- The viewpoints are quite thoroughly defined, with purpose, applicability, stakeholder interest, models to use, modeling scalability and advice on creating the views all presented. In most cases there is also guidance provided that often includes potential problems to be aware of.
- The viewpoints defined address data explicitly (via the Logical Data and Physical Data viewpoints).
- The viewpoints are all defined using UML as the primary modeling notation, which is widely understood and supported.

Problems we found when using this viewpoint set were:

- There are a lot of viewpoints in the set (14) and so the set can be quite unwieldy to explain and use.
- Many of the viewpoints are relevant to a large or complex system, and so there appears to be a real danger of the architectural description becoming fragmented. We take Garland and Anthony's point that you should only apply the viewpoints relevant to a particular system, but you should do this when applying any viewpoint set, and we feel that for many systems you will end up with quite a few viewpoints when using this set.
- There aren't any consistency rules defined for inter-view consistency. The other viewpoint sets don't tend to have these either but they seem all the more important when you many end up with 14 views.

Architectural descriptions based on this viewpoint set are likely to be a strong basis for information system implementation. Provided that the developers are prepared to understand a number of different views, the information that they require (including logical and physical data structure) can all be represented using views from this set. In addition, the Layered Subsystem view provides a bridge to implementation, which is well defined in the viewpoint definition (in [3]).

Overall, this viewpoint set is probably closest to the ideal set that we were searching for. Having said this, because it is a new set we haven't spent all that much time working with it. However, given that the set is well defined, based on practical experience and aimed at information systems, it appears to have a lot of potential for application to large information systems. The major concerns we have are explaining 14 viewpoints to anyone and creating a coherent, consistent architectural definition with a significant subset of this many parts.

Other Viewpoint Sets

Other viewpoint sets exist (such as Dana Bredemeyer's set) that we haven't talked about here, because we haven't spent enough time working with them and considering them to have informed opinions on their utility. We also probably aren't aware of all of the sets that exist.

Dana Bredemeyer's viewpoint set is potentially very relevant to our area of concern, being aimed at enterprise information systems development. It comprises Structural and Behavioral variants of Conceptual, Logical and Execution viewpoints (making 6 viewpoints in all). However, we aren't aware of any publicly available reference source for this viewpoint set (the normal source being Bredemeyer Inc.'s training courses) and this makes it difficult to research the viewpoint set further.

One other interesting set that is worth mentioning, is the set of "view types" introduced in [2]. We are aware of these view types and deliberately don't discuss them as a separate set of viewpoints, because their focus appears to be capturing knowledge and advice related to documenting an architecture rather than actually creating it. We have found the advice in this text to be credible and valuable, but it appears to be relevant irrespective of the viewpoint set in use, rather than being a definition of a new set of viewpoints.

General Observations

Having attempted the application of a number of viewpoint sets to the architectural design of information systems, we have made to a couple of general observations about the approach that are independent of the specifics of a viewpoint set. These observations are summarized below.

- *Viewpoints Are an Effective Approach.* We have found viewpoints to be a very effective approach to the problem of organizing the architectural design process and capturing its results (the architectural description). We have found viewpoints to be useful for both novice architects (as a guide) as well as by experts (as a set of aide-memoirs). We have found that a number of viewpoint sets can be very effective for information systems architecture, with the "4+1" and "Garland and Anthony" sets showing particular promise for further refinement and use.
- *Good Viewpoint Sets.* We have found that all of the viewpoint sets we have reviewed are coherent, logical and appear to be well thought out. In reality, it appears that they could all be applied successfully and this bodes well for the general acceptance of the approach.
- *No Standard Viewpoint Definitions.* A constant challenge when trying to understand new viewpoint sets was the fact that there is little standardization between the viewpoint set definitions in the published literature. We found that this meant that it was hard to compare viewpoint sets without a lot of analysis and that starting to use a new viewpoint set can be difficult.
- *General Lack of Cross-Viewpoint Consistency Rules.* In the viewpoint sets that we have reviewed and used, we have generally found a lack of cross-viewpoint consistency rules. Given the inherent fragmentation, that a view based approach to architectural description implies, this seems strange. Our experience is that cross-viewpoint consistency is a significant challenge and that even a simple set of rules helps architects to keep their views consistent, particularly when they are inexperienced with a viewpoint set.
- *Suggested Standard Viewpoint Content.* Based on our experience of trying to apply viewpoint sets, we would suggest that a viewpoint definition should contain:
  - *Concerns* that the view should address.
  - The *Stakeholders* that are likely to be interested in the view (and the reason for their interest) so that the architect can cater to them.
  - The *Activities* to perform to create the view, with guidance on performing each activity.
  - The set of *Models* (or other content) that can appear in the view, with guidance on creating each type.
  - Common *Pitfalls* that the architect should be aware of when creating the view, with pointers to possible solutions for them.

It is worth noting that this content is compliant with IEEE 1471, as the standard states that a viewpoint definition includes stakeholders; concerns; modeling language and modeling techniques; (and optionally) consistency tests; analysis techniques; and heuristics to guide successful view creation.

We would also suggest that the definition of a viewpoint set should also include:

- An *overall model* of how the views are used to represent an architecture (in other words an overview of what goes where and the rationale for this organization).
- A set of *consistency rules* to allow cross-view consistency to be assessed.
- A *presentation* that can serve both a novice architect looking for guidance and an experienced architect needing an aide-memoir. (Realistically, this is likely to imply a hybrid presentation that includes explanation coupled with reference material such as checklists and summary tables.)

Further Work

After initial work with the available viewpoint sets (at that time, "4+1", Siemens and RM-ODP) we decided that we needed a fully defined, information system centric, viewpoint set to use ourselves and with our clients. We felt that such a set would be useful for teaching, consultancy, mentoring and during practice.

In response to our need, we designed such a set as a clear evolution of the "4+1" set, which appeared to provide the best basis to work from. The aim of this paper is to compare other people's viewpoint sets rather than to introduce another, but the brief descriptions in Table 5 give a flavour of the content of the set.

Table 5. Proposed Information Systems Viewpoint Catalog.

Viewpoint	Description
Functional	Describes the system's runtime functional elements, their responsibilities, interfaces and primary interactions
Information	Describes the way that the architecture stores, manipulates, manages, and distributes information (including content, structure, ownership, latency, references, and data migration).
Concurrency	Describes the concurrency structure of the system, and maps functional elements to concurrency units to clearly identify the parts of the system that can execute concurrently and how this is coordinated and controlled.
Development	Describes the constraints that the architecture places on the software development process.
Deployment	Describes the environment into which the system will be deployed, capturing the hardware environment, the technical environment requirements for each element and the mapping of the software elements to the runtime environment that will execute them.
Operational	Describes how the system will be operated, administered and supported when it is running in its production environment. For all but the smallest simplest systems, installing, managing and operating the system is a significant task that must be considered and planned at design time.

We also decided to follow our own advice and define some consistency rules that can be used to help check a view set for consistency. Some example consistency checks between the Functional and Development views are shown in Table 6.

Table 6. Example Consistency Checks.

1	Does the code module structure include all of the functional elements that need to be developed?
2	Does the Development View specify a development environment for each of the technologies used by the Functional View?
3	If the Functional View specifies the use of a particular architectural style, does the Development View include sufficient guidelines and constraints to ensure correct implementation of the style?
4	Where common processing is specified, can it be implemented in a straightforward manner over all of the elements defined in the Functional View?
5	Where reusable functional elements can be identified from the Functional View, are these modeled as libraries or similar features in the Development View?
6	If a test environment has been specified, does it meet the functional needs and priorities of the elements defined in the Functional View?
7	Can the functional structure described in the Functional View be built, tested and released reliably using the codeline described in the Development View?

While these checks aren't complex or terribly sophisticated, they do reflect the sorts of mistakes that we all make when creating architectural descriptions and aim to help architects – particularly those inexperienced with the viewpoint set – to avoid the most common mistakes. The rules also help those using the viewpoint set to improve their understanding of it and help to resolve confusions about the role of each viewpoint.

We are currently completing the development of this viewpoint set (along with further work to help architects address quality properties for their systems) and hope to publish this work during 2004.

Acknowledgements

The work described here has been performed with Nick Rozanski, an IT architect with the French-Thornton Partnership in London, UK.

References

1. Ambler S., Constantine L.: The Unified Process Transition and Production Phases, CMP Books (2001). See also http://www.enterpriseunifiedprocess.info.
2. Clements P., Bachmann F., Bass L., Garlan D., Ivers J., Little R., Nord R., Stafford J.: Documenting Software Architectures, Addison Wesley (2003).
3. Garland J., Anthony R.: Large Scale Software Architecture, John Wiley (2003).
4. Hofmeister, C., Nord, R., and Soni, D.: Applied Software Architecture, Addison Wesley (1999).

5. Recommended Practice for Architectural Description: IEEE Std-1471-2000, IEEE Computer Society (2000).
6. Reference Model for Open Distributed Processing: International Standard 10746-1, ITU Recommendation X.901, International Standards Organization (1996).
7. Kruchten P.: Architectural Blueprints – The 4+1 View Model of Software Architecture, Software, Vol. 12, Number 6, IEEE (1995).
8. Kruchten P.: The Rational Unified Process: An Introduction, Second Edition, Addison Wesley (2000).
9. Putman J.: Architecting with RM-ODP, Prentice Hall PTR (2001).

Software Architecture: The Next Step

Jan Bosch

University of Groningen, Department of Computing Science
PO Box 800, 9700 AV Groningen, The Netherlands
Jan.Bosch@cs.rug.nl
http://segroup.cs.rug.nl

Abstract. This position paper makes the following claims that, in our opinion, are worthwhile to discuss at the workshop. 1) The first phase of software architecture research, where the key concepts are components and connectors, has matured the technology to a level where industry adoption is wide-spread and few fundamental issues remain. 2) The traditional view on software architecture suffers from a number of key problems that cannot be solved without changing our perspective on the notion of software architecture. These problems include the lack of first-class representation of design decisions, the fact that these design decisions are cross-cutting and intertwined, that these problems lead to high maintenance cost, because of which design rules and constraints are easily violated and obsolete design decisions are not removed. 3) As a community, we need to take the next step and adopt the perspective that a software architecture is, fundamentally, a composition of architectural design decisions. These design decisions should be represented as first-class entities in the software architecture and it should, at least before system deployment, be possible to add, remove and change architectural design decisions against limited effort.

Introduction

For those that have followed the emergence of the notion of software architecture over the last decade or more, the field must have represented a classical example of technology innovation. Although references to the concept of software architecture were made earlier, the paper of Perry and Wolf [4] formed the starting point for an evolving community that actively studied the notion and practical application of software architecture. In the years to follow, software architecture was broadly adopted in industry as well as in the software engineering research community. Today, virtually all conferences in the field of software engineering mention software architecture as a topic of interest and in industry is the role of software architect well established.

The definition of software architecture, although for a long time an issue of lively debate, has been concluded (for now) with the adoption of the IEEE 1471 standard that defines software architecture as the fundamental organization of a system embodied in its components, their relationships to each other and to the environment and the principles guiding its design and evolution [2]. With this definition, the component and the connector are reinforced as the central concepts of software architecture.

The research in the area of software architecture, including workshops, e.g. the ISAW series, conferences, e.g. the WICSA series, special issues of journals and

F. Oquendo et al. (Eds.): EWSA 2004, LNCS 3047, pp. 194–199, 2004.
© Springer-Verlag Berlin Heidelberg 2004

books, has focused on the careful design, description and assessment of software architecture. Although some attention has been paid to evolution of software architecture, the key challenge of the software architecture community has been that software architectures need to be designed carefully because changing the software architecture of a system after its initial design is typically very costly. Many publications refer to changes with architectural impact as the main consequence to avoid. Interestingly, software architecture research, almost exclusively, focuses on this aspect of the problem. Very little research addresses the flip side of the problem, i.e. how can we design, represent and manage software architectures in such a way that the effort required for changes to the software architecture of existing systems can be substantially reduced. As we know that software architectures will change, independent of how carefully we design them, this aspect of the problem is of particular interest to the community.

To reduce the effort in changing the architecture of existing software systems it is necessary to understand why this is so difficult. Our studies into design erosion and analysis of this problem, e.g. [1] and [3], have led us to believe that the key problem is knowledge vaporization. Virtually all knowledge and information concerning the results of domain analysis, architectural styles used in the system, selected design patterns and all other design decisions taken during the architectural design of the system are embedded and implicitly present in the resulting software architecture, but lack a first-class representation. The design decisions are cross-cutting and intertwining at the level at which we currently describe software architectures, i.e. components and connectors. The consequence is twofold. First, the knowledge of the design decisions that lead to the architecture is quickly lost. Second, changes to the software architecture during system evolution easily cause violation of earlier design decisions, causing increased design erosion.

The message of this position paper is twofold. First, we claim that the traditional software architecture research addressing the components and connectors has matured and disseminated to industry to an extent that diminishes the relevance of further research in this domain. The first phase of software architecture research has, in this sense, ended. Second, this does not mean that research in software architecture is finalized. Instead, we need to fundamentally change our view on software architecture. Rather than components and connectors, we need to model and represent a software architecture as the composition a set of architectural design decisions, concerning, among others, the domain models, architectural solutions, variation points, features and usage scenarios that are needed to satisfy the requirements. Once we are able to represent software architectures, in several phases of the lifecycle, in terms of the aforementioned concepts, changing and evolving software architectures will be considerably simplified.

The remainder of the position paper is organized as follows. In the next section, we discuss the problems of the current perspective on software architecture. Subsequently, we present what in our opinion should be the future perspective on software architecture. Then, we present the concept of an architectural design decision and architectural fragment. Finally, the paper is concluded with a short summary of our position and statements.

Problems of Software Architecture

Software architecture has become a generally accepted concept in research as well as industry. The importance of stressing the components and their connectors of a software system is generally recognized and has lead to better control over the design, development and evolution of large and increasingly dynamic software systems.

Although the achievements of the software architecture research community are admirable, we should not let ourselves believe that no issues remain in this area. In this section, we present a set of problems that we feel are of particular importance to be addressed in the next phase of software architecture research. The discussion of these problems is organized around the concept of an architecture design decision. We define an architecture design decision as consisting of a restructuring effect on the components and connectors that make up the software architecture, design rules imposed on the architecture (and resulting system) as a consequence of the design decision, design constraints imposed on the architecture and a rationale explaining the reasoning behind the decision. In our definition, the restructuring effect includes the splitting, merging and reorganization of components, but also additional interfaces and required functionality that is demanded from components. For instance, when a design decision is taken to use an object-oriented database, all components and objects that require persistence need to support the interface demanded by the database management system. Architecture design decisions may be concerned with the application domain of the system, the architectural styles and patterns used in the system, COTS components and other infrastructure selections as well as other aspects needed to satisfy all requirements.

The problems that are inherently present in the current definition of software architecture and insufficiently addressed by the research community are the following:

- **Lack of first-class representation**: Architecture design decisions lack a first class representation in the software architecture. Once a number of design decisions is taken, the effect of individual decisions is implicitly present, but almost impossible to identify in the resulting architecture. Consequently, the knowledge about the "what and how" of the software architecture is quickly lost. Some architecture design methods stress the importance of documenting architecture design decisions, but experience shows that this documentation often is difficult to interpret and use by individuals not involved in the initial design of the system.
- **Design decisions cross-cutting and intertwined**: Architecture design decisions typically are cross-cutting the architecture, i.e. affect multiple components and connectors, and often become intimately intertwined with other design decisions.
- **High cost of change**: A consequent problem is that a software architecture, once implemented in the software system, is, sometimes prohibitively, expensive to change. Due to the lack of first-class representation and the intertwining with other design decisions, changing or removing existing design decisions is very difficult and affects many places in the system.
- **Design rules and constraints violated**: During the evolution of software systems, designers, and even architects, may easily violate the design rules and constraints imposed on the architecture by earlier design decisions.
- **Obsolete design decisions not removed**: Removing obsolete architecture design decisions from an implemented architecture is typically avoided, or performed only

partially, because of the (1) effort required, (2) perceived lack of benefit and (3) concerns about the consequences, due to the lack of knowledge about the design decisions. The consequence, however, is the rapid erosion of the software system, resulting in high maintenance cost and, ultimately, the early retirement of the system.

Software Architecture: The Next Step

In the first two sections, our aim has been to convince the reader of two things. First, the first phase of software architecture research, where the key concepts are components and connectors, has matured the technology to a level where industry adoption is wide-spread and few fundamental issues remain. Second, the traditional view on software architecture suffers from a number of key problems that cannot be solved without changing our perspective on the notion of software architecture.

In our research, we have evolved to an approach to software architecture that addresses the problems discussed in the previous sections. The key difference from traditional approaches is that we do not view a *software architecture* as a set of components and connectors, but rather as *the composition of a set of architectural design decisions*.

An architectural design decision consists of a solution part and a requirements part. The solution part is the first-class representation of a logically coherent structure that is imposed on the design decisions that have already been taken. The design decision may (1) add components to the architecture, (2) impose functionality on existing components, (3) add requirements on the expected behaviour of components and (4) add constraints or rules on part or all of the software architecture. A design decision may not (1) remove components from the software architecture, although components may be isolated and (2) split or merge components, although part of the functionality of a component may be ignored.

The requirements part of a design decision is present because of the fact that no design decision can be a complete architectural design, except for perhaps toy examples. Each design decision addresses some of the requirements of the system, but leaves others to be resolved. In addition, a design decision may introduce new requirements on components in the system.

An architectural design decision may represent a number of solution structures, including a reusable domain architecture, an architectural style or pattern, a design pattern or a component selection, e.g. a COTS component, a reusable component from a system family or a system specific component. In the next section, we define the concept of an architecture design decision in more detail.

Architecture Design Decisions

Designing a software architecture can be viewed as a decision process, i.e. a sequence of easy and difficult design decisions. The software architect, in the process of translating requirements into a design, basically takes, potentially many, design decisions that, combined, give the software architect its final shape.

We, as a software design community, have a tendency to freely speak about design decisions, but few have addressed the notion of design decisions in detail. In our experience, one can identify four relevant aspects of a design decision:

- **Restructuring effect**: The most visible effect of a design decision is the effect on the structure of the software architecture. As a consequence of the design decision, components may be added, split, merged or removed. Although this effect is very clear at the time the decision is taken, the accumulated restructuring in response to a series of design decisions is not at all so easy to understand any more. Current notations and languages do not provide support to describe design decisions individually.
- **Design rules**: A second aspect of a design decision is that it may define one or more design rules that have to be followed for some or all components in the system. A rule typically specifies a particular way of performing a certain task.
- **Design constraints**: In addition to design rules, a design decision may also impose design constraints on a subset of the components. A design constraint defines what the system, or parts of it, may not do.
- **Rationale**: Finally, each design decision is taken in response to some functional or quality requirement(s). The software architect reasons about the best way to fulfill the requirement(s) and then decides. The rationale, including possible new principles, guidelines and other relevant information about the design of the system, should be documented.

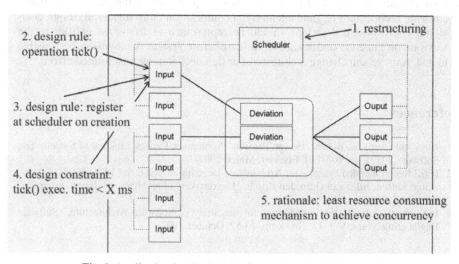

Fig. 1. Application-level scheduler for small, embedded system.

In figure 1, the different aspects of design decisions are illustrated. In the example, for a small embedded system, the decision is taken to use an application-level scheduler to achieve concurrency in the system. As shown, this decision results in one added component (Scheduler), two design rules, one design constraint and a described rationale.

In the traditional perspective on software architecture, most of the information above is lost during the design process. Consequently, when, during the evolution of the system, some component is added that requires concurrency, there is a considerable likelihood that the software engineer violates some rules or constraints, resulting in either errors in the behaviour of the component or the failure of the system as a whole.

Conclusion

This position paper makes the following claims that, in our opinion, are worthwhile to discuss at the workshop:

- The first phase of software architecture research, where the key concepts are components and connectors, has matured the technology to a level where industry adoption is wide-spread and few fundamental issues remain.
- The traditional view on software architecture suffers from a number of key problems that cannot be solved without changing our perspective on the notion of software architecture. These problems include the lack of first-class representation of design decisions, the fact that these design decisions are cross-cutting and intertwined, that these problems lead to high maintenance cost, because of which design rules and constraints are easily violated and obsolete design decisions are not removed.
- As a community, we need to take the next step and adopt the perspective that a software architecture is, fundamentally, a composition of architectural design decisions. These design decisions should be represented as first-class entities in the software architecture and it should, at least before system deployment, be possible to add, remove and change architectural design decisions against limited effort.

References

1. Jilles van Gurp, Jan Bosch, 'Design Erosion: Problems & Causes', Journal of Systems and Software, 61(2), pp. 105-119, Elsevier, March 2002.
2. IEEE Recommended Practice for Architecture Description, IEEE Std 1471, 2000.
3. Anton Jansen, Jilles van Gurp, Jan Bosch, 'The recovery of architectural design decisions', submitted, 2004.
4. D.E. Perry, A.L. Wolf, 'Foundations for the Study of Software Architecture,' Software Engineering Notes, Vol. 17, No. 4, pp. 40-52, October 1992.

Using Architectural Models at Runtime: Research Challenges

David Garlan and Bradley Schmerl

Department of Computer Science
Carnegie Mellon University
5000 Forbes Ave, Pittsburgh PA 15213 USA
{garlan,schmerl}@cs.cmu.edu

1 Introduction

One crucial aspect of high quality software engineering is the development of a well-defined software architectural model. Such a model describes the runtime manifestation of a software system in terms of its high level components and their interconnections. A good architectural model can be used as the basis for design-time analysis to determine whether a software system will meet desired quality attributes.

Despite advances in using software architectural model to clarify system design, there remains a problem that is typical of design-time artifacts: Does the system as implemented have the architecture as designed? Without some form of consistency guarantee the relationship between the architecture and the implementation will be hypothetical, and many of the benefits of using an architecture in the first place will be lost. One approach to addressing this problem is to enforce correspondence by generating code from the architectural model or by forcing developers to implement against a specific code library, which can then be used to provide some guarantees (e.g., [1,8,10]). Another approach is to use static code analysis techniques to determine the architecture of the code, subject to some constraints about code modularization and code patterns [5,6,7].

An alternative approach is to monitor the running system and translate observed events to events that construct and update an architectural model that reflects the actual running system. One can then compare this dynamically-determined model to the correct architectural model. Discrepancies can be used to flag implementation errors, or, possibly, to effect run-time adaptations to correct certain kinds of flaws.

At Carnegie Mellon University, our research group has been investigating the use of system monitoring and reflection using architectural models. In the process of exploring this area we have identified a number of significant research challenges. In this paper we outline our experience, and use that as a way to lay out an agenda for architecture-based approaches to system monitoring and system self-repair. We then briefly outline the ways in which we have been addressing some of these challenges.

2 Research Challenges

The notion of using architecture models at runtime to monitor and repair a running system is attractive for a number of reasons: First, different architectural models or

F. Oquendo et al. (Eds.): EWSA 2004, LNCS 3047, pp. 200–205, 2004.
© Springer-Verlag Berlin Heidelberg 2004

views can be chosen depending on the system quality of interest. Second, externalized mechanisms can support reuse, since they are not application-specific. Third, the details of how models are derived and of what to do if something is wrong can be easily modified, since they are localized in the external mechanisms and not distributed throughout the application. Fourth, the models used as the basis for external reasoning can exploit a large body of existing work on analytical methods for improving attributes such as performance, reliability, or security.

However, achieving these benefits requires that one address a number of research challenges. These challenges can be divided into four categories:

1. **Monitoring.** How do we add monitoring capabilities to systems in non-intrusive ways? What kinds of things can be monitored? Is it possible to build reusable monitoring mechanisms that can be added to existing systems?
2. **Interpretation.** How do we make sense of monitored information? How do we produce architectural models from this information? How can we determine whether a problem exists with the running system and whether repair, or more generally improvement, is required? How can we pinpoint the source of a problem? What models are best paired with specific quality attributes and systems?
3. **Resolution.** Once we know there is a problem – that the running system is at variance with the intended architectural design and its behavior – how do we decide what to do to fix it? How can we select the best repair action from a set of possible actions? What can we guarantee about a repair? Can we "improve" a system even if there is no specific problem?
4. **Adaptation.** How can we cause the adaptation to occur in a running system? What do we do if something goes wrong during the process of adaptation? How do we know that the adaptation actually worked to repair the system?

Ideally solutions to these problems would lead to mechanisms that not only add new capability to existing systems, but do so in a cost-effective manner. That is, we would like to find reusable infrastructure that addresses many of these issues, and have ways to adapt that infrastructure to specific systems.

3   Experience with Architecture-Based Monitoring and Repair

In an attempt to gain some experience with these issues we have been exploring the use of architectural models at run time in the context of a project called Rainbow [2]. To address issues of cost-effectiveness, our approach to providing dynamic architecture discovery and repair is to provide an "externalized" *generic infrastructure* that is independent from an executing system and that can be *specialized* for particular target systems. Such an approach allows us to target existing systems for which (a) the code was not written with any particular convenient library or code pattern; (b) an architectural model may not exist; or (c) adaptation was not designed a priori.

The externalized approach supports a form of closed-loop control system, where system behavior is monitored, analyzed, and (if required) adapted. In such a case, the architectural model acts as a basis for reasoning about the observations of the system, and also for reasoning about changes that may need to be made.

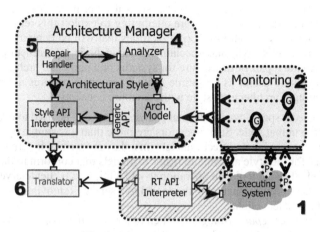

Fig. 1. Adaptation Framework.

The approach is illustrated in Figure 1. In the Rainbow framework, architectural models and styles are central to providing externalized self-adaptation mechanisms. An executing system is (1) is monitored to observe its run time behavior (2). Monitoring information is abstracted and related to architectural properties and elements in an architectural model (3). Changes in the architectural model trigger rule evaluation (4) to determine whether the system is operating within an envelope of acceptable ranges. Violations of rules are handled by a repair mechanism (5), which adapts the architecture. Architectural changes are propagated to the running system (6).

Our approach to dynamically discovering an architecture and issuing repairs based on observations about that architecture requires a generic framework that can be used in many systems, and a means of specializing this framework for particular domains to effect useful and meaningful discovery and repair in that domain.

The specialization of the framework requires us to specify many parts. A key challenge is how to maximize reuse so that details can be shared in the same domain. For example, if we are detecting and adapting systems in the domain of automotive software, we should be able to reuse many of the details regardless of the system. Part of this challenge is identifying what can be reused, and when, in a methodical manner.

3.1 Architectural Style

Key to solving the reuse challenge is the use of architectural style to parameterize our generic infrastructure. We consider an architectural style to be a collection of types for components, connectors, interfaces, and properties together with a set of rules for how elements of those types may be composed. Properties are associated with elements in the architecture to capture behavior and semantics. For example, a property on a connector type might be used to indicate its protocol or capacity. Rules can, for example, specify that some property value must be within certain ranges.

The benefits of associating a style with an architecture include support for analysis, reuse, code generation, and system evolution [3,9,10]. In particular, the knowledge, rules, and analyses can be defined at the style level and reused in all instances of that style. This has proved extremely useful at design-time for providing tools to guide an architect in developing a model. We are attempting to exploit this reuse for dynamic repair by factoring repair and monitoring facilities that will be common for all architectures of a particular style and specializing our generic infrastructure with these facilities to provide repair infrastructure for systems of a particular architectural style.

To make the style useful as a runtime artifact for repair requires us to extend the traditional notion of architectural style with two more concepts:

1. A set of style-specific *architectural operators* that can be used to change an architecture in that style. Such operators are more than just simple operations for adding or removing architectural elements; they are written in terms of the vocabulary for the style and should result in models that conform to the architectural style. For example, an operation to add a client in a client-server style would also involve connecting the model to a server. Removing a server may relocate or delete clients.
2. A collection of *repair strategies* written in terms of these operators associated with the style's rules. If a dynamic observation is interpreted as violating a rule of the architecture, then a repair is issued which uses properties of the style to pinpoint the error, and operators of the style to adapt the architecture.

The operators and repair strategies are chosen based on an examination of the analyses associated with a style, which formally identify how the architecture should change in order to affect desired characteristics.

The key to making this work is to parameterize the Architecture Manager (Figure 1) with an architectural style. Within a style, or domain, the Architecture Manager will remain largely unchanged – the analyzer will analyze the same rules, the Style API will use the same operators, and the repair handler will likely use the same repair strategies or tactics. To reuse the infrastructure in another domain requires specializing the framework with a different architectural style.

A second critical issue is then getting the information out of the system and effecting changes back into the system. To address the *Monitoring* challenges, we divide the problem into system-level information, which can be ascertained by using off-the-shelf probing technologies (such as network monitors, debugging interfaces, etc.), and architecture level information. To bridge the gap between system-level information and architectural properties we use a system of adapters, called "gauges," which aggregate low-level monitored information and relate it to the architectural model [4]. For example, gauges may aggregate measurements of the round-trip time for a request and the amount of information transferred to produce bandwidth measurements at the architectural level. Gauges thus interpret monitored events as properties of an architectural model.

To address the challenge of *Adaptation*, we use a knowledge base to map architecture operations into system-level operations to make changes to the system. This knowledge base uses customized translations in addition to collecting information from gauges.

3.2 Architecture Discovery

Until recently, gauges in our work were restricted to monitoring properties of architectural models. They were used merely to monitor the system and interpret those observations as properties on a pre-existing architecture. In order to address the challenge of determining the architecture of a running system, and to help determine whether architectural repairs have been enacted in the system, we need a method for taking observations about the running system and discover its architectural structure.

DiscoTect [11] is a system for discovering the architectures of running, object-oriented systems and can be used to construct architectures dynamically. The novelty of DiscoTect is the way that the mapping between the system and the architecture specified. A form of state machine is used to keep track of the progress of system-level events and emit architectural events when combinations of system-level events are detected. We require a state machine because a given architectural event, such as creating a connector, might involve many runtime events. Conversely, a single runtime event might correspond to multiple architectural events. For example, a simple method invocation may signal the creation of a connector, its associated interfaces, and connecting the connector to particular components. Complicating this further is the fact that many architectural events may be interleaved in an implementation. For example, a system might be midway through creating several components and connectors.

Again, the notion of style is helpful in providing reuse for this complicated process. The architectural events will be in terms of the operators of the style. We may also be able to take advantage of particular pairings of architectural style and implementation conventions to garner common parts of the state machine, thus generalizing detection more. For example, if the implementation is written in CORBA, many CORBA events will map to the same architectural events for a particular architectural style.

4 Conclusion

In this position paper, we outlined a set of challenges that need to be addressed in order to make architectures available and useful at runtime. We argued that using architectural information dynamically has benefits of providing a feasible and flexible approach for discovering a system's architecture, and for detecting faults, reasoning about them, and deciding repairs. We then indicated some of the challenges that fall within the categories of monitoring, interpretation, resolution, and adaptation. Next we outlined research that we believe addresses some of those challenges. As we have tried to indicate, architecture-based monitoring and adaptation is a rich area of ongoing research, and ripe for contributions along many lines, from engineering to foundations.

References

1. Aldrich, J., Chambers, C., and Notkin, D. ArchJava: Connecting Software Architectures to Implementation. In Proc. 24th International Conference on Software Engineering (ICSE 2002), Orlando, FL., pp. 187-197, 2002.
2. Cheng, S.-W., Garlan, D., Schmerl, B., Sousa, J., Spitznagel, B., Steenkiste, P. Using Architectural Style as the Basis for Self-repair. Proc. the 3rd Working IEEE/IFIP Conference on Software Architecture, pp. 45-59, 2002.

3. Garlan, D., Allen, R., Ockerbloom, J. Exploiting Style in Architectural Design. Proc. SIGSOFT'94 Symposium on the Foundations of Software Engineering, New Orleans, 1994.
4. Garlan, D., Schmerl, B., and Chang, J. Using Gauges for Architecture-based Monitoring and Adaptation. Proc. Working Conference on Complex and Dynamic Systems Architecture, Brisbane, Australia, 2001.
5. Jackson, D., WainGold, A. Lightweight extraction of object models from byte-code. In Proc. 21st International Conference on Software Engineering, Los Angeles, CA, 1999.
6. Kazman, R., Carriere, S. Playing Detective: Reconstructing Software Archtiecture from Available Evidence. Journal of Automated Software Engineering 6(2):107-138, 1999.
7. Murphy, G., Notkin, D., Sullivan, K. Software Reflexion Models: Bridging the Gap Between Source and High-Level Models. In Proc 13th ACM SIGSOFT Symposium on Foundations of Software Engineering, Washington D.C., pp. 18-28, 1995.
8. Shaw, M., Deline, R., Klein, D., Ross, T., Young, D., Zelesnik, G. Abstractions for Software Architecture and Tools to Support Them. IEEE Transactions on Software Engineering (TOSEM) 21(4):314-335, 1995.
9. Shaw, M. and Garlan, D. Software Architectures: Perspectives on an Emerging Discipline. Prentice Hall, 1996.
10. Taylor, R., Medvidovic, N., Anderson, K., Whitehead, E., Robbins, J, Nies, K., Oriezy, P., Dubrow D. A Component- and Message-based Architectural Style for GUI Software. IEEE Transactions on Software Engineering 22(6):390-406, 1996.
11. Yan, H., Garlan, D., and Schmerl, B. DiscoTect: A System for Discovering Architectures from Running Systems. In Proc. 26th International Conference on Software Engineering, Edinburgh, Scotland, 2004.

Maintainability through Architecture Development

Bas Graaf

Faculty of Electrical Engineering, Mathematics and Computer Science
Delft University of Technology
b.s.graaf@ewi.tudelft.nl

Abstract. This position paper investigates on the need to put software architecture evaluations for maintainability in a broader perspective than is done until now.

1 Introduction

Embedded systems are getting increasingly complex. Consequently developing software for embedded systems becomes more difficult. Nevertheless an industrial survey we conducted confirmed that the embedded systems industry is very cautious in adopting new development technologies [1]. One reason was that some of the industry's practical problems are not solved satisfactory by available technologies.

Industry is rarely developing new products from scratch. This implies that development artefacts can be reused; not only code, but also architectural design. This is one aspect of industrial development that is insufficiently addressed by current approaches. Although more effective reuse is promised by software (product line) architecture technologies, reuse is done ad-hoc in most companies, e.g. by using 'copy-paste'. Therefore these technologies did not yet fulfilled their full potential.

Continuously changing requirements, caused by changes to stakeholder objectives or the environment in which the software is embedded, is another aspect that is insufficiently supported by current technologies. Due to the increased complexity of embedded systems this is very difficult to handle using current development technologies.

Both examples put embedded-specific type of demands on the development of embedded systems. One is related to the capability of a software product to be reused, for which it possibly needs to be (slightly) modified. The other is about the capability of a software product to be adapted to changing stakeholder objectives or environment. Both are closely related and are about the ease of reusing existing software products for new products or for the same (adapted) product. In this paper we use the term maintainability to refer to this desired property of embedded software products.

In this paper we claim that there are already many technologies available to help software engineers to better understand the software architecture and its implications from this maintainability perspective. However, these technologies only shed light on one side of the problem as will be explained in this paper.

F. Oquendo et al. (Eds.): EWSA 2004, LNCS 3047, pp. 206–211, 2004.
© Springer-Verlag Berlin Heidelberg 2004

2   Related Work

According to [2] different concerns regarding a software system should be addressed in different views on the architecture. A view conforms to a corresponding viewpoint, of which many have been defined [3],[4],[5]. Some of these viewpoints partly address the maintainability concern as explained in the introduction, e.g. the module dependency view.

Architecture description languages provide a formal semantics that makes it possible to analyze the architecture with respect to several properties such as time behaviour. Other design level properties such as liveness, safety, and deadlock can be verified as well. However, it is not easy to see how these properties are related to specific stakeholder requirements. Furthermore these approaches in general only allow for analysis of operational properties of software systems and their applicability to realistic, industrial situations is limited.

Another type of techniques for architecture analysis uses scenarios. Mostly these techniques are based on ATAM or SAAM [6]. By identifying the key-concerns and analyzing the architecture for its support for different scenarios a software architecture can be evaluated. An advantage of these techniques compared to ad-hoc evaluations is that the evaluators do not have to be domain experts. Furthermore the use of scenarios makes it possible to evaluate non-operational attributes, e.g. by using change scenarios. However, the analysis is mainly based on the experience of the evaluators, who typically are highly skilled and experienced architects. This makes people that can do this type of analysis scarce, and as systems become increasingly complex, even more so in the future.

3   Maintainability and Architecture

Some of our observations during the survey we conducted, suggested that it is not always clear what kind of architecture is under consideration: is it the architecture as documented, or as the architects understand it, or maybe as it is implemented. We believe that it is very important to be aware of what is actually considered when evaluating a software architecture for maintainability. This led to the idea that the impact of software architecture on maintainability is easier understood if one considers how each architecture development activity contributes to it. For analysis the same is true: what has been done in each activity to realize maintainability? This idea led to the hypothesis:

The maintainability of a software system can be more effectively evaluated by separately considering three different aspects of software architecture: design decisions, documentation, and implementation.

In Table 1 the three aspects in the hypothesis are clarified by a corresponding question. These aspects are derived from our view on the software architecture development process (Figure 1) and are discussed in the subsections below.

Table 1. Maintainability questions.

Aspect	Question
Design decisions	Does a design decision support maintainability?
Documentation	Can the rationales for a design decision be recovered, e.g. by traceability to requirements?
Implementation	Is this design decision respected in the implementation?

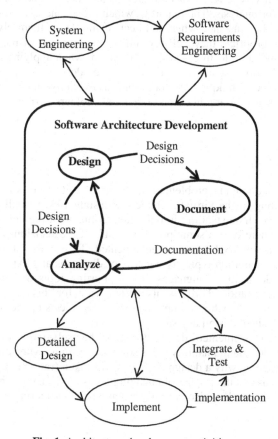

Fig. 1. Architecture development activities.

3.1 Design Decisions

Design is one of the activities in the software architecture development process (Figure 1). During this activity design decisions are taken. Software architecture design is concerned with global design decisions. Little support for this activity is available, besides guidelines in the form of architectural styles [7],[8], patterns [9] or tactics [10]. Consequently its outcome is very dependent on the architect's skills and experience. The result of this activity is a virtual architecture of the system. It is virtual in the sense that the decisions are neither documented nor implemented during this activity.

The architectural design decisions taken at the beginning of a project have a significant impact on the maintainability of a software system. For example the decision to merge two components can make maintaining the system more difficult.

In order to raise the confidence that these important design decisions are indeed appropriate, different technologies are available to analyze them, another core activity of architecture development. In practice design decisions are continuously analyzed, most times implicitly. The result of both architecture design and documentation can be used as input for analysis. The extent to which either one is used depends on the type of technique. For instance when architects evaluate for themselves if some design decision is appropriate they will use mostly the outcome of the design activity alone, i.e. the virtual architecture. On the other hand, when applying formal verification techniques, the documentation in the form of models and properties is the main input. Scenario-based techniques use both inputs as they rely on the documentation as well as on the presence of architects and other stakeholders during an evaluation session.

3.2 Documentation

One of the most challenging problems in software architecture is how to achieve a shared understanding of the virtual architecture designed by a small group of architects. Such a shared understanding is important to maintain the conceptual integrity [11] of a design. Therefore, at some point the result of the decisions taken during the architecture design activity have to be documented. This is also shown in Figure 1. The resulting documentation typically consists of diagrams and explaining text. Several architecture description languages and supporting tools are available for the architecture documentation. UML is also often used for this. The documentation serves various purposes, such as communicating design decisions to programmers, or as a basis for analysis of design decisions (Figure 1).

Considering the (documented) design decisions themselves is not enough to make statements about the maintainability of a software system. After all, suppose it is impossible to determine why a design decisions was taken (rationale). That will make it very difficult to assess the impact of changing a design decision. This suggests that the documentation by itself is also very important when considering maintainability.

3.3 Implementation

Besides the virtual architecture as designed by the architects and (partially) documented, there is the implemented architecture. As the designed and documented architecture in principal represent the 'software-to-be', the implemented architecture represents the 'software-as-is'. Due to architectural erosion [12] and miscommunications these are not necessarily the same.

Conformance is the extent to which the implemented architecture corresponds to the virtual architecture and is an important aspect of maintainability. This is illustrated by a project that was considered during the survey we conducted [1]. In this project the maintainability of architectural components was analyzed by determining the complexity of the components. In fact this is an analysis of the design decisions. By the use of metrics one component was identified as very complex. However, when asked, the architects pointed out a different component to be difficult to change. This component only had a modest score on the complexity metric. Further analysis revealed an unexpected relation in the implementation to another component. This difference between the designed and implemented architecture (i.e. conformance) was an important reason for this component to be difficult to change.

Several techniques are available to ensure this conformance, such as change management, code generation and the use of product family architectures. Furthermore by the use of reverse engineering techniques views on the implemented architecture can be generated, which can be compared to the documented and virtual architectures.

4 Contributions

The contributions of our research will involve software architecture development techniques that address the three aspects discussed in this paper. Furthermore the integration, consolidation, and interpretation of the results of these techniques will be addressed. Hence the result of this research provides more insight in how different aspects of architecture development affect software maintainability. Consequently, it will result in the definition of architectural views that specifically address the maintainability concern. Finally, it will increase the insight in the applicability and tailorability of technologies for architecture development that have been defined.

5 Methods

Besides literature research the ideas in this paper are currently based on discussions we had with over 35 software practitioners during a survey. It was conducted in the context of an ITEA (www.itea.org) project called MOOSE (www.mooseproject.org). This industry driven project aims at improving software quality and development productivity for embedded systems. It offers possibilities to validate ideas and developed or tailored technologies. We pursue a series of small-scale industrial experiments, each addressing a different aspect of architecture development (Table 1). Currently two industrial experiments have been defined. In one of them the behaviour of an architectural component is redocumented. In this case the approach is bottom-up: we try to identify what information engineers need to (re)use or change a component. In the other experiment we consider the effect of design decisions on the maintainability of a reference architecture. By conducting a SAAM-like assessment the reference architecture is evaluated with respect to its support for future product generations. We intend to augment the SAAM with architectural strategies that embody explicit architectural knowledge, such as tactics [10].

Additionally we have defined a small in-house project at our department in which we consider conformance. This project addresses questions such as: how can be ensured that architecture decisions are implemented and how can the conformance be analyzed, i.e. what criteria are relevant when considering conformance from a maintainability perspective.

References

1. B. Graaf, M. Lormans, and H. Toetenel. Embedded Software Engineering: state of the practice. IEEE Software, November 2003.
2. IEEE Recommended Practice for Architectural Description of Software-Intensive Systems. Std 1471-2000, IEEE, 2000
3. P. B. Kruchten. The 4+1 view model of architecture. IEEE Software, November 1995.
4. C. Hofmeister, R. Nord, and D. Soni. Applied Software Architecture. Addison-Wesley, 1999.
5. P. Clements, F. Bachmann, L. Bass, et al. Documenting Software Architectures. Addison-Wesley, 2002.
6. P. Clements, R. Kazman, and M. Klein. Evaluating Software Architectures. Methods and Case Studies. Addison Wesley, 2001.
7. M. Shaw and D. Garlan. Software Architecture: Perspectives on an Emerging Discipline. Prentice Hall, 1996.
8. F. Buschmann, R. Meunier, H. Rohnert, et al. Pattern-Oriented Software Architecture: A System of Patterns. John Wiley, 1996.
9. J. Bosch. Design & Use of Software Architectures: Adopting and evolving a product-line approach. Addison-Wesley, 2000.
10. F. Bachmann, L. Bass, and M. Klein. Illuminating the Fundamental Contributors to Software Architecture Quality. CMU/SEI-2002-TR-025, Software Engineering Institute, Carnegie Mellon University, August 2002.
11. F. Brooks, Jr. The Mythical Man-Month. Addison-Wesley, anniversary edition, 1995.
12. D. Perry and A. Wolf. Foundations for the Study of Software Architecture. ACM SIGSOFT Software Engineering Notes. October 1992.

An Architecture Description Language for Mobile Distributed Systems

Volker Gruhn and Clemens Schäfer

University of Leipzig
Faculty of Mathematics and Computer Science
Chair for Applied Telematics / e-Business*
Klostergasse 3, 04109 Leipzig, Germany
{gruhn,schaefer}@ebus.informatik.uni-leipzig.de

Abstract. Mobile software applications have to meet new requirements directly arising from mobility issues. To address these requirements at an early stage in development, an architecture description language (ADL) is proposed, which allows to manage issues like availability requirements, mobile code, security, and replication processes. Aspects of this ADL, Con Moto, are exemplified with a case study from the insurance sector.

1 Motivation

We can observe in our daily life, that existing and emerging communication technologies and the growing availability of powerful mobile communication and computing devices are the enablers for software systems with mobile parts. Regardless whether we look at fleet management systems or point-of-sale systems, all applications with mobile parts have in common that the point where the information technology is used is moved towards the point where the business process is really executed.

Although these mobile applications bring new requirements with them, we usually apply development methods and modeling methods used for 'conventional' applications. In this work, we will show how the development of mobile applications can benefit from an approach explicitly addressing mobility issues.

The remainder of this paper is organized as follows. In section 2 we motivate the necessity of an architecture description language (ADL) for mobile systems. Section 3 contains an application of this mobile ADL to a case study from the insurance sector. Finally, the conclusion in section 4 rounds out the paper.

2 Con Moto as Mobile ADL

As discussed in the previous section, more and more software systems are determined by some sort of mobility. In the following we call a software system part which is used at different locations (without these locations being known in advance) a "mobile component". We call a business process mobile, if its execution depends on a mobile component. For a more precise definition of the term "mobile" we refer to [1].

---

* The chair for Applied Telematics / e-Business is endowed by Deutsche Telekom AG.

F. Oquendo et al. (Eds.): EWSA 2004, LNCS 3047, pp. 212–218, 2004.
© Springer-Verlag Berlin Heidelberg 2004

If a software system contains mobile components, its management has to deal with a number of tasks and challenges which do not occur in the management of systems without mobile components. Examples of such tasks and challenges are:

- A functionality which is crucial for a number of mobile business processes has to be available on client systems. Usually it is not sufficient to keep it running at a central site and to allow mobile access to it. Thus, the availability requirement for this functionality may clash with service level agreements which can be obtained for telecommunication infrastructure.
- If huge amounts of data are needed in a mobile business process, then it is usually necessary to provide a only readable copy of these data at the mobile location. This immediately raises the question whether or not these data can be downloaded when needed or if they should be installed at the remote location in advance.
- If certain functionality are to be handled confidentially, then this may collide with mobility requirements, simply, because components implementing this functionality should not be made available at local devices.
- Updates and patches of mobile components demand either precautions from a software update process point of view (e.g. to register which versions of which components are installed where) or they require that mobile components are not made persistent at mobile locations.

Further challenges exist in the context of compatibility between mobility on the one hand and other non-functional requirements (robustness, scalability, security, traceability, etc.) on the other hand. Summing this up, requirements with respect to the mobility of software systems determine not only substantial parts of the software processes for the development and maintenance of these systems, but they also have an important impact on the architecture of these systems.

Our approach to an architecture centric software development of mobile software systems is to express all aspects of software systems' mobility in a software architecture. This software architecture is described from different views (application view, software view, system view [2]). All these views onto the architecture should clearly describe which components and which business processes are mobile, which kind of mobility applies to them (ranging from mobile web-based access to central systems to mobile code in the sense of the FarGo approach [3, 4]) and which side effects a change of mobility properties could have.

Our approach is based on the architecture description language Con Moto. Describing all three views onto a software architecture in terms of Con Moto means to grasp all aspects of mobility. A Con Moto-based description of a software architecture is used for different purposes:

- understanding the architecture of the system, paying particular emphasis on mobility issues
- using the architecture description for configuration management and change management tasks

- scheduling work including tasks and packages related to infrastructure support enabling mobility
- analysis of the architecture, in particular for the identification of performance bottlenecks and incompatibilities between mobility requirements and non-functional requirements.

In the next section we will introduce the key elements of Con Moto along the lines of a concrete example. This examples covers a point-of-sale software system for insurance agents. We put emphasis on those elements of Con Moto which focus on mobile components and mobile business processes. We are aware of the fact, that this introduction does not give a complete overview about Con Moto, but it hopefully will provide sufficient insights into the role a Con Moto based architecture description plays in an architecture centric development of mobile system.

During the introduction of Con Moto we refer to other ADLs (a good overview can be found in the paper of Medvidovic and Taylor [5]) wherever appropriate in order to point out what the benefits of considering mobility as first class property of software systems look like.

3   A Case Study: uniPOS

In the insurance sector, insurance and financial products are more and more sold actively to the customer instead of being bought by the customer. From the viewpoint of insurance agents, this produces new requirements like rapidity, actuality, and demand for diversity (for services as well as for products), which have to be fulfilled by sales supporting systems.

Existing sales support systems are mostly realized as fat client applications, which are extensive and allow autarkic (offline) execution. However, their architecture implies a number of problems (e.g. replication issues) and fails to meet the needs described above.

Since a mobile system is predestinated to provide the above-mentioned sales support, we decided to create the case study *uniPOS*.

The uniPOS system supports different target groups. Tied intermediaries, brokers, multiple agents, policy holders as well as staff members of the insurance company are provided with an optimized view on stock data and support for their daily business processes by

- integration of different lines of business in one view,
- support for different sales channels, and
- online deal- or case-closing transactions.

Additionally, uniPOS provides fast introduction of new products and avoids multiple plausibility checks.

Figure 1 shows a part of the uniPOS system, expressed in Con Moto. There are two devices, namely the *uniPOS Server* and the *uniPOS Client*, both represented by rectangles with triangles in their edges. On these devices, there are

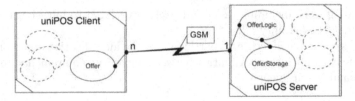

Fig. 1. Offer Component in uniPOS

several components, namely *Offer*, *OfferLogic* and *OfferStorage*, which are represented by ovals. The lines between the components and the components and the devices depict connectors, meaning that e.g. *Offer* can use services from *OfferLogic*, since the two devices are connected by a attributed connector representing a GSM telecommunications channel.

With this representation (and the formalism behind) it is possible to judge about the operational availability of e.g. the *Offer* component. If we request a high availability, a Con Moto checker can show the clash between the GSM channel (which is not always available) and the requirement of availability. Hence, availability requirements for systems and subsystems can be answered by analyzing a system depicted in Con Moto.

Since we want to use Con Moto during the component based design of mobile systems, the need for a graphical representation is clear. Although the ADL *Wright* [6] can model distributed systems, it lacks a graphical representation. Other ADLs allow the graphical modeling of distributed systems. *Darwin* [7] is based on the pi calculus. From these precise semantics, Darwin's strength lies in modeling hierarchically constructed systems and distributed systems. *Rapide* [8] provides comprehensive modeling, analysis, simulation and code generation capabilities. However, as it is strictly event based, it clashes with the service-oriented nature of component-based systems. *C2SADL* [9] is an ADL also suitable for dynamic systems.

However, none of these ADLs implies constructs similar to our notion of the device and the attributed channel. These ADLs also do neither support such constructs directly nor support non-functional properties, which could be used to extend the existing ADLs in a way to make them suitable for mobile systems.

Weaves [10] addresses issues that seem to be related to mobile systems like dynamic rearrangement. However, the concept of the stream-like weaves do not fit into the component-based approach that is used for mobile systems today. A recent contribution to the field of ADL research is *xADL 2.0* [11]. It is an XML-based ADL that is highly extensible. Although it does not support the mobility issues we want to point out, that ideas from it can be valuable contributions to Con Moto.

We now continue with our example. Before, we detected a system which fails to meet the availability requirements. Con Moto also supports the modeling of a system variant that is superior at this point.

In Figure 2 two equivalent variants of uniPOS are depicted that make use of mobile code. The components that shall be mobile have been marked with

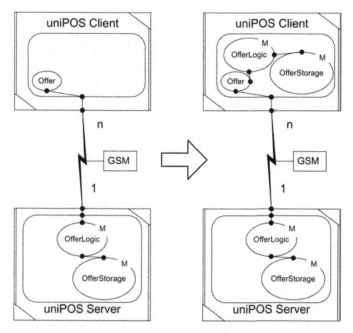

Fig. 2. Mobile Code

an 'M'. But to check whether a system configuration with this kind of mobile component is possible, we need to introduce the notion of *execution environment*, depicted by a rounded rectangle. This indicates that there are different execution environments like application servers, lightweight application servers etc., that may be compatible in a way that they allow mobile components to move around the system in order to cope with availability problems. With the specified mobile components, the availability requirement for the component *Offer* can be satisfied, as the mobile components may travel from the server to the client.

Furthermore, with this representation Con Moto allows the discussion of security aspects as it is able to determine which components on which execution areas and hence on which devices a component will be available.

However, just making a component mobile is not sufficient: in our example, the *OfferStorage* component has to work on some data from a database. This directly leads to replication problems in the mobile case. Hence, we have to express in our architecture, where replication has to be performed. Figure 3 shows two equivalent architectures this for the database with offer data. The replication areas have been drawn as dotted rounded rectangles. The dotted line between them indicates that they belong together and that there is a replication relationship between them.

In Figure 2 and in Figure 3, two equivalent variants of the same system have been displayed. In both cases, the left variant (with the components *OfferLogic* and *OfferStorage* on the server) is sufficient, as the "mobile" cases (the right

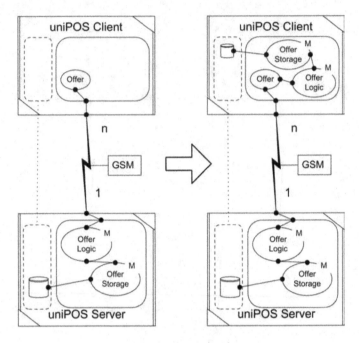

Fig. 3. Replication

sides of the figures) are covered as well due to the specification of the execution environments and the replication areas.

4   Conclusion

In this paper we discussed the idea of an architecture description language matching the requirements of mobile architectures. Due to the increasing mobility and distribution of business processes and supporting software systems, the mobility aspect deserves emphasis and this emphasis should be reflected in the architecture description. Even though our ADL Con Moto is no formally defined yet and even though the language itself is still subject to minor updates, it turned already out to be useful in managing the complexity of mobile architectures. We consider this and—even more—the strong demand for architectures whose mobile aspects are easy to recognize as encouragement on the further way to full syntax and semantics definition for Con Moto.

References

1. Roman, G.C., Picco, G.P., Murphy, A.L.: Software Engineering for Mobility: A Roadmap. In: Proceedings of the Conference on the Future of Software Engineering, ACM Press (2000) 241–258

2. Gruhn, V., Thiel, A.: Komponentenmodelle *(in German)*. Addison-Wesley (2000)
3. Holder, O., Ben-Shaul, I., Gazit, H.: Dynamic Layout of Distributed Applications in FarGo. In: Proceedings of the 21st International Conference on Software Engineering, IEEE Computer Society Press (1999) 163–173
4. Weinsberg, Y., Ben-Shaul, I.: A Programming Model and System Support for Disconnected-Aware Applications on Resource-Constrained Devices. In: Proceedings of the 24th International Conference on Software Engineering, ACM Press (2002) 374–384
5. Medvidovic, N., Taylor, R.N.: A Classification and Comparison Framework for Software Architecture Description Languages. IEEE Transactions on Software Engineering **26** (2000) 70–93
6. Allen, R., Garlan, D.: A Formal Basis for Architectural Connection. ACM Transactions on Software Engineering and Methodology **6** (1997) 213–249
7. Magee, J., Dulay, N., Eisenbach, S., Kramer, J.: Specifying Distributed Software Architectures. In Schafer, W., Botella, P., eds.: Proc. 5th European Software Engineering Conference (ESEC 95), Springer-Verlag, Berlin (1995) 137–153
8. Luckham, D.C., Vera, J.: An Event-Based Architecture Definition Language. IEEE Transactions on Software Engineering **21** (1995) 717–734
9. Medvidovic, N., Rosenblum, D.S., Taylor, R.N.: A Language Environment for Architecture-Based Software Development and Evolution. In: Proceedings of the 21st International Conference on Software Engineering, IEEE Computer Society Press (1999) 44–53
10. Gorlick, M.M., Razouk, R.R.: Using Weaves for Software Construction and Analysis. In: Proceedings of the 13th International Conference on Software Engineering, IEEE Computer Society Press (1991) 23–34
11. Dashofy, E.M., van der Hoek, A., Taylor, R.N.: An Infrastructure for the Rapid Development of XML-Based Architecture Description Languages. In: Proceedings of the 24th International Conference on Software Engineering, ACM Press (2002) 266–276

Model Checking for Software Architectures*

Radu Mateescu

INRIA Rhône-Alpes / VASY, 655, avenue de l'Europe
F-38330 Montbonnot Saint Martin, France
Radu.Mateescu@inria.fr

Abstract. Software architectures are engineering artifacts which provide high-level descriptions of complex systems. Certain recent architecture description languages (ADLs) allow to represent a system's structure and behaviour together with its dynamic changes and evolutions. Model checking techniques offer a useful way for automatically verifying finite-state ADL descriptions w.r.t. their desired correctness requirements. In this position paper, we discuss several issues related to the application of model checking in the area of software architectures, underlining the aspects of interest for current and future research (construction of state spaces, expression and verification of requirements, state explosion).

1 Introduction

Software architectures [27] are essential engineering artifacts used in the design process of complex software systems. They specify at a high abstraction level various aspects of a system: gross organization into components, protocols for communication and data access, functionality of design elements, etc. Over the last decade, a significant number of architecture description languages (ADLs) were proposed and supported by dedicated tool environments (see [20] for a survey). Recently defined ADLs such as π-SPACE [5] and the ARCHWARE ADL [22] aim at describing the structure and behaviour of software systems that are subject to dynamic changes and evolutions. Inspired from mobile process calculi, such as the higher-order polyadic π-calculus [21], these ADLs provide mobility of communication channels, dynamic process creation/destruction, and higher-order process handling, enabling one to design evolvable, industrial-scale systems. To ensure the reliability of such complex systems, computer-assisted verification methodologies become a necessary step in the design process.

Model checking [6] is a verification technique well-adapted for the automatic detection of errors in complex systems. Starting from a formal representation of the system under design, e.g., an ADL description, a corresponding model (state space) is constructed; then, the desired correctness requirements, expressed in temporal logic, are checked on the resulting model by using specific algorithms. Although limited to finite-state systems, model checking provides a simple and efficient verification approach, particularly useful in the early phases of the design process, when errors are likely to occur more frequently.

* This study was supported by the European IST-2001-32360 project "ArchWare".

F. Oquendo et al. (Eds.): EWSA 2004, LNCS 3047, pp. 219–224, 2004.
© Springer-Verlag Berlin Heidelberg 2004

During the last decade, model checking was successfully applied for analysing software architectures described using different ADLs inspired from process algebras, the most prominent ones being WRIGHT [2] and DARWIN [17]. WRIGHT is based upon CSP, thus allowing to use FDR [25] to perform various architectural consistency checks amenable to deadlock detection and behavioural refinement. DARWIN uses the π-calculus to describe the structural aspects of the architecture (configuration and coordination) and FSP (a dialect of CSP) to describe the behaviour of individual components; this allows to check properties expressed in Linear Temporal Logic (LTL) using LTSA [16].

However, so far relatively little work was dedicated to model checking for ADLs that provide mobility and dynamicity mechanisms. Dynamic WRIGHT [3] allows to describe dynamic reconfiguration and steady-state (static) behaviour orthogonally, by introducing special reconfiguration-triggering events handled by a configuror process; reconfigurable architectures are translated into CSP by instantiating a finite number of possible configurations and by tagging events with the configuration in which they occur. A similar approach was used for ΔPADL [1], where dynamic architectures are simulated by instantiating finite numbers of replicas and by adding transparent routers to model dynamic reconfiguration. In addition to these general results concerning the extension of ADLs with dynamicity, the problem of model checking was also considered for dynamic systems belonging to specific domains, such as publish-subscribe systems [12].

In this position paper, we discuss three different aspects related to the application of model checking techniques for analysing dynamic ADL descriptions: construction of the state space corresponding to an ADL description (Section 2), expression and verification of correctness requirements (Section 3), and handling of the state explosion problem (Section 4). Finally, we give some concluding remarks and directions for future research (Section 5).

2   Constructing State Spaces

We can identify two ways of building the state space of an architectural description written in a dynamic ADL: either by developing from scratch an ADL simulator able to explore all reachable states of an architectural description, or by translating the ADL into another formal specification language already equipped with a state space generator. The first solution would certainly be the most efficient and accurate w.r.t. the operational semantics of the ADL, but may require a considerable effort (e.g., simulators for the polyadic π-calculus, such as MWB [29], are complex pieces of software). On the other hand, the second solution can be much simpler to achieve and may take advantage of the software tools already available for the target language. In the sequel, we examine the latter solution by considering as targets LOTOS [14] and E-LOTOS [15], two languages standardized by ISO, which combine the best features of classical value-passing process algebras (CCS and CSP) and are equipped with state-of-the-art software engineering environments such as the CADP verification toolbox [9].

Dynamic Process Creation. To obtain finite-state ADL descriptions in presence of dynamic process creation, one must statically bound the maximum number of process replicas that may coexist. LOTOS can describe dynamic process creation by using recursion through parallel composition (e.g., processes like P := a; stop ||| P), but most of the existing compilers do not handle this construct, since it may yield infinite, non regular behaviours. A solution would consist in statically expanding each dynamic process into the parallel composition of its n allowed replicas (all initially idle): this can be expressed concisely in E-LOTOS by using the indexed parallel composition operator [11]. Alternatively, one may directly construct the sequential process equivalent to the interleaving of n parallel replicas [13].

Mobility of Communication Channels. LOTOS and E-LOTOS assume that the process network has a fixed communication topology. Nevertheless, mobility of communication channels can be simulated in LOTOS by defining a data type "channel name", which allows to send and receive channel names as ordinary data values. The LOTOS processes produced by translating ADL (dynamic) processes will still communicate along a fixed network of gates, but each communication on a gate G will carry the name of an underlying mobile channel (e.g., G !c !0 denotes the emission of value 0 along channel c). The number of gates can be reduced due to the powerful synchronization mechanisms of LOTOS, which allow several channels to be multiplexed on a single gate. Also, the fact of bounding the number of replicas for dynamic processes also induces a bound on the set of (private) channel names that can be created by individual processes.

Higher-Order Process Handling. Since LOTOS provides only first-order constructs (data values and behaviours are clearly separated), it does not allow a direct representation of higher-order mechanisms such as sending a process along a channel. However, a significant part of a higher-order dynamic ADL can be translated into first-order by applying the translation from higher-order to first-order π-calculus [26, chap. 13].

By developing a translation according to the guidelines above, and by subsequently using a compiler for LOTOS (such as the CÆSAR [10] compiler of CADP), one can obtain a state space generator for a dynamic higher-order ADL. Such a tool would allow to handle finite-state configurations of ADL descriptions presenting a limited amount of dynamic process creation, channel mobility, and higher-order communication.

3   Checking Correctness Requirements

Temporal logics and μ-calculi [28] are well-studied formalisms for expressing correctness requirements of concurrent systems. During the last decade, many algorithms and model checking tools dedicated to these formalisms were developed; now, the research focuses on the application of these results in industrial context. We can mention two areas of interest w.r.t. the analysis of software architectures using temporal logics:

Optimized Verification Algorithms. The speed and memory performance of verification algorithms can still be improved, namely when they are applied to particular forms of models. For instance, *run-time verification* consists in analysing the behaviour of a system by checking correctness requirements on execution traces generated by executing or randomly simulating the system. In this context, memory-efficient verification algorithms have been designed for μ-calculus [18]; further improvements (e.g., memory consumption independent from the length of the trace) can be obtained by specialising these algorithms for particular temporal logics.

Advanced User Interfaces. User-friendliness is essential for achieving an industrial usage of temporal logic. Several aspects must be considered when integrating model checking functionalities into an engineering environment: extension of the basic temporal logics with higher-level constructs, e.g., regular expressions [19]; identification of the interesting classes of requirements, which should be provided to the end-user by means of graphical and/or natural language interfaces; and automated interpretation of the diagnostics produced by model checkers in terms of the application under analysis.

4   Handling Large Systems

When using model checking to analyse large systems containing many parallel processes and complex data types – such as ADL descriptions of industrial systems – the size of the state space may become prohibitive, exceeding the available computing resources (the so-called *state explosion* problem). Several techniques were proposed for fighting against state explosion:

On-the-fly Verification. Instead of constructing the state space entirely before checking correctness requirements (which may fail because of memory shortage), on-the-fly verification explores the state space incrementally, in a demand-driven way; this allows to detect errors in complex systems without constructing their whole state space explicitly. An open platform for developing generic on-the-fly verification tools is provided by the OPEN/CÆSAR environment [7] of CADP, together with various on-the-fly verification tools (guided simulation, searching of execution sequences, model checking, etc.).

Partial Order Reduction. Due to presence of independent components which evolve in parallel and do not synchronize directly, the state space of a parallel system often contains redundant interleavings of actions, which can be eliminated by applying partial order reductions [24]. A form of partial order reduction useful in the context of process algebras is τ-confluence, for which several tools are already available [23].

Compositional Verification. Another way to avoid the explicit construction of the state space is by using abstraction and equivalence. Compositional verification consists in building the state spaces of the individual system's components, hiding the irrelevant actions (which denote internal activity), minimising the resulting state spaces according to an appropriate equivalence relation, and recomposing them in order to obtain the state space of the whole system. The SVL environment [8] of CADP provides an efficient and versatile framework for describing compositional verification scenarios.

Sufficient Locality Conditions. For specific correctness requirements (e.g., deadlock freedom), there exist sufficient conditions (e.g., acyclic interconnection topology) ensuring the satisfaction of the requirement on the whole system by checking it locally on each component of the system [4]. In this way state explosion is avoided, since only the state spaces of the individual components need to be constructed. An interesting issue concerns the extension of these results for more elaborate correctness requirements.

Experience has shown that analysis of large systems can be achieved effectively by combining different methods. A promising direction of research would be to study the combination of the aforementioned verification methods in the field of software architectures, and to assess the results on real-life industrial systems.

5 Conclusion

In this position paper we have attempted to make precise several directions of research concerning the integration of model checking features within the design process of industrial systems based on software architectures and dynamic ADLs. At the present time, the theoretical developments underlying model checking have become mature, and robust, state-of-the-art tool environments are available. Therefore, we believe that a natural and effective way to proceed is by reusing, adapting, and enhancing the existing model checking technologies in the framework of software architectures.

References

1. P. Abate and M. Bernardo. A Scalable Approach to the Design of SW Architectures with Dynamically Created/Destroyed Components. In *Proc. of SEKE'02*, pp. 255–262, ACM, July 2002.
2. R. J. Allen. A Formal Approach to Software Architecture. Ph.D. Thesis, Technical Report CMU-CS-97-144, Carnegie Mellon University, May 1997.
3. R. J. Allen, R. Douence, and D. Garlan. Specifying and Analyzing Dynamic Software Architectures. In *Proc. of FASE'98*, LNCS vol. 1382, pp. 21–37.
4. M. Bernardo, P. Ciancarini, and L. Donatiello. Detecting Architectural Mismatches in Process Algebraic Descriptions of Software Systems. In *Proc. of WICSA'01*, pp. 77–86. IEEE Computer Society, August 2001.
5. C. Chaudet and F. Oquendo. Pi-SPACE: A Formal Architecture Description Language Based on Process Algebra for Evolving Software Systems. In *Proc. of ASE'2000*, pp. 245–248, September 2000.
6. E. Clarke, O. Grumberg, and D. Peled. *Model Checking*. MIT Press, 2000.
7. H. Garavel. OPEN/CÆSAR: An Open Software Architecture for Verification, Simulation, and Testing. In *Proc. of TACAS'98*, LNCS vol. 1384, pp. 68–84.
8. H. Garavel and F. Lang. SVL: a Scripting Language for Compositional Verification. In *Proc. of FORTE'2001*, pp. 377–392. IFIP, Kluwer Academic Publishers, August 2001.
9. H. Garavel, F. Lang, and R. Mateescu. An Overview of CADP 2001. *EASST Newsletter*, 4:13–24, August 2002.

10. H. Garavel and J. Sifakis. Compilation and Verification of LOTOS Specifications. In *Proc. of PSTV'90* pp. 379–394, IFIP, June 1990.
11. H. Garavel and M. Sighireanu. Towards a Second Generation of Formal Description Techniques – Rationale for the Design of E-LOTOS. In *Proc. of FMICS'98*, pp. 187–230. CWI, May 1998.
12. D. Garlan, S. Khersonsky, and J. S. Kim. Model Checking Publish-Subscribe Systems. In Proc. of SPIN'03, LNCS vol. 2648, pp. 166–180.
13. J. F. Groote. A Note on *n* Similar Parallel Processes. In *Proc. of FMICS'97*, pp. 65–75. CNR, July 1997.
14. ISO/IEC. LOTOS — A Formal Description Technique Based on the Temporal Ordering of Observational Behaviour. ISO Standard 8807, 1989.
15. ISO/IEC. Enhancements to LOTOS (E-LOTOS). ISO Standard 15437:2001.
16. J. Kramer, J. Magee, and S. Uchitel. Software Architecture Modeling & Analysis: A Rigorous Approach. In *Proc. of SFM'2003*, LNCS vol. 2804, pp. 44–51.
17. J. Magee, N. Dulay, S. Eisenbach, and Jeff Kramer. Specifying Distributed Software Architectures. In *Proc. of ESEC'95*, LNCS vol. 989, pp. 137–153.
18. R. Mateescu. Local Model-Checking of Modal Mu-Calculus on Acyclic Labeled Transition Systems. In *Proc. of TACAS'2002*, LNCS vol. 2280, pp. 281–295.
19. R. Mateescu and M. Sighireanu. Efficient On-the-Fly Model-Checking for Regular Alternation-Free Mu-Calculus. *Sci. of Comp. Prog.*, 46(3):255–281, March 2003.
20. N. Medvidovic and R. N. Taylor. A Classification and Comparison Framework for Software Architecture Description Languages. *IEEE Transactions on Software Engineering*, 26(1):70–93, January 2000.
21. R. Milner. *Communicating and Mobile Systems: The Pi Calculus.* Cambridge University Press, 1999.
22. F. Oquendo, I. Alloui, S. Cîmpan, and H. Verjus. The ArchWare ADL: Definition of the Abstract Syntax and Formal Semantics. Project Deliverable D1.1b, European project IST 2001-32360 "ArchWare", December 2002.
23. G. Pace, F. Lang, and R. Mateescu. Calculating τ-Confluence Compositionally. In *Proc. of CAV'2003*, LNCS vol. 2725, pp. 446–459.
24. D. A. Peled, V. R. Pratt, and G. J. Holzmann, editors. *Partial Order Methods in Verification*, vol. 29 of DIMACS series. American Mathematical Society, 1997.
25. A.W. Roscoe. Model-Checking CSP. In *A Classical Mind, Essays in Honour of C.A.R. Hoare*. Prentice-Hall, 1994.
26. D. Sangiorgi and D. Walker. *The Pi-Calculus: A Theory of Mobile Processes.* Cambridge University Press, 2001.
27. M. Shaw and D. Garlan. *Software Architecture – Perspectives on an Emerging Discipline.* Prentice Hall, Englewood Cliffs, NJ, 1996.
28. C. Stirling. *Modal and Temporal Properties of Processes.* Springer Verlag, 2001.
29. B. Victor and F. Moller. The Mobility Workbench – A Tool for the π-Calculus. In *Proc. of CAV'94*, LNCS vol. 818, pp. 428–440.

Distilling Scenarios from Patterns
for Software Architecture Evaluation – A Position Paper

Liming Zhu, Muhammad Ali Babar, and Ross Jeffery

National ICT Australia Ltd. and University of New South Wales, Australia
{limingz,malibaba,rossj}@cse.unsw.edu.au

Abstract. Software architecture (SA) evaluation is a quality assurance technique that is increasingly attracting significant research and commercial interests. A number of SA evaluation methods have been developed. Most of these methods are scenario-based, which relies on the quality of the scenarios used for the evaluation. Most of the existing techniques for developing scenarios use stakeholders and requirements documents as main sources of collecting scenarios. Recently, architectures of large software systems are usually composed of patterns and styles. One of the purposes of using patterns is to develop systems with predictable quality attributes. Since patterns are documented in a format that requires the inclusion of problem, solution and quality consequences, we observed that scenarios are, though as informal text, pervasive in patterns description, which can be extracted and documented for the SA evaluation. Thus, we claim that the patterns can be another source of collecting quality attributes sensitive scenarios. This position paper presents arguments and examples to support our claim.

1 Introduction

The software architecture (SA) constrains the achievement of various quality attributes (such as performance, security, maintainability and modifiability) in a software intensive system [1, 2]. Since SA plays a crowning role in achieving system wide quality attributes, it is very important to evaluate a system's architecture with regard to desired quality requirements as early as possible. The principle objective of SA evaluation is to assess the potential of the chosen architecture to deliver a system capable of fulfilling required quality requirements and to identify potential risks [3].

A number of methods, such as Architecture Tradeoff Analysis Method (ATAM) [4] and Architecture-Level Maintainability Analysis (ALMA) [5], have been developed to evaluate a system's software architecture with respect to desired quality. Most of these methods are scenario-based. The accuracy of the results of these methods is largely dependent on the quality of the scenarios used for the evaluation [6]. The main sources of collecting scenarios are problem domain, quality requirements and stakeholders [1, 6]. We claim that architectural patterns and styles are another important source of collecting quality attributes specific scenarios.

Most of the software architectures for large and complex systems have embedded patterns. One of the major purposes of using patterns is to develop software systems that are expected to provide the desired level of quality [7]. Since patterns are documented in a format that requires the inclusion of problem, solution, and quality consequences, we observed that patterns' description contain, though as informal text, sce-

F. Oquendo et al. (Eds.): EWSA 2004, LNCS 3047, pp. 225–229, 2004.

narios and other architecturally significant information, which can systematically be extracted and appropriately documented to support the SA evaluation process.

In this paper, we present arguments why we believe that architectural patterns can be an important source for collecting scenarios and architectural related information. We also show how quality attribute sensitive general scenarios can be extracted from a few known architectural patterns. Our future research is aimed at formalizing the process of distilling scenarios from architectural patterns for architecture evaluation.

2 Motivation

SA evaluation and architectural patterns and styles are two sub-disciplines of software engineering, which have been gaining a lot of attention since early 90s [8, 9]. SA evaluation is important to predict the level at which the SA will support various quality attributes. Different techniques can be used for SA evaluation. Most of them are scenario-based as scenarios are very useful in characterizing quality attributes to be evaluated. For a scenario-based evaluation method, developing appropriate sets of scenarios are one of the most important activities [1].

The SA researchers have developed various techniques to develop scenarios that can be used to precisely specify and evaluate almost any quality attribute [4, 6, 10]. There are some inherent problems with these techniques; they are expensive, time consuming and the coverage of the final scenario sets is uncertain, which contributes to the possible sensitivity problem of evaluation methods [11]. That is why there is a need to find complimentary or alternative scenario collection techniques to support SA evaluation process.

Nowadays, the architectures of the large software systems are composed of patterns and styles [12]. Each pattern helps achieve one or more quality attribute in a system; however, each of them may also hinder other quality attributes. In pattern-oriented design, an architect develops a desirable SA by composing a number of architectural patterns and tactics. Patterns are documented in a format that requires the inclusion of problem, solution and quality consequences. That means within each pattern, there is information on the description of the scenarios that characterize the quality attributes being achieved by the pattern as well as the quality consequences of using the pattern.

These are the vital pieces of information required to perform SA evaluation and interim results of the evaluation. However, patterns are documented in a way that such information is not readily available to the software architect and SA evaluators. This may be the reason that the information within patterns is normally not used in SA evaluation. While there is a need to provide complimentary or alternative scenarios development techniques and there is huge amount of information implicitly hidden in pattern descriptions, we believe that distilling quality attribute specific information from the patterns can improve the SA evaluation process.

3 A Proposal

In the last section, we mentioned the major drivers of our research to find effective techniques to collect quality attribute specific general scenarios for SA evaluation and to utilize the architecture related information found in patterns. We believe one of the solutions to the afore-mentioned issue is to extract the architecturally important information from patterns and organize it into a format that it can readily be used during architecture design and evaluation. The availability of general scenarios for desired quality attributes during architecture design can help an architect to precisely articulate the quality requirements [7].

Most of the scenario-based SA evaluation methods require the stakeholders to generate scenarios to evaluate the architecture using requirement documents and brainstorming technique. We believe that if the stakeholders are provided with the general scenarios that characterize the quality attributes satisfied by the patterns used in the SA, it will improve SA evaluation and reduce the time and resources required to generate scenarios. Apart from general scenarios, there is another important piece of information which we call proto-evaluation. Proto-evaluations are the quality consequences for each quality attributes and tradeoffs made in the pattern. Proto-evaluations can be used for attribute analysis and tradeoff analysis.

4 Example

In this section, we show a few general scenarios extracted from known architectural patterns in EJB enterprise application [13]. We have stated earlier, a pattern has three elements: problem, solution and quality consequence. Scenarios are described mostly in problem element. However the quality attributes it concerns are also in quality consequence part since explicit quality attributes description are usually not elaborated extensively in the early part of the pattern especially the quality attributes bearing negative quality consequence. We have extracted the quality attribute sensitive scenarios using a scenario development framework proposed in [7]. This framework has following six elements:

- *Stimulus*
- *Response*
- *Source of the stimulus*
- *An environment*
- *A stimulated artifact*
- *A response measure*

For the details of each element, please see [7]. Stimulus, source of stimulus and environment can be found in the problem part of the investigated pattern. Response and stimulated artifact are commonly encountered in the solution part of the pattern. Explanations of the purpose of different parts within a pattern will reveal the stimulated artifact and expected response of the system. Response measures are usually pervasive, especially in the quality consequence part of the pattern documentation.

One scenario from Data Mapper pattern [13] is presented here:

*A periodic data structure change request (**stimulus**) from stakeholders (**source of the stimulus**) arrives when data use case changes after the system is deployed (**environment**). The system (**stimulated artifact**) has to be modifiable (**response**) according to the data structure change request within certain scope under certain time and maintenance cost (**response measure**).*

Similar general scenarios can also be extracted from Direct Access to Entity Bean, Data Transfer Object, Domain Data Transfer Object, Custom Data Transfer Object and Hash Factory [13]. However, all the extracted scenarios may not focus on the positive quality consequence. We can also extract scenarios by looking at negative quality consequence of a pattern and unexpected stimulus.

The second scenario has been extracted from the Data Transfer Object [13] pattern on data transfer performance:

*A periodic large amount of data requests (**stimulus**) from an independent source (**source of the stimulus**) arrive at the system under normal condition (**environment**). The system (**stimulated artifact**) has to transfer the data (**response**) within a certain amount of time under a certain network limit (**response measure**).*

Similar scenarios can be extracted from States Holder, Value Object, Detailed Object [13].

Both of the examples of scenario extraction from the architectural patterns are very high level general scenarios. Patterns usually have extra rich context sensitive information, which can be used to refine the general scenarios into more specific ones. For example, by integrating some contextual information, the performance general scenario can be refined to as following:

*A periodic large amount of requests on an individual data entity attribute (**stimulus**) from a user interface (**source of the stimulus**) arrive at the system under normal condition (**environment**). The system (**stimulated artifact**) has to transfer the data (**response**) within a certain amount of time without generating too many network calls (**response measure**).*

In order to make the general scenarios directly usable by SA evaluation, we need to convert them into concrete scenarios by providing system specific numbers for various elements like periodic, large, time and bandwidth etc.

5 Discussion and Future Work

This position paper argues that architectural patterns are an important source of collecting general scenarios and other architectural information to support the SA evaluation process. We have argued that there is valuable architecture related information, though as informal text, implicitly hidden in the patterns. This information can be systematically captured and used to improve the quality of the SA evaluation. This paper extracts and presents a quality attribute sensitive general scenario from known architectural patterns using a scenario development framework [7] to provide an example. Our future research is aimed at formalizing the scenario extraction process and providing a set of guidelines to identify, capture, and document general scenarios for SA evaluation.

References

1. L. Bass, P. Clements, and R. Kazman, "Software Architecture in Practice," 2nd ed: Addison Wesley, 2003.
2. P. Clements, R. Kazman, and M. Klein, *Evaluating software architectures: methods and case studies.* Boston: Addison-Wesley, 2002.

3. N. Lassing, D. Rijsenbrij, and H. v. Vliet, "The goal of software architecture analysis: Confidence building or risk assessment," in *Proceedings of First BeNeLux conference on software architecture*, 1999.
4. R. Kazman, M. Klein, G. Barbacci, and T. Longstaff, "The Architecture Tradeoff Analysis Method," 1998.
5. N. Lassing, P. Bengtsson, J. Bosch, and H. V. Vliet, "Experience with ALMA: Architecture-Level Modifiability Analysis," in *Journal of Systems and Software*, vol. 61, 2002, pp. 47-57.
6. P. Bengtsson and J. Bosch, "An Experiment on Creating Scenario Profiles for Software Change," University of Karlskrona/Ronneby, Sweden, 1999.
7. L. Bass, F. Bachmann, and M. Klein, "Deriving Architectural Tactics-A Step toward Methodical Architectural Design," 2003.
8. F. Bushmann, R. Meunier, H. Rohnert, P. Sommerlad, and M. Stal, "Pattern-Oriented Software Architecture - A System of Patterns," John Wiley&Sons, 1996.
9. M. Shaw and D. Garlan, "Software Architecture: Perspectivies on An Emerging Discipline," Prentice Hall, 1996.
10. R. Kazman, G. Abowd, L. Bass, and P. Clements, "Scenario-based analysis of software architecture," in *IEEE Software*, vol. 13: Practical, 1996, pp. 47-55.
11. L. Dobrica and E. Niemela, "A survey on software architecture analysis methods," in *Software Engineering, IEEE Transactions on*, vol. 28, 2002, pp. 638-653.
12. M. Fowler, "Patterns of enterprise application architecture," in *The Addison-Wesley signature series*. Boston: Addison-Wesley, 2003, pp. xxiv, 533 p.
13. F. Marinescu, "EJB design patterns: advanced patterns, processes, and idioms." New York: John Wiley, 2002, pp. xxii, 259 p., [1] folded leaf.

Towards an MDA-Based Development Methodology*

Anastasius Gavras[1], Mariano Belaunde[2], Luís Ferreira Pires[3],
and João Paulo A. Almeida[3]

[1] Eurescom GmbH
gavras@eurescom.de
[2] France Télécom R&D
Mariano.belaunde@rd.francetelecom.com
[3] University of Twente
{pires,alme}@ewi.utwente.nl

Abstract. This paper proposes a development methodology for distributed applications based on the principles and concepts of the Model-Driven Architecture (MDA). The paper identifies phases and activities of an MDA-based development trajectory, and defines the roles and products of each activity in accordance with the Software Process Engineering Metamodel (SPEM). The development methodology presented in this paper is being developed and applied in the European 5th Framework project MODA-TEL, which aims at assessing the applicability and potential of MDA in the context of telecom services and applications. The paper claims that the proposed methodology is general enough to be applicable to distributed applications in other domains as well.

1 Introduction

The Model-Driven Architecture (MDA) [6], which is being currently promoted by the Object Management Group (OMG), consists of a set of concepts and principles for the development of distributed applications. The MDA standards define technologies to support these concepts and principles, but they do not prescribe nor require any specific *development methodology*, by which we mean that MDA gives no guidelines in terms of the processes (activities and phases), roles and responsibilities that are involved in the development trajectory of a distributed application. Furthermore, the MDA technologies are not explicitly related to identifiable activities within software development processes, since these technologies are being developed to be generally applicable in combination with development processes that may already be anchored in organisations.

Since MDA does not prescribe a development methodology, each MDA-based development project has to define its own methodology or apply existing ones. This paper outlines the MDA-based development methodology that is being developed and applied in the MODA-TEL project [2]. MODA-TEL is an European IST 5th Framework project that aims at assessing the applicability and potential of MDA in the context of telecom services and applications. This paper identifies phases and activi-

---

* An extended version of this paper is available at [9].

F. Oquendo et al. (Eds.): EWSA 2004, LNCS 3047, pp. 230–240, 2004.

ties in the development process, and defines the roles and products of each activity in accordance with the Software Process Engineering Metamodel (SPEM) [3]. The methodology presented in this paper can be seen as a framework for combining established software development processes with the MDA concepts, principles and technologies, and thus customising the specific software engineering process that may be used in an organisation. This allows organisations to profit from the benefits of applying MDA, like model reusability, preservation of application development investments and automated transformations, to name just a few.

The paper is further structured as follows: The next section below gives an overview of our methodology, in terms of its main activities and phases. After that a section discusses the activities of the project management phase, following by a section that discusses the project preparation activities and a section that presents the activities of the project execution phase. A final section draws some conclusions.

2   Development Activities and Phases

We start the identification of the development phases in an MDA-based project by classifying the users of MDA technology in three categories:

- *Knowledge builders*: people who build knowledge (repositories) to be used in multiple different MDA-based projects. This category includes systems architects, platform experts, quality engineers and methodology experts. We estimate that this group amounts approximately 5% of the total MDA users population;
- *Knowledge facilitators*: people who assemble, combine, customise and deploy knowledge for each specific MDA-based project. This category includes project managers and quality engineers. We estimate that this group amounts approximately 5% of the total MDA users population;
- *Knowledge users*: people who apply the knowledge built and facilitated by the other user categories, respectively. This category includes designers and software engineers. We estimate that this group amounts approximately 90% of the total MDA users population.

Fig. 1 illustrates the three categories of MDA technology users.

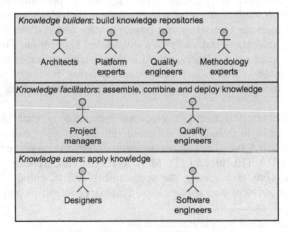

Fig. 1. Categories of MDA users.

Fig. 1 shows that different roles and skills can be identified in the MDA users population. These roles perform different activities and require different tools.

In any MDA-based project, the distinction between preparation activities and execution activities is essential. Preparation activities are those that structure and plan the work, and as such they enable knowledge reuse, which is one the main benefits of the MDA. Preparation activities are mainly performed by knowledge builders and should start before the project execution activities. However, it should be possible to switch between preparation and execution activities, allowing the preparation activities to be revisited while the execution activities are being carried out. This is necessary because project requirements may change (e.g., change of platform), more detailed requirements may be defined (e.g., some requirements were not detailed enough) and problems may occur in the execution phase (e.g., selected modelling language is found too limited or not expressive enough), amongst others.

The MODA-TEL methodology identifies the following phases:

1. *Project management*: aims at organising and monitoring the project;
2. *Preliminary preparation*: aims at identifying modelling and transformation needs;
3. *Detailed preparation*: aims at obtaining the modelling and transformation specifications;
4. *Infrastructure setup*: aims at making tool support and metadata management facilities ready to use;
5. *Project execution*: aims at producing the necessary software artefacts and the final products.

Fig. 2 shows the five phases of the MODA-TEL methodology and their relationships. For reasons of conciseness, in **Fig. 2** we have omitted the relationships between the project management phase and the other phases.

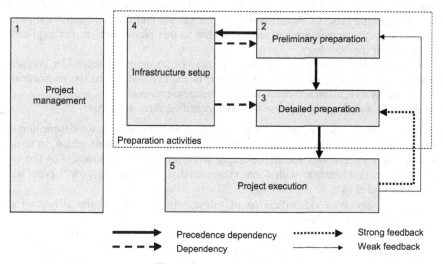

Fig. 2. Development phases.

The phases of our methodology correspond to the available and required expertise identified before, and, therefore, these phases can be directly associated with the partitioning of the MDA users expertise shown in **Fig. 1**: phase 1 is mainly performed by knowledge facilitators, phases 2, 3 and 4 are mainly performed by knowledge build-ers, while phase 5 is mainly performed by knowledge users.

Fig. 2 shows how the preparation activities have been structured in different phases. These phases are useful to understand and to describe the dependencies be-tween the activities. Project management activities have a direct impact on all the other activities; in particular, the activity that defines the whole software development process prescribes the list of the execution activities to be performed, such as, e.g., the sequence of transformations to be implemented. Activities of the preliminary and detailed preparation phases, such as selecting a platform and deciding on the usage of a modelling language, are the key elements to enable reuse of knowledge in the pro-ject execution phase. Finally, the activities of the infrastructure set-up phase, such as, e.g., tool selection, influence the preliminary and detailed preparation phases, even if project managers have decided to be as much tool-independent as possible.

Fig. 2 also shows that many dependencies have been identified between the devel-opment phases of our methodology, which means that these phases should be per-formed iteratively and incrementally. Feedback from the execution activities to the preparation activities, and vice-versa, should be taken into account in an effective way. The availability of model-to-model transformations, code generation techniques and well-defined traceability strategies are crucial for this purpose.

3   Project Management Phase

We distinguish between typical process management activities, such as keeping track of milestones and resource consumption, and activities that are directly related to management decisions absolutely necessary to setup the project, such as the selection of the engineering process. Additional activities known and applied from "best prac-tices" in project management can still be added to this phase, but are not explicitly covered by our methodology.

The management activities identified here may be strongly influenced by prepara-tion activities, e.g., in case SPEM [3] is used to explicitly describe the engineering process, and by execution activities, such as requirements analysis.

In the project management phase we have identified three activities:

- *Software Development Process (SDP) selection*, which results in the description of the software development process to be followed at the execution phase, in terms of specific sub-activities and the resulting work products. A discussion on the use of MDA in combination with some established software development processes can be found in [4];
- *Project organisation* (identification of roles), which results in the allocation of activities to process roles;
- *Quality management*, which defines procedures to enhance the quality of the de-velopment projects. Some aspects of quality management can be orthogonal to the SDP, such as, for example, the maturity levels of the Capability Maturity Model (CMM) [7].

Fig. 3 depicts the activities of the process management phase and the relationships between these activities.

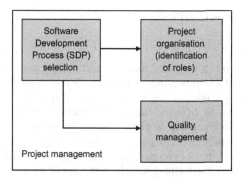

Fig. 3. Project management activities.

Since MDA is based on the principles of object-orientation and component-based development it fits well into most contemporary software development processes. MDA has been conceived to allow the existing development processes in organisations and projects to be reused to a large extent, since MDA concepts can be applied in the scope of these processes.

We use the term *Model Driven Engineering* (MDE) to denote the process of applying an MDA-based SPD. The engineering aspects, i.e., the designing, building and maintaining pieces of software, are dynamic and contrast with the static nature of a set of models. There is no single way to engineer software and many different alternatives can be found by reusing elements of some established software development processes.

Fig. 4 shows the relationship between the SDP selection activity of the process management phase and the project execution phase.

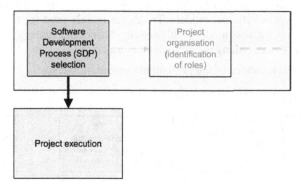

Fig. 4. Influence of the SDP on the project execution phase.

4   Preparation Activities

The preparation activities have been grouped in three phases, namely preliminary preparation, detailed preparation and infrastructure setup. Each of these phases and their relationships with other phases are discussed below.

4.1 Preliminary Preparation Phase

In the preliminary preparation phase we identify four activities:

- *Platform identification*: a platform refers to technological and engineering details that are irrelevant to the fundamental functionality of a system (or system part). What is irrelevant and what is fundamental with respect to a design depends on particular design goals in different stages of a design trajectory. Therefore, in order to refer to platform-independent or platform-specific models, one must define what a platform is, i.e., which technological and engineering details are irrelevant, in a particular context with respect to particular design goals. In this activity we identify the concrete target platform(s) on which the application is supposed to be implemented and their common abstraction in terms of an abstract platform [1]. Concrete platforms may also include legacy platforms;
- *Modelling language identification*: models must be specified in a modelling language that is expressive enough for its application domain. This activity identifies the specific needs for modelling languages. Since models can be used for various different purposes, such as data representation, business process specification, user requirements capturing, etc., many different modelling languages may be necessary in a development project. Process roles for performing this activity include domain experts;
- *Transformations identification*: transformations define how model elements of a source model are transformed into model elements of a target model. This activity identifies the possible or necessary transformation trajectories from the abstract to the concrete platforms. These transformations have to take into account the modelling languages identified before;
- *Traceability strategy definition*: traceability in model transformation refers to the ability to establish a relationship between (sets of) model elements that represent the same concept in different models. Traces are mainly used for tracking requirements and changes across models. This activity defines the strategy to be applied in the definition of traces along the development trajectory.

Fig. 5 shows the activities of the preliminary preparation phase.

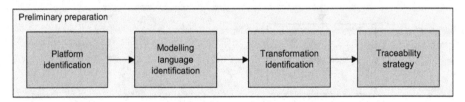

Fig. 5. Preliminary preparation activities.

The activities of the preliminary preparation phase often depend on the requirement analysis activity of the project execution phase (see next section), as depicted in **Fig. 6**.

In case model-driven techniques are used for requirement analysis, certain preliminary preparation activities may precede requirement analysis. For example, this can be the case if a UML profile or a metamodel is available for the User Requirement

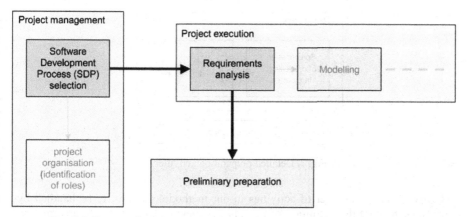

Fig. 6. Influence of requirements analysis on the preliminary preparation phase.

Notation (URN) [8]. Identifying such a profile or metamodel is a preliminary preparation activity to be performed before requirements analysis.

4.2 Detailed Preparation Phase

In the detailed preparation phase we have identified two activities:

- *Specification of modelling languages*: in accordance with the specific needs for modelling languages identified before, this activity identifies the concrete general purpose or domain specific modelling languages that shall be used in the execution phase. Source and target metamodels used in the transformations are also defined in this activity. Process roles for performing this activity include domain experts;
- *Specification of transformations*: model transformations need rules and annotations to control the transformation process. Rules control the transformation of an annotated source model to a target model. Rules have to be defined at the metamodel level, in order to be applicable to any instance of the source metamodel that is transformed to an instance of the target metamodel. Rules can be formalized in a certain modelling language or metamodel, or they may be defined as code in a scripting or programming language. Annotations are information related to a model, optionally defined in terms of elements of this model's metamodel. This activity is concerned with the specification of the necessary transformation rules and annotations.

Fig. 7 shows the activities of the detailed preparation phase.

Language and transformation specifications produced in this phase are strong candidates for reuse, namely in future projects in similar application domains. Therefore these specifications should be somehow stored and catalogued for future use. These reuse considerations are also depicted in **Fig. 7**.

4.3 Infrastructure Setup Phase

In the infrastructure setup phase we have identified two activities:

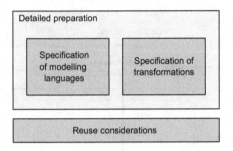

Fig. 7. Detailed preparation activities.

- *Tool selection*: a number of activities in our methodology have to be handled by tools, such as (i) the definition of models and metamodels, (ii) the transformation and code generation based on model information, (iii) the definition of constraints and rules to verify model compliance. This activity aims at selecting of one or more tools to support activities in the development process. For the selection of appropriate tools, all requirements from the software engineering perspective are identified and mapped to capabilities of existing tools available on the market;
- *Metadata management*: metadata provides in most cases information about the structure of data, e.g., which data types are available, the structure of these data types, what data aggregations are valid, etc. Different technology families usually define their own ways to manage metadata, as well as to generate and manipulate metadata repositories. Metadata can be used in different situations, like, e.g., to store information about transformations, to store information about available resources, to support migration or to support applications during runtime. In each project, the necessary support for metadata as well as the way to manage metadata is defined in this activity.

Fig. 8 shows the activities of the infrastructure setup phase.

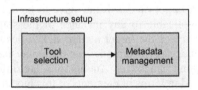

Fig. 8. Infrastructure setup activities.

The tool selection activity can be quite intricate. The choice of the most appropriate MDA tool depends mainly on the level of engineering support required in the project. In some projects, MDA tools may be required to support behaviour modelling and simulation. In general MDA tools should also give support to traceability, for example, to associate code fragments to their corresponding model elements in order to guarantee that changes in the code are reflected in the model and vice-versa. Extensibility, integration with XML-based techniques and interoperability with other tools may also be important requirements to consider. Furthermore, other circumstances like the availability of a certain tool in an organisation or the experience of the designers with some specific tool may strongly influence if not determine the choice. The tool selection activity may have an impact on each of the preparation activities, as well as on the metadata management activity.

5 Execution Phase

The project execution phase is the main phase of a project, since in this phase the developers apply the acquired knowledge to produce software artefacts and deliver the final products. The specific activities of this phase depend on the selected SDP, which is described in terms of sub-activities and work products. However, for the purpose of our methodology we have identified general activities that appear in virtually any object-oriented or component-based SDP. Our methodology has identified seven activities in the project execution phase:

- *Requirements analysis*: this activity generally aims at (i) establishing a dictionary with well-defined terminology and (ii) structuring the requirements. Both the dictionary and the requirements are normally used as input to produce conceptual domain models. Requirements should also be associated to their corresponding model elements, allowing traceability from requirements to models or even to code. It may be even possible to have some model-to-model transformation that creates an initial platform-independent model (PIM) from requirements models;
- *Modelling*: this activity comprises the formal specification, construction, documentation and (possibly) visualisation of artefacts of distributed systems, using one or more modelling languages. This activity is concerned with the development of software engineering specifications that are expressed as an object or component model or combinations thereof. The products of this activity are specifications of the structure of these artefacts, such as names, attributes and relationships with other artefacts. Behaviour specifications describe the behaviour of the artefacts in terms of states, allowed transitions and the events that can cause state changes. The interactions between artefacts may also be represented in behaviour specifications. These models are created with the help of tools that support the representation of the artefacts and their behaviour;
- *Verification/Validation*: this activity is concerned with (i) determining whether or not the products of the modelling activity fulfil the requirements established by the requirements analysis activity, and (ii) evaluating whether the products of the modelling activity are free from failures and comply with the requirements established in the requirements analysis activity. Some existing technologies allow these activities to be performed (semi-) automatically by using tool support. A verification/validation strategy for the produced models has to be explicitly defined in this activity;
- *Transformations*: this activity is concerned with the refinement of the models produced in the modelling activity by means of rules and annotations that control the transformation process. The artefacts defined by the modelling activity are refined by defining data structures and procedures, defining message protocols for the interactions, mapping the artefacts into classes and mapping these onto constructs of a programming language (model-to-code transformations);

- *Coding/Testing*: this activity is concerned with the development of code that is necessary to complement the automated code generation. With current technology, somecoding is still required by developers after a model-to-code transformation has been performed. The same applies for the execution of test cases. Automatic testing is possible to some extent, but usually manual testing is also necessary to complement the testing activities;
- *Integration/Deployment*: this activity is concerned with the embedding of the newly developed systems into their operational environment. In large organisations, new services and applications have to co-exist with established systems and work on existing infrastructures. The MDA prescribes that (new) functionality should be modelled at the platform-independent level. Since platform-independent models of the existing (legacy) systems can be developed by applying reverse engineering, integration issues can be addressed already at the platform-independent level. The deployment sub-activity is concerned with the management of the life-cycle of component instances running on the nodes of a platform. This sub-activity handles issues like, e.g., the transfer of implementations to the appropriate nodes, and instantiation, configuration, activation and deactivation of component instances;
- *Operation/Maintenance*: this activity is concerned with the overall management of the life-cycle of a distributed application, including issues like, e.g., dynamic configuration, dynamic service upgrade, and service migration to different nodes;

Fig. 9 shows the activities of the project execution phase.

Project execution

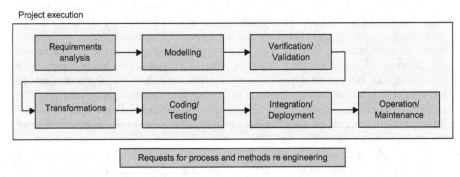

Fig. 9. Project execution activities.

In general, the activities in the project execution phase can be repeated more than once, e.g., if multiple development iteration cycles are applied or errors are found. In case failures, defects or other problems are discovered in one of the activities, the process should resolve the issue at the modelling activity, since models are supposed to drive the whole process execution phase. All activities of the project execution phase can generate feedback to refine and improve of the processes and methods, influencing in this way the preliminary or the detailed preparation phases or both, depending on the severity of the feedback.

6 Conclusions

A development methodology should define guidelines to be used in a development project, in terms of the necessary activities, roles, work products, etc. The methodology presented in this paper gives such guidelines and combines them with the concepts and principles of the MDA. The methodology itself is under development and its application on case studies that are being performed in the MODA-TEL project, will certainly provide the necessary feedback and refinement to improve its applicability. An MDA-based development trajectory can require many different meta-models, models, transformations and their supporting tools. From our first experience with use cases under study, we can conclude that the MDA approach requires that the engineering process is explicitly described and documented in terms of the necessary work products and activities. The explicit definition of the engineering process makes an MDA-based project manageable. An extended version of this paper [9] illustrates the activities of this methodology with a case study on the development of a VoiceXML application.

References

1. J.P.A. Almeida, M.J. van Sinderen, L. Ferreira Pires, D.A.C. Quartel. A systematic approach to platform-independent design based on the service concept. In *Proceedings of the Seventh IEEE International Conference on Enterprise Distributed Object Computing (EDOC 2003)*, Brisbane, Australia, September 2003.
2. http://www.modatel.org
3. MODA-TEL project. *Deliverable D3.1: Model-Driven Architecture definition and methodology*, 2003. http://www.modatel.org/public/deliverables/D3.1.htm
4. MODA-TEL project. *Deliverable D3.2: Guidelines for the application of MDA and the technologies covered by it*, 2003. http://www.modatel.org/public/deliverables/D3.2.htm
5. Object Management Group. *Software Process Engineering Meta-model V1.0* (SPEM), formal/02-11-14, November 2002
6. Object Management Group. *MDA-Guide, V1.0.1*, omg/03-06-01, June 2003
7. Software Engineering Institute. *The Capability Maturity Model: guidelines for improving the software process*. Carnegie Mellon Univ. Addison Wesley Publishing Company, 1995
8. ITU-T. Recommendation Z.150: User Requirements Notation (URN): Language requirements and framework. Geneva, February 2003.
9. A. Gavras, M. Belaunde, L. Ferreira Pires, J.P.A. Almeida, Towards an MDA-based development methodology for distributed applications, in M. van Sinderen, L. Ferreira Pires (eds.): Proceedings of the 1st European Workshop on Model-Driven Architecture with Emphasis on Industrial Applications, MDA-IA 2004, CTIT Technical Report TR-CTIT-04-12, University of Twente, ISSN 1381 - 3625, Enschede, The Netherlands, March 2004, 71-81.

Correct Development of Embedded Systems*

Susanne Graf[1] and Jozef Hooman[2]

[1] VERIMAG, Grenoble, France
Susanne.Graf@imag.fr
[2] University of Nijmegen and Embedded Systems Institute, Eindhoven, The Netherlands
jozef.hooman@embeddedsystems.nl

Abstract. This paper provides an overview on the approach of the IST OMEGA project for the development of correct software for embedded systems based on the use of UML as modelling language. The main contributions of the project are the definition of a useful subset of UML and some extensions, a formal dynamic semantics integrating all notations and a tool set for the validation of models based on this semantics.

1 Introduction

Building embedded real-time software systems of guaranteed quality, in a cost-effective manner, is an important technological challenge. In many industrial sectors, such as automotive and telecommunications, a proper development process supported by validation and formal verification tools is requested. Furthermore, the relations between suppliers and manufacturers are changing; the suppliers provide components which are integrated by manufacturers to produce goods and services of guaranteed quality. This requires new software engineering environments supporting architecture-based engineering practice for building complex systems by composing available components with known properties and evaluating the impact of local design choices on their global behaviour. There is now a general agreement that a means to achieve this is a *Model based approach* which has the following characteristics:

- This approach is based on the existence of a global model of a software system, consisting of possibly heterogeneous components. This model should address different aspects of the system - functional, architectural, non-functional, etc. Changes may be made for some aspects during the development from very high level requirements down to code; nevertheless the consistency of the global model must be maintained throughout the development.
- At any level of abstraction, models should be executable. In the context of embedded systems a model of the environment is also needed in order to allow "testing at model level"; this is interesting as in a model there exists a better controllability of the system and the explicit modelling of non-functional aspects (especially time and memory) allows to avoid the "probe effect" due to the presence of a "tester".

Such a model-based development approach is only useful if it is accompanied by tool support for the validation of design choices. This is particularly true in the context

---

* This work has been supported by the IST-2002-33522 OMEGA project –
http://www-omega.imag.fr

F. Oquendo et al. (Eds.): EWSA 2004, LNCS 3047, pp. 241–249, 2004.

of real-time systems, where non-functional properties, such as reactivity of the system, are as important as its functionality. In order to detect design errors early, it is necessary to take non-functional aspects into account, in particular time-related ones, in high-level abstract models. Early decisions on the ordering of independent activities may later need important redesign when it turns out that time constraints cannot be met. Resolving non-determinism when timing constraints are already taken into account allows avoiding this problem.

Formal validation of different aspects (functional, non-functional) is usually done on specialised analysis models. In order to guarantee consistency, these models should be obtained by tool-supported extraction of the relevant information from the global model, and results of the analysis must be fed back into the global model. To avoid divergence between model and code, which would make the model useless, it is important to have automatic generation of code, depending on the target platform. Moreover, to avoid that "bugs" are eliminated at code level only, also support for round-trip-engineering is needed, where changes in the code are reflected in the model automatically.

In order to be able to implement an environment for such a model-based approach, one needs (1) notations for representing all aspects of heterogeneous systems and their environment, by separating as much as possible different aspects, (2) a formal semantics integrating all notations into a global model of both static constraints and dynamic behaviour, and (3) tools and methods for simulation and formal validation for both functional and non-functional properties of the system. The Unified Modelling Language (UML), which has been developed with the goal to enable model-based development, has become a de facto standard in the domain of software development and is imposing itself also in the domain of real-time and embedded systems.

In this paper we report on work done in the EU-IST project OMEGA. The goal of this project is to provide a framework the development of embedded software systems based on UML and formal verification. The project has 6 academic partners, Verimag, CWI, OFFIS, Weizmann Institute and the universities of Kiel and Nijmegen and 4 industrial users, EADS, France Telecom R&D, Israeli Aircraft Industries and National Aerospace Lab of the Netherlands. The academic partners provide the formal semantics and validation tools based an requirements and feedback from industrial users. The approach is being validated and continuously improved on 4 industrial case studies.

Section 2 gives a brief overview on UML and the state-of-the-art of UML tools as well as formal validation techniques. Section 3 presents the approach chosen by the Omega project and section 4 contains some feedback and lessons learned from the progress achieved within the first two years of the project.

2   Towards UML Based Development: State-of-the-Art and Problems to Be Solved

This section has 3 parts, giving a critical overview on the three main ingredients of the problem the Omega project wants to solve, UML and its semantics, formal validation methods and tools and UML-based CASE tools.

UML, its aims and deficiencies: UML aims at providing an integrated modelling framework encompassing architecture descriptions, as supported by the various Architecture Description Languages (ADL), and behaviour descriptions, as supported by various behavioural specification languages such as languages based on the concept of communicating state machines. Nevertheless, in UML some aspects of model based design are not sufficiently addressed:

– Semantic issues are hardly addressed. The UML meta-model solves a part of the static semantics, but most of the dynamic semantics is left to the CASE tools. Not fixing the dynamic semantics is intentional to provide a unified framework for various domains with different needs. Nevertheless, this means that validation tools are dependent on the semantic choices of each CASE tool. Notions for distinguishing successive refinements of models as well as an appropriate notion of refinement are lacking. In particular, there is no means to distinguish within a single refinement step between the "model" of the system under development and "properties" which can be used as a consistency check of this model and should be implied by it. All properties expressed - in an operational or declarative manner - have a priori the same status.

– Some of the UML notations are not expressive enough or have no appropriate semantics.

  • UML Sequence Diagrams are not meant for fully characterising the set of possible scenarios of a system. We want however use them for this purpose as an alternative to temporal logic which is less well accepted by users than scenario based specifications.
  • The notions for expressing architecture and components were very weak in the initial versions of UML. UML 2.0 has improved the situation, at least at the syntactic level.
  • UML has not been developed in the context of safety or performance critical systems, and initially, time and performance related features have not been considered otherwise than in the form of informal annotations. The Profile for scheduling performance and real-time (SPT) [OMG02] has brought some additional notation, but no concrete syntactic framework, and no semantics.

In the Omega project, we address the above mentioned issues by defining a UML Kernel model with extensions and a formal semantics. We provide also a notation for an explicit distinction between diagrams being part of the model definition and those representing requirements which must be implied by the model and represent the properties to be verified.

Formal verification: Little tool support exists so far for the formal verification of all aspects of this kind of systems. There exists many model checking tools [QS82,CES83] for verifying properties on finite state models. Similarly, there are tools for validating properties of timed systems [Yov97,JLS00] based on timed automata [AD94] and frameworks for scheduling analysis and performance evaluation. These tools suppose that models of a particular form are provided. Some tools claim to handle UML models (e.g. [LP99,CHS00]), but a closer look shows that they validate state charts [Har87] or UML activity diagrams. There are also many tools for the verification of properties of some form of scenarios. Nevertheless, it is impossible to use the different existing tools together for a more complete analysis on a common model which is, amongst others, due to incompatibilities of semantics between tools.

Besides obvious problems of syntax compatibility, there are two main fundamental problems to be addressed when building validation tools that are smoothly integratable into a UML based software development process:

- The problem of adapting the verification techniques and making them scalable. In particular, the use of UML poses several challenges:
  - Verification of systems defined using object-oriented features, such as dynamic object creation and destruction, inheritance and parameterisation.
  - Verification of complex requirements on systems with a complex structure, and including non-functional aspects, such as time related features.
- The problem of model extraction: in UML, different diagrams are used to represent different aspects of a system which all together represent a unique model.
  - To obtain a faithful semantic model (e.g., for interactive or guided simulation) all these must be combined in a consistent manner into a unique semantic model.
  - Different aspects are verified in different steps, possibly using different tools. It is important to extract for the validation of each aspect all the necessary information, but not more than that.

Within OMEGA, UML models are translated into the formats of several existing validation tools. In particular, we consider a tool for handling scenario based requirements [DH99,HKMP03], an untimed model-checking tool [BDW00] and a model-checking tool for timed and untimed specifications [BFG⁺99,GM02]. We also provide a mapping, dealing with general OCL constraints, to PVS [SOR93], an interactive theorem prover allowing general reasoning about models, and thus potentially allowing to overcome some of the problems occurring with object-orientation.

The problem of scalability is addressed in several ways. General compositionality results are applied, and in particular, two aspect-depending abstract models are extracted: an untimed model dealing only with the functional aspects, and a timed model taking into account only control, interaction and timing and scheduling related aspects. In the future, both analysis methods should profit from each other. Presently each of these models is simplified using abstraction and static analysis algorithms implemented in the individual tools.

Finally, model transformation approaches are considered, in the form of scheduler synthesis and the synthesis of a state chart model from a complete set of scenario specifications. Nevertheless, the underlying synthesis problems have a prohibitive complexity, except when applied in restricted contexts.

UML CASE tools: There is a large number of generic CASE tools for UML, which allow mainly to edit diagrams and to generate templates for code production. They only deal with the static structure of a software. For the object-oriented development of real-time systems, there exists a number of specialised CASE tools, such as Rhapsody of I-Logix [Ilo], Real-time Studio of ARTiSAN [Art01b], TAU Generation-2 of Telelogic [Tel02], Rose-RT of IBM/Rational [SR98]. Contrary to general purpose UML tools, they all implement some *dynamic semantics* of UML and allow the user to interactively simulate models, as well as to generate executable code. Nevertheless, most of them pose one or several of the following problems:

- They are visual programming tools rather than modelling tools; non-determinism which is not modelled explicitly - in the environment - is forbidden or eliminated in some way by the tool.
- Some timing features, such as timers, are in general available, but no tool implements a framework as sketched in the SPT profile.
- Some notations, in particular the Object constraint Language, OCL [WK98] which is very useful for constraining models, never really made their way into any CASE tool.
- Apart from some simple static checks, the only available validation method is model-based testing, i.e. interactive or guided simulation of the directly executable part of the model. Tools for formal validation of models are lacking.

In the Omega project, our intention is not to improve CASE tools, but to develop tools that can be used together with any CASE tool exporting models in the standard XMI format. We achieve inter-operability by using mainly the extension mechanisms provided by UML itself. Our tools, however, are not made to be compatible with the dynamic semantics of any particular tool, but propose a rather non-deterministic semantics in which a part of the non-determinism is to be eliminated by timing, scheduling and user defined priority constraints, and not only by predefined rules.

Many important topics are not addressed in Omega, such as code generation, test case generation, general automatic model transformation and refinement, how to get appropriate estimations on execution times and other durations used in the high level model, as well as dealing with other non-functional characteristics, such as memory or power constraints. Moreover, we do not address meta-tools for model and proof management, which is an issue that should typically be handled within a commercial CASE tool.

3   The Omega Approach and Initial Developments

Within Omega, we intend to build a basis for an environment for rigorous model based development of real-time and embedded systems addressing basic issues, such as an appropriate set of notations with common semantic foundations, tool supported verification methods for real-life systems, as well as real-time related aspects. This section gives an overview on how we have addressed these problems.

3.1   UML Notations and Semantics

Concerning the problems of **expressiveness**, we mention here the most crucial issues in the context of real-time systems:

- In a given UML specification, we distinguish between the model and requirements to be verified on this model. Class and architecture diagrams, as well as state-machines are used for the definition of the model. To strengthen the model or to define requirements, (1) Scenarios in a formalism called Live Sequence Charts (LSC), which are more expressive than the standard UML sequence diagram and have a defined semantics[], (2) a subset of OCL extended with history depending constraints [KdB02,KdBJvdZ03] and (3) particular state machines, stereotyped as "observers" [OGO04] can be used.

- In typical embedded systems several execution and communication modes are used[1]. We consider a system as a hierarchically structured set of components. *Activity groups*, which may be part of and contain components, define a mono threaded behaviour, interacting with the environment and revealing their state only at well defined points in between so called run-to-completion steps; no implicit choice concerning the execution order of concurrently active activity groups is made. Communication is either by synchronous method calls or asynchronous signals. This semantics is defined in the form of a unique symbolic transition system in [DJPV03]. A more abstract version by means of an interpretation in PVS is defined in [vdZH03].
- A concrete timing framework, consistent with the SPT profile, has been developed, allowing to define a timed extension of any model. This framework is based on the notion of *timed event*, which can also be used to define a user-defined notion of *observability*, where durations between occurrences of events and constraints on them can be expressed by particular OCL expressions. The semantics of time extensions are orthogonal to the operational semantics.
- We consider architecture diagrams as static constraints and use components in order to define an appropriate notion of encapsulation for compositional reasoning and property preserving refinement. The interface between a component and its environment is defined by ports, where the communication between a component and its environment is only via these ports.

Thus, in order to achieve *semantic integration*, we consider a quite small, but powerful, subset of notations. Presently, activity diagrams are not considered but later they could be integrated easily as an alternative way to define "tasks", as needed in the context of timing and scheduling analysis.

3.2   Tool Support for Verification

The aim of the Omega project is to not impose a particular development methodology, but to provide methodological support for the use of the modelling language and tools in combination, as validation is only feasible for models respecting some structure. To be able to provide useful verification results in the context of software development in the Omega framework, we propose to extend and adapt a number of existing verification tools integrating state-of-the-art technology where each one solves a particular verification problem. The work has two parts, adapting tools to the UML technology and extending the verification technology, as described below.

Adapting tools to the UML *technology:* We have chosen to build upon the existence of the UML exchange format XMI which includes a standard extension mechanism useful to adapt UML to a particular framework. All the validation tools will rely on the same XMI format, and the common semantic framework allows to ensure consistent interpretation of a model amongst the different tools. The problems we had to face are the weakness of the XMI standard (in particular, there exists no structured representation of OCL or the action language, and the representation of sequence diagrams is too

---

[1] E.g. so-called GALS - globally asynchronous, locally synchronous systems are often considered. Our model is close to this view.

poor to represent the more powerful LSC) and the fact that XMI is still not sufficiently adopted, or used in different ways, by the different CASE tool builders.

Extending the verification technology: The main techniques for making formal verification scalable consist in exploiting the principles of compositionality (composing properties of subsystems to derive system properties) and abstraction (extracting just the necessary information from the model of a system or a component for the verification of a given aspect or property). It is well-known that time related aspects are by their nature not very compositional and the object-oriented setting makes the static analysis used for model extraction hard to apply. The methodology used - and its support by the notational framework - plays an important role for obtaining models in which the relevant component can be composed to system properties. This kind of methodological support is out of the scope of the project[2].

Our aim is to provide model-checking tools for establishing properties of components, where the notion of component interface plays an important role for establishing the notion of externally observable behaviour. We use composition theories and support of interactive theorem provers and composability results for timing properties to deduce system properties.

Overview on the Omega tool set: There are four main validation tools in the tool set:
- The play-in/play-out tool [HKMP03] allows user friendly editing of LSC (called play-in), interactive simulation and verification of consistency of LSC (called play-out) and an extension for state machine synthesis.
- A model-checking tool [BDW00] allows the verification of functional properties on an untimed model (time is counted in terms of run-to-completion steps). Properties can either be described by LSC or by a set of temporal logic patterns, integrated in the user interface of the verification tool.
- The IF verification platform [BFG+99,OGO04] allows timed and untimed verification. Nevertheless, it is more appropriate for the verification of coordination and timing properties and scheduling analysis. It takes into account the Omega real-time extensions and represents the UML model by a set of extended timed automata by abstracting a variable amount of attributes. The consistency of a model can be validated by interactive or exhaustive simulation of such a more or less abstract model. Properties, expressed by Omega time constraints or observers can be verified. In some cases, automata representing the externally observable behaviour can be generated. Also schedulability analysis is formulated as a consistency problem and validated in the same way on a particular abstraction.
- A set of tools [KdBJvdZ03,KdB03,vdZH03] built upon the interactive theorem prover PVS. They rely all on the same translation from UML, including OCL constraints, into a PVS expression. The aim is to verify systems which may have configurations of unbounded size and unbounded message queues and data. The tools aims at the verification of type-checking conditions, consistency checks, and proving properties of systems expressed either as temporal logic formulas or as OCL constraints.

---

[2] There is presently much effort devoted to this subject, e.g., in the Artist Network of excellence, see http://www.artist-embedded.org/

An important aspect of the Omega tool set is that all tools are based on a common reference semantics of UML, the only way to ensure that all tools analyse the same model. An effort will be made to provide feedback to the user in a user-friendly manner (e.g. error traces are provided in the form of scenarios), but beyond the already mentioned limited synthesis approaches no feedback in the form of a corrected or refined UML models in XMI format can be provided within the duration of the project. The tools will only provide relevant information, helping the user to manually update or refine the model.

4   Some Lessons Learned

A very preliminary analysis of the feedback from the work with the case studies allowed us to identify some critical points from which we mention only the most important ones:

- Object orientation makes static analysis and constraint propagation, e.g., methods which are important to make the model-checking approach feasible, are very hard to apply due to potential aliasing. Moreover, in the context of embedded systems, the only object oriented feature frequently used is static inheritance which can be compiled away for validation.
- Presently, different tools handle somewhat different subsets of the Kernel UML, for example, only one tool handles OCL, and each tool has its own internal format. A common semantic level format, which keeps the structure and concepts useful for validation and maps all others into more primitive ones, would be interesting for exchanging some effort (e.g. translation of OCL constraints, operational meaning of LSC, ...)
- Users are very satisfied with LSC for the expression of requirements, as long as they are not required to provide complete specifications. This means that we might have to revise our approach to synthesis of state charts from LSC.
- Interactive verification using PVS based on the general semantic model is rather complex and requires many user interactions. This can be improved by restricting the semantics to the features that occur in the model under investigation and by using the powerful strategies of TLPVS, which mechanises proof rules for temporal logic. For the verification of large models, the use of compositionality is essential.
- concerning scalability, there is still quite some effort to be made.

References

[AD94]   R. Alur and D. Dill. A Theory of Timed Automata. *Theoretical Computer Science*, 126:183–235, 1994.

[Art01b]   *ARTiSAN*, 2001.

[BDW00]   T. Bienmüller, W. Damm, and H. Wittke. The STATEMATE Verification Environment – Making it real. In *International Conference on Computer Aided Verification, CAV*, number 1855 in LNCS, 2000.

[BFG+99]   M. Bozga, J.C. Fernandez, L. Ghirvu, S. Graf, J.P. Krimm, and L. Mounier. IF: An Intermediate Representation and Validation Environment for Timed Asynchronous Systems. In *Formal Methods'99, Toulouse, France*, number 1708 of LNCS, 1999.

[CES83]   E.M. Clarke, E.A. Emerson, and E. Sistla. Automatic verification of finite state
            concurrent systems using temporal logic specification: a practical approach. In
            ACM Symposium on Principles of Programming Languages (POPL), 1983.
[CHS00]   K. Compton, J. Huggins, and W. Shen. A semantic model for the state machine in
            the unified modelling language. In *Dynamic Behaviour in UML Models: Semantic
            Questions, UML2000 Workshop*, 2000.
[DH99]   W. Damm and D. Harel. LSCs: Breathing life into Message Sequence Charts. In
            *FMOODS'99, Int. Conf. on Formal Methods for Open Object-Based Distributed
            Systems*. Kluwer, 1999.
[DJPV03]   W. Damm, B. Josko, A. Pnueli, and A. Votintseva. A formal semantics for a UML
            kernel language. In F. de Boer, M. Bonsangue, S. Graf, and W.-P. de Roever, edi-
            tors, *1st Symp. on Formal Methods for Components and Objects, revised lectures*,
            volume 2852 of *LNCS Tutorials*, 2003.
[GM02]   M. Bozga S. Graf and L. Mounier. IF-2.0: A validation environment for compo-
            nent-based real-time systems. In *Conference on Computer Aided Verification,
            CAV*, LNCS 2404, 2002.
[Har87]   D. Harel. Statecharts: A visual formalism for complex systems. *Sci. Comput.
            Programming 8, 231-274*, 1987.
[HKMP03]   D. Harel, H. Kugler, R. Marelly, and A. Pnueli. Smart play-out. In *Compan-
            ion of the ACM SIGPLAN conference on Object-oriented programming, systems,
            languages, and applications*, 2003.
[Ilo]   Ilogix. Rhapsody development environment.
[JLS00]   H. Jensen, K.G. Larsen, and A. Skou. Scaling up UPPAAL: Automatic verification
            of real-time systems using compositionality and abstraction. In *FTRTFT*, 2000.
[KdB02]   M. Kyas and F. de Boer. D1.2.1: Assertion Languages for Object Structures in
            UML. Deliverable of the IST-2001-33522 OMEGA project, 2002.
[KdB03]   M. Kyas and F. de Boer. On message specification in OCL. In *Compositional
            Verification in UML*, Workshop associated with UML 2003.
[KdBJvdZ03] M. Kyas, F.. de Boer, J. Jacob, and M. v. d. Zwaag. Translating UML and OCL
            to PVS. In *Submitted*, 2003.
[LP99]   J. Lilus and I. Porres Paltor. vUML: a tool for verifying UML models. Technical
            Report No 272, Turku Centre for Computer Science, 1999.
[OGO04]   I. Ober, S. Graf, and I. Ober. Model checking of UML models via a mapping to
            communicating extended timed automata. In *SPIN Wshop on Model Checking of
            Software*, LNCS 2989, 2004.
[OMG02]   OMG. Response to the OMG RFP for Schedulability, Performance and Time,
            v. 2.0. OMG document ad/2002-03-04, March 2002.
[QS82]   J-P. Queille and J. Sifakis. Specification and verification of concurrent systems in
            Cesar. In *Int. Symp. on Programming, LNCS 137*, 1982.
[SOR93]   N. Shankar, S. Owre, and J.M. Rushby. The PVS proof checker: A reference
            manual (draft). Tech. report, Comp. Sci.,Laboratory, SRI International, 1993.
[SR98]   B. Selic and J. Rumbaugh. Using UML for Modeling Complex Real-Time Sys-
            tems. Whitepaper, Rational Software Corp., March 1998.
[Tel02]   Telelogic. *TAU Generation 2 Reference Manual*, 2002.
[vdZH03]   M. v. d. Zwaag and J. Hooman. A semantics of communicating reactive objects
            with timing. In *Proc. of Workshop on Specification and Validation of UML models
            for Real-Time Embedded Systems (SVERTS)*, 2003.
[WK98]   J. Warmer and A. Kleppe. *The Object Constraint Language: Precise Modeling
            with UML*. Addison-Wesley, 1998.
[Yov97]   S. Yovine. KRONOS: A verification tool for real-time systems. *Journal of Soft-
            ware Tools for Technology Transfer*, 1(1-2), 1997.

Expressing Domain Variability for Configuration

John MacGregor

Robert Bosch GmbH, Eschborner Landstrasse 130-132
60489 Frankfurt am Main, Germany
john.macgregor@de.bosch.com

Abstract. Ideally, product development in a product line context should consist of selecting the appropriate components, assembling them and setting their parameters. That is, configuring the components. In industrial contexts, component variability varies exponentially with the hundreds, even thousands of products that are realised. Even such a simple direct configuration process, when applicable, is daunting. The problem is compounded when potential modification of the components or component selection based on their effect on overall product capability are taken into account.

The EU-IST project ConIPF is defining a methodology to support product line product development under these conditions with product configuration methods from artificial intelligence. It has defined CKML (Configuration Knowledge Modelling Language) to combine the aspects of feature and component variability and interaction with the procedural aspects of configuring features and components. This language is used to specify the development support environment and to assess the applicability of commercial configuration tools for that development environment.

This paper describes key elements of the ConIPF methodology and shows its relevance to architectural considerations.

Introduction

For industry, the benefits of reuse; reduced effort, shorter development cycles and increased quality, are very seductive. The problem is that they come at a high cost: mastering the complexity of industrial development processes. Industrial product development contexts are sometimes staggeringly complex.

Variability contributes to this complexity, where variability in this case embodies the characterisation of *which* product component is used *where*. There can be hundreds, even thousands, of similar but not identical products. Individual products can consist of hundreds of modules and contain thousands, even tens of thousands, of compile-time or run-time parameters. Sometimes the term "variability management" is used with the emphasis on variability, but the management aspect should not get the short-shrift.

But combinability also contributes to industrial complexity. Combinability addresses that part of variability which deals with the inclusion or exclusion of parts and as such embodies the consideration of *how many* of the components are used in a product. Principally, it consists of cardinality considerations of (mandatory, optional, alternative, limiting to a certain number) and the interdependency considerations (includes, excludes) between peer elements (modules or classes, for example).

F. Oquendo et al. (Eds.): EWSA 2004, LNCS 3047, pp. 250–256, 2004.

In the industrial context, the tremendous product variability manifests itself with corresponding challenges in product architecture variability. Architecture addresses these challenges through structure: product structure (encapsulation), but also through patterns, and through variability management.

Variability management [3][7][13][14]defines the points in the architecture where variability occurs: *variation points*. Since the same basic variability can be realised with different mechanisms at different points in the development process, variation management also defines the binding time as a specific point in the development process where the variability mechanism is invoked and the variability is eliminated, or bound.

The product line approach (PLA) has two differentiating ingredients: the use of feature models to characterise the commonalities and variabilities in the product line's domain and the definition of a platform architecture that codifies these them for re-use[2]. It attacks the variability problem by grouping the products to be developed and classifying their similarities. Platform engineering develops the reuse platform, composed of assets, while application engineering uses the assets to develop the individual products.

Additionally, product line engineering incorporates the explicit consideration of combinability at the requirements level, where atomic requirements are aggregated into features. There are two related methodologies that deal explicitly with combinability: FODA[9] and FORM[10]. While the first deals exclusively with platform engineering, the second addresses both application and platform engineering.

Some work has been done on characterising combinability at the product component level in the product line context [1][4][5][8][12], but work on combinability in terms of actively combining components (i.e. configuring) in product line product engineering is still in its early stages.

Configuring physical product components is a quite mature discipline, in artificial intelligence rather than in product line engineering , however [6]. Structure-based configuration encompasses, among other things, expression for compositional and taxonomic elements, and cardinality and interdependence relations that are very close to those defined in FODA.

Structure-based configuration introduces procedural considerations. That is consideration of the sequence of decisions in which the variability is resolved and how to backtrack when a particular decision results in an interdependency conflict.

ConIPF

The EU Research Project ConIPF (**Con**figuration in **I**ndustrial **P**roduct **F**amilies) is developing a product engineering product derivation methodology based on structure-based configuration.

The ConIPF consortium consists of Robert Bosch GmbH (Germany), an electronics manufacturer, Thales Naval Nederland (Netherlands), a defence systems manufacturer, the University of Groningen (Netherlands), representing software engineering and the University of Hamburg (Germany), representing artificial intelligence.

The ConIPF project is divided into two streams: methodology and experiments. The methodological stream consist of a requirements phase, where the requirements for the methodology are defined based on interviews with personnel from the industrial partners, a development phase where the methodology is defined and a validation phase where the methodology is tested under realistic conditions at the industrial partners.

The experiment stream consists of a planning phase, a preparatory phase where an appropriate product development environment is developed and an experimental phase where the methodology is tested and the results are packaged.

The project is currently at the stage where the methodology has been completely defined, the experimental environments are ready and representative products from each industrial partner are being developed using the methodology.

The *leitmotiv* of the approach is to infer the components of a particular product by selecting features from a feature model which describes all feature variability in the domain. Structure-based configuration is used to guide this process. Only feasible features are offered based on inferences from the cardinality and dependency rules. The approach is especially attractive, as there are commercial tools which perform structure-based configuration.

It is clear that the product derivation process in a product line depends heavily on the platform architecture. One of the bases of the project is the proposition that configuration is an essential activity in product line product development and the design and implementation of the infrastructure to support configuration is a discipline in itself. As such, configuration considerations are significant factors in the platform architecture.

The ConIPF Methodology

The ConIPF methodology is directed at organizations where, as outlined in the introduction, there is the potential for massive reuse. The investment in the analysis required to implement the methodology is clearly justified. In fact, some type of reuse is unavoidable. In cases where reuse is less massive, it is also possible to implement parts of the methodology.

The methodology, per se, consists of three parts: a notation describing the essence of configuring technology, guidance in modelling product line assets (features, components, etc.) using configuration technology and a process for applying the technology in product line configuration.

The following section presents the key ingredients of the methodology. The actual methodology will not be finalized until the experiments are completed.

Capability Features

Configuration is a selection process. The implicit assumption is that the person making the selection understands the effects of the selection. In the product derivation process, a system engineer selects components that provide the qualities required for the product. It is not unusual in industrial contexts that the system engineers that can indeed select the right components are experts with many years of experience. They are often scarce and overloaded. They are therefore also often a bottleneck in the development process.

Features are usually defined to be any useful attribute of a product. The goal of ConIPF is to use feature models that specify, at the top-most level the *capabilities* of the product to be developed. Alternatively, there are features that are attributes of the components. These we term *product attribute* features.

The approach thus attempts to codify the system engineer's expert knowledge to ensure that more personnel can configure products optimally. Overall product quality and development time improve correspondingly.

Note the implication of this approach, however. In order to use product capability features in product derivation, the contribution of component selections to product capabilities must be captured and modeled. This is a not a trivial task.

Process

The methodology addresses 3 aspects to the product line product development process:

☐ Direct Derivation
☐ Calibration
☐ Evolution

Direct derivation refers to the case where available components meet the requirements at hand. Product derivation then consists of selecting the desired features. Personnel surveyed at both industrial partners indicated that direct derivation rates of 75-80% should be achievable in their organisations.

Existing capability models are not exact and often contain approximations or heuristics, or even are based on rigorous testing. Feature selection thus often represents an over-engineered or under-engineered first approximation of the ultimate solution. In this context, "over-engineered" means that the first approximation is either overly-complex, uses overly-expensive components or too many components. "Under-engineered" would be the converse.

Both industrial partners have *calibration* processes that consist of exchanging components or varying parameters to tune the performance of a particular product until it is satisfactory. That is, until the solution represents the optimal trade-off between considerations such as cost, reliability, performance, safety, etc.

Evolution is the converse of direct derivation. The capabilities of the available components do not meet the requirements. When reuse is possible at all, existing components must be adapted or new components must be developed. The task at hand is to identify which components can still be reused directly and how much must be changed and where.

Structure-based configuration can be used in all 3 activities. Features can be selected to identify components that can be reused directly. Requirements that exceed the capabilities of defined features cause conflicts, which can be investigated to estimate modifications. In calibration, configuration models can be used to ensure the consistency of component reselections and parameter changes.

Notation

ConIPF has defined a notation to be used with the methodology: Configuration Knowledge Modelling Language (CKML). It is used to define the knowledge base for configuration. CKML consists of conceptual and procedural knowledge models, where conceptual knowledge describes the entities to be configured and their relationships and procedural knowledge describe the process used to configure them. It is an abstraction from languages used in known configuration tools.

The elements of the conceptual knowledge is similar to the feature description notations used in domain engineering. ([9], [5]) whereby they apply to all artefacts to be configured, not just the features.

Concepts are the entities to be configured. They have properties that are described by parameters. Concepts can be features, components and intermediate representations used in the transformation from features to concepts.

The current hypothesis is that functions in a product are the main software features and the parameters describe the qualities associated with the feature.

Concepts are associated through relations; taxonomic (is-a), compositional (is-part-of) and constraints (mandatory, optional, alternative, requires, excludes, recommended and discouraged).

Configuration consists of executing a sequence of strategies. A strategy is the knowledge of which objects are to be configured, the order to configure them and how to configure them. The procedural knowledge specifies configuration steps which set the concept properties to more specific values. That is, selecting parts, specific instances of generic components or setting property values, for instance. Procedural knowledge also consists of:

☐ Focus knowledge
☐ Selection knowledge
☐ Execution knowledge

Focus knowledge specifies which properties of a concept are to be configured. (Some properties are informational.)

The selection knowledge is embodied in an agenda which specifies the order of the configuration steps.

Execution knowledge specifies how to determine the solution for a particular configuration step. Parameters can be set or the value can be inferred. Constraints can be evaluated. Values can be computed based on algorithms, etc. Execution knowledge also consists of conflict resolution knowledge. That is, how to backtrack to previous decisions after constraint processing detects a conflict.

Conclusions

This paper has presented the ConIPF approach to product line product development. The approach emphasizes the direct reuse of available components while supporting the adaptation or new development of components when necessary. It also emphasizes the use of capability modelling to lessen the reliance on expert knowledge in the selection of components.

It combines traditional product line feature notation with configuration technology from artificial intelligence. The consistency and feasibility of the solution is thus guaranteed insofar as there are no errors in the model.

The methodology addresses all essential aspects of industrial product development processes and offers mechanisms to manage the complexity of industrial product lines through managing both variability and combinability.

CKML, the notation behind the methodology, offers mechanisms for expressing and resolving variability, combinability and procedural considerations in the design of the platform architecture and as such is also a notation for the platform architecture.

Current State and Outlook

The first version of the methodology has been defined and the project is now in the experiment phase. The development environments for the experiment have been implemented, using commercial tools and the assessment plans have been finalised.

The methodology will be published in a book, tentatively titled "Configuration in Industrial Product Families: Challenges, Solutions and Examples"

Acknowledgements

This paper represents the work of the ConIPF project team. ConIPF is partially funded by the European Union.

References

1. D. Batory, S. O'Malley: The Design and Implementation of Hierarchical Software Systems with Reusable Components: ACM Transactions on Software Engineering and Methodology, October 1992.
2. J. Bosch: Design and Use of Software Architectures – Adopting and Evolving a Product-Line Approach: Addison-Wesley, 2000.
3. J. Bosch, G. Florijn, D. Greefhorst, J. Kuusela, H. Obbink, K. Pohl: Variability Issues in Software Product Lines: Proceedings of the Fourth International Workshop on Product Family Engineering PFE-4, Bilbao, Spain, October 3-5, 2001.
4. L. Baum, M.Becker, L. Geyer, G. Molter: Mapping Requirements to Reusable Components using Design Spaces: Proceedings of the IEEE International Conference on Requirements Engineering (ICRE2000), Schaumburg, Illinois, USA June 19-23, 2000.
5. K. Czarnecki, U. W. Eisnecker: Generative Programming. Methods, Tools, and Applications, Addison-Wesley, 2000.
6. A. Günter, C. Kühn: Knowledge-Based Configuration – Survey and Future Directions. XPS-99, Knowledge-Based system, Würzburg, Germany.
7. J. van Gurp, J. Bosch, M. Svahnberg: On the Notion of Variability in Software Product Lines", Proceedings of the 2001 IFIP/IEEE Conference on Software Architecture, August 2001.
8. A. Hein, J. MacGregor, S. Thiel: Configuring Software Product Line Features: Proceedings of the Workshop on Feature Interaction in Composed Systems, 15th European Conference on Object-Oriented Programming (ECOOP 2001), Budapes, Hungary. June 18-22, 2001.

9. K. C. Kang, S. G. Cohen, J. A. Hess, W. E. Novak, A. S. Peterson: Feature-Oriented Domain Analysis (FODA). Feasibility Study, Technical Report CMU/SEI-90-TR-21. Carnegie Mellon University, Software Engineering Institute. 1990.
10. K. C. Kang, S. Kim, J. Lee, K. Kim: FORM: A Feature-Oriented Reuse Method with Domain-Specific Reference Architectures. Annals of Software Engineering. Vol. 5. pp. 143-168. 1998.
11. P. Kruchten: The Rational Unified Process – An Introduction (Second Edition): Addison-Wesley, 2000.
12. T. Männistö, T. Soininen, R. Sulonen : Product Configuration View to Software Product Families. Software Configuration Workshop (SCM-19), Toronto, Canada, 2001
13. M. Svahnberg, J. Van Gurp, J. Bosch: A Taxonomy of Variability Realization Techniques, Technical Paper ISSN: 1103-1581, Blekinge Institute of Technology, Sweden
14. S. Thiel, A. Hein: Systematic Integration of Variability into Product Line Architecture Design.: G. J. Chastek (ed.): Software Product Lines, Lecture Notes in Computer Science, Vol. 2379, pp 130 – 153, Springer Verlag, 2002.

ARCHWARE: Architecting Evolvable Software

Flavio Oquendo[1], Brian Warboys[2], Ron Morrison[3], Régis Dindeleux[4],
Ferdinando Gallo[5], Hubert Garavel[6], and Carmen Occhipinti[7]

[1] InterUnec/University of Savoie – France
`http://www.arch-ware.org`
[2] University of Manchester – UK
[3] University of St Andrews – UK
[4] Thésame – France
[5] Consorzio Pisa Ricerche – Italy
[6] INRIA – France
[7] Engineering Ingegneria Informatica – Italy

Abstract. This paper gives an overview of the ArchWare European Project[1]. The broad scope of ArchWare is to respond to the ever-present demand for software systems that are capable of accommodating change over their lifetime, and therefore are evolvable. In order to achieve this goal, ArchWare develops an integrated set of architecture-centric languages and tools for the model-driven engineering of evolvable software systems based on a persistent run-time framework. The ArchWare Integrated Development Environment comprises: (a) innovative formal architecture description, analysis, and refinement languages for describing the architecture of evolvable software systems, verifying their properties and expressing their refinements; (b) tools to support architecture description, analysis, and refinement as well as code generation; (c) enactable processes for supporting model-driven software engineering; (d) a persistent run-time framework including a virtual machine for process enactment. It has been developed using ArchWare itself and is available as Open Source Software.

1 Introduction

ArchWare applies an innovative approach to the architecture-centric model-driven engineering of software systems that sets the "ability to evolve" as its central characteristic. Evolution arises in response to changes to requirements as well as to run-time feedback. Within this focus, ArchWare comprises:

- the definition of formal languages (with textual and graphical notations) for modelling dynamic[2] architectures (including expression of run-time structure, behaviour, and semantic properties from a run-time component-and-connector viewpoint) and expressing their analyses and refinements;

---

[1] The ArchWare European Project is partially funded by the Commission of the European Union under contract No. IST-2001-32360 in the IST-V Framework Program.

[2] The architecture of a software system is dynamic if it can change during the course of its execution.

F. Oquendo et al. (Eds.): EWSA 2004, LNCS 3047, pp. 257–271, 2004.
© Springer-Verlag Berlin Heidelberg 2004

- the implementation of a customisable environment for architecture-centric software engineering, including processes and tools for supporting architecture description, analysis, refinement, code generation, and their evolution;
- the validation of ArchWare languages and environment through industrial business cases and its dissemination as Open Source Software.

The novelty of the ArchWare approach lies in its holistic view of software. This starts with the capturing of the key architectural decisions by the definition of architecture styles, which might also involve the specification of invariant properties of the software (w.r.t. aspects such as structure, behaviour and qualities). Such properties may then be checked/proved using analysis tools throughout the software life cycle. Since ArchWare accommodates both static and dynamic qualities, it is essential that the run-time system can provide feedback and evolve while preserving the defined properties according to any policy and constraint defined at the level of the architectural style.

ArchWare goes beyond existing software environments in supporting architecture-centric engineering of software systems. In ArchWare both the software engineering process and its products at every stage of the software life cycle, including specification, implementation, qualities and indeed architectural styles themselves, are run-time evolvable. While existing software environments have proposed and implemented mechanisms for particular evolutionary scenarios, ArchWare addresses the problem of evolution at all levels of abstraction throughout the lifecycle of a software system.

The engineering of evolvable software systems requires the capture of key design decisions about "how" the software is to function in terms of expected behaviours, "what" is its structure in terms of components and their connectors, and "which" qualities are to be guaranteed. Furthermore, an appropriate refinement process (describing "how to build" the software) is also to be effectively supported.

The core of ArchWare is its integrated set of architecture-centric languages: an architecture description language, an architecture analysis language, and an architecture refinement language. These integrated languages are supported by an integrated tool-set including a UML-based visual editor, a hyper-code textual editor, a graphical animator, a property checker, a refiner, a virtual machine, and a code-generator synthesizer.

ArchWare provides a process-integrated software engineering environment. The ArchWare software engineering process is itself influenced by its architecture-centric nature, in which the software architecture description is used to organise development activities. This architecture-centric approach guarantees that compliant implementations conform to the architecture description (including structural, behavioural, and quality properties).

A further central aspect of ArchWare is the support for the dynamic evolvability of applications and embedded processes. ArchWare enables deployed software architectures to evolve, in a controlled manner, in order to address aspects such as run-time evolution of requirements and technology.

This paper gives an overview of ArchWare. The remainder of the paper is organised as follows. Section 2 introduces architecture-centric model-driven software engineering. Section 3 briefly presents the ArchWare architecture-centric languages: the description, analysis and refinement languages. Section 4 introduces the ArchWare architecture-centric integrated development environment. Section 5 addresses related work and concludes the paper.

2 Architecture-Centric Model-Driven Software Engineering

All forms of engineering rely on models to design real-world systems. Models are used in many ways: to understand specific system aspects, predict system qualities, reason about impact of changes, and communicate major system features to stakeholders.

Figure 1 shows the spectrum of modelling approaches in software engineering [13]. Each category identifies a particular use of models in assisting software engineers to create running applications (code) for a specific run-time platform as well as the relationship between the models and the code.

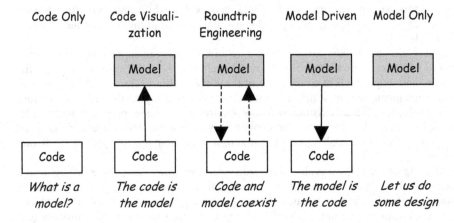

Fig. 1. The Modelling Spectrum.

Models are at the heart of the ArchWare approach. ArchWare provides a model-driven approach, i.e. the system models have sufficient detail to enable the generation of a full system implementation from the models themselves. Indeed, "the model is the code", i.e. the focus is on modelling and code is mechanically generated from models. In ArchWare, models are architecture-centric (run-time) models. They are executable and support analysis and refinement. This is illustrated in Figure 2 which shows a variety of architecture-centric model-driven activities and stakeholders that may be used when developing applications in ArchWare.

Typical architecture-centric activities are "define style", "define architecture", and "refine architecture" (the last refinement is code generation). Typical stakeholders are "style architect", "application architect", and "application engineer".

"Define style" activities, whose principal actors are the "style architects", represent the top level inception of a family of software architectures. An architecture style defines a domain specific architecture description "profile", including formal definitions of what an architectural element is, and what its invariant properties (including qualities) are, how elements can be combined, which constraints apply, and which processes can be applied to architecture elements and whole architecture descriptions (notably w.r.t. refinement and evolution).

"Define architecture" activities, whose principal actors are the "application architects", may use the domain specific styles defined by the style architect to describe a

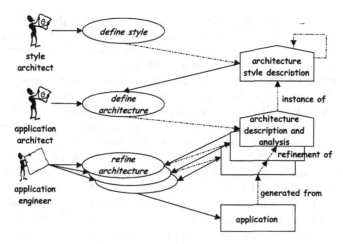

Fig. 2. ArchWare Architecture-centric Model-driven Software Engineering.

specific software architecture. In ArchWare an architecture description conforms to the properties and constraints defined by its style and can represent a system at various levels of abstractions (w.r.t. the detail of implementation decisions provided by the application engineer).

"Refine architecture" activities, whose principal actors are the "application engineer", support refinement transformations from abstract to more concrete architecture descriptions. Thus, an abstract – platform independent – architecture description can be refined to a concrete – platform specific – description of a specific application. The role of the application engineer is to derive that concrete description by applying correctness preserving refinements that conform to the constraints defined by the application architect and by the adopted architecture styles.

It is worth noting that this software engineering process model is not hard-coded in ArchWare. It is one possible architecture-centric software engineering process model that can be explicitly defined and enacted in ArchWare. ArchWare provides a library of software engineering process models that includes this one and they are all evolvable.

3 ARCHWARE Architecture-Centric Languages

ArchWare provides languages for describing dynamic architectures, analysing architecture structural and behavioural properties, and refining architecture descriptions. These languages are implemented using a software environment for supporting the evolution of architectural models, and this environment includes the processes used to develop the environment.

3.1 ARCHWARE Architecture Description Language

In ArchWare, architecture description encompasses two aspects: the expression and verification of architectural styles (typically carried out by style architects) and of software architectures themselves (typically carried out by application architects).

The ArchWare Architecture Description Language (ADL) [50][48] provides the core structure and behaviour constructs for describing dynamic software architectures. It is a formal specification language designed to be executable and to support automated analysis and refinement of dynamic architectures.

The ARCHWARE ADL has as formal foundation the higher-order typed π-calculus [54], a higher-order calculus for communicating and mobile systems. The ARCHWARE ADL is itself a formal language defined as a domain-specific extension of the higher-order typed π-calculus: it is a well-formed extension for defining a calculus of communicating and mobile architectural elements.

The ARCHWARE ADL takes its roots in previous work concerning the use of π-calculus as semantic foundation for architecture description languages [15][14]. Indeed, a natural candidate for expressing dynamic (run-time) behaviour would be the π-calculus as it is [43], which provides a general model of computation and is Turing-complete. This means that in π-calculus "every computation is possible but not necessarily easy to express". In fact, the classical π-calculus is not suitable as an architecture description language since it does not provide architecture-centric constructs to easily express architectures in particular w.r.t. architectural structures. Therefore, a language encompassing both structural and behavioural architecture-centric constructs is needed. The ARCHWARE ADL is this encompassing language, defined as a domain-specific extension of the higher-order typed π-calculus. It achieves Turing completeness and high architecture expressiveness with a simple formal notation.

The following general principles guided the design of ARCHWARE ADL:

- formality: ARCHWARE ADL is a formal language: it provides a formal system, at the mathematical sense, for describing dynamic software architectures and reasoning about them;
- run-time viewpoint: ARCHWARE ADL focuses on the formal description of software architectures from the run-time viewpoint: the (run-time) structure, the (run-time) behaviour, and how these may evolve over time;
- executability: ARCHWARE ADL is an executable language: a virtual machine runs specifications of software architectures;
- user-friendliness: ARCHWARE ADL supports different concrete syntaxes – textual [17][59] and graphical [6][7] (including UML-based) notations – to ease its use by architects and engineers.

Based on these general principles, the design of ARCHWARE ADL followed the following language design principles [47][57][58]:

- the principle of correspondence: the use of names are consistent within ARCHWARE ADL, in particular there is a one to one correspondence between the method of introducing names in declarations and parameter lists;
- the principle of abstraction: all major syntactic categories have abstractions defined over them (in ARCHWARE ADL, it includes abstractions over behaviours and abstractions over data),
- the principle of data type completeness: all data types are first-class without any restriction on their use.

In first-class citizenship, i.e. in addition to rights derived from type completeness (i.e. where a type may be used in a constructor, any type is legal without exception), there are properties possessed by all values of all types that constitute their civil rights in the language. In ARCHWARE ADL they are:

- the right to be declared,
- the right to be assigned,
- the right to have equality defined over them,
- the right to persist.

Additionally, ARCHWARE ADL provides an extension mechanism, i.e. new constructs can be defined on top of the language using user-defined mixfix abstractions. This extension mechanism provides the basis for providing style-based definitions.

In ArchWare, a style notation [16], built on the ARCHWARE ADL, provides the style constructs from which the base component-and-connector style and other derived styles can be defined. Conceptually, an architectural style includes:

- a set of abstractions for architectural elements,
- a set of constraints (i.e. properties that must be satisfied) on architectural elements, including legal compositions,
- a set of additional analyses that can be performed on architecture descriptions constructed in the style.

ArchWare provides a novel ADL that is general-purpose and Turing-complete. The advantage w.r.t. other ADLs is that the ARCHWARE ADL supports user-defined architectural component-and-connector abstractions (instead of being obliged to use hard-coded abstractions provided by particular ADLs that very often do not meet architect needs). It can be seen as a second generation ADL: in first generation ADLs, languages were not complete and architectural (run-time) concepts were hard-coded as language constructs; in second generation, languages should be complete and architectural (run-time) concepts should be customisable.

3.2 ARCHWARE Architecture Analysis Language

In ArchWare, architecture analysis encompasses two aspects: the expression and verification of properties of architectural styles (typically carried out by style architects) and of software architectures themselves (typically carried out by application architects).

The ArchWare Architecture Analysis Language (AAL) [4] provides a uniform framework for specifying relevant properties of styles and architectures. These properties have different natures: they can be structural (e.g. cardinality of architectural elements, interconnection topology) or behavioural (e.g. safety, liveness, and fairness defined on actions of the system). The ARCHWARE AAL complements the ARCHWARE ADL with features allowing architects to express and verify properties of software architectures and styles in a natural way. Analysis is intended to be performed according to three approaches: model-checking, theorem proving and specific external tools.

The ARCHWARE AAL is a formal property expression language designed to support automated verification. Thereby, one can mechanically check whether an architecture described in ARCHWARE ADL satisfies a property expressed in ARCHWARE AAL.

The ARCHWARE AAL has as formal foundation the modal μ-calculus [35], a calculus for expressing properties of labelled transition systems by using least and greatest fixed point operators. ARCHWARE AAL is itself a formal language defined as an extension of the μ-calculus: it is a well-formed extension for defining a calculus for expressing structural and behavioural properties of communicating and mobile architectural elements.

The ARCHWARE AAL takes its roots in previous work concerning the extension of modal operators with data-handling constructs [41], the use of regular expressions as specification formalism for value-passing process algebras [23], and the extension of fixed point operators with typed parameters [30].

Indeed, a natural candidate for "pure" behavioural properties would be the modal μ-calculus, which is a very expressive fixed point-based formalism subsuming virtually all temporal logics defined so far in the literature [55]. However, since ARCHWARE AAL must also provide features for expressing structural properties of architectures [5], the modal μ-calculus is not sufficient. Therefore, a formalism encompassing both the predicate calculus and the modal μ-calculus is needed. The ARCHWARE AAL is, thereby, this encompassing formalism, defined as a domain-specific extension of the μ-calculus.

The ARCHWARE AAL combines predicate logic with temporal logic in order to allow the specification of both structural and behavioural properties. It enables automated verification of property satisfaction by model checking (through on-the-fly model checking) or theorem proving (through deductive verification using tabled logic programming).

3.3 ARCHWARE Architecture Refinement Language

Software applications are usually developed in several steps. Indeed, the concrete architecture of a software system is often developed through vertical and horizontal refinements of related architectures that differ respectively w.r.t. abstraction and partition dimensions.

Vertical refinement steps add more and more details to abstract models until the concrete architectural model is described. A vertical refinement step typically leads to a more detailed architecture description that increases the determinism while implying properties of the abstract description. Generally, an abstract architecture is smaller and easier to understand and a concrete architecture reflects more implementation concerns.

Horizontal refinement is concerned with partitioning of an architecture. For instance, partitioning an abstract component in its parts at the same abstraction level.

ArchWare supports both vertical and horizontal refinement. In ArchWare, the underlying approach for architectural refinement is underspecification, i.e. at a high-level of abstraction, when specifying an architectural element, certain aspects can be left open. The decrease of this underspecification establishes a refinement relation for architectural elements.

A refinement relation in ArchWare, from an external or internal point of view, comprises four forms of refinement:

− behaviour refinement,
− port refinement,
− structure refinement,
− data refinement.

In behaviour refinement, the underspecification may concern the external (observable) behaviour or the internal behaviour of an architectural element. The external behaviour of an architectural element is the behaviour that its environment can observe, i.e. its behaviour from an external point of view. The internal behaviour concerns the internal expression of behaviour within the scope of the architectural element. The structure of an architectural element is its internal structure in terms of subarchitectural elements and their connected ports, i.e. the structure within the scope of the architectural element from an internal point of view. The ports of an architectural element provide the interaction points (i.e. connections) between the element and its environment, i.e. its ports from an external point of view.

The most fundamental notion of refinement in ArchWare is behaviour refinement. The other forms of refinement imply behaviour refinement modulo port, structure and data mappings.

In general, architectural refinement is a combination of the four forms of refinement. For instance, an architect can define an abstract architecture, then "data" refine that architecture in order to introduce base and constructed data types, then "port" refine the architecture to have ports with finer grain connections carrying data of different types, then "structure" refine its composite behaviour by adding new finer grain connectors, and so on.

The ArchWare Architecture Refinement Language (ARL) [49] provides constructs for defining refinements of the four forms cited so far, according to external or internal points of view. Composite refinements can be defined in terms of refinement primitives and composite refinements themselves. Refinement primitives comprise:

- adding, removing, replacing or transforming data type declarations of an architecture,
- adding, removing, replacing or transforming ports of an architecture,
- adding, removing, replacing or transforming output and input connections of ports of an architecture,
- transforming the behaviour of an architecture or the behaviour of a component or connector in an architecture,
- adding, removing, replacing or transforming components or connectors in an architecture,
- exploding or imploding components or connectors in an architecture,
- unifying or separating connections of ports in an architecture.

These primitives, applied step by step, allow the incremental transformation of an architecture description. These transformations are enforced to be refinements if preconditions of refinement primitives are satisfied and proof obligations discarded. A refinement engine based on rewriting logics [40][12] runs the refinement descriptions expressed in ARCHWARE ARL generating further refined architectures. Code is generated from refined (concrete) architectures.

The ARCHWARE ARL is a formal (executable) refinement language providing architecture-centric refinement primitives and supporting refinement compositions in both vertical and horizontal dimensions, from external or internal points of view. When applied, they refine architectural models described in ARCHWARE ADL outputting new refined architectural models also in ARCHWARE ADL.

ARCHWARE ARL provides the required key features for supporting architecture-centric model-driven formal development. By addressing software development as a set of architecture-centric model refinements, the refinements between models become first class elements of the software engineering process. This is significant because a great deal of work takes places in defining these refinements, often requiring specialized knowledge on source and target abstraction levels, for instance knowledge on the source application logics and on the targeted implementation platforms. Efficiency and quality of software systems can be improved by capturing these refinements explicitly and reusing them consistently across developments. Thereby, user-defined refinement steps can be consistently defined, applied, validated, and mechanically automated.

4 ARCHWARE Integrated Development Environment

ArchWare implements a software development environment, i.e. the ArchWare Integrated Development Environment (IDE), to support the application of architecture-centric processes. The ARCHWARE IDE is composed of:

- The ArchWare Core Environment which provides the ARCHWARE ADL Compiler and Virtual Machine that supports the enactment of architecture descriptions.
- The ArchWare Core Meta-Process Models which provide the support for software processes that are used to build and evolve software applications.
- The ArchWare Environment Components which provide the ArchWare tools that support architecture description, analysis, and refinement processes.

The ARCHWARE ADL Virtual Machine provides the basic support for an evolvable persistent store used to both control the execution of applications and the processes used for their development and subsequent evolution [28]. Architecture descriptions expressed in ARCHWARE ADL will be enacted after compiling the ADL into the Virtual Machine executable code and thus will be preserved (and, more significantly, can be dynamically evolved) in the target persistent store.

The main ArchWare Core Meta-Process Model is the Process for Process Evolution (P2E) [29]. This provides a recursive mechanism for selecting a process abstraction (written in ARCHWARE ADL) from a library of existing abstractions or for producing a new (or evolved) abstraction if a suitable one is not available. The recursion means that abstractions for abstraction production are developed (and evolved) in the same way. This recursion can apply to any depth.

The ARCHWARE ADL Virtual Machine persistent store provides a repository for storing, retrieving and refining architectural models. Basic support is provided through the concept of an architecture "node" which is a reference to a element description written in ARCHWARE ADL. Nodes are related through a graph structure where the directional arcs represent different dimensions of refinement supported by ArchWare. The ARCHWARE IDE provides operations to support the creation and evolution of this graph structure. There is a refine operation which allows for one node to be related to another in terms of the child node being a more concrete vertical refinement of its parent. There is a partition operation which allows for nodes to be related by horizontal refinement in terms of the child(ren) being parts explosion of the parent. Methods of vertical and horizontal refinements are written in ARCHWARE ARL. There is also a satisfy operation to support verification of properties written in ARCHWARE AAL. The nodes (and graph structure) are evolved using the P2E meta-process cited so far.

ArchWare Environment Components are implemented either as ADL enactable descriptions (and hence wholly stored in the ADL Virtual Machine persistent store) or as COTS[3]-like components integrated by wrapping them using ARCHWARE ADL as with other application software. Wrapped application components are essentially the end-user components of an ArchWare-based application in operation.

From the viewpoint of ArchWare users, the establishment of an integrated persistent environment that supports higher-order code yields a new software development paradigm, hyper-code [61], in which source code may include direct links to data and code values that exist in the persistent environment. Hyper-code unifies source code and executable code. The result is that the distinction between them is completely removed: the software engineer sees only a single code representation form throughout the software engineering process, during software construction, execution, debugging, and viewing existing code and data.

The integration of hyper-code into the ARCHWARE ADL supports this unified view [8]: an architecture can be described, then compiled to be executed, afterwards during execution composed with other descriptions via hyper-code, and so on.

The ARCHWARE IDE is itself an example of an evolutionary software system. ArchWare adopts the methods and principles it itself is developing in the development of the ArchWare Engineering Environment.

5   Related Work and Concluding Remarks

Several architecture description languages (ADLs) have been proposed in the literature, including: ACME/Dynamic-ACME [26][27], AESOP [25], AML [60], ARMANI [44], CHAM-ADL [32][33], DARWIN [39], META-H [11], PADL [9], RAPIDE [52][38], SADL [45][46], $\sigma\pi$-SPACE [15][36], UNICON-2 [19], and WRIGHT/Dynamic-WRIGHT [2][3].

ADLs provide both a concrete syntax and a formal, or semi-formal, semantics. Typically, they embody a conceptual framework reflecting characteristics of the domain for which the ADL is intended and/or an architectural style [42].

The focus of ArchWare is on languages and tools for the formal modelling of dynamic software architectures (evolvable at design and run-time), and for the computer-aided formal analysis and refinement of these models. In a broad sense the ARCHWARE ADL is composed of a set of integrated notations: the architecture description notation (the core), the style definition notation, the property expression notation, and the refinement definition notation. No other ADL provides a comprehensive set of notations for describing dynamic architectures.

But how does ArchWare compare with related work? Comparing ADLs objectively is a difficult task because their focuses are quite different. Most ADLs essentially provide a component-and-connector built-in model of architecture description and formalise topological constraints. The reason for this is probably that structure is certainly the most understandable and visible part of an architecture. But behavioural and quality aspects are not completely neglected. They are often taken into account (even if partially) in most ADLs. They are certainly an essential part of architecture description.

---

[3]   Commercial off-the-shelf (COTS).

ARCHWARE ADL is the most general among studied ADLs. Instead of hard coding a specific component-and-connector viewpoint model, it is a general-purpose ADL that can be used to define, in a compliant way, different user-defined component-and-connector viewpoint models.

ARCHWARE AAL provides the notation to express properties of architectures described in ARCHWARE ADL.

ARCHWARE AAL combines predicate logic with temporal logic in order to allow the specification of both structural properties and behavioural properties concerning architecture descriptions obtained by instantiating a given style.

Regarding behavioural properties, the choice of modal μ-calculus as the underlying formalism provides a significant expressive power. Moreover, the extension of μ-calculus modalities with higher level constructs such as regular formulas inspired from early dynamic logics like PDL [21] facilitates the specification task of the practitioners, by allowing a more natural and concise description of properties involving complex sequences of actions. The extension of fixed point operators with data parameters also provides a significant increase of the practical expressive power, and is naturally adapted for specifying behavioural properties of value-passing languages such as the ARCHWARE ADL.

In the context of software architectures, several attempts at using classical process algebras and generic model-checking technology have been reported in the literature. In [31], various architectural styles (e.g., repository, pipe-and-filter, and event-action) are described in LOTOS, by using specific communication patterns and constraints on the form of components, and verified using the CADP toolbox [20][24]. In [53], several variants of the pipe-and-filter style are described in LOTOS and analysed using CADP. In [34], the transformation of software architectures specified in LOTOS and their verification using the XTL model-checker [41] of CADP are presented. Finally, an approach for checking deadlock freedom of software architectures described using a variant of CCS is described in [10]. All these works provide rather ad-hoc solutions for a class of software architectures limited to static communication between architectural elements, and can be subsumed by the more general framework provided by ARCHWARE ADL/AAL and verification tools.

Regarding structural analysis, ACME, ARMANI, CHAM-ADL, DARWIN, RAPIDE, SADL, WRIGHT and others addressed mainly properties like completeness and consistency of software architectures. Most of those approaches propose a less or more sophisticated language for describing properties to analyse.

The main limitation of most of these approaches with regard to ArchWare objectives is that they address either structural or behavioural properties, but not both as in ArchWare.

As regards architecture refinement, with the exception of a variant of FOCUS [56], i.e. FOCUS/DFA [51], RAPIDE and SADL, there is no proposal for a rigorous calculus based on architectural terms. In the case of SADL the refinement is only structural. In the case of RAPIDE it is only behavioural (supported by simulations). In both cases, clear architectural primitives for refining architectures are not provided and the refinement supported is only partial. ARCHWARE ARL, like the B [1] and Z [18] formal methods, provides operations to transform specifications. However, unlike FOCUS, B and Z, ARCHWARE ARL has been specially designed to deal with architectural elements of any architectural style. Unlike SADL, ARCHWARE ARL supports underspecification. In FOCUS/DFA, refinement is essentially logical implication. In SADL, it is restricted by faithful interpretation. In RAPIDE, it is defined by simulations. In ArchWare, it is based on property implication, where the properties to be preserved are defined by the architect.

The ARCHWARE ARL provides a novel language that on the one side has been specifically designed for architectural refinement taking into account refinement of behaviour, port, structure, and data from an architectural perspective and on the other side is based on preservation of properties. The core of ARCHWARE ARL is a set of architecture transformation primitives that support refinement of architecture descriptions. Transformations are refinements when they preserve properties of the more abstract architecture. Core properties are built-in. Style-specific or architecture-specific properties are user defined. The underlying foundation for architected behaviours is the higher-order typed π-calculus. Satisfying proof obligations in ARCHWARE ARL is supported by the ArchWare analysis tools, which comprises a model checker, a prover and specific evaluators.

A detailed positioning of ARCHWARE ADL, AAL and ARL w.r.t. the state-of-art is given in [22][37][49].

ARCHWARE languages have been applied in several realistic case studies and industrial business cases at Thésame (France) and Engineering Ingegneria Informatica (Italy). The pilot project at Thésame aims to develop and evolve agile integrated industrial process systems. The pilot project at Engineering Ingegneria Informatica aims to develop and evolve federated knowledge management systems. ARCHWARE languages have also been used by the CERN (Switzerland) for architecting human computer interfaces for monitoring particle accelerator restart. Ongoing work focuses on customisations of the ARCHWARE IDE for automating engineering processes in these applications.

Besides providing languages, frameworks, processes, and tools for architecture-centric model-driven engineering, ArchWare enforces a novel relationship between software systems and their development environments. Indeed, in ArchWare, software systems and the software development environments that support their engineering are both evolving artefacts; the keystone of ArchWare is recognising that compositional, architecture-centric evolutionary approaches (supported by adequate formal languages, frameworks, processes and tools) are needed to effectively construct and operate both kinds of systems. Thus, ArchWare solutions are applied consistently to the software systems being engineered as well as to the software engineering process and environment themselves. Jointly, they exploit the many advantages of the ArchWare architecture-centric compositional and evolutionary framework. This gives the possibility of an ongoing link between software systems and their software engineering processes in order to support continuous evolution, thereby accommodating change over their lifetime.

References

1. Abrial J.-R.: The B-Book: Assigning Programs to Meanings. Cambridge University Press, 1996.
2. Allen R.: A Formal Approach to Software Architectures. PhD Thesis, Carnegie Mellon University, 1997.
3. Allen R., Douence R., Garlan D.: Specifying and Analyzing Dynamic Software Architectures. In Fundamental Approaches to Software Engineering, LNCS 1382, Springer Verlag, 1998.

4. Alloui I., Garavel H., Mateescu R., Oquendo F.: The ArchWare Architecture Analysis Language: Syntax and Semantics. Deliverable D3.1b, ArchWare European RTD Project, IST-2001-32360, January 2003.
5. Alloui I., Oquendo F.: Supporting Decentralised Software-intensive Processes using ZETA Component-based Architecture Description Language. Enterprise Information Systems, Joaquim Filipe (Ed.), Kluwer Academic Publishers, 2002.
6. Alloui I., Oquendo F.: The ArchWare Architecture Description Language: UML Profile for Architecting with ArchWare ADL. Deliverable D1.4b, ArchWare European RTD Project, IST-2001-32360, June 2003.
7. Alloui I., Oquendo F.: Describing Software-intensive Process Architectures using a UML-based ADL, Proceedings of the 6th International Conference on Enterprise Information Systems (ICEIS'04), Porto, Portugal, April 2004.
8. Balasubramaniam D., Morrison R., Kirby G., Mickan K.: Integration of Hyper-code and Structural Reflection into ArchWare ADL. Deliverable D1.5, ArchWare European RTD Project, IST-2001-32360, February 2003.
9. Bernardo M., Ciancarini P., Donatiello L.: Architecting Systems with Process Algebras. Technical Report UBLCS-2001-7, July 2001.
10. Bernardo M., Ciancarini P., Donatiello L.: Detecting Architectural Mismatches in Process Algebraic Descriptions of Software Systems, Proceedings of the 2nd Working IEEE/IFIP Conference on Software Architecture, Amsterdam, IEEE-CS Press, August 2001.
11. Binns P., Engelhart M., Jackson M., Vestal S.: Domain-Specific Software Architectures for Guidance, Navigation, and Control. International Journal of Software Engineering and Knowledge Engineering. 1996.
12. Bolusset T., Oquendo F.: Formal Refinement of Software Architectures Based on Rewriting Logic, ZB2002 International Workshop on Refinement of Critical Systems: Methods, Tools and Experience, Grenoble, Janvier 2002.
13. Brown A.W.: An Introduction to Model Driven Architecture – Part I: MDA and Today's Systems. The Rational Edge, February 2004.
14. Chaudet C., Greenwood M., Oquendo F., Warboys B.: Architecture-Driven Software Engineering: Specifying, Generating, and Evolving Component-Based Software Systems. IEE Journal: Software Engineering, Vol. 147, No. 6, UK, December 2000.
15. Chaudet C., Oquendo F.: A Formal Architecture Description Language Based on Process Algebra for Evolving Software Systems. Proceedings of the 15th IEEE International Conference on Automated Software Engineering (ASE'00). IEEE Computer Society, Grenoble, September 2000.
16. Cimpan S., Leymonerie F., Oquendo F.: The ArchWare Foundation Styles Library. Report R1.3-1, ArchWare European RTD Project, IST-2001-32360, June 2003.
17. Cimpan S., Oquendo F., Balasubramaniam D., Kirby G., Morrison R.: The ArchWare Architecture Description Language: Textual Concrete Syntax. Deliverable D1.2b, ArchWare European RTD Project, IST-2001-32360, December 2002.
18. Davies J., Woodcock J.: Using Z: Specification, Refinement and Proof. Prentice Hall International Series in Computer Science, 1996.
19. DeLine R.: Toward User-Defined Element Types and Architectural Styles. Proceedings of the 2nd International Software Architecture Workshop, San Francisco, 1996.
20. Fernandez J-C., Garavel H., Kerbrat A., Mateescu R., Mounier L., Sighireanu M.: CADP (CAESAR/ALDEBARAN Development Package) – A Protocol Validation and Verification Toolbox, Proceedings of the 8th International Conference on Computer-Aided Verification, New Brunswick, USA, LNCS 1102, Springer Verlag, August 1996.
21. Fischer M.J., Ladner R.E.: Propositional Dynamic Logic of Regular Programs. Journal of Computer and System Sciences Vol. 18, 1979.
22. Gallo F. (Ed.): Annual Report: Project Achievements in 2002. Appendix B: Survey of State-of-the-Art and Typical Usage Scenario for ArchWare ADL and AAL. Deliverable D0.4.1, ArchWare European RTD Project, IST-2001-32360, February 2003.

23. Garavel H.: Compilation et Vérification de Programmes LOTOS. Thèse de Doctorat, Univ. Joseph Fourier (Grenoble), November 1989. Chapter 9: Vérification (In French).
24. Garavel H., Lang F., Mateescu R.: An Overview of CADP 2001. European Association for Software Science and Technology (EASST) Newsletter, Vol. 4, August 2002.
25. Garlan D., Allen R., Ockerbloom J.: Exploiting Style in Architectural Design Environments. Proceedings of the ACM SIGSOFT Symposium on Foundations of Software Engineering, New Orleans, 1994.
26. Garlan D., Monroe R., Wile D.: ACME: An Architecture Description Interchange Language. Proceedings of CASCON'97, Toronto, November 1997.
27. Garlan D., Monroe, R., Wile D.: ACME: Architectural Description of Component-Based Systems. Foundations of Component-Based Systems, Leavens G.T, and Sitaraman M. (Eds.), Cambridge University Press, 2000.
28. Greenwood M., Balasubramaniam D., Cimpan S., Kirby N.C., Mickan K., Morrison R., Oquendo F., Robertson I., Seet W., Snowdon R., Warboys B., Zirintsis E.:Process Support for Evolving Active Architectures, Proceedings of the 9th European Workshop on Software Process Technology, LNCS 2786, Springer Verlag, Helsinki, September 2003.
29. Greenwood M., Robertson I., Seet W., Snowdon R., Warboys B.: Evolution Meta-Process Model. Deliverable D5.3, ArchWare European RTD Project, IST-2001-32360, December 2003.
30. Groote J. F., Mateescu R.: Verification of Temporal Properties of Processes in a Setting with Data. Proceedings of the 7th International Conference on Algebraic Methodology and Software Technology, Amazonia, Brazil, LNCS 1548, January 1999.
31. Heisel M., Levy N.: Using LOTOS Patterns to Characterize Architectural Styles, Proceedings of the International Conference on Theory and Practice of Software Development, LNCS 1214, Springer Verlag, 1997.
32. Inverardi P., Wolf A.: Formal Specification an Analysis of Software Architectures using the Chemical Abstract Machine Model. IEEE Transactions on Software Engineering, Vol. 21, No. 4, April 1995.
33. Inverardi P., Wolf A., Yankelevich D.: Static Checking of System Behaviors using Derived Component Assumptions. ACM Transactions on Software Engineering and Methodology, Vol. 9, No. 3, July 2000.
34. Kerschbaumer A.: Non-Refinement Transformation of Software Architectures. Proceedings of the ZB2002 International Workshop on Refinement of Critical Systems: Methods, Tools and Experience, Grenoble, Janvier 2002.
35. Kozen D.: Results on the Propositional μ-Calculus. Theoretical Computer Science 27:333-354, 1983.
36. Leymonerie F., Cimpan S., Oquendo F. : Extension d'un langage de description architecturale pour la prise en compte des styles architecturaux : application à J2EE. Proceedings of the 14th International Conference on Software and Systems Engineering and their Applications. Paris, December 2001 (In French).
37. Leymonerie F., Cimpan S., Oquendo F., "État de l'art sur les styles architecturaux : classification et comparaison des langages de description d'architectures logicielles", Revue Génie Logiciel, No. 62, September 2002 (In French).
38. Luckham D.C., Kenney J.J., Augustin L.M., Vera J., Bryan D., Mann W.: Specification and Analysis of System Architecture Using RAPIDE. IEEE Transactions on Software Engineering, Vol. 21, No. 4, April 1995.
39. Magee J., Dulay N., Eisenbach S., Kramer J.: Specifying Distributed Software Architectures. Proceedings of the 5th European Software Engineering Conference, Sitges, Spain, September 1995.
40. Martí-Oliet N., Meseguer J.: Rewriting Logic: Roadmap and Bibliography. Theoretical Computer Science, 2001.
41. Mateescu R., Garavel H.: XTL: A Meta-Language and Tool for Temporal Logic Model-Checking. Proceedings of the 1st International Workshop on Software Tools for Technology Transfer, Aalborg, Denmark, July 1998.

42. Medvidovic N., Taylor R.: A Classification and Comparison Framework for Architecture Description Languages. Technical Report UCI-ICS-97-02, Department of Information and Computer Science, University of California. Irvine, February 1997.
43. Milner R.: Communicating and Mobile Systems: The Pi-Calculus. Cambridge University Press, 1999.
44. Monroe R.: Capturing Software Architecture Design Expertise with ARMANI. Technical Report CMU-CS-98-163, Carnegie Mellon University, January 2001.
45. Moriconi M., Qian X., Riemenschneider R.A.: Correct Architecture Refinement. IEEE Transactions on Software Engineering, Vol. 21, No. 4, April 1995.
46. Moriconi M., Riemenschneider R.A.: Introduction to SADL 1.0: A Language for Specifying Software Architecture Hierarchies. Computer Science Laboratory, SRI International, Technical Report SRI-CSL-97-01, March 1997.
47. Morrison R.: On the Development of S-algol. PhD Thesis, University of St Andrews, 1979.
48. Oquendo F.: The ArchWare Architecture Description Language: Tutorial. Report R1.1-1, ArchWare European RTD Project, IST-2001-32360, March 2003.
49. Oquendo F.: The ArchWare Architecture Refinement Language. Deliverable D6.1b, ArchWare European RTD Project, IST-2001-32360, December 2003.
50. Oquendo F., Alloui I., Cimpan S., Verjus H.: The ArchWare Architecture Description Language: Abstract Syntax and Formal Semantics. Deliverable D1.1b, ArchWare European RTD Project, IST-2001-32360, December 2002.
51. Philipps J., Rumpe B.: Refinement of Pipe and Filter Architectures. Proceedings of FM'99, LNCS 1708, 1999.
52. RAPIDE Design Team: Guide to the RAPIDE 1.0. Language Reference Manuals, Stanford University, July 1997.
53. Rongviriyapanish S., Levy N.: Variations sur le Style Architectural Pipe and Filter. Actes du Colloque sur les Approches Formelles dans l'Assistance au Développement de Logiciels (AFADL'00), Grenoble, France, January 2000.
54. Sangiorgi, D., Expressing Mobility in Process Algebras: First-Order and Higher-Order Paradigms. PhD Thesis, University of Edinburgh, 1992.
55. Stirling C.: Modal and Temporal Properties of Processes. Springer Verlag, 2001.
56. Stolen K., Broy M.: Specification and Development of Interactive Systems. Springer Verlag, 2001.
57. Strachey C.: Fundamental Concepts in Programming Languages. Oxford University Press, Oxford, 1967.
58. Tennent R.D.: Language Design Methods based on Semantic Principles. Acta Informatica 8, 1977.
59. Verjus H., Oquendo F.: The ArchWare Architecture Description Language: XML Concrete Syntax. Deliverable D1.3b, ArchWare European RTD Project, IST-2001-32360, June 2003.
60. Wile D.: AML: An Architecture Meta Language. Proceedings of the 14th International Conference on Automated Software Engineering, pp. 183-190. Cocoa Beach. October 1999.
61. Zirintsis, E.: Towards Simplification of the Software Development Process: The Hypercode Abstraction. PhD Thesis, University of St Andrews, 2000.

The FABRIC Project

Peter van der Stok[1], Jan Jelle Boomgaardt[2], Helmut Burklin[3], Gabriele Cecchetti[4], Jean-Dominique Decotignie[5], Hermann de Meer[6], Gerhard Fohler[7], Johan Lukkien[8], and Gerardo Rubino[9]

[1] Philips Research, prof Holstlaan 4, 5656 AA Eindhoven, Netherlands
Peter.van.der.Stok@philips.com
[2] Netherlands Organisation for Applied Scientific Research (TNO)
[3] Thomson (TMM)
[4] Scuola Superiore St Anna (SSSA)
[5] Centre Suisse d'Electronique et de Microtechnique (CSEM)
[6] University of Passau (UP)
[7] Maelardalen Hoegskola (MDH)
[8] Technische Universiteit Eindhoven (TUE)
[9] Institut National de Recherche en Informatique et Automatique (INRIA)

Abstract. The FABRIC project aims at the integration of middleware standards used in home networks to provide high quality streaming over a heterogeneous network without introducing new standards.

1 Introduction

At this moment we are confronted by a large set of communication and interoperability standards in the home-networking domain. Within the context of a single standard, devices can be introduced into the home by simply unpacking them and switching them on, possibly accompanied by connecting them to some wiring infra-structure (see [1]). Currently, devices from different standards are completely isolated from each other. Each standard offers specific advantages to the equipment adhering to it and we can safely assume that these standards are here to stay. At the same time the advance of new technology (like 3G roaming devices) will result in newer standards. The users and purchasers of this equipment are not interested and probably not aware of the incompatibilities of standards. Confronted with the cited incompatibilities future customers will NOT acquire these new technologies. Integration of the different standards is absolutely essential to allow a transition from the current islands of technology to one integrated provision of services (roaming or wired) within the home and between the home and service providers.

FABRIC aims at developing *an architecture* in which several interoperability standards and technologies in the home networking context can be integrated. More than integration alone, a FABRIC application manages the complete network to satisfy *Quality of service (QoS)* requirements. The design is guided in this process by the requirements of a chosen application: multiple roaming multimedia streams.

F. Oquendo et al. (Eds.): EWSA 2004, LNCS 3047, pp. 272–278, 2004.

The FABRIC-architecture especially caters for dynamic network configurations allowing frequent additions, removals and roaming of devices.

The FABRIC-architecture supports the provision of real-time multimedia streaming. The timing specification and realization by the FABRIC communication media provides the end-to-end Quality of Service (QoS) required by the multimedia streaming. Reactions to system changes need to be done in a timely manner to support high quality video streaming over wireless media with rapid bandwidth fluctuations (smaller than 10 ms). Configuration changes and video stream settings need to be communicated to the involved devices within time scales of a few 100 ms.

1.1 HLA Integration

The FABRIC project investigates the application of the High Level Architecture (HLA) standard [2] to provide the services mentioned above. HLA addresses the inter-operability of applications in the large-scale (interactive) simulation domain. (e.g. simulation to support the training of a fighter pilot). HLA assists the integration of the middleware islands. An HLA *federation* is composed of collaborating federates. One federate can be equated to one set of devices belonging to a given standard. Federates can interact in a meaningful way by a common interpretation of the exchanged data. A communication layer, called Run Time Infrastructure (RTI), provides communication services with an Application Programming Interface (API) defined by the HLA Interface Specification. All transfer of data between federates passes through the RTI. The RTI permits to translate the communication between partners. In this way, members of a federate communicate according to their standard. Members of different federates communicate meaningfully a subset of translatable items. HLA supports the dynamic addition and removal of members of a federate. This is realized at the federate level by the standard used within a federate. Between federates it is supported by the 'subscribe and publish' facilities of HLA.

Once real-time constraints can be specified and realised under controlled conditions, the distributed decision making algorithms that support stream management, can be simplified and improved. Accordingly, the real-time character of the FABRIC network is exploited to change dynamically the setting of the network in a managed and timely manner and to communicate network changes in a timely manner. This timely management infrastructure is used to support the decision making process on many QoS aspects such as: timeliness, responsiveness, security, flexibility, and reproduction quality of A/V streams. The infrastructure allows a flexible response to changing user needs with limited (managed) network and computing resources.

2 Project Organization

FABRIC is funded by the fifth framework IST program of the European Union. There are two industrial partners: Thomson (TMM) and Philips (PR), three large scientific institutes: Centre Suisse d'Electronique et de Microtechnique (CSEM), Institut National de Recherche en Informatique et Automatique (INRIA) and Netherlands Organisation for Applied Scientific Research (TNO), and four universities, Technische Universiteit Eindhoven (TUE), Maelardalen Hoegskola (MDH), University of Passau (UP) and Scuola Superiore St Anna (SSSA). The project is divided in three phases spread over an 18 month period. The project terminates end February 2004.

3 Middleware Functionality

The network middleware serves to describe devices and services on the network in a standardized way. These descriptions are communicated to all other connected devices running the same middleware. According to the received descriptions, an application can control a device or service or invoke a service. Such middleware standards are necessary to support the plug and play properties of the connected CE devices in a home network (e.g. see [1]).

An in-home digital network consists of a set of interconnected *physical devices* (devices for short). A device is connected to the network via a digital connector that is realized with one or more chips. Examples of digital connectors are interface cards for an Ethernet cable, or a wireless transceiver. A device, A, is connected to another device, B, when:

a. The digital connector of A can send bit patterns to the digital connector of B such that B can interpret these bit patterns.
b. A is connected to some device C and C is connected to B.

Physical Device

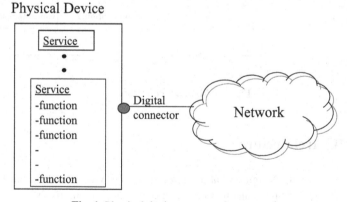

Fig. 1. Physical device connected to network.

For example two devices are connected when they are attached to the same Ethernet wire, or the signal emitted by one device can be received and decoded by the second device. Two devices are also connected when there exists a path via a set of connected devices. On the network, a physical device is identified by the identifier of the digital connector. Therefore, a device has as many identifiers as it has digital connectors. For example a device with two Ethernet cards has two identifiers.

Device *resolution* is making the identifiers of the devices connected to a device, A, available to the applications running on device A. Device *advertisement* is the proclamation by a device of its identifier to a subset of all connected devices. *Discovery* usually covers both aspects.

On a device a set of *services* (see Figure 1) can deliver a "service" to applications situated on connected physical devices. A service is an instance of a *service type* or service class. An example of a service type is a printing service or a clock service. The meaning and interface of service types is defined by a committee, or by manufacturers, or by individual people. E.G. an individual service type may be the returning of video images of the last 5 minutes taken by a home webcam. A service provides a set of functions that can be invoked, and a set of variables that can be read or set. Functions can modify or monitor the software and associated storage or may act on the physical operation of the device. Service *resolution* is making the identifiers of the services available to an application on a connected device. Service *advertisement* is the proclamation by a device of its services to a subset of all connected devices. Service advertisement and service resolution are often referred to as *Service Discovery*.

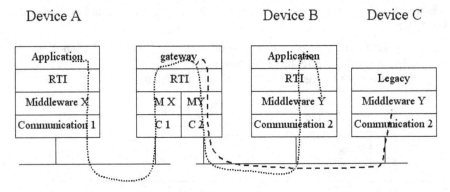

Fig. 2. FABRIC architecture.

4 FABRIC Architecture

Central to the FABRIC design is that all content (music, videos at different levels of quality) is published. This means that communication is anonymous: beforehand subscribers do not know the identity of the publisher and vice versa. The FABRIC architecture is shown in Figure 2. Devices of a given middleware are interconnected by a communication medium. Devices with different middleware are interconnected by a gateway. Four layers are identified within a device: (1) the application layer where applications publish objects (descriptions of a service instance) and subscribe to classes (description of a service), (2) the Run Time Infrastructure (RTI) that realizes the communication between applications, (3) the middleware layer of standard X or Y that provides and application with standardized access to the services of a device, and (4) the communication layer that interconnects devices. The dotted line shows an example thread of control for an application in device A that publishes information, subscribed to by an application in device B, and transmitted to the underlying service provided by the middleware. The dashed line shows an alternative when the application, for device specific reasons, is made middleware sensitive. The information is then sent directly to the middleware of the destination device. The dotted option is the recommended design. The dashed option is an alternative for specific cases where the functionality of the destination device cannot be handled by the RTI. Three essential FABRIC applications are described in more detail to explain the interoperability results: (1) streaming a video from a server to a renderer, (2) service discovery over middleware standards, and (3) QoS management.

4.1 Streaming Video

A streaming application involves the following collaborating entities. The *renderers*, which display a video on a connected display, publish their availability and state. The *video servers,* which produce video, publish the content they can deliver. Consequently, all applications that are connected to a given content or display via the network can subscribe to information about that content or display. A *controller*, which can connect servers to renderers, can decide to show a given content on an available rendering device without knowing beforehand which rendering device to choose. After establishment of the relation between video content and renderer by the controller, the renderer subscribes to the video. Irrespective of the presence of the controlling device, the video will be shown on the rendering device as long as there is a path of sufficient bandwidth between video server and rendering device, and rendering device and video server remain active. New controlling devices may be switched on and connected to the network. By subscription to the contents and rendering devices, the new controlling device can stop or modify on-going video streams.

The following scenario is taken as example

> *"Owner O arrives home with his PDA, which he uses as remote control and positioning device. The home network and the PDA discover each other and an alert appears on the TV. It states that the new DVD movie in the multimedia jukebox is available. O uses the PDA to start the video, which is presented on the TV. The quality of the video is low due to the limited bandwidth. Unfortunately, the jukebox is not able to provide the video in different qualities. After watching, O closes the video stream."*

To realize the scenario, the PDA has subscribed to the published objects in the home network to which it has connected. After reception of the alert, a browser application shows the video with its quality attributes. The video player subscribes to requests for video. On reception of a request from the PDA, the player publishes the video. The chosen renderer receives a request and subscribes to the specified video.

It is important to note that a specific player is selected. The player identity has been communicated to the PDA in the object that is published by the player service.

4.2 Service Discovery

The purpose of the FABRIC service discovery is to push interoperability as far as possible. The discovery service should hide the differences between the different middleware standards without any loss of functionality provided by the discovered services. Although not encouraged, for diverse reasons an application may want to exploit specific attributes provided by the description of a service by a particular middleware standard. The proposed FABRIC discovery allows application programmers, at a cost, to define their **own** (local) service interface, possibly conformant to a given middleware standard.

We use the HLA classes to provide the translation between application objects and discovered devices and services. Applications or services can publish objects instantiated from a given class. Applications can subscribe to a set of attributes of a given class. A FABRIC-enabled application subscribes to the descriptions of the services and devices present in the heterogeneous network. It is not known beforehand which devices and services will exist in a network. Consequently, it seems reasonable to define an abstract service and device class that has attributes that allow the identification of the service and contains enough information to reconstitute the complete service description for the application.

The discovery design is split in two parts; (1) FABRIC-enabled Directory Services (FDS-X) that is part of the RTI that links to the discovery middleware of standard X, and (2) the FDS-application (FDS-A) that can publish and subscribe to discovery objects, has access to RTI functionality and coexists with the FDS-X. The service-descriptions and the device-description are published by the FDS-A on the hosting device.

4.3 QoS Management

This section introduces a more detailed view of the QoS management approach, called *Matrix*. The Matrix will be composed of several entities that constitute an effective mechanism for monitoring and scheduling available resources in the system. The constituting parts are:

(1) Resource manager schedules and reserves resources
(2) Status Matrix contains information about available resources
(3) Order Matrix contains requests for resource allocations
(4) Order manager allocates resources at a particular device to a specified application
(5) Local scheduler allocates local CPU resources and schedules packets
(6) Local monitor will perceive changes in bandwidth availability.

The resource manager subscribes to quality requests, expressed in the status matrix, that are published by streaming applications. The order manager subscribes to the order matrix to receive orders from the resource manager. Locally the order manager, local scheduler and local monitor enforce the orders, observe the system and publish changes in bandwidth availability in the status matrix.

5 Evaluation

The FABRIC project has successfully completed what it set out to do. The anonymity of the publish/subscribe paradigm can be overridden elegantly when requests needed to be sent to a specific renderer. The HLA standard is very rigid in a predefinition of published classes. This is particular to the development process specified by the HLA standard, but is not a technical necessity. A dynamic addition of new types of devices will need a change to the HLA standard.

Acknowledgements

The FABRIC project is funded in the context of the IST program of the EC fifth framework. Hugh Maaskant and Michael van Hartskamp have improved the presentation of this paper.

References

1. Universal Plug and Play Device Architecture, version 1.0, 2000.
2. IEEE, Standard for modelling and Simulation High Level Architecture, IEEE standard 1516-2000.

Author Index